The A

FAUX TITRE

306

Etudes de langue et littérature françaises
publiées sous la direction de

Keith Busby, M.J. Freeman,
Sjef Houppermans et Paul Pelckmans

The Art of Instruction

Essays on Pedagogy and Literature in 17th-Century France

Edited by
Anne L. Birberick

AMSTERDAM - NEW YORK, NY 2008

Cover illustration: from a original design by Jacques Antoine Derôme.

Cover design: Pier Post.

The paper on which this book is printed meets the requirements of
'ISO 9706: 1994, Information and documentation - Paper for documents -
Requirements for permanence'.

Le papier sur lequel le présent ouvrage est imprimé remplit les prescriptions
de 'ISO 9706: 1994, Information et documentation - Papier pour documents -
Prescriptions pour la permanence'.

ISBN: 978-90-420-2335-2
© Editions Rodopi B.V., Amsterdam - New York, NY 2008
Printed in The Netherlands

Acknowledgements

I am grateful to a number of individuals and institutions whose generosity has made this collection of essays come to fruition. Material support was provided by the College of Liberal Arts and Sciences at Northern Illinois University. I would particularly like to thank Joseph Grush, Acting Dean of the College, for his continued advice, encouragement and support. Christa Stevens of Rodopi Press deserves a special debt of gratitude for once again artfully guiding us through the production process. Very special thanks go to Grant Olson; this is our second collaboration and, as in the first, his keen sense of humor has been invaluable to completing our project as has his expertise with the computer in creating the final manuscript. I would also like to thank the scholars who contributed to the volume. Working with them has been both pleasurable and instructive. The engravings of Pierre de Loysi that accompany the essay "The Prince and the Subject" are reproduced here with the kind permission of the Bibliothèque Municipale de Besançon, and I would like to extend my thanks to them. Finally, I wish to dedicate this volume to my parents, Delphine and the late Donald Birberick, whose art of instruction over the years has been the inspiration for my own.

Introduction

From the establishment of new schools to the publication of treatises on educational theory to the circulation of etiquette manuals, seventeenth-century France witnessed a veritable explosion of interest in instructional practices and theories. The preoccupation with education was not, however, limited to those who were trained and working as educators; religious figures, salon women, literary men and women, nobles, bourgeois, all, revealed the degree to which they held a stake in the development of educational practices. Indeed, pedagogy became one of the most controversial issues in the early modern culture war known as The Quarrel between the Ancients and the Moderns for, as Joan DeJean has shown in *Ancients against Moderns: Culture Wars and the Making of a Fin de Siècle*, the Modernist defeat in the formulation of a new educational curriculum was as much the result of their failure to articulate the benefits of their new program as it was of their rivals, the Ancients, orchestrating a propaganda campaign against modern literature. DeJean's important study figures as one among several to examine the relation among education, literature and culture. Although studies by Ursula A. Kelly, *Schooling Desire: Literacy, Cultural Politics, and Pedagogy*, and Carolyn Merchant, *The Death of Nature: Women, Ecology, and the Scientific Revolution*, focus primarily on this relationship within the context of gender roles in contemporary culture, their studies may be understood, at one level, as a continuation of Linda Timmermans's magisterial work *L'Accès des femmes à la culture, 1598-1715*. Two additional works bear mentioning: *La pédagogie en France aux XVIIe et XVIIIe siècles* by Georges Snyders and *L'Education en France au XVIIe et XVIIIe siècles* by Roger Chartier, M.-M. Compère and Dominique Julia. Published in 1965 and 1964 respectively, these works form the cornerstone of scholarship on French seventeenth- and eighteenth-century educational institutions and pedagogies.[1]

The Art of Instruction: Essays on Pedagogy and Literature in Seventeenth-Century France aims to add a new dimension to the scholarly discussion on how culture is inculcated. The nine essays comprising the volume call attention to the ways in which seventeenth-century French writers embraced both sides of the Horatian ideal that literary works combine the *utile* with the *dulce* so as to be pleasingly instructive. Or, to put it differently, the volume emphasizes the interplay between aesthetic forms and pedagogical agendas. In doing so, it takes into account the full range of meanings associated with the term *art*: learning, science, method, means, artifice, beautiful expression, aesthetic creation or artifact.[2] Hence, the notion of "art," standing as it does at the junction of form (aesthetic artifact) and content (knowledge), becomes central to the volume. This is most immediately apparent in the diversity of literary genres – both established (comedies, tragedies, lyric poetry) and nascent (novels, manuals, gazettes) – as well as the different writers – Chassignet, La Bruyère, Lafayette, Molière, Scarron, Subligny, Racine, de Visé – examined by the contributors. Yet despite this variety, all the essays share the common purpose of contributing to our understanding of how aesthetic form shapes, and is in turn shaped by, knowledge and learning.

The essays in the collection have been organized into three sections. While each section, in many ways, may be viewed as a discrete unit, the essays contained in one section enter into dialogue with those that proceed or follow in another section. In other words, each essay contributes to the overall focus of the volume as major themes circulate among essays and across units. The first section explores the ways in which seventeenth-century French writers used stories – in particular, the narrative strategy of the *exemplum* – to construct, reconfigure or manipulate pedagogical agendas. In the second, the focus is on how authors negotiate between aesthetic values and didactic concerns as they seek to inculcate more overt moral lessons in their audience. The final section probes the political dimension of pedagogy as it examines the intersection between art and politics within the context of princely or royal instruction.

As the world of print changed during the seventeenth century, so too did the needs and expectations of the reading public. By the 1670s, coterie literary production and reception was on the wane and soon to be replaced by the idea of the anonymous reader; in addition, social and scientific journalism were challenging both the nature of information circulation and readers' conceptions of discursive referentiality. In the volume's opening essay, "Relearning to Read: Truth and Reference in Subligny's *La Fausse Clélie*, Nicholas Paige shows how Subligny, in his novel *La Fausse Clélie*, proposes a new model of reading to his public by means of an updated use of embedding tales

within a frame narrative. A technique familiar since the time of Boccaccio and Chaucer, the intercalated tale assumes in Subligny's work,
as Paige argues, a covertly didactic purpose, for it reeducates readers
to view reading not so much as a moral act but a cognitive one.
Embedded tales also stand at the heart of Jennifer Perlmutter's essay
"Sociopolitical Education and the *Nouvelles* of *Le Mercure galant*."
Focusing on the *nouvelles* interspersed among the news stories in *Le
Mercure galant*, Perlmutter demonstrates how Donneau de Visé's use
of these tales evolved over time as he transformed them from amusing
filler meant to entertain readers into exemplary texts aimed at making
readers better subjects of the king. In this way, the later tales supported
the broader narrative progression, echoed in the news stories, towards
absolutism in France's history.

Essays by Twyla Meding and Larry Riggs continue to explore
the use of exemplary storytelling. In "Keys of Iron, Keys of Gold:
Enclosure, Example and Alchemical Teachings in the Novella and
L'École des femmes," Meding analyzes the "précaution inutile" theme
in María de Zayas's *El prevenido engañado*, Paul Scarron's *La Précaution inutile* and Molière's *L'École des femmes*. Her analysis reveals
how the pedagogical tool of *exempla* is transformed from author to
author in such a way that it comes to reinforce the hero's error. The
failure of example to correct behavior occurs most notably in *L'École
des femmes* as Molière fragments key exemplary episodes and, in
doing so, makes Arnolphe a figure of sterility and belatedness who
never learns the lesson of his predecessors in the novellas.

Molière's two plays, *L'École des femmes* and *Les femmes
savantes*, as well as Mme de Lafayette's *La Princesse de Clèves* serve
as the textual basis for Riggs's essay entitled "Prudes, *Précieux*, and
Patriarchs: Pedagogies of Paranoia and Repression." He takes as his
point of departure Ursula A. Kelly's notion of "critical literacy" as a
means of exploring how the characters of Mme de Chartres, Arnolphe
and Philaminte each fashion an educational curriculum whose purpose
is to regulate desire. What ultimately emerges from the juxtaposition
of these three works is a sense of how pedagogy becomes an expression of the educator's paranoiac fear.

The second grouping of essays concentrates on works preoccupied with immediate moral utility and explicit didacticism. Plays
intended for performance by school children as well as those intended
for the public stage offer one such example. Indeed, dramatic theory
throughout the early modern period insisted that comedies are morally
beneficial because they hold human follies and vices up to public ridi-

cule. In his essay, "Didactic Strategies in French Classical Comedy," Perry Gethner catalogues the diverse strategies, tactics and techniques used by authors – both professional dramatists (Boursault, Dancourt, Regnard) and skilled educators (Mme de Maintenon) – to convey moral lessons. Yet his essay goes beyond offering a simple catalogue, for he also reveals the ways in which these strategies are modified according to location and historical moment. My own essay, "Behind Closed Doors: Theater, Pedagogy and the 'Crisis' of *Esther*," examines theater's didactic role from another perspective: the pedagogical practices of Saint-Cyr. By reading *Esther* within its educational context, I show that while Racine sought to respect the injunction by Mme de Maintenon to write a moral drama, the aesthetic choices he made in both composition and staging ultimately subverted the play's didactic message and, as a result, foreshadowed the crisis to come.

While Gethner and I examine how edifying messages are integrated into literary works, Claire Carlin studies how literariness is infused into a traditionally didactic genre in her essay "Perfect Harmony: Love and Marriage in Early Modern Pedagogy." Seventeenth-century marriage manuals serve as Carlin's point of departure as she examines the ways in which authors incorporated theories of *honnêteté*, with its expectations of social performance within salon culture, in their manuals and, by doing so, transformed the marriage manual into a new literary form. She distinguishes among three kinds of manuals – facetious, *galant* and moralizing – in order to trace what she terms the "nuptial imagery" of the *Grand Siècle*.

The two essays in the last section of the volume investigate the intersections among art, instruction and politics. In "Satirical Realia: The *Caractères*' Conversion of Royal Pedagogy to Social Critique," Mark A. Cohen focuses on La Bruyère's experiences as royal tutor to the Duke of Condé to document the ways in which he reworks subjects traditionally taught in the monarchial curriculum (for example, the study of genealogy, geography and history) into sketches of social critique in *Les Caractères*. For Cohen, consideration of La Bruyère's position in the aristocratic household of the Grand Condé allows us not only to track the author's passage from preceptor to moralist but also to understand the role he accorded instruction ("enseigner") in *Les Caractères*. The volume's final essay by Christine McCall Probes, "The Prince and the Subject at the Intersection of Emblematic Poetry and Art: Moral and Pragmatic Reflection in Jean-Baptiste Chassignet's Poetry and Pierre de Loysi's Engravings," examines the art of instruction in Chassignet's *Sonnets franc-comtois* and the related engravings by Loysi. Through her detailed analyses, Probe reveals how the constituent elements of text and image enter into dialogue with one another so as to create an emblematic whole whose purpose is doubly didactic: to instruct readers on the divine rights of kings and to remind kings of their rightful place before God.

As these brief synopses illustrate, *The Art of Instruction* is born out of a desire to explore how instructional agendas, no matter their focus, rely as much on manipulating artistic forms as they do on articulating didactic principles. This volume makes no pretense of offering a definitive study on the art of instruction. It does, however, expand the current discussion on the inculcation of culture in early modern France by focusing attention on aesthetic concerns as well as by suggesting new avenues of further study. Accordingly, it is the hope of the volume that the articles presented here will be pleasingly instructive to readers.

Notes

[1] To detail the history of works published on seventeenth-century educational practices goes beyond the scope of this introduction.

[2] As the dictionary *Le Robert* indicates, the term *art*, in its more ancient etymological sense, means "science, savoir" as well as "moyen, méthode."

Works Cited

Chartier, Roger, M.-M. Compère, and Dominique Julia. *L'Education en France aux XVIIe et XVIIIe siècles*. Paris: Presses Universitaires de France, 1964.

DeJean, Joan. *Ancients against Moderns: Culture Wars and the Making of a Fin de Siècle*. Chicago: University of Chicago Press, 1997.

Kelly, Ursula A. *Schooling Desire: Literacy, Cultural Politics, and Pedagogy*. London: Routledge, 1997.

Merchant, Carolyn. *The Death of Nature: Women, Ecology, and the Scientific Revolution*. San Francisco: Harper, 1989.

Snyders, Georges. *La pédagogie en France aux XVIIe et XVIIIe siè-cles*. Paris: Presses Universitaires de France, 1965.

Timmermans, Linda. *L'acces des femmes à la culture (1598-1715)*. Paris Champion, 1993.

Relearning to Read:
Truth and Reference in Subligny's La Fausse Clélie

Nicholas Paige

> It would be quite foolish to assume that one can lightheartedly move away
> from the constraint of referential meaning.
>
> – Paul De Man

Adults, too, must learn to read.[1] Reading is only in the most
basic sense a skill acquired once and for all, when a person, usually a
child, is taught to recognize letters and phonemes. Adults need reading
lessons partly because their tastes change and expand; they must learn
to recognize codes and conventions other than those previous reading
has acquainted them with. But (re)learning to read is also a historical
problem: new genres and subgenres emerge, often as a result of
changed social, technological or even epistemological circumstances,
and readers must continually be taught to perform the unfamiliar
operations that such texts demand. Authors and critics are of course
the primary agents of this permanent reeducation; their prefaces and
treatises declare one mode of reading outdated, while promoting their
own alternatives, very often touted as more "natural" or "realistic."
More discreet figures – editors, printers, booksellers – also help groom
readers to respond to what they read in new ways.[2] All contribute to
the horizon of expectations of any given literary public, which must be
taught the operations and assumptions that following generations will
take for granted. Many of the assumptions we bring to the reading of a
novel, for instance, are in fact historically bound: scholars have demonstrated how familiar concepts such as empathetic identification,
deep character, and even the modern idea of fiction itself – a discourse
that seems to take place in the real world but that is understood to be
invented – may well have been unknown to readers before the Enlightenment, and thus needed at some point to be internalized.[3]

I would like in what follows to analyze one episode in the
reeducation in reading that accompanied what most scholars agree was
a massive upheaval in the literary landscape of Europe – the replace-

ment of the fictional form we now call romance with the beginnings of the modern novel.[4] Certainly, one can exaggerate the suddenness of romance's fall from fashion: its age-old topoi survive well into the eighteenth century, and many of its best-known examples – the historical romances of La Calprenède and Scudéry, certainly, but also, already, d'Urfé's *L'Astrée* – anticipate the novel's subsequent use of history to guard against charges of idle fancifulness.[5] Still, the change was substantive enough to be registered by a number of contemporaries (Sorel, Du Plaisir, and others), and it is not difficult to imagine that readers familiar with sprawling, episodic pastoral and heroic romances might approach the closely drawn settings and tightly plotted narratives of Saint-Réal's *Don Carlos* (1672) or Lafayette's *La Princesse de Clèves* (1678) with some perplexity. This perplexity might account for the insistence with which some novels of the time integrate the idea of teaching reading into their very substance, and figure within them, *en abyme*, characters whose confrontation with narrative are unambiguously lessons in good (and bad) reading techniques. *La Princesse de Clèves*, with its particularly sophisticated use of intercalated narratives, and its pedagogical motifs more generally, has been interpreted in such a way, but other authors provided reading reeducations as well.[6] Of these, Adrien-Thomas Perdoux de Subligny's *La Fausse Clélie* (1670) offers, I believe, a particularly instructive lesson on how to read in a world dominated by concerns of referentiality.[7]

As the title of Subligny's work indicates, *La Fausse Clélie* is a sort of "response" or postscript to Scudéry's last romance masterpiece, whose final volume appeared in 1660. The barest of plot summaries – the novel revolves around a woman, Juliette d'Arviane, who is subject to moments of extravagance during which she thinks she is the heroine of Scudéry's earlier work – reveals that Subligny also has in mind the paradigmatic example of a "bad" reader, Cervantes's Don Quixote. Quixote, of course, was a reader historically out of synch – he read chivalric romance as if it were referential discourse – and who needed to be "reprogrammed"; his reprogramming has come to be seen in retrospect as a decisive moment in the reeducation of the modern reader, taught now to enjoy more realistic (as opposed to idealistic) fare. By analogy, then, we might be led to expect from Subligny a satire intended to sweep away Scuderian romance, to ridicule its excesses, and to announce something new. The lesson of *La Fausse Clélie*, however, is not in fact so simple, nor so dismissive of its model. Subligny, I will argue, takes a number of related steps to encourage readers to adapt their knowledge of romance to the demands of discursive referentiality; that is, he rewrites *Clélie, histoire romaine* so as to permit romance tropes to live on in a world in which good readers read less for lessons on ideal conduct than to verify that utterances correspond to the empirically known world.[8] This "false" *Clélie* is thus, counter-intuitively, a "true" *Clélie*, a *Clélie* reformulated so as to seem real. Furthermore, I hope to show that this reformulation is of more general import for the historian of the novel: because *La Fausse Clélie* is in no meaningful sense of the word real*ist* even though it pretends to be real, Subligny's forgotten work is emblematic of a moment preceding the invention of modern fiction in which writers were struggling to articulate new possibilities for referring novels to the world around them.

Cogitations

Though Subligny's *La Fausse Clélie* does not have the heft of its Scuderian intertext, it is similarly difficult to summarize: its six episodic books, comprising myriad stories held together by a frame narrative, work against any unified plot. But a good place to start looking for the decisive changes Subligny imparts to his model is in *La Fausse Clélie*'s *in medias res* beginning. One day when the court is at Fontainebleau, the Marquis de Riberville decides to take the air at Vaux-le-Vicomte. Reading verse in the garden, his attention is caught by a young beauty accompanied by an older woman; he is making small talk with the former when all of a sudden this scene of banal flirtation turns into a veritable adventure. "'Monsieur,'" the young woman cries out, starting to run, "'sauvez-moi d'un homme qui me cherche partout pour m'enlever!'"(2).[9] And indeed, a man appears out of nowhere, pursues her, and eventually hustles his prey into a waiting carriage, which speeds off just as Riberville catches up. Riberville turns around, but the woman's guardian has disappeared. "'Ah!' dit-il, 'elle est complice de l'enlèvement'" (3). There is nothing to do but follow on horseback; onlookers he meets along his route tell him that yes, a carriage has just passed, containing only a man and a woman, and that it has taken the road for Combreux. Riberville rides on and comes across what he discovers to be a different carriage stopped in the road, and yet another adventure: four women are trying to stop two horsemen from murdering a gentleman with them. Riberville, acting like a "Héros de Roman" (4), drives the assailants off, after which he realizes that he already knows the people he has just obliged. (The four women and one man will be, along with Riberville, the main figures of the novel. They are: Mademoiselle de Barbesieux, Madame de Mulionne, Mademoiselle de

Velzers, Mademoiselle de Kermas, and the Chevalier de Montal.[10])
Alas, the trail of the mysterious abducted woman is now cold: his
friends tell Riberville that no such carriage passed them. At any rate,
they suspect him of inventing the whole story – "on lui dit qu'il fait
une histoire à plaisir" (5). While he did not invent, it will turn out that
he misinterpreted what did, it is true, look for all the world like a real
adventure. The following day, back at Vaux, the perplexed Marquis
goes to read in his *cabinet*, only to find the mysterious woman hiding
there; true to his heroic role, he asks her to name his "enemy," so that
he might avenge her. She then introduces herself as Clélie, daughter of
Clelius, and claims to be pursued by a Roman. Riberville, "comme
tombé des nues," realizes that he was wrong to have taken seriously
"une aventure si ridicule" (10): the woman who calls herself Clélie is
clearly deluded. Her "abductor," who shows up asking to speak with
Riberville, quickly fills in the details: Juliette d'Arviane was so struck
by the resemblance between her life and the events of Scudéry's novel
– foremost among which, a shipwreck and an earthquake – that for the
last six years she has been afflicted with these sudden episodes of
delirium, usually triggered by any mention of things Roman. (The
Marquis recalls, now, having flirtatiously compared her face to that of
a Roman just before she ran off.) The "abductor" is in fact a former
suitor, enlisted by d'Arviane's family to try to keep her from doing
herself harm.

These opening pages – merely the first twenty or so in a novel
of about 320 – are quite distinctive. Most obviously, we are *not* in a
pseudo-Roman narrative world, but in a familiar Ile-de-France peopled
with plausibly named characters. Names – a subject to which I will
return – are not the only thing that stands out. For one, Subligny offers
us in these pages access to a series of cognitive inferences on the part
of a protagonist acting on an initial assumption (the erroneous or
extravagant idea that "Clélie" has been abducted). Thus Riberville
notes the guardian's disappearance as a sign of her complicity; and
when he asks witnesses if a carriage has just passed, his judgment that
it must be that of the kidnapper is confirmed ("confirm[é]," 3) upon his
learning that it contains a man and a woman. Little by little, though,
Riberville is confronted with facts he is unable to make sense of – the
carriage stopped in the road is not, in fact, the one he was following;
and the whole "aventure" (the word is foregrounded through repeated
use) is found by his friends to be dubious. Riberville is additionally
baffled when the supposedly complicitous guardian shows up back at
Vaux and leaves word with his attendants that "Clélie"'s abductor, if

located, must not be harmed, since he was acting under her family's orders. "Ce n'était pas pour éclaircir le pauvre Marquis[,...qui] était au désespoir quand il voulait chercher quelque lumière parmi toutes ces obscurités" (6).

We have, then, a text that initially presents a cognitive problem, as much to the reader as to the protagonist, whose efforts to understand double or parallel our own. The reader of romance would immediately register the twist that Subligny is giving to the familiar device of the enigmatic event, presented *in medias res*, that then gives way to explanatory narrative, usually in the form of a flashback. (La Calprenède especially expands their use well beyond what one finds in the oft-imitated structure of Heliodorus's *Aethiopica*.) In earlier romances, this type of explanation was typically furnished by onlookers who all, unlike the protagonist, knew the story. By contrast, *La Fausse Clélie*'s flash-back (the abductor's tale of d'Arviane's past) occurs only *after* we have been allowed to try to put the pieces of the puzzle together ourselves. Perhaps picking up on the elaborate puzzle structure that characterized the main narrative of Scarron's *Roman comique* (1651-57), Subligny dilates the time separating enigma from explanation, thus opening up the possibility for both characters and readers to hesitate over how to interpret a certain number of clues.

For truth, in *La Fausse Clélie*, must be assembled. Subligny's novel constitutes a vast exercise in programming readers to expect novels to make sense: he produces a novelistic universe that one might call cognitively "thick." The novel's enigmatic opening, with its series of deductions and corrections, is but part of this. For the entire structure of the book – its incorporation of the embedded narratives typical of both romance and *devisant*-type collections like that of Marguerite de Navarre – is put into service of constituting an active reader who asks where stories come from, and who puts the stories he or she hears into relation with others, all so that their truth may be verified. One of Subligny's most serious commentators, Jean Serroy, who examines *La Fausse Clélie* in light of the tradition of the comic tale, is certainly right to maintain the thematic unity of many of *La Fausse Clélie*'s embedded narratives – say, duping, or the way women love, or the possibility of ghosts – and to point out their many antecedents. *La Fausse Clélie* also seems familiar on account of the main characters' discussions about the exemplary moral value of the tales they tell, since such commentary is a constant as much in the *Heptaméron* as in Scudéry's romances. What distinguishes *La Fausse Clélie*, what marks it off qualitatively from all the famous works of which it reminds us, is its persistent staging of reading less as a moral action (that is, as a way to police and codify social and amorous behavior) than as a cognitive one. So it is that when Montal, the character attacked at the novel's beginning and then rescued by Riberville's arrival, tells the gallant story behind the attempted murder, skeptical readers repeatedly intervene: his adventures are "si peu vraisemblables," mere "follies" (34). Yet listeners do more than denounce what they hear as lies, and tellers, likewise, do not merely affirm they tell the truth. Instead, stories can be evaluated, tested, and read against other things we have heard or that we know to be true. Montal's protestations of truth are at least partially backed up when Riberville interrupts to say that he has already heard of this "aventure": "'mais je ne croyais pas,' dit-il au Chevalier [de Montal], 'que tu en fusses le Héros, et on ne nommait personne'" (37).[11] When the number of coincidences involved increases, Riberville's skepticism reasserts itself: "'Et par quelle aventure,' dit le Marquis au Chevalier, '[ton ennemi] t'est-il venu rencontrer si à propos sur ces chemins?'" (41). Riberville's pejorative use of "aventure" is clearly the same one he used when he dismissed d'Arviane's madness as "une aventure si ridicule" (10). But adventures, Subligny tells us, do happen, and can be explained: "'Par quelle aventure?' reprit le Chevalier, 'je n'en sais rien, à moins que ce traître m'ait épié à Fontainebleau, où je le vis il y a quatre ou cinq jours'" (41). Montal, twice challenged, has been twice vindicated.

The assertion of narrative truth is nothing specific, of course, to 1670 France: it was a staple gambit of the *Heptaméron*, of Renaissance travel narratives, and before that of Chrétien's verse romances; the topos was old enough in Classical times for Lucian to mock it in his *True Story* (2nd century A.D.), and indeed seems to lead us all the way back to the *Odyssey*, where numerous characters make claims for the truth of their narrative (usually, it has been pointed out, when they are about to lie). But if *La Fausse Clélie* gives the impression of cognitive thickness whereas previous works do not, this is because its characters take such pains to verify what they are told, at least to the extent of reducing apparent improbability. In the example just cited, the teller counters his skeptics by adding new information that makes a coincidence seem less coincidental. This is a fairly frequent occurrence in the novel. Barbesieux recounts in Book 4 an anecdote about the gallant lover of the wife of a magistrate who, accused of murder, prefers being beheaded to naming his mistress as his alibi. The tale, similar in tenor to what one finds in François de Rosset's *Histoires tragiques* (1614), is intended as part of an argument about the exis-

tence of amorous discretion. Montal, however, immediately proposes a
series of objections. If, he reasons, the lover really did keep the secret
of his whereabouts on the night of the murder, then the story could
never be known; true, replies Barbesieux, but it came out later through
the maid, who was privy to the liaison and who subsequently leaked
the information after being mistreated by her mistress. But if that is
true, continues Montal, her testimony is suspect, since it is motivated
by revenge. True again – but the real assassin was arrested, and con-
fessed both his guilt and the lover's innocence (202-3).

This short story is followed in Book 5 by a number of tales
involving supernatural occurrences; these are especially scrutinized,
for while other narratives, such as Barbesieux's anecdote about how
men can keep secrets, had moral value, the ghost stories are essentially
about their own possibility or believability. The subject of the supernatural is prompted by another enigmatic event in the main narrative,
one whose elucidation will propel the novel to its conclusion: the
group of friends is informed that a man has just fainted in the gardens
of Vaux-le-Vicomte after seeing a ghost. This immediately furnishes
an occasion to raise the subject of credulity. Montal, the same skeptical
questioner who dogged Barbesieux with questions about her *histoire
tragique*, reveals himself to be an *esprit fort*, that is, someone who
thinks the age of supernatural occurrences (and divine intervention in
the natural world) to be past.[12] Mulionne, less disenchanted, counters
with the story of a certain Santois, who is both "ancien Echevin de
Paris" and well known to Mulionne: "'c'est dans mon quartier que
loge ce bonhomme-là, qui est un homme d'honneur s'il en fût jamais'"
(215). The story, which Mulionne maintains happened only last Thurs-
day, involves some papers mysteriously torn up, apparently by a sprite
(*lutin*) of some sort. Montal, mirthfully incredulous, refuses
Mulionne's invitations to go see for himself: "'si j'y allais,'" he says,
"'il faudrait que je puisse soupçonner quelque possibilité à cela, et je
n'y en crois point du tout'" (218). The deadlock between believer and
nonbeliever is broken by Montal, who brings pressure to bear on
Mulionne's reassertion of the socially impeachable origins of witnesses ("'il faut ajouter foi aux honnêtes gens quand ils disent qu'ils
ont vu' [*sic*]" [218]).

> "D'accord, Madame," répondit-il; "mais montrez-moi un de ceux-là." "Ah!"
> dit-elle, "j'y consens de tout mon coeur, et je ne veux que l'Abbé de Lanciat, à
> qui feu Monsieur Fouquet de Croissy s'est apparu à Tours dans son allée. Je ne
> veux que Madame la Marquise de Tessau, dont il fut aussi tirer les rideaux
> comme elle était couchée. Ce sont là des gens irréprochables...." "Je n'en doute

pas, Madame," reprit Montal; "mais tenez-vous cela de l'Abbé et de la Marquise, ou de quelqu'un d'autre?" "Je le tiens," répondit Madame de Mulionne, "d'un de leurs amis seulement...." (218-19)

Mulionne tries to strike back by invoking an illustrious family – the house of Brandenburg – haunted by a ghost that appears each time a family member is to die; Montal quickly debunks this final assertion by pointing to a suspiciously similar tale in Lucian's *Dialogues*.[13]

Comparison with the traditions Subligny is clearly building on – and modifying, based on new imperatives – is instructive. In romance, the information furnished by internal narrators was invariably reliable; techniques of embedding served many functions, but none of them included the calling into question of the position of enunciation.[14] This applies to as much to the third-person narratives by reliable attendants that proliferate in La Calprenède and Scudéry as to earlier first-person narratives that were modeled on the eye-witness of the travel narrative.[15] The other model for embedded narrative that Subligny is also recalling, that of the Boccaccian tradition, is equally the domain of reliable narrators: argue as they may about gender politics, Marguerite de Navarre's *devisants* can only oppose one true story with another one, never claim that the story supporting such-and-such a position is simply invented.[16] In both romance and the *Heptaméron*, truth is a bare affirmation; no information is provided that would help other characters, or the reader, doubt or verify that affirmation. Following Michael McKeon, we can call familiar assertions like these "naïve empiricism": truth is ritually advanced, and accepted as such. Subligny, in re-introducing first-person narrators after their neglect in mid-century romance, practices a shrewder brand of empiricism: his affirmations beg to be interrogated. As it turns out, decorum is still safe, for Subligny's narrators all prove to be in perfectly good faith. Riberville, even if he was wrong about the abduction, was not in fact inventing things or hiding them from his friends. Subligny's empiricism is merely naïvely shrewd, and a far cry, certainly, from the more skeptical dismissal of testimony (in favor of circumstantial evidence) one can observe in eighteenth-century Britain (see Welsh). But the reliability of narrators and the truth of narrative have nonetheless moved from being an unprovable assumption to being the major point of interest of the narrative itself.

Reality Effects

The process of doubt and verification, now central to the reading experience, is in fact part of a larger project that consists of illustrating how narrative can be tied to the real world, made referential: characters in Subligny's frame tale are continually learning that the tales they hear are extensions of the world they move in. Few terms, perhaps, are more naïve and conceptually fuzzy as "real world"; by it, I do not mean to suggest that *La Fausse Clélie* is "realistic" – as I shall point out in a moment, it is not – but that the architecture of the novel carefully joins the world of tales told with the world of their tellers, shows them to be coterminous. The moral tale does not need to be part of the same spatio-temporal world as that of its audience or teller, because such examples function allegorically; the coherence of collections of such narratives is guaranteed by the illustration of complete spectrum of moral possibilities. The coherence of Subligny's universe, by contrast, is assured by the articulation of all narrative levels, by the production of a spatio-temporal continuum that has the effect of suggesting a world "out there" to which any narrative must belong.

On a basic level, of course, any homodiegetic narrative (that is, a narrative in which the teller is an actor) achieves an interpenetration of diegesis (the primary narrative, or, here, frame tale) and metadiegesis (the secondary narrative, or embedded tale).[17] But *La Fausse Clélie* reveals, upon analysis, a far more complicated sort of interpenetration. Serroy, for instance, has singled out as one of Subligny's innovations the fact that fairly systematically his characters are the heroes of the stories they tell, and that "il se noue...tout un système de relations entre les protagonistes" (672).[18] For narrative accretion in Subligny does not consist of piling independent stories one upon another so as to produce a compendium of exempla, as happens in Boccaccio and Marguerite de Navarre. This model, in which a group of characters take turns telling stories, is indeed evoked, but with the difference that the frame tale and the embedded tales of *La Fausse Clélie* belong to the same diegetic universe.[19] In older *devisant*-type collections, there exists – in spite of the frequent insertion of references to the truth of the embedded tales – a strict demarcation between narrative levels: embedded tales are the space of action, while the frame narrative allows for commentary. Subligny, by contrast, uses a similar conceit to quite different ends. Things actually happen in this frame narrative, for d'Arviane's various disappearances provide an unfolding action; each *devisant* has a past whose events continue to have ramifications in the

frame narrative; and the stories told complement each other not morally but factually. When Riberville's friends, at the outset, dismiss his
protestations to the effect that the story of the abduction of "Clélie"
happened as he maintains, this is not only because the abduction is in
itself improbable; it is also because his listeners know Riberville's past
too well not to suspect he is hiding something.

> "Tu te moques de nous, Marquis," répond Montal [à Riberville], "on ferait bien
> son rendez-vous d'un Jardin comme celui de Vaux, pour enlever une femme en
> plein jour, et encore de la manière que tu le viens de dire: cela ne peut
> seulement tomber dans l'esprit d'une personne qui a de la raison." "Mais, mon
> Dieu!" ajoute Mademoiselle de Barbesieux, qui connaissait aussi l'humeur
> galante du Marquis; "ne savez-vous pas que Mademoiselle de Sencelles ne
> demeure pas loin d'ici?" (5)

Sencelles, we will learn much later, once passed letters between Riberville and a certain Comtesse de Tourneüil; Barbesieux's knowledge of
this fact, she will later explain, lies behind this initial suspicion of
Riberville's abduction story. Riberville's past will remain murky even
as more details start to emerge. When Barbesieux does finally furnish
the story of his relation with Tourneüil, Riberville claims that her point
of view can only be clouded by her jealousy of Riberville's love for
d'Arviane, and then provides an alternate version of the story, one that
purports to explain in a manner favorable to himself the motives
behind the publicly acknowledged fact that Barbesieux ends with –
Tourneüil's delayed return from London (107-13). Even heroic
romance, which did integrate more than *devisant*-type fiction the frame
tale and various embedded "flash-back" tales, never achieved this level
of thickness, in which the author weaves a web of events that are ultimately inseparable from one another.[20] Thus, if it is difficult to
reconstitute for the purposes of this article all these interlocked narrative threads, this confusion is in a sense the point of the novel: *La
Fausse Clélie* is all about paying attention to who tells what, and to the
various clues that can be used to cross-reference narratives with a
wider horizon, that of the "real world."

Indeed, Subligny's narrative continuum does considerably
more than merely put each character's past into a separate compart-
ment: bits of Riberville's past seem to float free from any one self-
contained flash-back, and they interfere with the stories he tells and the
main narrative.[21] Another way of putting this would be to say that
homodiegetic stories continually gesture to a world *outside* of any one
particular narrative and *against* which any narrative must situate itself.
The long story of Velzers and the Chevalier de La Grancour in Book 2

is a case in point. Naturally, the story is advanced as true, with the intention, moreover, of convincing the audience of Velzers's virtue. As we have seen, however, it is not enough in *La Fausse Clélie* to say you tell the truth, you must create a plausible case for truth. And Velzers's case is made by gesturing to a place outside of both the metadiegesis (the narrative of La Grancour and herself) and the diegesis (the primary narrative of the group of friends at Vaux), to a world of publicly known facts to which both diegesis and metadiegesis are connected.

> "Vous savez," [asks Velzers,] "le bruit qui courut l'hiver passé, qu'on nous avait voulu voler la nuit?" "Oui," reprit Madame de Mulionne, "on dit qu'on avait trouvé sur le balcon des poignards et des noeuds coulants, avec quoi on vous devait tous étrangler, et cela servit d'entretien à tout Paris." (80)

Velzers reveals that this publicly attested fact was not as it appeared, for the daggers and ropes were part of a persistent lover's many stratagems.[22] Later, Mulionne reverses the direction of traffic between the independent world and her story when in her autobiographical tale of *galanterie* gone wrong, she motivates her own fear by appealing to a violent *fait divers* that had previously come to her attention.[23]

Crossing in such a way narrative lines with a reality defined as external to it produces the effect of a narrative world that is, notwithstanding the fragmentation of its multiple plot lines, or perhaps because of this fragmentation, of a single piece. And significantly, this reality effect is only enhanced by those cases in which characters do in fact narrate tales in which they play no role. Barbesieux, Montal, Riberville produce their own narratives, but they also pass on and evaluate other narratives, in such a way that the diegetic world of the characters, instead of being a rarefied or self-contained *locus amoenus*, deliberately opens out onto a less familiar, but still coterminous, world. These unconnected tales (generally viewed by Subligny's few commentators as a manifest weak spot, a reversion to conventional "filler") are notably situated with more than a perfunctory nod in the direction of truth. Book 3, for instance, contains only three stories, all unrelated to the characters, and each a fairly conventional tale of roguery with occasional bawdy accents. (*Bienséance* excludes such narrative from the gallant register of the main [noble] protagonists, and only time spent at the home of Madame de Mulionne, whose husband is of the robe, allows for its integration.) All three contain varying noteworthy authentifying devices.

• The first, told by the elderly but good-natured Monsieur de Mulionne, "Conseiller de la Cour," comes from a court case recently prosecuted. Historians have shown that court cases in the early modern period were an object of much general interest, both in England and in France; although the circulation of legal briefs, or factums, was probably still rather limited in the 1660s and 1670s, evidence does exist that they were being read.[24] Monsieur de Mulionne's tale is not at all a factum, nor even particularly legal; it is merely the tale of a young lady's guardian – one thinks of course of Arnolphe – who refuses to let his charge marry, and of the ensuing (comical) complications. Its significance lies chiefly in its foregrounding of the empirical alibi courts were starting to provide for narrative in these years.[25]

• The second involves a man, Monsieur de Luchères, who arrives to see Monsieur de Mulionne; his story is embedded in the world of our protagonists by means of a sort of triangulation.

> Quand [Luchères] fut parti, le Marquis [de Riberville] prenant la parole[:] "Si," dit-il, "j'étais aussi hardi que Montal, je vous conterais une plaisante histoire de ce Monsieur de Luchères, qui, si je ne me trompe, est un gros homme de Normandie, et dont la femme est aussi innocente qu'il est fin et spirituel." "Il est de Normandie?" reprit Montal[;] "Ah, si c'est Monsieur de Luchères de Normandie, je le connais aussi bien que toi, et sa femme aussi; et j'en vais conter l'Histoire si l'on veut." "Conte-la donc," reprit le Marquis, "je t'en cède la gloire." (123)

This short introduction allows Subligny to do more than simply relate a tale: he introduces a minor character into the frame narrative who is subsequently placed on the map of France, and whose identity (and history) is confirmed by the fact that two other characters have heard of him independently of one another.

• The last story of Book 3 offers a final variation on narrative integration: the tale of a man fleeced of 4000 francs is told by none other than the victim, the Procureur Tigean, also visiting Monsieur de Mulionne on business. Normally, tales of roguery or comic humiliation adopt a point of view close to that of the rogue; in *La Fausse Clélie*, the novelty of having the *berné* himself relate his victimhood – here one thinks of George Dandin's monologues – is what allows the narrative a different type of relation with the frame.

As Serroy disappointedly points out, all these stories are perfectly formulaic and have long lines of antecedents (673-74). From a different perspective, however, their interest has little to do with literary originality *per se*, and still less with their status as actual historical anecdote; whether the story of Luchères is true is of as little concern as knowing if Monsieur de Mulionne's story can actually be traced to a court case. On the other hand, what does fully motivate their inclusion in *La Fausse Clélie* is the fact that Subligny is interested in producing a compendium of techniques for relating different types of narrative, in inventing new modes of enunciation that would accentuate their reality effect, and of thereby making them seamlessly part of the world of his characters. Subligny is not content with making the world of his main protagonists of a piece, for he takes the further step of integrating their gallant adventures with generically more diverse narratives. Be it comic hearsay or the discourse of amorous experience, all narratives, finally, take place against the same backdrop.

The reason *La Fausse Clélie* invites us to use a term such as the "real world," then, is not simply because characters claim their stories as true, or because Subligny places them against an existing, recognizable geography. Rather, he predicates the integration of narrative levels and genres on the underlying ground that is reality; that is, the reading of *La Fausse Clélie*, which amounts to connecting and articulating its various narrative strands, produces an effect of reality in the reader. That all these numerous strands would have this effect may be surprising for the modern – or modernist – reader, more acquainted with the idea that the more narrative types and layers multiply, the more problematic the existence of some extra-discursive reality becomes. This reader – the reader of Proust, Joyce, or Gide, or the viewer of Welles's *Citizen Kane* – may well, faced with a mass of contradictory testimony, conclude that layers upon layers of cultural and discursive mediation separate us even from our own experience, and that the only reality we can know is, as the saying goes, narratively constructed. (If this is bad for partisans of the real world and referential discourse, it is good for modernist art, which is able to reveal itself to be more tenacious than the real world, and more deeply attuned to psychological truth.) Nor does the "reality effect" of *La Fausse Clélie* much resemble the one Roland Barthes discerned in the realist novel – an effect generated by details that by their intrusive gratuitousness, their flagrant disregard for narrative economy, proclaimed to the reader, "This is true!" Finally, Subligny's "real world" must be distinguished from the conception of the real evinced by the previous comic novels, which confronted airy idealization with the prosaic elements of daily life such as shaving bowls, windmills, taverns, and other examples of the everyday. Rather than establish reality through juxtaposition with something denigrated as false, Subligny makes the entire reading practice into an exercise in cognitive coherence.

Subligny produces, therefore, a complicated mix of techniques for ascertaining the truth of narratives we hear, for truth is what we, like the cogitating Riberville at the novel's outset, are after. We can confront narratives with what we know about the motives of the teller, as when Barbesieux assumes Riberville's abduction story is a bogus cover. We can dismiss stories that seem on some fundamental level improbable as Riberville's daylight kidnapping or supernatural stories seem to Montal. We can cross them with information we have received from other sources, as in the case of the tools found on the balcony of Velzers's house. And we can accept narratives if two people know them, as when Montal and Riberville have both heard Luchères's tale. The fact that *La Fausse Clélie* is hardly a skeptical text merits emphasis: only in one or two cases of the supernatural are stories revealed to be downright false. Subligny's world is, massively, one of truth – a truth repeatedly put to the test, to be sure, but truth nonetheless. Suspected of lies or inventions, his characters inevitably confirm their reliability, no matter how far-fetched their stories may be. That Montal objects to the idea of daylight kidnappings in the gardens at Vaux, or that the group concludes that Velzers's tale of her affairs with La Grancour must be true because "elle n'avait pas assez d'esprit, toute spirituelle qu'elle était, pour avoir inventé sur le champ une intrigue si bien suivie" (105) serve as examples that clearly suggest that Subligny's characters possess some criteria of intrinsic plausibility.[26] But because listeners are so quick to be satisfied, *La Fausse Clélie*, in spite of its satiric ancestors, is hardly an anti-*Clélie*: it does not subvert romance commonplaces, it fortifies them against the possible reproach that they are unreal, preparing them, as it were, for a new sort of discursive economy in which referentiality is the assumed function of prose.

For the novel's ending, which largely revolves around the mystery of the "ghost" seen by the man who has fainted in the garden at Vaux, is unmistakably romance-like. Faced with explaining the apparition, as well as the equally mysterious fact that Kermas has decided to don a mask before joining them, the members of the group ask the man, the Marquis de Kimperbel, to tell his story. Kimperbel claims to have seen the ghost of his dead and much regretted mistress, whom he had been prevented from marrying years ago on account of a family feud. The mistress, naturally, will be identified as Kermas herself, who, after an intervening story involving a new character, Lusigny, will explain just how it happened that she did not die in childbirth as Kimperbel thought, and ended up alive and well at Vaux.

Kermas's "étrange aventure" (276) – she had been erroneously thought dead, buried alive, rescued, only to be shipwrecked and marooned for three years on an island – as well as the coincidence of her turning up masked at Vaux immediately strike all concerned as worthy of romance: "'il n'y a pas dans les Romans d['histoire] mieux intriguée que celle-là, sur ma parole,'" says Lusigny (284). Serroy expresses surprise at this sort of plot, given what he takes to be Subligny's intention to "peindre la société de son temps" (677). Judging from the way the novel functions, this is not Subligny's intention at all: *La Fausse Clélie* simply adapts romance storytelling to an audience that is now supposed to read for truth. *La Fausse Clélie* does not refuse or ridicule improbable devices – abductions, pirates, shipwrecks, and a final recognition scene – but it validates them through the construction of the fact-checking reading apparatus I have been examining.

Doubtless, Subligny's willing return to the topoi of romance is counter-intuitive for the literary historian trained to think of the rise of the novel as the steady triumph of increasing realism; after all, Ian Watt long ago pointed to an explicit mistrust of traditional plots as a signal characteristic of the realist mode (13-15). *La Fausse Clélie*'s evident and overriding concern with truth must not, however, be confused with realism. Certain devices may indeed be evaluated as improbable (again, "'cela ne peut seulement tomber dans l'esprit d'une personne qui a de la raison,'" says Montal of the purported abduction of "Clélie"), but Subligny's narrative cannot do without them, for it has nothing to put in their place. All he can do is present the devices to his readers in a way that fortifies them against attacks founded on the criterion of intrinsic plausibility; and this is why Juliette d'Arviane is never satirized in the way the reader of *Don Quixote* or *Les Précieuses ridicules* is prepared for. Again, Serroy expresses surprise, this time at Subligny's lack of satirical edge: "Juliette n'a qu'un seul tort, celui d'avoir connu un destin tellement romanesque qu'il aurait été digne, en effet, de figurer dans un roman précieux" (672). No one, Serroy continues, even takes advantage of her illness, as occurs in all of Subligny's comic predecessors. On the contrary, and as the abductor who fills Riberville in on the events he has incorrectly interpreted is the first to point out, "une étrange sympathie" (20) exists between d'Arviane's life and Clélie's: "elle a raison dans la comparaison, si elle ne l'a pas dans l'application" (17). Much later, after a second disappearance, a new carriage, and another pursuit, the group of friends returns again to the fundamental resemblance of life and literature: "[O]n raisonna longtemps sur la nouveauté de ces incidents qu'on

trouva tout à fait dignes d'une personne qui s'imaginait être Clélie"
(308). The wide comic gap between life and (idealistic) literature that
was the motor of quixotic satire is closed, because d'Arviane was *right*
to make the comparison, even if her conclusion that she must be in the
Rome of *Clélie* was wrong.

How, then, is d'Arviane a "bad" reader? What lesson is she to
offer Subligny's own readers, what is the trap we need to avoid? Ide-
alism is not in question here, as it was in the *Quixote*; nor is implausi-
bility, as I have said, for as long as the implausible can be verified, it
can be admitted into the novel. D'Arviane is hardly the only character
here to note a close correspondence between what happens in life and
what happens in books. Riberville, we have seen, behaves bravely as
would a "Héros de Roman" (4); and the abductor prefaces his story by
noting that he seems to be playing "le personnage d'un Ecuyer de
Roman" (16). Later mysterious events in the frame narrative –
Velzers's attempted repossession, for example, of the dropped letter
Riberville has impolitely started to read – also furnish "de quoi faire la
matière du plus joli Roman du monde" (43). D'Arviane, by contrast,
takes the historical alibi of romance (ancient Rome, Egypt, and so on)
too seriously, and has failed to realize that the genre in fact describes
contemporary life. To put the matter differently, one can say that faced
with the fact (undisputed by any of the characters) that her life parallels Clélie's, d'Arviane concludes that she must be Clélie, rather than
following the resemblance in the opposite direction: the proper conclusion, according to Subligny's reading lesson, would be closer to realizing that Clélie is in fact Juliette d'Arviane, or less literally, that the
adventures we read about are transpositions of our lives. Romance, it
would seem, is merely the name we give to adventures we are not able
to recognize as our own; as Velzers exclaims upon hearing the unfa-
thomable coincidences of Kermas's and Kimberbel's relationship, "On
nomme les Aventures des autres des histoires Romanesques" (311).
The lesson, obviously, is far from quixotic; Subligny does not propose
to reform prose fiction by pointing out or eliminating its unreality, but
by showing how the lives his readers live resemble books. Romance is
already real, if only people would stop attributing to themselves those
silly Roman names.

Name Games

Indeed, naming lies at the heart of Subligny's enterprise, and
not only because, as part of their efforts at verification, characters

attempt to fit names of people and places they already know to the new
narratives they hear. More important, Juliette d'Arviane's modified
quixotism is at bottom a problem of names. D'Arviane has identified
resemblances between *Clélie* and her own life – and rightly so, for, as
d'Arviane's brother has already remarked, "*elle a raison* dans la comparaison" (17, *my emphasis*). Rightly, moreover, because her comparison recalls what so many readers of Scudéry had already done and
would continue to do for centuries more – to wit, notice that certain
elements of the Roman world of romance uncannily recall the contemporary world of the salonnière's Samedis. Her mistake, her malady, is
simply that she does not know how to use a key; instead of concluding,
as Scudéry's readers clearly did, that these historical characters might
just be disguised versions of her contemporaries, d'Arviane reasons, in
reverse, that she must be a figure from historical romance. Her illness,
then, is a historical symptom that has nothing to do with the truism that
one must not take books for life, but with a literary context in which
strategies for referring novels to the present-day world had taken on
acute importance. One such strategy was the key.

As we have seen, *La Fausse Clélie* depicts characters that are
continually shuttling back and forth between the stories they hear and
the shared, known world in which they all exist; their narratives' correspondence to that world must be ascertained. And a good part of the
process of evaluation hinges on naming: fitting names to narrative
becomes central to the type of reading Subligny is teaching. This is
obvious even in the way the protagonists of the novel's third-person
(that is, heterodiegetic) embedded narratives – *faits divers*, tales of
roguery, and so on – are carefully named.[27] The man whose papers are
torn up by a sprite is "Santois, échevin de Paris"; the bawdy tale of
Luchères is told at Mulionne's chateau precisely when the protagonist's name comes to light; even Barbesieux's *histoire tragique* about
the lover who refused to compromise his mistress's alibi contains his
name (the Comte de Bernilly). On occasion names are missing, but
other information is supplied that would seem to encourage readers to
find a name to go with the narrative, as in the case of the magistrate (*le
président*) from Ardivilliers, who finds his chateau "haunted" by some
crooks who want to force him from it. Meanwhile, the embedded narratives revolving around the past of the main characters also highlight
the act of fitting names and places to narrative. As we have seen,
Riberville is able to verify Montal's story – felt by most listeners to be
highly improbable – because it enables him to fill in a blank opened up
by a previously heard story: "'J'ai ouï parler de cette histoire...; mais je

ne croyais pas,' dit-il au Chevalier, 'que tu en fusses le Héros, et on ne
nommait personne'" (37). Anonymity is an invitation to be curious,
and to start the process of identification. Hence speculation regarding
Riberville's past reaches a fever pitch when d'Arviane reveals that she
knows "'celle avec qui [sa] dernière aventure est arrivée'" (51). Riberville begs her not to name names if she continues with his story, but
only succeeds in piquing everyone's interest even further: "'il craint
qu'on ne nomme les gens...; ce doit être une Histoire d'importance'"
(52). D'Arviane obeys Riberville's request for anonymity to the letter,
but certainly not in spirit, for as he laughingly points out at the end,
"'Il est vrai, Madame...que la chose est bien malaisée à deviner, après
que vous avez nommé Toulouse et dit que la Dame allait au rendezvous pendant que son mari allait au Palais'" (59). Such details, Riberville implies, are intended to be clues, and the consumption of narrative has become an explicit game of identifications, as the alert reader
penetrates temporary anonymity so as to produce a narrative map of
the known social world.

　　If, as I have been contending, *La Fausse Clélie* offers, *en
abyme*, a model for reading, the interest Subligny's characters take in
names gives us cause to wonder: perhaps Subligny would have his
readers fit real-world names to the narratives he spins? After all, the
author puts the question of naming front and center in a short preface
often cited in histories of literary realism. "Il me reste maintenant," he
writes, after a few standard remarks about hoping to please his reader,
"à parler de [la] nouvelle façon d'écrire qu'il pourra sembler que j'ai
introduite. Peu de gens avant moi s'étaient avisés de donner des noms
français à leurs Héros" (n.p.).[28] Indeed, from this point on plausible-
sounding French names will become a feature of the *nouvelle galante*
especially, most of which are formed from a fairly predictable number
of suffixes – "-ville," "-sac," "-cour," and so on.[29] But plausibility may
not be what is at issue, or at least not only what is at issue, for these
"noms français" for the most part beg to be read as anagrams.[30] Hence,
Alain Niderst has suggested that the Abbé de Ruper can hide only the
Abbé de Pure, and that Lusigny must be Subligny himself: "Il est à
peine besoin d'une clef, car les noms réels sont respectés, ou à peine
déformés" (*Essai d'histoire littéraire* 54). A contemporary key, moreover, does exist, and was printed and included in at least one copy of
the 1672 Amsterdam edition, published by Jacques Wagenaar.[31] It confirms the anagrams Niderst detected, and offers others: "Clélie"'s
abductor, the Comte de Sarbedat, is given as a certain Saubedac; Santois, who was spooked by the sprite, is "Monsieur de Santeüil, Echevin

de Paris"; another walk-on character, the Marquis de Luseau, is the
Chevalier de Lauzain. Most of the identifications, however, do not
work through onomastic resemblance. Montal, is not, as Niderst
hypothesizes, given as François de Montsaulvin, "deuxième fils du
fameux comte de Montal, qui combattit pour Condé après la Fronde"
(*Essai d'histoire littéraire* 54), but as the Chevalier de Cavois. The key
identifies most, if not absolutely all, of the characters in the novel,
down to the most minor *comparses* ("l'ami au justaucorps bleu," featured in one short anecdote, is, apparently, the Marquis de Carvois). So
much for *La Fausse Clélie* denouncing literal reference: on the contrary, its characters' constant mapping of narrative onto their "real
world" has, it seems, spread outward to Subligny's own readers, now
expected to relate his tales to the real "real world" of 1660s France.

The female Quixote that is Juliette d'Arviane is not mad
because she reads too literally, but because she does not read literally
enough; she insists on viewing her own life through the lens of
Scudéry's historical fictions, whereas it is Scudéry who must be read
through the lens of contemporary society. And so if d'Arviane unnec-
essarily renames herself Clélie, Subligny, by contrast, constructs his
novel on the opposite principle, and converts all those romance names
back into French. His preface continues:

> [I]l est à craindre que quelques esprits Romanesques voyant un nom de *Mar-
> quis de Riberville, de Mirstain, de Franlieu, et autres*, au lieu de celui d'un
> *Tiridate* ou d'un *Cléante*, ne fassent d'abord le procès à mon livre. Mais je
> demande pardon à ces esprits délicats, si pour leur plaire je ne fais pas des
> Grecs ou des Arabes de ceux que veux faire passer pour des Français un peu
> galants. Je suis un bon Picard qui appelle un chacun du nom qui lui est propre.
> (n.p.)[32]

Subligny does not argue that the adventures of a Tiridate are more
ridiculous or improbable than the ones he will narrate, for they are, at
bottom, the same adventures all around; in the passage from Scuderian
romance to *La Fausse Clélie*, only the names have been changed. Two
things follow from Subligny's remarks. First, d'Arviane does not stand
in for *the* reader of Scudéry; she is merely a *bad* reader of Scudéry –
bad because she has not understood that conventional Roman names
were made to be read through, or keyed to the French world. Second,
Subligny proposes something new to avoid altogether this problem. He
will give readers the lesson in direct and truthful referentiality we have
seen; he will strip contemporary culture of its classical alibi; and most
important, he will reformulate Scudéry's keying practice, designed

with the closed world of the coterie in mind, to suit the infinite universe of modern print culture.

A robust critical interest in the history of reading practices has in the last few years called keyed forms of reading back from the disrepute in which they had long been held: even if modern readers tend to be put off at the idea of keys – for thoroughly historical reasons I will address below – the latter were demonstrably, and in remarkably diverse ways, part of an earlier horizon of expectations that can be reconstructed.[33] The relevant context of Subligny's particular use of keys is – unsurprisingly, given his novel's title – Scuderian romance. The extent, nature and significance of Scudéry's use of keys has been hotly debated ever since Victor Cousin proposed in 1858 that the plots and characters of *Artamène* and *Clélie* offered a veritable a window onto the lives of the aristocrats in the circle of Scudéry's famous Samedis. The authenticity of the manuscript key, purportedly dated 1657, that Cousin reported having dug up in the Bibliothèque de l'Arsenal has been put into doubt, partially on the basis of its disappearance (suspiciously, Cousin was the only one to have seen it); moreover, various internal problems make Cousin's view of *Artamène* as a barely disguised relation of Grand Siècle life highly problematic.[34] Other doubts riddle attempts to use keys to decipher Scudéry's works: not only are the keys proposed usually bewilderingly contradictory, but the author herself also refuted their existence in a letter ("je n'ai jamais donné de clef ni de Cyrus, ni de Clélie, et je n'en ai pas moi-même" [cited in Godenne 88]). Still, as suggested by Scudéry's denial itself, not to mention other anecdotal evidence – from letters of Lafayette to a remark in Christian Huygens's journals – the *possible* reference of romance characters to people in the real world was very much on the minds of readers at the time.[35] The abundantly testified propensity of contemporaries to view Molière's protagonists as having specific real-world models or the printed keys to La Bruyère's later *Les Caractères* only confirms the suggestion.[36] The point that keyed reading is most definitely not anachronistic projection on the part of Cousin is brought home by the fact that Scudéry herself incorporates such expectations into the *Clélie*: her characters wonder about, and then exchange, possible keys before going on to discuss the pros and cons of this type of reading (1:496-501). Moreover, the burgeoning genre of the literary portrait, which patently depends on real-world referents, is imported by Scudéry into a novel whose very title subliminally spurs us, perhaps, to look for keys.

The problem of Subligny's heroine is thus a historical one, linked to developments in keyed reading practices in the 1650s and 1660s: d'Arviane lacks the code that would allow her to profit from the increasingly intricate web being spun between novels and contemporary society. She can be pardoned her ignorance, for readers of romance prior to Scudéry had long been spared the task of ferreting out possible resemblances between this or that character and this or that person. D'Urfé's *L'Astrée* is the most apposite example. What is curious about this pastoral romance is precisely that it almost completely does away with the types of pseudonymous games that had characterized Renaissance pastoral. As Françoise Lavocat has detailed in *Arcadies malheureuses*, d'Urfé, following his Spanish predecessors Montemayor and Cervantes, severs his pastoral world from the first-person poet-narrator that in Sannazaro's highly influential *Arcadia* (pub. 1508) – and indeed in the lyric Virgilian tradition more generally – had made of the genre a transparent allegory of relations between the poet, his colleagues, his rivals, and his patrons. Nor does d'Urfé do much to encourage readers to view his labyrinthine narrative as keyed, save including a prefatory denial of real-world referents unaccompanied by any obvious markers of irony.[37] Indeed, no evidence exists to suggest that d'Urfé's immediate contemporaries violated his wishes; and when a member of a later generation, the jurist Olivier Patru, searched the romance for what he called its "fondement véritable" (559), he was essentially concerned with understanding the techniques by which d'Urfé may have transposed his own experience into fiction.[38] None of this much resembles Scudéry's use of keys, which if anything marks something of a return to Sannazaro's academic model. In *Clélie*, readers who are presumed to be "in the know" or who at least fancy themselves as such are encouraged to view characters as pseudonymous covers of members of a conspicuous social group. Juliette d'Arviane is simply the last to know.

Subligny's keying, however, is distinctive. Crucially, Subligny eliminates the very device that was the pivot of keyed reading in Scudéry – the portrait. For, as Chantal Morlet-Chantalat has argued, it was principally the portrait that provoked guessing games, not this or that narrative: *Clélie* is not a compendium of contemporary gossip.[39] Gossip, by contrast, is what *La Fausse Clélie* is all about. Subligny was a man of the nascent "society" press, since his weekly newsletter in verse, *La Muse de la cour*, which appeared in the mid 1660s, catered to the news demands of those at court and in the city. And indeed, reading his novel is very much like reading a gazette – only one that does not limit itself to the goings-on of a given group, but one that, anticipating the *Mercure galant* (1672), canvasses all of France for appropriately diverting tales. That Subligny drop Scudéry's practice of pseudonyms, which came straight from the extra-literary games that characterized gallant society (Denis 189-235), appears fully logical – not so much a move in the direction of increasing "realism" as a recognition that the ideal of the coterie was inadequate to the type of reading he was attempting to put into place. Anagrams and more minor onomastic deformations, by contrast, suited much better his purpose. They were not a code, but clues capable of underwriting investigation, as we have seen Riberville point out: "'la chose est bien malaisée à deviner, après que vous avez nommé Toulouse et dit que la Dame allait au rendez-vous pendant que son mari allait au Palais'" (59). Moreover, there are at least a couple of indications that Subligny, unlike Scudéry, is actually keying the action of his novel, or at least its embedded stories. The key identifies Riberville as the Chevalier de Rohan, while the unhappily married Comtesse de Tourneüil, whom Riberville helps escape from her jealous husband, and who takes refuge in England, is keyed to Madame de Mazarin.[40] Here, the parallels with what we know – indeed, what everyone at the time knew – are clear, for Hortense Mancini did indeed enlist her presumed lover the Chevalier de Rohan so as to flee to Italy, in June of 1668. It is also doubtless significant that the adventure that occurs between Riberville and the unnamed Dame de Toulouse (the one about whom the friends learn enough to identify her, Riberville thinks) is keyed not to Rohan, but to "Le Marquis de Trerigni et Mademoiselle de Keravioir, soeur de la Présidente Laelant." Riberville's character can, it would seem, serves as a "host" for miscellaneous pieces of gossip. Further biographical research into the identity of this "Keravioir" or anyone else for that matter is probably unnecessary. Whether or not all the adventures recounted here refer to real-world affairs, Subligny wants us – with an insistence that never characterized the age-old topos of the "true story" – to think they do. Hence the inclusion of hints that enable his readers to do more or less what his characters do, which is to undertake the work of fitting narratives to the world they know.

　　　　Yet one thing that does not change between Scudéry and Subligny, and indeed characterizes much discourse about keys in these years, is that reference was almost always blurred, intentionally and necessarily. For with the exception of the related but distinct practices of satire and the *chronique scandaleuse*, keyed reading seems to have been a much more open-ended, labile practice than is often supposed.[41]

Artamène and *Clélie*, for instance, probably did not have one "author-ized" complete key, now regrettably lost. On the contrary, it would appear that some parts of the work were more clearly keyed than others; that some characters could have obvious models while others did not; and that, finally, keys were intended not as an end to reading but as part of the reading process itself. Hence scholars who argue on principle against the pertinence of keys – the principle, dear to professors of literature, that keys reduce literature to historical documents – are misdirected, in that the seventeenth-century conception of the key was in no sense positivist. Indeed, authors who, like Scudéry, raise the possibility of a key typically go on to discount it; and those who protest against keyed readings often say or do something else that give cause for thinking the warnings ironic. Whence Furetière, whose preface to the *Roman bourgeois* (1666) begs for a general and not specific reading of his characters, but who then goes on to hint that his text is indeed referential – only cryptically so: "[La clef] ne te servira de rien, car la serrure est mêlée. Si tu crois voir le portrait de l'un, tu trouveras l'histoire de l'autre" (901). Or La Bruyère, whose paratextual dismissal of keys is both laden with irony and in manifest conflict with the onomastic guessing games that his text begs the reader to play (see Tourette). Or, finally, Subligny. For Subligny, who seems to do so much to teach his readers to perform an incessant back-and-forth between narrative and reality, remains coy in his preface about the name game he proposes.

> J'ajouterai une très humble prière aux personnes dont le nom peut avoir quelque ressemblance avec ceux que j'ai inventés, de ne pas croire que je l'aie fait à dessein. Ils verront bien par le peu de conformité qu'il y aura de leurs aventures avec celles de mes Histoires que c'est plutôt l'effet du hasard que de mon intention. Et en tout cas, je n'y introduis guère de galants que ce ne soit à leur avantage. (n.p.)

Save one pro forma sentence excusing eventual typographical errors, this is the end of Subligny's preface. It is a denial of real-world reference whose ironic final twist quite plainly encourages readers to look for "resemblance" and "conformity" between book and world.

Such a Janus-like position might well be useful for reasons of decorum, or even to preserve a quasi-legal "deniability" in the wake of Bussy-Rabutin's imprisonment over *L'Histoire amoureuse des Gaules* in 1665. These were years, after all, when expanding print markets were making the ideal of a closed community increasingly anachronistic, and the indecorous circulation of gossip was a problem many writers needed to think about. *La Princesse de Clèves*, too, can be viewed

as a lesson on the dangers of referential discourse that circulates too
promiscuously, a reply of sorts to books such as Bussy-Rabutin's.[42]
But there is no doubt another factor that explains the slippery nature of
discussion about keys in these years, and that is the lack of any clear
concept of fiction in a modern sense. Whence a second reason why
seventeenth-century keys cannot possibly reduce "literature" to "historical documents": the period did not possess modern notions of character and fictionality, and was instead experimenting with other ways
of linking text and world. The reader of *Le Rouge et le noir* is not
encouraged even to think there exists a real person of whom Julien
Sorel may be the mask. Stendhal has no need of awakening in the back
of our mind such a possibility; and should someone point out that
Stendhal based the character's trajectory on the newspaper account of
a real young man, we might be interested in this window onto the
author's work processes, but we would not, certainly, understand such
a source as a key. This is not because we are less naïve that seventeenth-century readers, but because circumstances have altered considerably from the time of Scudéry and Subligny. Keys, in short, had been
a way of countering the reproach long directed at the work of poets,
and with which Stendhal would no longer have to reckon: that is was
empty of truth, purely imagined – "fiction" in the venerable sense of
"lies." But writers also needed to refuse to commit to a one-to-one correspondence that would make of them historians, that might get them
in legal trouble, and most important perhaps, that would imply that
readers not in possession of a key – say, the German readers of a
translated *Clélie*, or people in Brittany who have no idea of who's who
in Subligny's Toulouse – have no reason to read. Hence, the existence
of a key was a necessary fantasy underwriting novel reading at a time
when "fiction" did not yet mean what it would well over a hundred
years later.

   And if keys were a historically necessary fantasy for readers of
the seventeenth century, the modern dismissal of keys is an inevitable
consequence of a concept of fiction that Scudéry and Subligny did not
have available; that is, the idea that narrative discourse can purport to
take place in the real world without being literally true. It may at first
appear curious that Cousin produced his key to *Artamène* and *Clélie* in
precisely the years that fiction had triumphed: after all, one would
think that he should be a less literal reader, given the realist codes of
the mid-nineteenth century. His thesis no doubt owes much to his profession, that of the historian who validated his status via the erudition
he deployed (Ribard). But his literal reading actually makes broader

literary-historical sense. Once one is equipped with the concept of fiction and the types of characters that people it, Scudéry's characters, who did not seem in any way "deep," could legitimately be supposed to operate according to different principles.[43] Unfortunately, Cousin's perspicacity extended only so far, for "pre-fictional" did not mean literal-minded. On the contrary, writers of Scudéry's time and well after occupied themselves with inventing strategies for making the bond between book and world both firm and supple. Keys were one such strategy, and one moreover with their own intricate history. Subligny was engaged in an effort to think about how the device that Scudéry had returned to the center of literary preoccupations could be reused in a print economy that bore little resemblance to the closed world of the salon. *La Fausse Clélie* might be said to be representative of the leading edge of a mode that would dominate the novel throughout the eighteenth century, one that Barbara Foley has usefully called the "pseudo-factual," so as to differentiate it from nineteenth-century realism. These were narratives that advanced claims to literal truth, but ironized and undercut them, leaving the reader to surmise that novels must maintain some sort of ambiguous relation with the world. The contradiction inherent to the pseudo-factual was necessary given the absence of any firmly articulated concept of what Foley calls "analogous configuration" – the idea that fiction could be like reality without being real.[44]

Subligny's puzzling novel provides one of the pseudo-factual's early incarnations – call it the pseudo-false, perhaps, since the author says his novel is made up, hints that it is not, and then goes ahead and uses it to show how narrative refers to the real world. Terms like this are inevitably idiosyncratic, but they cannot be avoided. The modern categories of fiction and non-fiction simply do not map onto the early novel. Properly speaking, and without broaching the quite different issue of the extent to which the conceits of fiction contaminate all purportedly historical discourse, or the question of "just how much" Subligny might have distorted real events, *La Fausse Clélie* is neither fiction nor non-fiction. The difficulty of naming the type of reading it calls for is, however, the interest of the text. Subligny demonstrates no particular prescience; *La Fausse Clélie* is not even a good early example of the pseudo-factual, never mind a harbinger of some later realism. One might go so far as to say that the reading lesson it offers – a lesson in reading for truth, but a masked and slightly altered truth that can never quite admit it is true – is an example of a historical dead end. For as a mechanism for underwriting a slippery, pre-fictional link between book and world, the device of keys was clumsy and con-straining – not only dangerous, as the example of Bussy-Rabutin proved, but largely incompatible with the anonymous book market and the invention of the general reader. Later writers – d'Aulnoy and her *Voyage en Espagne* (1691) come to mind, though the process begins before then – would maintain truth without hinting at keys, while all the while serving up those affirmations in an ever more ironic sauce. But Subligny's lesson in referential reading still teaches us how to unlearn the dominant modern modes of reading we call fiction and realism, and recognize that novel reading has never been intuitive or natural as it may now seem.

Notes

[1] I would like to thank Juliette Cherbuliez and The Group for Theorizing Early Modern Sovereignty at the University of Minnesota for giving me the opportunity to discuss and present very early versions of many of the ideas that I deal with here. I would also like to gratefully acknowledge the Hellman Fund for providing the resources to do much of the primary research on and around Subligny. Finally, thanks to Órlaith Creedon for much last-minute research help.

[2] See, for example, Chartier, Jordan and Patten, Benedict, Paige *Being Interior*, and Séité. For a less obviously historicized look at how the rhetorical apparatus of the text implies its own reader and shapes its own reception, see Iser.

[3] See, respectively, Marshall, Lynch, and Gallagher. I will return to the question of fiction in my conclusion.

[4] The bibliography on this shift is extensive. For two influential accounts, see Davis and McKeon. The French case specifically is covered by Showalter 11-37.

[5] For the critical tradition that insists on the continuity between the modern novel and previous prose fiction, see Bakhtin and Doody. For an account of how romance, through recourse to more specifically drawn historical settings, tried to refute criticism of its fancifulness, see again McKeon 52-58.

[6] Lafayette's heroine's relation to the historical narratives she hears has been an object of inquiry ever since its publication; see especially Lyons, Beasely 212-24, and Stone 150-69. It remains to point out that in referring to the teaching of reading within novels of the time, I am using "reading" metaphorically: I assume that the relation of characters to stories they hear orally, while not *identical* to the relation of readers to books, is at least analogous to it, and that the former provides a way of figuring the latter.

[7] Subligny's work was fairly popular at the time, as is evidenced by repeated publica-tions, both in the 1670s and again in the 1710s, as Marivaux and Challe were experi-menting with the future of French fiction. The original Paris edition of 1670, cited by

Lenglet-Dufresnoy, is lost; the first Dutch editions (1671, 1672, 1680) are nearly identical (the 1680 edition especially may be a repackaging of unsold volumes of an earlier printing); early eighteenth-century editions (1710, 1712, 1716, 1718) vary in format. Scholarship on Subligny's text is limited; see especially Serroy 670-79, Coulet 258-59, and Sermain 71-73. For additional studies, see Lathuillère, Niderst *Essai d'histoire littéraire*, and Garsault; the latter two take up especially the novel as possible ancestor of Challe's *Les Illustres Françaises* (1713).

[8] My reading here is thus directly opposed to interpretations of seventeenth-century comic novels (be they *Don Quixote*, Sorel's *Le Berger extravagant* [1627-1628] or *La Fausse Clélie*) as denouncing narrative referentiality; for an example of such an interpretation, see Hodgson.

[9] In citing Subligny's text, I have both modernized spelling and corrected the obvious misprints that riddle the Dutch editions; to facilitate presentation of dialogue, I have also added quotation marks around reported speech.

[10] For consistency and brevity, and except in cases where confusion might result, I will refer to all characters by their last name.

[11] For reasons that Subligny does not explain, Riberville and Montal *tutoient* each other.

[12] "*Esprit fort* est une espèce d'injure qu'on dit à ces libertins et incrédules qui se mettent au-dessus des croyances et des opinions populaires. La plupart des beaux *esprits* font les *esprits forts*, qui ne s'étonnent de rien, qu'on ne persuade pas aisément" (Furetière).

[13] Montal's association of superstitious discourse with socially inferior sources is typical of an inversion in the Western history of the marvelous, by which phenomena that had been the subject of elite interest become stigmatized as popular error; see Daston and Park. The ending of Racine's roughly contemporary *Iphigénie* (1674) furnishes an example of skepticism's intrusion into myth (normally exempt from such considerations on account of its manifest fabulousness): the task of asserting that Diane descended to claim Eriphile is devolved to a potentially unreliable or credulous soldier (ll. 1781-84).

[14] Thomas Pavel's description of *L'Astrée* holds for romance more generally: "[A] part quelques cas de tromperie volontaire, les récits de *L'Astrée*...sont racontés par des narrateurs parfaitement au courant des événements, véridiques et scrupuleux. Ces narrations, de surcroît, ne sont presque jamais contestées. Elles ne présentent pas le point de vue d'un des personnages sur les faits, point de vue qui serait susceptible d'être contredit ou du moins modifié par un témoignage différent" (251). This romance reliability had previously been pointed out by Horowitz 128.

[15] That is, before approximately 1630, romances included a high proportion of first-person narratives; for reasons of aristocratic decorum, later authors would modify this procedure. For more information on romance narrators, with special attention to early modern transformations of the topoi of the Greek novels of Heliodorus and Achilles Tatius, see Plazenet 597-624.

[16] On the truth topos in Marguerite de Navarre, see Mathieu-Castellani 7-22; for a wider view, see also Pérouse.

[17] The narratological terms are Genette's; by and large, *La Fausse Clélie* can be discussed easily without them, but I will occasionally include them when I feel they might add clarity for some readers. For a very brief presentation of the terms I use here (in reference moreover to Saint-Amant's *Moïse sauvé* [1653]), see Genette.

[18] Serroy seems to be following Coulet, who states: "Subligny engage dans une action unique un groupe de personnages qui nous sont donnés à connaître par leur conduite au cours de cette action, par les histoires qu'ils racontent d'eux-mêmes ou des autres, par les commentaires que ces histoires suscitent" (254). As I have mentioned, in late French romances decorum prevented aristocratic characters from providing accounts of their own heroic actions; instead, secondary characters provided the stories of their masters. This elimination of the first person was especially thorough by Scudéry's time; of the 39 embedded narratives of *Artamène, ou le Grand Cyrus* (1649-53), only three are in the first person (Godenne 97n1).

[19] "'Si c'est une histoire,'" says Montal to Velzers, "'vous la conterez donc, aussi bien que nous en avons conté les nôtres....' 'Vraiment, dit Madame de Mulionne, voilà de quoi faire la matière du plus joli Roman du monde, si chacun veut conter la sienne'" (43); the rest of the group immediately agrees.

[20] As Chantal Morlet-Chatalat has remarked, Scudéry for instance does not actually pursue the possibility of interweaving her various narrative threads. Between embedded tales and frame tale there is at best "un vague rapport d'antériorité qui...ne donne lieu à aucune surprise exploitable dans la suite des événements romanesques" (236). A better model for Subligny's interweave might be the extremely intricate structure of *L'Astrée* (see Aragon) or the enigmatic story of Destin and L'Etoile in the *Roman comique,* although both these works are exempt from worries about narrative truth. Subligny's interest in the interweaving of narrative threads is shared by some of his contemporaries – notably, Lafayette, in *Zayde* (1670-71), and Villedieu, in *Les Exilés de la cour d'Auguste* (1672). Challe's *Les Illustres Françaises* is typically seen as the finest (and final, at least until Balzac) example of this sort of interweave.

[21] I would, however, take care to separate Subligny's construction of characters with multiple or complicated pasts from characters that seem psychologically "deep" in a Romantic sense. Coulet suggests that Subligny's characters may be proto-Romantic when he describes the effect of the multiple interlocking narratives as follows: "en confrontant entre eux ces divers éléments, on saisit chaque personnage non dans son portrait achevé et arrêté, mais dans son dynamisme et dans ses relations avec les autres[;] on comprend que sa vérité est au-delà des indications contradictoires données sur lui" (254). But Riberville is not unknowable or dynamic in any psychological sense; his complicated past has only factual interest. I will return to the problem of character in my concluding remarks.

[22] Similarly, Velzers will validate her story by entwining it with another publicly known fact, the death of the suitor (cf. 95).

[23] "'Ce qui me confirma dans cette résolution était l'exemple tout frais d'une fille qu'un brutal avait empoisonné, parce qu'il n'avait pu l'obtenir de ses père et mère'" (183).

[24] The murder of the Marquise de Ganges in 1667 was the subject of a number of factums whose republication suggests widespread interest. In the 1670s, the factums pro-

duced around the Brinvilliers case and the affair of the poisons were widely reprinted, and even appended to new editions of François de Rosset's famous *Histoires tragiques*. For more information on factums around this time, see Biet 143-71 and O'Hara; as Maza has established, factums became ever more public in the following century.

[25] Jean Donneau de Visé's *Nouvelles galantes, comiques et tragiques* (1669), which contains a variety of innovative means of presenting narratives whose actual content is often unremarkable, features a number of tales said to come straight from court. Early issues of his *Mercure galant* also contained purported court cases.

[26] What I am calling intrinsic plausibility, based on a sense of probability, logic, experience, and the laws of nature, differs from the classical idea of *vraisemblance*, which is inseparable from questions of social decorum and literary tradition. This is not to say that some criteria of plausibility are "natural," as opposed to conventional, but that the conventions governing intrinsic plausibility are specific.

[27] In contrast with the *Heptaméron*, in which "true" tales feature at best characters whose names are onomastic plays on character traits; see for example Winn. To be sure, scholars have made efforts to identify, with apparent success, many of the tales' real-world referents; see Cazauran 30-33. For a broad look at Renaissance name play, see Rigolot.

[28] A presentation and reproduction of Subligny's preface can be found in Esmein 352-55.

[29] See for example Showalter, who discusses Subligny's naming practice specifically on 164-65. For some general remarks, see also Watt 18-21. "Romance" (chiefly pseudo-Greek) names – Philandre, Clitandre, Philis – continue to be used well into the eighteenth century, however.

[30] That such a decoding was well within contemporary expectations is clear from the fact that anagrammatical reading was practiced both in erudite circles (Hallyn) and in salon literature (Denis 225-27).

[31] The example consulted is in the collection of the Bancroft Library, University of California, Berkeley (PT1100.F7 no. 1061 \t\). Niderst to all appearances was unaware of this key when he made his identifications of Subligny's protagonists.

[32] Subligny might be responding here to a wish expressed by one of the *devisantes* in Segrais's *Nouvelles françaises*, where the question of names is foregrounded: "[J]e m'étonne que tant de gens d'esprit, qui nous ont imaginé de si honnêtes Scythes et des Parthes si généreux, n'ont pris le même plaisir d'imaginer des chevaliers ou des princes français aussi accomplis, dont les aventures n'eussent été moins plaisantes" (1:19).

[33] The most notable sign of a change in critical winds has been the appearance of a volume of *Littératures classiques* devoted to the subject (Bombart and Escola). For pioneering work on the subject, see Beugnot, who argues that the significance of keys far outstrips the "sociologie primaire" (229) often practiced by their nineteenth-century champions; and Stewart, who provides a brief overview of the post-romance use of keys in France.

[34] For instance, the key covered too few of the book's many characters to authorize us to view the entire opus as keyed. For a critique of Cousin's position, see Godenne 83-96. Since Cousin, other researchers have attempted to devise keys from scratch, based on various biographical clues; see especially Niderst *Madeleine de Scudéry, Paul Pellisson et leur monde* and "Sur les clefs de *Clélie*."

[35] Lafayette refers on two occasions, in 1657 and 1658, to keys to *Clélie* (544, 566); for the contents of Huygens's remark, see Mesnard 371; Mesnard's article offers a spirited defense of the relevance of keys to Scudéry's fiction.

[36] As Norman has shown, Molière was at pains to demonstrate that his comedies had general applicability and were not in fact satire, a genre which had freely admitted of specific targets hidden under a pseudonymous veil. For the case of La Bruyère, see Couton 106-14.

[37] "Si tu te trouves parmi ceux qui font profession d'interpréter les songes, et découvrir les pensées plus secrètes d'autrui, et qu'ils assurent que Céladon est un tel homme, et Astrée une telle femme, ne leur réponds rien, car ils savent assez qu'ils ne savent pas ce qu'ils disent" (Urfé 1:6).

[38] The author therefore becomes, in Lavocat's words, an "archi-référent" "rayonnant vers plusieurs entités fictionnelles" ("Lectures" 38). Such curiosity, directed more at the author's personal experience than at the real identities of a circle of protagonists, is of a piece with, say, contemporary interest in Montaigne the man (Paige *Being Interior* 39-50).

[39] "Il semble donc que, tandis que le portrait laisse apparaître de plus en plus clairement ses liens avec l'actualité, l'histoire intercalée, dans ses parties proprement narratives, reste tributaire d'une tradition de réflexion morale" (Morlet-Chantalat 214). One should perhaps nuance this with the observation that a limited number of intercalated narratives, advanced as *divertissements* that further the romance's *diversité*, are claimed to be recent gallant adventures recounted under supposed names; notably, it is the "histoire d'Artaxandre" (1:435-95), recounted by Amilcar, that actually leads to the discussion on keys. The case is somewhat complicated, however, by the fact that Amilcar's cast of characters is unknown to the main group. As Clélie herself observes, stories coming from outside the coterie do not need name changes in the first place, since no one possesses the knowledge that will permit identifications. Additional information on the keys to Scudéry's portraits in *Clélie* can be found in Plantié 725-35.

[40] Rohan was a brilliant member of court society who has the distinction of being the only member of the upper nobility executed during Louis XIV's long reign after a failed plot against the crown in 1674.

[41] The *chronique scandaleuse*, "keyed" in that it patently referred to well-known events (usually the loves of the politically influential), became in the later part of the century a significant subset of the *nouvelle historique* (Harth 190-206); this type of keying was widely practiced in the eighteenth century as well (in the oriental tale, for instance), and prospered in England, too – perhaps because strict liable laws discouraged direct naming (see Gallagher, chap. 3). While such keying to publicly known figures is present in *La Fausse Clélie* (indeed, the author incorporates a discussion of *la chronique*

scandaleuse [292-96]), the novel generally seems to refer to myriad events that have no immediate claim on readers' imaginations other than that they occurred.

[42] DeJean, in "Lafayette's Ellipses," has provided a pioneering contextualization of Lafayette's novel in terms of an ambient culture of printed gossip. Gevrey has articulated a similar reading, although without reference to DeJean's work (esp. 195-97). For the argument that trends in print circulation threatened to upend earlier modes of literary production and consumption, see DeJean's *Reinvention of Obscenity*. The increasing difficulty of conceptualizing literature as a type of coterie practice is addressed by Paige in "The Storyteller and the Book."

[43] For an argument regarding the late eighteenth-century origins of character conceived of as round or deep, see Lynch. See also Woloch on the particular "character space" of the nineteenth-century novel.

[44] For another effort to understand how modern "fiction" is qualitatively different from the pretension to literal truth, see again Gallagher. The tradition of the "truth topos," and its prevalence in purportedly true memoirs and letter collections, is too well known and vast a subject to delve into here.

Works Cited

Aragon, Elisabeth. "L'enchâssement dans *L'Astrée.*" *Cahiers de littérature du dix-septième siècle* 3 (1981): 1-43.

Bakhtin, M. M. *The Dialogic Imagination: Four Essays*. Trans. Caryl Emerson and Michael Holquist. Ed. Michael Holquist. Austin: University of Texas Press, 1981.

Barthes, Roland. "L'effet de réel." 1968. *Littérature et réalité*. Eds. Gérard Genette and Tzvetan Todorov. Paris: Seuil, 1982. 81-90.

Beasley, Faith E. *Revising Memory: Women's Fiction and Memoirs in Seventeenth-Century France*. New Brunswick, N.J.: Rutgers University Press, 1990.

Benedict, Barbara M. *Making the Modern Reader: Cultural Mediation in Early Modern Literary Anthologies*. Princeton: Princeton University Press, 1996.

Beugnot, Bernard. "Oedipe et le sphinx: Des clés." *La Mémoire du texte: Essais de poétique classique*. Paris: Champion, 1994. 227-42.

Biet, Christian. *Droit et littérature sous l'Ancien Régime. Le jeu de la valeur et de la loi.* Paris: Champion, 2002.

Bombart, Mathilde, and Marc Escola, eds. *Lectures à clef. Littératures Classiques* 54 (2005).

Cazauran, Nicole. *L'Heptaméron de Marguerite de Navarre.* 2nd ed. Paris: SEDES, 1976.

Chartier, Roger. *L'Ordre des livres: Lecteurs, auteurs, bibliothèques en Europe entre XIVe et XVIIIe siècle.* Aix-en-Provence: Alinéa, 1992.

Coulet, Henri. *Le Roman jusqu'à la Révolution.* 9th ed. Paris: Armand Colin, 2000.

Couton, Georges. *Ecritures codées: Essais sur l'allégorie au XVIIe siècle.* Paris: Klincksieck, 1991.

Daston, Loraine, and Katherine Park. *Wonders and the Order of Nature, 1150-1750.* New York: Zone Books, 1998.

Davis, Lennard J. *Factual Fictions: The Origins of the English Novel.* New York: Columbia University Press, 1983.

DeJean, Joan. "Lafayette's Ellipses: The Privileges of Anonymity." *PMLA* 99 (1984): 884-902.

_____. *The Reinvention of Obscenity: Sex, Lies, and Tabloids in Early Modern France.* Chicago: University of Chicago Press, 2002.

Denis, Delphine. *Le Parnasse galant: Institution d'une catégorie littéraire au XVIIe siècle.* Paris: Champion, 2001.

Doody, Margaret Anne. *The True Story of the Novel.* New Brunswick, N.J.: Rutgers University Press, 1996.

Esmein, Camille. *Poétiques du roman: Scudéry, Huet, Du Plaisir et autres textes théoriques et critiques du XVIIe siècle sur le genre romanesque.* Paris: Champion, 2004.

Foley, Barbara. *Telling the Truth: The Theory and Practice of Documentary Fiction.* Ithaca: Cornell University Press, 1986.

Furetière, Antoine. *Le Roman bourgeois.* 1666. *Romanciers du XVIIe siècle*. Ed. Antoine Adam. Paris: Gallimard, 1958. 899-1104.

Gallagher, Catherine. *Nobody's Story: The Vanishing Acts of Women Writers in the Marketplace, 1670-1820*. Berkeley: University of California Press, 1994.

Garsault, Alain. "Une Source des *Illustres Françaises* de Robert Challes: *La Fausse Clélie* de Subligny." *Dix-septième siècle* 79 (1986): 57-66.

Genette, Gérard. "D'un récit baroque." *Figures II*. Paris: Seuil, 1969. 195-222.

Gevrey, Françoise. "Lectures à clés de *La Princesse de Clèves* au XVIIIe siècle." *Littératures Classiques* 54 (2005): 191-203.

Godenne, René. *Les Romans de Mademoiselle de Scudéry*. Geneva: Droz, 1983.

Hallyn, Fernand. "L'anagramme et ses styles au XVIIe siècle." *Littératures Classiques* 28 (1996): 239-54.

Harth, Erica. *Ideology and Culture in Seventeenth-Century France*. Ithaca: Cornell University Press, 1983.

Hodgson, Richard G. "'Une Prodigieuse aliénation d'esprit': The Referential Fallacy in the Seventeenth-Century French Novel." *Selecta: Journal of the Pacific Northwest Council on Foreign Languages* 7 (1986): 66-70.

Horowitz, Louis K. *Honoré d'Urfé*. Twayne World Author Series. Boston: G. K. Hall & Co., 1984.

Iser, Wolfgang. *The Act of Reading: A Theory of Aesthetic Response*. 1978. Baltimore: Johns Hopkins University Press, 1991.

Jordan, John O., and Robert L. Patten, eds. *Literature in the Marketplace: Nineteenth-Century British Publishing and Reading Practices*. Cambridge, U.K: Cambridge University Press, 1995.

Lafayette, Marie-Madeleine Pioche de La Vergne, Comtesse de. *Oeuvres complètes*. Ed. Roger Duchêne. Paris: Editions François Bourin, 1990.

Lathuillère, Roger. "Persistance du langage précieux dans la conversation mondaine: *La Fausse Clélie*, 1670." *Mélanges de langue et de littérature françaises offerts à Pierre Larthomas*. Paris: Ecole Normale Supérieure de Jeunes Filles, 1985. 267-78.

Lavocat, Françoise. *Arcadies malheureuses: Aux origines du roman moderne*. Paris: Champion, 1998.

_____. "Lectures à clefs de *L'Arcadia* de Sannazar et de *L'Astrée* d'Honoré d'Urfé: Allégorie et fiction dans le roman pastoral." *Littératures Classiques* 54 (2005): 29-44.

Lynch, Deidre Shauna. *The Economy of Character: Novels, Market Culture, and the Business of Inner Meaning*. Chicago: University of Chicago Press, 1998.

Lyons, John. D. "Narrative, Interpretation and Paradox: *La Princesse de Clèves*." *Romanic Review* 72.4 (1981): 383-400.

Marshall, David. *The Surprising Effects of Sympathy: Marivaux, Diderot, Rousseau, and Mary Shelly*. Chicago: University of Chicago Press, 1988.

Mathieu-Castellani, Gisèle. *La Conversation conteuse: Les Nouvelles de Marguerite de Navarre*. Paris: Presses Universitaires de France, 1992.

Maza, Sarah. *Private Lives and Public Affairs: The Causes Célèbres of Prerevolutionary France*. Berkeley: University of California Press, 1993.

McKeon, Michael. *The Origins of the English Novel, 1600-1740*. Baltimore: Johns Hopkins University Press, 1987.

Mesnard, Jean. "Pour une clef de *Clélie*." *Les trois Scudéry*. Ed. Alain Niderst. Paris: Klincksieck, 1993. 371-408.

Morlet-Chantalat, Chantal. *La Clélie de Mademoiselle de Scudéry. De l'épopée à la gazette: Un discours féminin de la gloire*. Paris: Champion, 1994.

Niderst, Alain. *Essai d'histoire littéraire: Guilleragues, Subligny, et Challe. Des Lettres portugaises aux Illustres Françaises*. Saint-Genouph: Nizet, 1999.

_____. *Madeleine de Scudéry, Paul Pellisson et leur monde*. Paris: Presses Universitaires de France, 1976.

_____. "Sur les clefs de *Clélie*." *Papers on French Seventeenth-Century Literature* 21 (1994): 471-83.

Norman, Larry F. *The Public Mirror: Molière and the Social Commerce of Depiction*. Chicago: University of Chicago Press, 1999.

O'Hara, Stephanie. "Tracing Poison: Theater and Society in Seventeenth-Century France." Ph.D. diss. Duke University, 2004.

Paige, Nicholas. *Being Interior: Autobiography and the Contradictions of Modernity in Seventeenth-Century France*. Philadelphia: University of Pennsylvania Press, 2001.

_____. "The Storyteller and the Book: Scenes of Narrative Production in the Early French Novel." *Modern Language Quarterly* 67.2 (2006): 141-70.

Patru, Olivier. "Eclaircissements sur l'histoire de L'Astrée." *Oeuvres diverses de Mr. Patru de l'académie française...* 3rd ed. Paris: Michel David, 1734. 557-67.

Pavel, Thomas. *L'Art de l'éloignement: Essai sur l'imagination classique*. Paris: Gallimard, 1996.

Pérouse, Gabriel-André. "Des Nouvelles 'vraies comme Evangile': Réflexions sur la présentation du récit bref au XVIe siècle." *La Nouvelle: Définitions, transformations*. Eds. B. Alluin and F. Suard. Lille: Presses Universitaires de Lille, 1990. 88-99.

Plantié, Jacqueline. *La Mode du portrait littéraire en France (1641-1681)*. Paris: Champion, 1994.

Plazenet, Laurence. *L'ébahissement et la délectation: Réception comparée et poétiques du roman grec en France et en Angleterre aux XVIe et XVIIe siècles*. Paris: Champion, 1997.

Ribard, Dinah. "Politique de la littérature: Les romans à clef du XVIIe siècle." *Littératures Classiques* 54 (2005): 257-68.

Rigolot, François. *Poétique et onomastique: L'exemple de la Renaissance*. Geneva: Droz, 1977.

Scudéry, Madeleine de. *Clélie, histoire romaine.* 1654-1660. Ed.
    Chantal Morlet-Chantalat. 5 vols. Paris: Champion, 2001-05.

Segrais, Jean Regnault de. *Les Nouvelles françaises ou les Divertisse-
    ments de la princesse Aurélie.* 1656. Ed. Roger Guichemerre. 2
    vols. Paris: STFM, 1990-92.

Séité, Yannick. *Du livre au lire:* La Nouvelle Héloïse, *roman des
    Lumières.* Paris: Champion, 2002.

Sermain, Jean-Paul. *Le Singe de don Quichotte: Marivaux, Cervantes
    et le roman postcritique.* Oxford: Voltaire Foundation, 1999.

Serroy, Jean. *Roman et réalité: Les histoires comiques au XVIIe siècle.*
    Paris: Minard, 1981.

Showalter, English. *The Evolution of the French Novel, 1641-1782.*
    Princeton: Princeton University Press, 1972.

Stewart, Philip. "Le Roman à clefs à l'époque des Lumières." *Les
    Dérèglements de l'art: Formes et procédures de l'illégitimité
    culturelle en France (1715-1914).* Eds. Pierre Popovic and
    Erik Vigneault. Montreal: Presses de l'Université de Montréal,
    2000. 183-95.

Stone, Harriet. *The Classical Model: Literature and Knowledge in
    Seventeenth-Century France.* Ithaca: Cornell University Press,
    1996.

Subligny, Adrien-Thomas Perdoux de. *La Fausse Clélie, histoire fran-
    çaise, galante et comique.* 1670. Nimègue [Nijmegen]:
    Regnier Smetius, 1680.

Tourette, Eric. "L'argument onomastique dans la clef de 1697 des
    Caractères." *Littératures Classiques* 54 (2005): 181-89.

Urfé, Honoré d'. *L'Astrée.* Ed. Hugues Vaganay. 5 vols. Lyon: Pierre
    Masson, 1925.

Villedieu, Marie-Catherine Desjardins, dit Madame de. *Mémoires de
    la vie de Henriette-Sylvie de Molière.* 1672. Ed. René
    Démoris. Paris: Desjonquères, 2003.

Watt, Ian P. *The Rise of the Novel: Studies in Defoe, Richardson, and
    Fielding.* Berkeley: University of California Press, 1957.

Welsh, Alexander. *Strong Representations: Narrative and Circumstantial Evidence in England*. Baltimore: Johns Hopkins University Press, 1992.

Winn, Colette. "Le Clin d'oeil de l'onomaturge: Les Nouvelles VIII, XI et XXXVII de *L'Heptaméron*." *Romance Notes* 26.2 (1985): 149-54.

Woloch, Alex. *The One vs. the Many: Minor Characters and the Space of the Protagonist in the Novel*. Princeton: Princeton University Press, 2003.

Sociopolitical Education
and the Nouvelles of Le Mercure galant

Jennifer R. Perlmutter

The *nouvelle* has piqued the interest of many literary scholars of the early modern period concerned with questions of generic boundaries. Some undertake chronological studies of the *nouvelle*'s rise in popularity, seeking to situate its originality and thereby to distinguish it from better-known genres such as the *roman*. Others focus on individual authors such as Jean-Pierre Camus, Charles Sorel and Mme de Villedieu who established their reputations primarily as writers of such short stories. Still others interpret the implications of embedding a series of *nouvelles* in a fictional framework as we find in Marguerite de Navarre's *Heptaméron*, Scarron's *Le Roman comique* and Mlle de Scudéry's *Clélie*.[1] All of these studies share a concern for the *nouvelle* as literature, as a fictional narrative distinct from the romanesque in its immediacy of both time and place. The present article contributes to the above characterization of the *nouvelle*, but considers in particular those of the newspaper *Le Mercure galant* as exemplary texts constitutive of French history.[2] Rather than reading them for their literary merits, I will instead focus my attention on these *nouvelles*, translated here as "novellas," as self-conscious constructions that contribute to and strengthen the historical narrative of a nation.[3] As I will show, the dependence of the *Mercure*'s editor Donneau de Visé on Louis XIV's financial support determined in great part the creation and implications of that narrative.

The novellas of *Le Mercure galant* serve as an intriguing complement to John D. Lyons's study of the example, which examines Marguerite de Navarre's *Heptaméron* in addition to other "exemplary" texts.[4] While the latter boasts a narrative framework for discussion and judgment of the exemplary novellas that punctuate it, *Le Mercure galant* lacks an internal narrative structure. Instead, a hodgepodge of historical and social information comprises that which surrounds the novellas, and such information, in many ways, functions as a series of examples itself. Our inquiry here, however, will focus not on this historical and social information, but on the novellas as exemplary texts in a newspaper whose overarching narrative, external but omnipresent, is the history of a nation. By adopting Lyons's terminology, we may see how this external narrative becomes the "general statement" of which the novella, "the example," is a "dependent statement" (Lyons x). The novella thus illustrates specific instances that support "the general statement." Through a comparative study of select novellas published during the newspaper's early years (1672-77) and others published in the few years preceding the Revocation of the Edict of Nantes (1682-85), we may discern that the "orderly functioning of the overall argument" (Lyons 78) of *Le Mercure galant* is in effect its fashioning of France's history which depends on the exemplary nature of this genre.

For Lyons, "[t]he novella is the genre that attempts or pretends to show the world through examples" (72). French writers of the seventeenth century frequently define "history" as a public narrative of memorable events.[5] These events are memorable largely because they provide models for readers to emulate. Those who write history, who select the events to remember, thus participate in the social and moral education of their readers.[6] A historian, one self-proclaimed or so recognized by his or her audience, functions, on one level, as a mentor. In selecting events for the public to remember, he or she creates an educational agenda, one that is more often than not both personal and political.[7] In the opening pages of the May 1677 issue of *Le Mercure galant*, its editor, Donneau de Visé, foregrounds his characterization of the journal as a historical document and implicitly acknowledges the pedagogical role he himself proposes to play for his reader. He writes, "vous regardez les Lettres que je vous écris comme une Histoire journaliere, & [...] vous m'assurez que plusieurs en font de mesme" (11).[8]

Like the already established *La Gazette* (1631) and the *Journal des Savants* (1665), *Le Mercure galant* benefited from royal pensions which shaped its content from the beginning, tacitly prescribing a political agenda from which de Visé was not free to stray without risking financial ruin.[9] Articles that flattered the king and supported his conquests appeared in profusion. Although these three publications shared loyalty to the crown, *Le Mercure galant* distinguished itself in its first issue, published in 1672, by addressing a broader, non-specialized public "qui, le raffinement des mœurs aidant, entendait s'orner l'esprit et embellir sa conversation de tous les menus événements de la vie intellectuelle" (Moureau 130).[10] This salon public drawn from the upper bourgeoisie and the aristocracy sought useful information and social strategies within its pages. At the same time, as they felt their status slipping,

> [n]obles thirsted to know the essential of their survival: who was the up-and-coming favorite at court, which royal or noble mistress was the preferred, which minister was about to be disgraced, what were the latest military maneuvers. The clergy needed to know which important livings were going to be available. Financiers' speculations depended on the latest news of the Bourse. Was the fashion in ladies' headgear about to change? Merchants needed to know. (Harth 171)

De Visé did not disappoint his readers, including not only an account of the most recent events he deemed noteworthy but also a hodgepodge of verses, melodies, engravings, literary reviews, obituaries, marriage and birth announcements and, of greatest interest here, novellas that were interspersed throughout almost every issue.

What role these novellas were meant to play among such entries seemed to baffle de Visé himself who referred to them alternately as "nouvelles," "histoires" and "avantures." On occasion, he even called a story an "avanture" in the body of the text and a "histoire" in the table of contents and vice versa. Erica Harth notes that in the seventeenth century, "the *nouvelle* was presented directly as a history. Either fictional characters appeared as historical figures in a historical setting, or else actual historical figures were fictionalized; in both cases fiction was disguised as history without the mediation of keys" (147). I maintain that as an integral part of a "Histoire journalière," the novellas of *Le Mercure galant* serve as exemplary texts that complement the surrounding articles. As the content of the articles surrounding these stories changed to reflect the political climate, so did that of the stories themselves. During the early years of *Le Mercure galant*, 1672-1677, Donneau de Visé imagines his ideal readership and, through the novellas, suggests to readers who they should be.[11] The novellas serve to construct a readership, one that will likely be amenable to the political agenda that becomes apparent in the four years leading up to the Revocation of the Edict of Nantes in 1685. During these later years, moral virtue and loyalty to the crown are one and the same. The injunctive function of the novellas of this period is

starkly evident. Having suggested to readers who they should be, de
Visé now begins telling them what they should and should not do.

The visual aspect of novellas from each period underscores
these two exemplary functions. The novellas published between 1672
and 1677 have descriptive titles – "Celle qui aima mieux se brûler,"
"Mary qui se croit cocu par luy-mesme," "Mariage par hazard," for
example – that appear in the tables of contents as well as at the beginning of each story. They are also set apart visually from the news stories by typographical flourishes. For a readership as attentive to visual
cues as that of the seventeenth century must have been – the printing
press was a recent invention – these cues alerted them to a change in
the text that reflected a change in genre. We can liken these earlier
novellas to the quotation, a figure of rhetoric set off graphically from
the main text.[12] Unlike the quotation, however, these novellas do not
interrupt the narrative and silence the narrator. They do, however, provide support for the primary discourse in much the same way as does
the example. Readers pick up on the visual cues and anticipate stories
that differ from the weighty news they have been reading. The editor
refers them to an outside world and describes the adventures of characters whom he may or may not name; through these imprecise references, the narrator provides direct and indirect social commentary that
serves an exemplary function.

The novellas published from 1682 to 1685 appear quite differently in the pages of *Le Mercure galant*. Listed as "histoires" in the
tables of contents, they lack distinguishing titles. Likewise the editor
does not indicate any textual change within the body of the journal.
There are no typographical flourishes separating the news articles and
these novellas; even "Histoire" does not appear before the latter.
Through these seamless transitions de Visé presents the novellas as an
integral part of the newspaper, suggesting that they are as historically
significant as the surrounding news articles. They do not obviously
"gesture toward an 'elsewhere'" as do quotations and most examples,
but they do require "the speaker…to appropriate…an experience that
is not present and may never have been that of the speaker […,] to
adopt or bring closer something that may come from far away" (Lyons
29, 31). The editor of *Le Mercure galant* presents these novellas as
historical truths, "histoires," that are relevant to the history of France
that the surrounding articles shape. In this way, they convey immedi-

acy, a sense of urgency to the reader to whom these stories serve as examples.

* * *

The first five years of *Le Mercure galant*'s publication, termed "les années difficiles" by Monique Vincent (*Donneau de Visé* 149), were marked by a profound self-consciousness on the part of its editor. From 1672 through 1677, de Visé experimented with its format and struggled to establish the legitimacy of his project at a time when journalists were widely thought to spread falsehoods. He was preoccupied by the idea of success and set out to construct the ideal readership that would guarantee it. This entailed attracting women and men whose desire for social status made them thirsty for knowledge and guidelines to follow. Part of de Visé's early struggles stemmed from the fact that he believed that women and men appreciate articles that differ significantly. While women would be more attracted to the romanesque and gallant tales of love, men would more likely engage with the more ostensibly learned news items. In his mind, playing the role of historian to both sexes thus meant pursuing his pedagogical goal in two distinct ways. In the "Lettre d'un inconnu a l'autheur du Mercure Galant" published in May 1677, its author mentions a female friend who was seeking de Visé's guidance. The author writes, "Elle espere que comme les Hommes ont leurs Historiens, vous ne dédaignerez point d'estre quelque jour celuy des Femmes" (108-9). Following the example of other historians by including detailed war stories in the *Mercure*, de Visé provided examples of valor for male readers who could easily imagine themselves as the military heroes mentioned therein.[13] The question of how to create examples of behavior for women without burdening them with details of France's ongoing struggles for European supremacy, an ongoing preoccupation of de Visé, thus arose. For him, becoming a women's historian did not mean chronicling the accomplishments of France's female citizens, but educating them in other ways through his entertaining and generally light-hearted novellas.

In the foreword to the volume of December 1677, which marks the end of this period, its bookseller announces the success of the journal in constituting a mixed readership, which meant that it had earned a certain amount of respect in the eyes both of men and women, *mondains* and *savants*. The bookseller writes,

> Je sçay que le Titre a fait croire d'abord que le Mercure estoit simplement
> galant, & qu'il ne devoit tenir place que dans la Bibliotheque des Femmes,
> mais on est sorty de cette erreur quand on y a veu des Pieces d'éloquence, des
> Harangues, des Relations fidelles & exactes, des Sieges & des Batailles, des
> Evenemens remarquables, des morceaux d'Histoire, & des Memoires glorieux
> à des Familles. Alors il est devenu le Livre des Sçavans & des Braves, apres
> avoir esté le divertissement du beau Sexe; & une marque incontestable de son
> succés, c'est qu'il a esté assez heureux pour plaire à Monseigneur le
> DAUPHIN, & que ce Grand Prince veut bien soufrir qu'il paroisse toûjours à
> l'avenir sous son Nom. (n.p. Visé)

By dedicating *Le Mercure galant* to the dauphin, de Visé further legitimizes it and provides a male counterpoint that represents the male readership to the "Madame" figure to which he addresses each issue of the journal. He has succeeded in making the journal an exemplary text for both women and men. He has provided models of social conduct, constructed his ideal readership that anticipates each month's publication and, I argue, more eagerly participates in the shaping of France's history.

"Leonidas," the longest novella at over one hundred pages, stands out among these early ones for its length and its romanesque qualities. It is a gallant tale whose plot is shaped by a quest for social status. Published in the fourth of four volumes to appear in 1673, it tells the story of two sisters of the minor nobility who follow the court of their country in hopes that the younger will gain *esprit* by keeping such illustrious company. Lucille, forty years old and thus well past her prime, takes it upon herself to educate her sixteen-year-old sister, Celie, by taking her to a play that the whole court is sure to attend. (All names have been fictionalized, according to the narrator, allegedly to protect the identity of those mentioned.) She hopes that the courtiers will serve as models of *esprit* for her sister, examples that she can follow in developing her own social identity. Prince Polexandre, struck by Celie's beauty, approaches her in the theater, but goes unrecognized and suffers her dismissive behavior. Lucille soon remedies the situation and satisfies the prince's curiosity by telling him everything he hoped to learn about her sister. The prince relays this information to his court, which includes Leonidas, who immediately falls for Celie. He and the prince then pursue her with equal determination. The prince, at first a main character of the story, soon becomes secondary as Leonidas gains the upper hand; Licinius, Leonidas's relative, and his lover, Hortense, are then introduced. After many romanesque plot twists, Leonidas and Hortense die, leaving Celie and Licinius to pursue their passion unobstructed. The narrator claims to have heard this story at a *ruelle galante* and adds, "L'Histoire de Leonidas estant finie, on en parla diversement; mais chacun demeura d'accord qu'elle estoit vraye, & plusieurs dirent les veritables noms de ceux à qui elle estoit arrivée & adjoûterent qu'ils croyoient qu'Hortense estoit Gréque" (106).

Set in another country, full of plot twists and secondary characters, "Leonidas" is a novella that shares qualities with the romance. While the romance offers a somewhat plausible yet distant view of reality, the novella "is the genre that attempts or pretends to show the world through examples" (Lyons 72).[14] By watching Celie move her way up the social ranks and secure her place among the elite, readers, particularly female ones, can imagine for themselves or for their intimates what is possible.[15] Shaped by her sister to appeal to those of the highest ranks, Celie is a social construct formed through her attention to exemplary forms of witty discourse. Noble, beautiful and docile, Celie makes a social blunder in not recognizing the prince but this is quickly remedied by her sister who is now too old to matter socially but who can pass along her education to those who still do. If unattractive, merely of the upper bourgeoisie or past her prime, the reader can only hope to find herself one day in the same position as Celie.

"Leonidas"'s exemplarity does not lie in the possibility of immediate identification – the tale is set abroad and is therefore far removed from the daily life of those in France – but it does encourage desire and provide entertainment as well as a happy ending for the worthy protagonist. Like the *roman*, this romanesque novella was written for readers who were not actively participating in wars – after all, they would not benefit from much leisure time to devote to reading if they were fighting battles – but for readers who were increasingly left out of the establishment of France as a sovereign nation.[16] It nevertheless exemplifies something worthy of imitation and validates the desire to acquire social status that would facilitate participation in their country's history. Annie Bruter explains that "non seulement [l'usage de l'histoire] doit…donner [à l'honnête homme] le moyen de briller dans la conversation, il le prépare aussi à tenir sa place dans la vie mondaine en l'habituant à observer et à interpréter les comportements" (127). While the news articles informed readers and provided them with a common ground for conversation, the glimpses into the daily life of individuals that many novellas provided served as models of conduct for readers who sought to achieve social success.

An untitled June 1682 novella suggests an alternative for young women who are eager to marry well but whose ambitions are thwarted by their social greed. The main character's ambitions and the anxieties to which they give rise serve as a model of what not to do. At the outset, the narrator ominously remarks that, "Dieu se sert de tout pour nous attirer à luy" (122), suggesting a precept to be illustrated in the tale that follows. The story is that of a young woman who is to inherit her father's fortune on the condition that she marry. Eager to espouse a wealthy man in particular, she is one day won over by a knight who is also a marquis. They plan to marry. Cautious after learning of a fake marquis who was known for trying to marry the daughters of widows, her friends begin to look into his background and discover that he is indeed the imposter. The young woman is so deeply embarrassed by her "trop hautes espérances" (127) that led her to overlook the prospective husband's false social posturing that she flees to the countryside, then to a convent. According to the narrator, God's grace "luy a fait ouvrir les yeux sur la vanité de ce qui flate le plus les jeunes Personnes; & le peu que les choses de la terre luy ont paru avoir de solidité, l'en a si fort dégoûtée, que depuis un mois elle a pris l'Habit de Religieuse" (128). The narrator both cautions against social ambitions and promotes religious devotion as the alternative to social shame.

While "Leonidas" rewards social ambition and offers a model for how to achieve status, the negative exemplarity of this later novella warns against the blindness that may result from being overly ambitious. The young woman has disrupted the social order by seeking more than she deserves and the only sensible response to social embarrassment is for her to remove herself from the system that gave rise to it. The young woman whose humiliation warns readers against pursuing their greedy desires thus becomes a model of piety for those who do not know their place in society. By becoming a nun, she cures herself of the vanity that disrupted the established social order and redeems herself. Remarkably, the narrator does not blame the imposter for the woman's social downfall; he remains free to pursue future manipulative schemes. Many have argued that women represented the greater threat to France's established order and therefore needed to be reined in to ensure its stability.[17] One way to accomplish this was by fostering a fear of public disgrace that would occur if they challenged their position in society, and by presenting the convent as an appealing, alternate order. Although the tone of this later novella does not differ significantly from that of the earlier "Leonidas," its promotion of a model of piety stands in stark contrast to the former's rewarded model of social status.

In an earlier novella, the main character chooses a religious life for very different reasons. "L'Histoire du Cabinet des miroirs," published in the first volume of *Le Mercure galant* in 1672, addresses a man's preoccupation with his social status in a light-hearted manner and comments on the relative validity of three possible roles. While waiting for his fiancée and her mother, Cléante, contemplates his future while standing in front of four mirrors dressed in borrowed outfits that represent his three possible paths in life. Dressed as a member of the old warrior nobility ("noblesse d'épée"), he breaks one of the mirrors while brandishing his sword. He finds himself convincing as a government official ("conseiller" of the "noblesse de robe"), but decides to try on the habit of a religious man nevertheless. As he is changing, Cléante realizes that working for the government means having to serve as an audience to too many people's opinions. His fiancée and her mother now enter the room while Cléante is considering himself as a cleric. Noticing the outfit, the mother asks him whether his decision to leave his fiancée for the church is firm. He says "yes" and remarks that he cannot be blamed for lack of fidelity since he is leaving her daughter for God. Aware of his reputation for fickleness, the mother had already chosen an alternate mate; her daughter is thrilled by the new choice and not the least bit disappointed. With a change of heart, Cléante tries to win her back and when he fails, becomes a monk.

Couched in this humorous and gallant novella is a parabole, a fictitious but possible exemplary tale that suggests models of social status.[18] On the most obvious level, Cléante fashions himself as a member of three different social groups, assessing their respective values. His ineptitude is confirmed by his breaking the mirror, so he clearly lacks the required self-control and discipline to serve in the king's army. As a government official, he would lack independence, as he would be responsible to too many citizens. His final decision to devote his life to religion is not his own and is merely circumstantial. All three options are presented as valid and they mirror those available

to the male reader of *Le Mercure galant* who will either serve the king
as a soldier or a government official, or serve God. Cléante experiences each profession in a cursory manner and, in a comic twist,
exemplifies the consequences of social folly. Upheld as an alternative
to the war stories that valorize France's heroes, "L'Histoire du Cabinet
des miroirs" provides divertissement as well as equal validation for the
choices available to men of a certain class. This humorous tale provides one example of how someone came to accept his social status
and serves as a thematically related, yet comic interlude within the
journal. As such, it was thought to appeal to female readers and others
thought to be easily bored by the war stories and lists of sieges that
surround it.

While also dramatizing the differences between the *noblesse
de robe* and the *noblesse d'épée*, an untitled October 1683 novella
lacks the humor of the previous tale. Also a story of love, it foregrounds instead social tensions but accepts them as inevitable. At the
outset, the narrator prepares the readers for an unfavorable outcome
and blames the fickleness of love.

> Il y auroit plus d'Amans heureux que l'on n'en voit, si on laissoit l'amour
> maistre de ses entreprises; mais s'il peut toucher les coeurs quand il luy plaist,
> il n'a pas toûjours le pouvoir de les unir. Des obstacles invincibles renversent
> souvent ses plus grands desseins, & ce qui est le plus chagrinant, c'est qu'il se
> rencontre des occasions où il se nuit par luy-mesme. (111)

The writer then defines the main characters in terms of their position
within the nobility: the man is a "Marquis à bon titre," the woman he
loves is from a robe family, and her only brother is a "Conseiller au
Parlement de sa Province," but hopes for a higher position when he
gets older. The Marquis takes advantage of the brother's absence to try
to win over the woman. At the same time, he is the tutor to his own
female cousin, the sole heir to her late parents' fortune. Without consulting him, she accepts the attentions of a gentleman who anticipates
using her to gain the title of "count." When he returns from his trip, the
brother falls in love with her as well, and the marquis begins to imagine how well advised it would be to join the families in a double alliance. The cousin refuses yet the marquis insists, explaining the advantages of "les gens de robe" and denigrating those of the sword. His
arguments fail to persuade her – she is young and easily dazzled by a
man in uniform – and he turns his attentions to dissuading the brother,
who stands in the way of what she and the aspiring count want, by

causing him to lose interest in her. This fails as well. The count-to-be, out of spite, decides to break up the union between the marquis and the sister by pretending to love her. She is impressed by him and is won over by his attentions. The brother insists on marrying the cousin since the count is no longer a rival. The marquis refuses to allow it because the sister is no longer interested in him. In the end, no one marries. Not surprisingly, the narrator's final commentary lacks optimism: "Peut-estre quand la belle Heritiere sera en âge de disposer d'elle, elle fera choix du Comte qui l'aime toûjours; mais dans le temps qu'il faudra attendre, c'est grande merveille, si l'une des deux passions ne s'affoiblit. Apres tout pourtant, elles pourront ne s'affoiblir pas, car les deux Amans ne se voyent guére" (135).

A story of defeated love, this *nouvelle* serves as a pretext for a dramatization of the importance of the social distinction between the robe and sword. The narrator does not take sides and, in blaming love rather than social tensions for the outcome, he accepts such tensions as inevitable. The assumed reader would sense the naïveté of the young woman, easily seduced by outward signs of status such as clothing and title. Like the marquis whose title accurately reflects his noble birth, the reader is meant to sense that a union between the families would secure their social status and increase their economic standing. That the characters do not fall into the desired order and all go without ful-filling their love reflects a moral judgment on the part of the editor. Their solitude at the end serves both as a punishment for their blind-ness to the advantages of an alliance between the robe and sword and as a warning to the reader. The matter-of-fact tone lacks levity and reinforces the gravity of such decisions, reinforcing this novella's injunctive quality. Thematically similar to "L'Histoire du Cabinet des miroirs," this story provides a model of negative exemplarity that con-trasts with the earlier one's amusing model of social choice.

Concerns for social status are inevitably linked to questions of honor and marriage, the latter a social construct that not only ensures the perpetuation of social and economic order but also facilitates social mobility. Both serve as the focus of an August 1677 story entitled "Histoire du Solitaire." The story of a provincial man of the minor nobility whose social ambitions for his son backfire in a rather amus-ing way, this novella makes light of the father's social disgrace and instead celebrates the son's disregard for his family honor. The man sends his son to Paris to study, but rather than see him take up the sword, the father calls him back to the provinces and buys him a government post that he keeps for ten years. During this time, he remains indifferent to women, much to the chagrin of his father who had hoped for heirs. The son eventually decides to sell his station and retire to a country house away from his father's incessant pleas to marry. At wit's end, the father decides to weaken his son's apathy towards women in an unusual way. He arranges for a prostitute and a boatman to feign a shipwreck in front of his son's house so that his son would be morally obliged to save the woman. The woman would then initiate the son to the pleasures of the opposite sex, after which the father could introduce him to someone more appropriate with greater success. The plan works much better than the father intended. Soon after meeting in this manner, the son and prostitute marry without the father's knowledge. Shocked, the father insists that they separate, but they refuse. The narrator comments, "Je les trouve tous deux à plaindre, & je serois bien embarassé si j'avois à prononcer là-dessus. Les raisons de l'un & de l'autre me paroissent bonnes, & je trouve que l'Amour de [*sic*] condamnable, mais il ne reconnoist point de Juges, & ne fait jamais ce qu'il luy plaist" (71). The narrator's loyalties obviously lie with the son, who is content to live a simple life, free from concerns for his family's honor.

While the narrator of "L'Histoire du Cabinet des miroirs" remains indifferent to the choices Cléante faces thereby validating all three, this narrator mocks the father's concern for his family's honor. By placing him in a ridiculous situation that he is unable to resolve to his satisfaction, the narrator calls into question his conception of what his son should be. The father attempts to establish a familial order, to ensure his legacy first through his son's honorable position and then through his grandchildren. However, the man's ridiculous scheme backfires and his ambitions are thwarted, suggesting that perhaps he is not worthy of such honor. The exemplarity of this early novella lies in its validation of another kind of happiness, the personal happiness of the son and his prostitute wife at the expense of public or familial social standing. Already outside of Parisian society, these two men need not concern themselves with that which preoccupies characters such as Cléante. This comic story lacks the injunctive quality of the October 1683 novella cited earlier; although the father is punished, the son is happy and that is what the narrator chooses to focus on in the end.

A March 1685 story paints a contrasting image of betrayal and its shameful consequences. A young woman whose reason usually dominates her feelings, always waits to make a decision about a suitor until she knows his character well for "la bienséance regloit tous les régards complaisans qu'elle croyoit leur devoir" (108). A knight takes an interest in her and pursues her persistently despite her tepid response. Eventually she begins to soften. He begins talking to her of marriage, but mentions an uncle whose consent he needs because he is to receive a large sum of money from him. After waiting a year for word of the uncle's permission, the woman discovers that her intended has also been frequenting a young widow. Jealous, she decides to take revenge. Dressed as a man, she waits for him in a street he often takes to return home. She confronts him and asks him to choose between marriage, the honorable choice, or his life. He responds jokingly, not imagining her to be serious. The woman then stabs him twice. As he lies dying, he apologizes and asks those who have come to his aid to recognize her as his wife by promise, thereby bestowing his inheritance on her. The narrator then defends the woman's crime of passion since her honor was at stake: "Je n'ay point sçeû ce que la Justice avoit ordonné contre elle. Son crime est de ceux que l'honneur fait faire, & il en est peu qui ne semblent excusables, quand ils partent d'une cause dont on n'a point à rougir" (125-26).

De Visé underscores the exemplarity of this novella at the outset: "ce qui s'est passé depuis peu de temps dans une des plus grandes villes du Royaume confirme les sanglans exemples que nous en trouvons dans les Histoires" (March 1685, 108). This illustration of a specific instance, this example, confirms and therefore supports the general idea the reader has of France's "Histoires." With a capital "H," this word recalls both a story ("histoire") about something that occurs within the country and of the history ("Histoire") of a nation. This novella therefore functions both as an illustration of an instance, a moral tale about one woman and one man, and as an example of a step in the process of nation building. While the narrator of "Histoire du Solitaire" mockingly dismissed family honor as a valid concern for those in the provinces, this narrator starkly defends the quest for personal honor by one big-city woman who always follows the rules of propriety. Marriage is serious business, he cautions, and one should promise it to a worthy mate only when planning to make good on the promise. The bloody ending warns those prone to trickery and mockery of the importance of marriage and accentuates the injunctive quality of this tale. Published just a few months prior to the Revocation of the Edict of Nantes and only six years after "Histoire du Solitaire" but thematically similar in that it addresses the questions of honor and marriage, this novella is characteristic of the moralizing tales of the period.

The question of marriage inevitably gives rise to that of children and how one should best raise them. The 1672 novella entitled "L'Histoire de la Fille Soldat" provides a comic look at the consequences of a father's greed and, to use Lyons's terminology, is an example, an improbable tale (fable) that provides pleasure for its own sake (23). Upon learning that his wife is pregnant, a man despairs for he has already calculated the necessary expenses associated with having a child. Together, they recognize that raising a boy would be cheaper than raising a girl and decide to do just that, without regard for the child's actual sex. Months later, the wife bears a daughter whom they raise as a son; the father mistreats her and she flees from home to join the army. Not entirely sure of who she is, she lives nevertheless as though she has something to hide. The daughter of the family with whom she is staying while serving the king falls in love with her and, finding herself pregnant by a man who has recently died, decides to regain her honor by marrying the soldier. The soldier agrees and they marry before the pregnancy begins to show. One night while they are in bed, a female cousin comes in the room to awaken her pregnant relative. She glimpses the uncovered breast of the female soldier and announces aloud what she has just found. In her naïveté the cousin spreads the rumor that a girl has gotten another girl pregnant.

Like "L'Histoire du Cabinet des miroirs" that appears in the same issue of *Le Mercure galant*, this story portrays the ridiculous consequences of making a misguided choice. Strictly motivated by financial concerns, the father's decision to raise his daughter as a son is short sighted. He and his wife perpetuate her ignorance, which ultimately leads to a loss of family honor. De Visé, however, does not choose to focus on this consequence and emphasize the negative exemplarity of the father's greed. Instead, he amuses the reader by focusing on the cousin's naïve reaction. This improbable and comic novella allegedly explains the origins of the rumor that a girl has gotten another girl pregnant that "tant d'Ignorans ont publié depuis quelques jours" (147), a weak claim to truth that in fact underscores this novella's quality of urban myth, its fictitiousness. It is an example that has the power "to interest us, even to fascinate and astonish us" whose effect "does not depend on the moral quality of its content" (Lyons 119). Like the examples Montaigne includes in his *Essais* that Lyons studies, this novella is astonishing and demonstrates that "[w]hat is rare in 'real life' is typical in fiction." An author need not always provide models of conduct through his or her use of examples. Instead, "[t]he discrepancy between the rare and the typical is itself a motivating factor in the use of example" (Lyons 121) and when presented from this point of view, the novella entertains the reader first and foremost. In the case of "L'Histoire de la Fille Soldat," what lies behind the example remains "something of a mystery."

A novella published in August 1685 offers an alternate ending to a thematically similar story. Published just a few months prior to the Revocation of the Edict of Nantes, its injunctive exemplarity reflects the moral fervor of this later time. The narrator underscores the exemplary nature of the main character's life from the outset.

> Vostre aimable Amie, dont vous me demandez des nouvelles, a fait un Voyage de deux mois, & est de retour icy depuis peu de jours. En rĕdăt visite dans un Convent de Province, on luy a fait voir une Personne fort bien faite, qui mene une vie tres-exemplaire, aprés avoir couru dans ses premieres années, le peril du plus grand desordre où une Fille soit capable de tomber. (196)

The risk of disorder is established when the girl's father arranges for her to marry an old man against her wishes. When she refuses, he begins to treat her badly. The girl then disguises herself as a man and enrolls in the army where she remains a solider for five years. When she begins to grow breasts and arouse suspicion at her first station, she leaves and goes to another where she stays two more years. The daughter of the man hosting her unit falls in love with her and her passion becomes so violent that she reveals her intention to marry her. Asking the daughter to keep her secret, the female soldier reveals her true identity (it remains unclear whether she accepts the proposal). Understandably astonished, the host's daughter divulges it and accuses her of hiding her sex "pour s'abandonner avec moins de retenuë au libertinage & à la débauche" (203-4). The girl proclaims her innocence and is believed, but understands that her reputation has suffered irremediable harm. She asks her host to take her to a convent where she lives an exemplary life.

What was an amusing and racy story free of religious overtones in an earlier incarnation has become a means of promoting convent life as the only viable option for those whose virtue seems to be in
peril. Similar to the June 1682 novella cited above, this one champions
religious devotion as a desirable alternative to those who fail to make
appropriate marriages. Unlike the earlier "L'Histoire du Fille Soldat,"
however, in which the girl's fate remains unknown to us and the light
tone of which suggests that her deception is not punished, this later
novella allows for no alternative. The girl's susceptibility to disorder
must result in her returning to an order of a religious kind. This model
of piety does not leave the reader hanging, seduced by the entertaining
predicament of the women in "L'Histoire du Fille Soldat" that does not
represent a return to order. By referring to the girl's behavior as libertine and debauched, the narrator challenges the morality of the choices
a young, unmarried woman makes to avoid her father's old-school
system of choosing a mate. This exemplary tale's injunctive power lies
in great part in its proclaimed truth-value. Allegedly, de Visé's
acquaintance saw the girl, heard her remarkable story and relayed it to
him directly after her trip. Her testimony, which is necessarily selective, was then culled by de Visé himself; only the most exemplary
accounts appear in *Le Mercure galant*. At the end of the novella, this
editor again insists on its truth-value. Referring to the witness's visit to
the convent, he adds, "C'est où vostre Amie l'a veuë. Elle a appris
d'elle-mesme tout ce que je viens de vous conter" (204-5). The storyteller and by extension de Visé align themselves with preachers who
provide examples through their sermons that are "intended to teach a
moral lesson and to enjoin a specific conduct" (Lyons 75) that reflects
their devotion to God.

Hypocrisy nevertheless finds its reward in "Histoire de
l'heureux Hipocrite" (April 1677). In this early novella, a younger
brother devises a scheme to inherit his father's money, which was
intended for his older sibling. He informs him that he is going to live in
a cloister to undo his attachment to material goods. The brother is easily swayed by this logic and decides to join him in his resolution.
When the day comes for them to take their vows, the younger man persuades his brother to go first. He then pretends to faint as the latter
pronounces them and succeeds in escaping the cloister. His father's
inheritance, a government post and a wife of good social standing are
his rewards for his deceit. The narrator closes the novella in a neutral

tone, stating, "On ne luy peut disputer la Succession, mais elle ne seroit pas à luy s'il n'avoit pas joüé le Personnage d'Hypocrite" (12-13). The exemplarity of this novella lies in its rarity and its fictional excess. Bordering on the blasphemous, it incites incredulousness and laughter while allowing for and, it can be argued, inviting the possibility of "a single counterexample" by its sheer improbability (Lyons 33).

Non-believers enjoy a much less sympathetic representation in two stories published during the later period. Examples of punishment incurred by those who do not live virtuously distinguish these tales of virtue. The first novella, published in the first of two volumes to appear in September 1682, begins with the admonition that: "Quoy que les jugemens de Dieu soient impénetrables, il est difficile de ne pas croire qu'une mort funeste qui suit une vie pleine de scandales, en est la punition" (191-92). It then chronicles the story of three young male friends in Lyon who are so close that they call each other "brother." They all have a lot of *esprit* but little religion, and they live a very libertine life. Each dies in a remarkable way, which, it is suggested, results from their hypocrisy. The first friend falls backwards in fright while witnessing the interrogation of a criminal and cracks open his head. The second impales himself accidentally. The third looks up at the sky while he is out walking with a priest and declares that he only has an hour to live. The priest tells him to confess if that is the case, and he responds that he will do so the next day. He then falls dead. The second novella published in November 1683 tells of a Calvinist woman and a Catholic woman, both pregnant, who are having a fight. The topic turns to religion and the Calvinist asks God to give them a sign as to who belongs to the wrong religion by having her bear a devil. Soon after, she goes into labor and bears a monster that is then smothered between two mattresses. Although the narrator ends the story with, "Vous tirerez telles consequences qu'il vous plaira de cette avanture. Je vous dis le fait sans raisonnement" (136), the moral of the story is quite transparent.

De Visé presents both stories as true and describes how he learned of them.[19] That he has heard them from reliable witnesses who reported what they themselves learned from worthy sources adds to the weight and importance of their message. They enjoin readers to ensure their salvation by doing the opposite of what the characters do. They reflect back at readers their "sinful nature" and providing this knowledge "is the goal of exemplary discourse" (Lyons 113). At the same time, they threaten them into following the only opportunity presented, that offered by the Catholic Church. As Bruter remarks, "l'histoire appelle la censure plutôt que l'imitation" (126) and these allegedly historical examples of sin enjoin readers to do the very opposite of the characters therein. Two of the most transparently ideological novellas, they reflect France's impending return to officially sanctioned religious intolerance. While de Visé who narrates the "Histoire de l'heureux Hipocrite" is still able to find humor in religious disobedience, he also intimidates by evoking death and monstrosity.

Sharing themes of social status, honor, marriage, children and religious devotion, the novellas from these two periods reveal an exemplary quality with distinct functions. Most stories published between 1672 and 1677 suggest models of social status to readers and provide entertainment for entertainment's sake. Through them, Donneau de Visé constructs his ideal readership through light-hearted examples, a readership that understands the importance of reasonable social ambition, marriage and family honor. These novellas lack the transparently injunctive function of those published between 1682 and 1685 that often took the form of negative exemplarity. De Visé includes eighteen fables among the twenty-eight novellas that appear during this later period, which reinforces the overall moral tone of these issues of *Le Mercure galant*.[20] While these fables are set apart typographically from the rest of the journal's contents, the novellas blend in seamlessly with the news articles to shape an overall image of France's history.

The "Avanture des Thuilleries," itself a novella that appears in October 1677, suggests ways of interpreting the exemplarity of the novellas of the first period. A gentleman, struck by the beauty of a woman he notices while walking in the Tuileries, decides to eavesdrop on her conversation to find out whether she has as much *esprit* as she does beauty. He overhears her telling her male cousin about her penchant for reading many different types of books. The cousin responds by encouraging her to read *Le Mercure galant* since everyone who reads as avidly as she knows of it. "Je m'imagine, ma belle Parente," he begins, "que vous ne manquerez pas à commencer par le Mercure Galant. Il n'y a point de Livre qui soit plus en vogue, & il seroit honteux qu'il vous échapast, puis que vous faites profession de tout lire" (169). They discuss the subjects addressed by the journal, after which the cousin explains what he sees to be its only weakness, the lengthy descriptions contained in its news stories.

> Pour moy, j'en suis si satisfait, que je serois tres-fâché qu'il ne le continuast pas; ce qui divertit, l'emporte de beaucoup sur ce qui seroit capable d'ennuyer; & si j'y trouve quelque chose à redire, c'est qu'il loüe avec profusion, & qu'il s'étend un peu trop sur les Articles de Guerre, car il perd plus de temps à décrire la prise des Villes, que le Roy n'en a employé à les conquérir. (170)

In response, the woman justifies the amount of space devoted to the praising of individuals and war stories by emphasizing their exemplary nature. In this way, she defends and represents Donneau de Visé and his choices.

> Quant aux loüanges, vous pouvez passer par dessus, si vous en soufrez; mais mille & mille honnestes Gens qui sont en France, ne meritent-ils pas qu'on parle d'eux? & le desir de se rendre digne d'estre loüé, servant quelquefois d'aiguillon à la Vertu, doit-on envier à tant de Braves qui hazardent tous les jours leur vie pour servir l'Etat, une récompense si légitimement deüé à leurs grandes actions? La justice qu'aparemment leur rend le Mercure, redouble la curiosité que j'ay de le voir, & je ne crains point que le trop de Guerre importune. (175-76).

Not only might these lengthy descriptions serve as incentives for others to behave virtuously by serving the State, they also resemble those that many people are used to reading. The belle speaks to the *Mercure*'s universal appeal and defends de Visé's approach to historical writing. In this way, "Avanture des Thuilleries" is a novella that defends the inclusion of lengthy yet exemplary news stories while it is itself an exemplary tale at the service of the entire journal.

In these early years of *Le Mercure galant*'s publication, the novellas frequently begin on a separate page from the surrounding news stories and are introduced with a title and a flourish, as mentioned above. These stories provide insight into the daily life of the *mondains*, remaining distinctive by their content and typography. De Visé and those who serve as mouthpieces for him throughout, narrators and characters in the stories, categorize them as diversions meant to entertain his female readers who, he claims, would otherwise be easily bored by the military news that makes up the bulk of the volumes. As entertaining filler, stories such as "L'Histoire du Cabinet des Miroirs" draw the reader's attention to the surrounding news while broadly addressing readers' social anxieties. In the June 1677 issue, de Visé writes,

Vous sçavez, Madame, que les plus beaux endroits d'un Ouvrage paroissent
toûjours moins en fragmens, que lors qu'ils sont placez où ils doivent estre; ce
qui les devance ou ce qui les suit, leur donne souvent des graces qu'ils
n'auroient pas sans cela, & tout ce que l'on en dit lors qu'on ne les fait pas
voir de suite est toûjours infiniment au dessous de ce qu'il seroit dans le corps
entier de l'Ouvrage. (242-43)

I argue, however, that these stories function as well to support the historical narrative created by *Le Mercure galant* as a whole. The novellas provide a break from the seriousness of the news and then redirect
the reader's focus onto the war stories, the details of sieges, the lists of
officers killed, and so forth that make up the bulk of the journal in its
early years. These facts seemed to speak for themselves – lists are easily verified, for instance – and de Visé rarely feels the need to insist on
their accuracy. He imagines that this information will appeal primarily
to his male readers who are more likely to have participated in the
military or to consider doing so. The female readers will sooner appreciate the novellas whose entertainment value never wavers, but whose
usefulness varies significantly as we saw above. By insisting on the
genuineness of such stories as "L'Histoire de la Fille Soldat," which de
Visé very frequently does, he categorizes them as a historical addition
to his overall narrative. While the news stories informed readers, the
novellas entertained and constructed an ideal readership through their
exemplarity.

At the same time, they function as integral parts of the overall
history of Paris and the court created by *Le Mercure galant*. Harth
argues that, "[t]he principal aim of history was utility, yet in order to
captivate a public rapidly succumbing to the fashionable new mania
for novels, history was obliged to borrow some of the 'pleasure' that
the novel advertised as its chief attraction" (134). At the *Mercure*'s
inception in 1672, de Visé makes clear his desire to inform and entertain. In the "Dessein de l'Ouvrage" that opens the very first issue
addressed to "Madame" who represents his female readers collectively, he writes,

Si je puis venir à bout de mon dessein, & que vous conservez mes Lettres,
elles pourront dans l'avenir servir de Memoires aux Curieux, & l'on y trouvera
beaucoup de choses qui ne pourront se rencontrer ailleurs, à cause de la
diversité des matieres dont elles seront remplies; mais il m'importe peu
qu'elles soient utiles à d'autres, pourveu qu'elles vous divertissent: c'est mon
unique but, & c'est pourquoy je commence par une Histoire, avant que
d'entrer dans le détail des nouvelles de cette Semaine. (12-13)

In his role of "historien des femmes," de Visé privileges pleasure and models of social status over overt models of piety and to this end, integrates novellas that were sure to elicit laughter and break up the monotony of the war stories. However, in incorporating them into his "histoire journalière" and claiming them to be true, de Visé aligns them with history and thus with utility. Even the most lighthearted ones served a purpose with their readers.

In December 1677, Donneau de Visé promises changes in the *Mercure*'s format that he will enact the following year. By this time, *Le Mercure galant* had become a predictable commodity, a source of current events and the circumstances surrounding them, of enigmas, poetry and music, and of anecdotes certain to elicit laughter and provoke discussion. Readers allegedly contribute to the journal's content by sending in solutions to enigmas presented therein, and sending any story of interest they might have heard. From 1678 onwards, this editor would strive to uphold his journal's earned reputation as "le Livre des Sçavans & des Braves" before that of "le divertissement du beau Sexe" (December 1677, n.p.). Although certain gallantries would be added, such as a second enigma and fashion drawings, these would be distinct from the "Pieces d'éloquence, des Harangues, des Relations fidelles & exactes, des Sieges & des Batailles, des Evenemens remarquables, des morceaux d'Histoire, & des Memoires glorieux à des Familles" (n.p.) that he will prioritize. The novellas, for their part, will fit into this latter part more seamlessly, edited "pour les mettre dans le stile serré du Mercure, qui doit estre le mesme par tout, ou pour oster quelquefois des choses qui sont trop libres, ou qui satirisant trop, pourroient chagriner les Intéressez" for "On ne sçauroit avoir trop de circonspection à rendre le Mercure digne d'estre toujours lû dans des lieux d'où la moindre liberté le banniroit" (9). In other words, they would no longer be considered part of the "divertissement du beau Sexe" but rather an integral part of the broader historical narrative.

From 1682 to 1685, in stark contrast with the journal's early years, the novellas are virtually indistinguishable from the news events both typographically and content-wise. These are the years that include the court's move to Versailles (May 1682), Louis XIV's secret marriage to the pious Mme de Maintenon (October 1683), and the Revocation of the Edict of Nantes (October 1685), formative years for France as a whole.[21] If the narrative created by the news stories in the *Le Mercure galant* can be called a general history, which Faith Beasley defines as "a broad view of events that is devoted uniquely to occurrences in the public sector" (12), then the novellas can be considered a series of "histoires particulières."[22] Defined by Beasley as stories that "seek to reveal the details and reasoning that underlie the public matters of general history, the motives and passions that determine officially recorded events" (29), they often include women as motivating forces. The majority of the novellas that appear during these later years have a cautionary or admonishing tone and an injunctive function. Entitled simply "histoire" in almost all cases, and indistinguishable typographically and often content-wise from the stories surrounding them, they differ as much from the early novellas as the latter did from the news that surrounded them. While those from 1672 through 1677 functioned as amusing filler within a historical narrative that they supported but from which they remained distinct, those of 1682 through 1685 functioned alongside the news stories to fashion a general history of Paris and the court.

* * *

Donneau de Visé stressed the significance and integrity of this joint historical narrative by insisting on the truth of these later novellas, which positioned them as more or less indistinct from the surrounding articles. As an integral part of his historical narrative, the novellas needed to have a purported truth-value equal to that of the news events; the August 1685 novella, a later version of "L'Histoire de la Fille Soldat" is one such example. Monique Vincent observes that, "C'est seulement à partir de 1677 que les Nouvelles méritent le nom d'*Histoires véritables* annoncé dans le titre du *Mercure*" (*Donneau de Visé* 318). De Visé reminds readers from time to time that he is seeking true stories and occasionally provides corrections to those that allegedly contain falsehoods. Referring to a story from November 1681 that aroused suspicions, he enjoins,

> Cette Feste me fait souvenir d'un avis que je me crois obligé de vous donner touchant celle de Charolles, dont vous avez veu les particularitez dans ma Lettre de Novembre. Les Memoires que l'on m'en avoit donnez ne se sont pas trouvez justes, & je ne puis dire par quelles raisons ceux qui ont pris la peine de les dresser, ont appliqué aux honnestes Gens de cette petite Ville, dont ils ont emprunté les noms, ce qui s'est passé dans un autre lieu de Bourgogne. Je ne voy pas quel avantage ils peuvent tirer de cette plaisanterie, dont apparemment ils ne voudroient pas se nommer autheurs. On m'a appris que la Ville de Charolles, bien que composée de quantité de Personnes d'honneur &

d'esprit, n'est nullement propre a des divertissemens de cette nature. (January 1682, 177-78)

De Visé follows this with a reminder and the threat of public embarrassment that the stories sent must be completely truthful.

C'est dequoy, Madame, j'ay voulu vous informer, & en mesme temps le Public, afin qu'on ne m'envoye plus d'Histoires qui ne soient vrayes dans toutes leurs circonstances. Si j'en reçois d'inventées, on les démeslera toûjours tost ou tard, au desavantage de ceux qui n'auront pas écrit juste. (178-79)

At the same time that de Visé wages war against fictitious novellas, the news reports themselves change. No longer an easily refutable list of officers or an account of a siege of which there were many witnesses, they appear in narrative form more often than not. No longer a series of undeniable facts, the news seems more subjective now. *Le Mercure galant* reads more or less as a continuous narrative, with the exception of the airs, engravings and verse poetry that interrupt its rhythm.

It is evident that truth, however, meant something very different for the seventeenth-century public than it does for the twenty-first century one. Whether or not the events occurred exactly as a historian depicts them was beside the point. What is more important is that what the historian claims to be true, that is to say, what he or she claims to be historical, serves as an illustration of a greater, ethical truth.[23] As Harth argues, historians blend verisimilitude with truth in order to more effectively convey their lessons, to make these examples more palatable. In particular, the novella imitates history, she asserts, "a genre that was not really a genre and that *had no positive truth*" (146). Although Harth goes on to claim that "[d]uring the height of the *nouvelles'* success, in the last few decades of the seventeenth century, their truth was simply a negation of official truth as broadcast in periodicals, pamphlets and other court literature" (178), the novellas of *Le Mercure galant*, expectedly, serve as a counter example. Because this journal is itself an officially sanctioned periodical and the novellas an integral part of it, they necessarily represent the moral truth it espoused. As Louis XIV worked to rid his kingdom of those whom he considered heathens, this moral truth became synonymous with Catholic ideology.

In contrast to his focus on war stories during the *Mercure's* early years, Donneau de Visé devotes a majority of pages from 1682 to 1685 to the Catholic cause. He creates a narrative that emphasizes the rewards bestowed on those who lived piously punctuated by examples of the punishments inflicted on those who do not. The fluidity of his narrative creates a more effective vehicle for de Visé's teachings.[24] As the stakes are raised and France's religious fervor mounts, de Visé creates a comparatively lively history within the pages of the *Mercure*. Instead of models of social status, he creates models of piety easily emulated by all readers. As Henriette Goldwyn remarks, this periodical, by dint of its title alone, is especially suited to such moral teachings.

> Œuvres de polémique, les mercures se distinguent en effet des autres périodiques par le raisonnement politique qu'ils véhiculent. Ce sont des œuvres hybrides dans lesquelles s'entrecroisent une multiplicité de nouvelles qui englobent l'actualité politique, littéraire, sociale et parfois même scientifique. Tout cela est traité avec beaucoup d'humour; on y admire la griffe ludique et la verve satirique destinées à divertir le lecteur. (248)

The humor of the early novellas has turned darker here, however, and rather than focusing on laughable characters, these later novellas concentrate on lamentable ones in most instances. Usually examples of what not to do, the novellas of this time frequently inspire pity and reflection, and often piety as well.

* * *

In Donneau de Visé's own words, *Le Mercure galant* went from being a "histoire journalière" in 1672 which contains a day-by-day account of memorable events, to a series of "lettres historiques" (November 1682) in 1685 which, although still historical in nature, focus on the narrative retelling of these events. Both incarnations of *Le Mercure galant* espouse an ideological agenda for its readers, determined in large part by the royal pension that supports it and that the exemplary novella support. While the novellas of the first years reinforce the groundwork for a social structure that prizes the bourgeoisie and their unthreatening social ambitions, the injunctive nature of the later ones recalls the *Heptaméron* in which "[e]xamples seem discredited as a means of providing any positive model" and "sin and ugliness convey a humiliating and negative exemplarity" (Lyons 73). A newspaper is a historical text by definition and the issues that appear just before the Revocation of the Edict of Nantes support Bruter's claim that "La nouveauté dans la manière de considérer l'histoire à la fin du XVIIe siècle réside en ceci qu'elle semble désormais se spécialiser dans cette fonction morale" (123). In addition to selecting facts that informed them of important events and their circumstances while illustrating the meritorious behavior of individuals, Donneau de Visé also includes novellas that reinforce this moral agenda. These stories are set in the recent past, take place usually in France, and contain anonymous characters who, much like the "Madame" by which de Visé addresses his female audience collectively, represents his constructed readership.[25] Unlike the news stories that almost always named those involved, thereby necessarily excluding others who could only hope to accomplish as much, the novellas address their readers broadly and presented them with a series of paradigms behind which lie a subtle or not so subtle injunctive force.

The Reformation and the benefits the Edict of Nantes accorded to non-Catholics interrupted the historical narrative the king envisioned for France by posing challenges to his authority. Because de Visé depends on Louis XIV's financial support, he necessarily serves as one of the monarchy's agents. *Le Mercure galant* with its lists of war heroes, fallen or not, battle reenactments and general praise for the current rule, mediates an ideological storyline external to its fragmented contents. This storyline, the history of a nation, is necessarily comprised of a series of events some of which de Visé presents both in the news articles and in his exemplary novellas. Camille Dumoulié provides a convincing account of the novella's relationship with events.

> De Boccacce à Joyce, le nouvelliste se donne des airs de moraliste. Mais ce n'est là encore qu'un effet secondaire par rapport à la véritable dimension éthique liée à l'essence de la nouvelle comme genre de l'événement, et que l'on peut exprimer simplement par cette formule: être à la hauteur de l'événement – principe déterminant aussi bien pour les personnages que pour le narrateur. (104)

The novellas of *Le Mercure galant* presented readers with examples culled from generalized if not actualized experiences that ultimately aim to make them better subjects of the king while supporting the broader narrative progression towards absolutism in France's history.

Notes

[1] Of the many sources on this topic, I suggest starting with Lennard Davis's *Factual Fictions: The Origins of the English Novel*, Frédéric Deloffre's *La Nouvelle en France*

à l'âge classique, René Godenne's *Histoire de la nouvelle française aux XVIIe et XVIIIe siècles*, Roger Guichemerre's introduction to *Dom Carlos et d'autres nouvelles françaises du XVIIe siècle*, Jean Lafond's introduction to *Nouvelles du XVIIe siècle* and finally Gabrielle Verdier's article "*Ceci n'est pas un roman*: Authorial Discourse in Early Seventeenth-Century Short Fiction and the Boundaries of the *Nouvelle*."

[2] Monique Vincent has written extensively on *Le Mercure galant*. See in particular her thesis published by Aux Amateurs de Livres entitled *Donneau de Visé et le* Mercure galant as well as her edition of select novellas taken from this journal. She, like others, reads these stories as separate from the news articles, a mere *divertissement* within a more serious context.

[3] Throughout this text, I will use the word "novellas" to refer to these stories, in keeping with Monique Vincent's terminology. See pages 312-15 of *Donneau de Visé et le* Mercure galant for justification of this choice.

[4] I have adopted this terminology from John D. Lyons's *Exemplum: The Rhetoric of Example in Early Modern France and Italy*, which will serve as the theoretical framework for this discussion.

[5] Faith E. Beasley cites two definitions of "histoire" in *Revising Memory*. The first, by Richelet in 1680, defines it as "Une narration continuée de choses vraies, grandes, et publiques, écrite avec esprit, avec éloquence et avec jugement pour l'instruction des particuliers et des Princes, et pour le bien de la société civile." According to Furetière in 1690, "['histoire'] [s]e dit de cette narration véritable suivie et enchaînée [*sic*] de plusieurs événements mémorables qui sont arrivés en une ou plusieurs nations" (11).

[6] Beasley notes that "The historian must judge events and choose those that are 'great' and 'memorable' for the account to fulfill its pedagogical function" (12).

[7] Annie Bruter argues that "l'histoire offre un terrain particulièrement propice à l'apprentissage de la morale parce qu'elle a l'avantage de la présenter sous une forme vivante, à travers des exemples [...]" (124).

[8] All citations from *Le Mercure galant* are from the original editions. I have maintained the contemporary spelling throughout.

[9] In his article on the beginnings of the French press, François Moureau remarks that "le *Mercure* fut pendant longtemps le seul mensuel littéraire autorisé en France" (131).

[10] Moureau explains that *La Gazette* provided readers with officially sanctioned versions of political events while the *Journal des savants* dedicated an increasing number of pages to book reviews and theological debates. Both journals, like *Le Mercure galant*, were written primarily in French rather than Latin, which leads Moureau to conclude that "en France, la presse d'érudition est originellement une œuvre de vulgarisation" (125).

[11] Although the novellas appear anonymously, many were attributed to de Visé himself and appear in his collection *Cent Nouvelles nouvelles*. De Visé often positions himself

as the narrator of these stories as well, but the question of narratology remains outside the scope of this article.

[12] See Lyons pages 29-31 for further discussion of the quotation.

[13] In "War Relations: A Journalist Writes the Sun King's Wars," Chloé Hogg raises some very intriguing questions concerning the connections between these war stories and royalist propaganda. She argues that *Le Mercure galant* creates a pedagogy of war while simultaneously creating support for it among its public. I am indebted to Hogg for several references that helped inform the present study.

[14] "[L]e roman propose au lecteur une fiction vraisemblable, à l'image de la vie même, suffisamment particulière pour que le lecteur puisse trouver sans difficulté matière à appliquer à son propre cas" (Grande 37).

[15] In her article on *Le Mercure galant*'s readership, Janet Letts notes that "fiction designed to sell well generally offers characters with whom readers can identify themselves either automatically or through wishful thinking that slightly raises their social status [...]" (218). In response, Arthur Herman argues that "large numbers of the *Mercure*'s readers understood how imitating the social intimacy of *galanterie* and related idioms was a projection of social power. We see a shift, from imitative desire as political and religious rivalry, to desire expressed through the pursuit of social status, and the anxieties it provokes [...]. The instruments of social striving, such as politeness and *galanterie*, provided imitative formulæ for acquiring a social role [...]. [T]he reader of the *Mercure Galant* finds his or her own image reflected in the periodical's ultimately inaccessible models, who are really models of desire" (233).

[16] As Erica Harth notes, the *roman* was "[w]ritten by nobles or intimates of nobles" and "appropriated history for those who were beginning to be excluded by it" (141).

[17] The characterization of women as disorderly in the seventeenth century is widespread. Michèle Longino provides a particularly clear and helpful elaboration of this characterization in *Orientalism in French Classical Drama*.

[18] As Lyons notes, Aristotle distinguishes three types of example: the parabole (comparison), the logos (fable) and the historical example. While the first is possible but fictitious, the logos is fictitious and entirely impossible. Similarly, Cicero distinguishes among the history (historia), the argument (argumentum), which corresponds to the parabole, and the fable (fabula) (7-8).

[19] He ends the first with this note: "J'ay leû ce que je vous dis dans une Lettre qu'a écrite icy le Supérieur d'une des Maisons les plus réformées de Lyon. Il marque qu'il a connu ces trois Freres, qu'il leur a parlé plusieurs fois [...]. Ces morts funestes m'ont esté confirmées de bouche par des Personnes tres-dignes de foy, venuës icy de Lyon depuis peu de jours" (septembre 1682, 197-98). The second begins "J'ay appris une chose fort surprenante d'un Homme tres-digne de foy, qui assure qu'il s'estoit trouvé à Orange le 25. du dernier mois chez Monsieur l'Evêque, lors que ce Prélat reçeut une Lettre d'un Gentilhomme, qui luy mandoit ce qui suit" (novembre 1683, 133-34).

[20] In comparison, the earlier period boasts a mere three fables. In both periods, the fables appear distinct typographically and have distinctive titles.

[21] It is notable that in the January 1682 issue, the first of this time period during which de Visé no longer expresses concern that he will bore his female public, he comments, "L'égalité des Sexes ne se conteste plus parmy les honnestes Gens" (92). Of course, this must be understood within its context. One of the articles in the February 1682 issue is entitled "De l'Art de se taire pour les Femmes" which de Visé presents in the following manner: "Voicy un terrible Chapitre, & je croy que dés le Titre mesme bien des Gens s'en moqueront. L'Art de se taire pour les Femmes, c'est comme qui diroit l'Art de ne mourir jamais" (221).

[22] This general history typically excludes women, Beasley adds. A notable exception for *Le Mercure galant*, however, would be the August 1682 issue devoted to the Duc de Bourgogne's birth. Described in detail, Madame la Dauphine's cries of pain attest to her service and devotion to France and therefore to her personal merit.

[23] "The moral dimension of history provided a corrective to truth, not exactly in rewriting history, but in adding reflections, in converting fact into example, so that truth became a lesson" (Harth 136).

[24] Bruter notes that "[L]es enseignements qu'on retire de l'histoire passent par le plaisir de sa lecture, qui lui-même provient du mouvement, de l'enchaînement des faits. D'où la nécessité d'éviter tout ce qui retarde le cours de la narration […]" (57).

[25] Writing about the newsbooks of seventeenth-century England, which share certain of these traits, Lennard Davis remarks that "the idea of continuity and recentness implies the reader's involvement in that externality." He further argues that "[t]he reader is brought within the frame of the discourse both spatially and temporally since his life is brought within the compass of print […]" (74).

Works Cited

Beasley, Faith E. *Revising Memory. Women's Fiction and Memoirs in Seventeenth-Century France*. New Brunswick, N.J.: Rutgers University Press, 1990.

Bruter, Annie. *L'Histoire enseignée au Grand Siècle. Naissance d'une pédagogie*. Paris: Editions Belin, 1997.

Davis, Lennard. *Factual Fictions: The Origins of the English Novel*. New York: Columbia University Press, 1983.

Deloffre, Frédéric. *La Nouvelle en France à l'âge classique*. Paris: Librairie Marcel Didier, 1967.

Demers, Jeanne. "Nouvelle et conte: des frontières à établir." *La Nouvelle: Écriture(s) et lecture(s)*. Ed. Agnès Whitfield and Jacques Cotnam. Montréal: XYZ, 1993. 63-72.

Dumoulié, Camille. "La Nouvelle: Genre de l'événement." *Nouvelle Revue Française* (1993): 94-105.

Godwin, Denise. "Le Nationalisme français dans la nouvelle de 1657 à 1700." *Papers on French Seventeenth-Century Literature* 16.31 (1989): 447-53.

Goldwyn, Henriette. "Journalisme polémique à la fin du XVIIe siècle: Le cas de Mme du Noyer." In *Femmes savantes, savoirs des femmes: Du crépuscule de la Renaissance à l'aube des Lumières*. Ed. Colette Nativel. Chantilly: Droz, 1995. 247-56.

Godenne, René. *Histoire de la nouvelle française aux XVIIe et XVIIIe siècles*. Geneva: Droz, 1970.

Grande, Nathalie. "Quand le roman oeuvre en moraliste: Madeleine de Scudéry et *Clélie*." *Dalhousie French Studies* 27 (1994): 31-41.

Guichemerre, Roger, ed. *Dom Carlos et d'autres nouvelles françaises du XVIIe siècle*. Paris: Gallimard, 1995.

Harth, Erica. *Ideology and Culture in Seventeenth-Century France*. Ithaca: Cornell University Press, 1983.

Herman, Arthur. "Print, Power, and Desire: 'La Presse periodique': Commentary." *Cahiers du dix-septième siècle* 5.2 (1991): 229-39.

Hogg, Chloé. "Strong Women, Illustrious Men: Constructing History and Civic Virtue in the *Grand Siècle*." *Papers on French Seventeenth-Century Literature* 26.50 (1999): 19-27.

_____. "War Relations: A Journalist Writes the Sun King's Wars." In *Relations and Relationships in Seventeenth-Century Literature: Actes du 36e congrès annuel de la North American Society for Seventeenth-Century French Literature, Portland State University, 6-8 mai 2004*. Ed. Jennifer R. Perlmutter. Tübingen: Narr, 2006. 197-208.

Lafond, Jean. *Nouvelles du XVIIe siècle.* Paris: Gallimard, 1997.

Le Mercure galant. Ed. Jean Donneau de Visé. Paris: Barbin, 1672-1710.

Letts, Janet T. "Responsive Readers of the *Mercure galant,* 1680-1710." *Cahiers du dix-septième siècle* 5.2 (1991): 211-28.

Longino, Michèle. *Orientalism in French Classical Drama.* Cambridge, U.K: Cambridge University Press, 2002.

Lyons, John D. *Exemplum: The Rhetoric of Example in Early Modern France and Italy.* Princeton: Princeton University Press, 1989.

Moureau, François. "Les Débuts de la presse en langue française (1631-1715)." *Australian Journal of French Studies* 2 (1981): 122-33.

Verdier, Gabrielle. *"Ceci n'est pas un roman:* Authorial Discourse in Early Seventeenth-Century Short Fiction and the Boundaries of the *Nouvelle." Papers on French Seventeenth-Century Literature* 16.30 (1989): 143-58.

Vincent, Monique. *Anthologie des nouvelles du Mercure galant (1672-1710).* Paris: Société des Textes Français Modernes, 1996.

_____. *Donneau de Visé et le* Mercure galant. 2 vols. Paris: Aux Amateurs de Livres, 1987.

Visé, Jean Donneau de. *Cent nouvelles nouvelles.* Geneva: Droz, 1966.

Keys of Iron, Keys of Gold:
Enclosure, Example and Alchemical Teachings in the Novella and L'École des femmes

Twyla Meding

Femme sotte se cognoist à la cotte.
Vous en avez la clef, & nous avons la serrure.[1]

Toutes choses se tiennent par quelque similitude, tout exemple cloche, et la relation qui se tire de l'experience est tousjours defaillante et imparfaicte: on joinct toutefois les comparaisons par quelque coin. – Montaigne, (III. 13, 1047)

Je te pardonne; mais tu le payeras. – Molière, *Le Médecin malgré lui* (I, 4)

Introduction: A Confraternity of Cuckolds

In the forty-first of *Les Cent nouvelles nouvelles* (1462), the protagonist, a recently widowed and world-weary knight reputed for his wisdom, takes as second wife a woman who is beautiful but "non pas des plus subtiles du monde" (178). Her slow wit suits him, since he hopes to profit from it in order to "mieulx la duyre et tourner a la fasson qu'avoir la vouldroit" (179); as he desires, she obeys him dutifully. Nonetheless, in order to curtail his new bride's appetite for "l'amoureux jeu," which is unequal to his own, he has her don a fetching hauberk ("jaserant"), reasoning through a military metaphor that "on ne se doit point trouver a l'assaut amoureux sans armes" (179). When the king calls him away to another kind of combat, she remains at home with her servants and an enterprising *clerc* endowed with a talent not only for playing the harp but for the game at which her husband balks. Ready to joust, then, she outfits herself in armor and awaits her new lover, who takes her for an armed knight and their rendezvous as a stratagem intended to entrap him. Startled, he takes a tumble down the stairs in his haste to escape, but once assured of his lady's identity and the desire she shares with him, he shows her "la coustume des clercs," according to him quite the opposite of "adoubement," the knights' custom of outfitting their ladies in armor. The *clerc* has her disrobe instead of suiting up – he removes her hauberk, and once in bed, the two "se desarmerent de leurs chemises" (180) – and spends many a pleasant hour with her during the husband's tour of duty at war. Upon the knight's return, the wife carelessly states her preference for the "coustume des clercs" at mealtime, but is shrewd enough to sense her husband's suspicions and to hide her transgression by hastily explaining, "Ilz boivent après graces" (181). The knight is satisfied with this response and decides to adopt that equivocal "coustume" in his household; for his part, the *clerc* is free to continue his tricks. In this case, the initial proverb's wisdom may be amplified to read: "Femme sotte se cognoist à la cotte de maille"; the wife's armor constitutes not only evidence of her docility and obedience to the whims of her husband, whose wisdom and wit ostensibly surpass her own, but signals by her eager acceptance of such unwieldy attire the danger inherent in unbridled feminine desire, enclosed paradoxically in a metallic and uncomfortable – but detachable – garment designed for combat between men. Regardless, it is she who has the last word: "Comme vous avez oy fut monseigneur par madame en sa response abusé" (181); her explanation of clerical table manners is designated as a "glose" (10) in the work's table of contents. The wife's verbal outsmarting of her horned husband and the *clerc*'s hijinks end by integrating "monseigneur" into the brotherhood of "noz amis" (181). The novella's conclusion is a distant reminder of Arnolphe's stunned complaint on his reversal of fortune in the final act of Molière's *L'École des femmes* (1662): "Ah! je l'ai mal connue; ou, ma foi! là-dessus / Une sotte en sait plus que le plus habile homme" (ll. 1543-44). Like the knight's new wife, Agnès is taken for a simpleton but still manages to outwit the older and ostensibly wiser Arnolphe, who appears to be on the verge of joining the ranks of the cuckolds he has mocked for more than twenty years, if indeed he can marry his young charge.

The origins of Molière's protagonists may be traced not to the medieval tale, but to contemporary novellas, which incorporate and amplify its elements. Seventeenth-century elaborations of this ribald tale of the absent husband hoodwinked by a doltish wife clad in armor feature the episode of marital dubbing and adulterous undressing as the culmination of the hero's folly: so preoccupied with protecting himself against feminine treachery is he that unlike the knight of *Les Cent nouvelles nouvelles*, he fails to consummate his long-desired marriage to a beautiful nitwit; he instead has her don his own armor and patrol the bedroom while he sleeps peacefully, secure in the knowledge that his wife is not deceiving him. When he is summoned to the court for six months, she promptly cuckolds him with the first passing stranger, whose name she never learns, and then reveals guilelessly to him the more pleasing pedagogical principles of that "autre mary" (Scarron 96), with no effort to conceal her misdeed, unlike the wife of *Les Cent nouvelles nouvelles* 41. The episode is nearly identical in María de Zayas's *El prevenido engañado*, the fourth tale in her *Novelas amorosas y ejemplares* (1637), and Paul Scarron's "Version" (32) of her "maravilla" (168), *La Précaution inutile* (1655), and is seen as the principal inspiration for Molière's version of the enlightened innocent, *L'École des femmes* (1662), where Agnès's recitation of the *Maximes du mariage* is a verbal reprisal of the wife's martial travesty in the novellas.[2] Onto the relatively simple structure of the medieval novella, both Zayas and Scarron superimpose architectural enclosure and the framework of example in order to lend plausibility to the wife's simplemindedness as well as the husband's foolish precautions. Contrary to the play's novelistic antecedents, in *L'École des femmes*, Arnolphe is neither husband nor cuckold, and he is fooled not by a simpleton but by a *femme habile* whom he took for a *sotte*.

It will be my purpose in this essay to show first that through excision, iterativity, enclosure and disjunction in the French and Spanish novellas, example functions to reinforce the hero's error – that is, in order to avoid women's trickery and the status of *mal-marié*, he must flee *femmes spirituelles* and instead marry a *sotte* – and finally to disabuse him, though too late to save him from falling victim to what he feared most. Next, I will show how the structure of example is fragmented and dispersed throughout Molière's dramatic adaptation of the novella, to the extent that the never-married Arnolphe never assimilates the lesson of his novelistic predecessors, whose undeceiving is based on their own experience. A keen observer and mocker of others' misfortunes, in his first foray into the experiential realm of marriage, Arnolphe is always already too late: Horace's father, Oronte, has already married his son to Agnès, daughter of the long-lost Enrique, before the play's opening scene. By staging the novella hero's perspectival "blind spot" (Lyons 91), Molière underscores Arnolphe's blindness to his dual status as mocking spectator of the misfortunes of others and unwilling and unaware actor in the spectacle that once provoked his derisive laughter.[3] Finally, I will show how in the novellas, objects made of metal – the key to the closet where the protagonist hides during his final tryst before his return home; the "cent pistoles" (Scarron 79) provided by his last conquest as compensation for his

"service" (76); the pass key that opens all the doors to the protagonist's dwelling inherited from his father; the armor he ought to have
transmitted to his own son – play a key role in storytelling and its connection to the ultimate impotence of the hero, who dies without heirs.
Through his preoccupation with power and the wealth exemplified by
the "cent pistoles" (l. 284) he offers so liberally to his rival, Horace,
Arnolphe contributes to the prolongation of a tale that results in his
own exit from the stage; the act of marriage that would ally him with
the confraternity of "noz amis" ultimately eludes Arnolphe.

Zayas and Scarron: Belated Exemplarity

The spectacle of cuckolds evoked by Arnolphe in *L'École des
femmes* (ll. 21-44) and his foolproof "méthode" (l. 124) for never
sharing the stage with them – he will marry a submissive, poor girl
raised in a "petit couvent, loin de toute pratique" (l. 135) and guarded
provisionally in his "autre maison" (l. 146), never frequented by visitors – differs sharply from the hero's journey across time and space in
María de Zayas's *El prevenido engañado*, in which the virtual incar-
ceration of women is reflected in the embedded structure of the narrative frame tale. Unlike the prologues of Boccaccio's *Decameron* or
Marguerite de Navarre's *Heptaméron*, which situate the frame characters' afternoon storytelling outdoors, in a temperate climate and in a
pastoral setting that recall Plato's *Phaedrus*, Zayas has Lisis and her
retinue of storytellers gather near Christmastime, when "los hielos y
terribles nieves" (167) cause all to keep to their houses.[4] The storytellers thus meet in Lisis's house, and conduct their nighttime "sarao" in
her bedroom, where she convalesces from an illness caused by jealousy, and where "costosos paños flamencos, cuyos boscajes, flores y
arboledas parecían las selvas de Arcadia o los pensiles huertos de
Babilonia" (169) create the semblance of the pastoral locale described
in the Italian and French prologues.[5] Architectural imbrication in *El
prevenido* thus reflects and prepares the structure of the frame, where
Zayas has each character tell a tale that is both preceded and followed
by continuation of the *sarao*; an embedded architectural frame thus
encloses a narrative frame.[6] Don Alonso's *maravilla* is explicitly
exemplary: his tale will be a "certificación" of maxims on the conduct
of "los más avisados" who often "[caen] en lo mismo que temen" and
on the fundamental incompatibility of simpleton and sage; his tale is
therefore a text "dependent" (Lyons 24) on the general statement that

precedes his narrative. At the same time, it serves as a cautionary tale to those men who might put too much stock in their own judgment or venture to test women; such fools would do better to fear the outcome of their risky behavior (Zayas 293). By showing the punishment that awaits those who would dare to put women's virtue to the test, don Alonso's novella will counter and correct the paradigm of wifely obedience outlined in Boccaccio's version of the Griselda story (*Decameron* 660-69).

In the story proper, women are generally confined to the houses of their fathers or husbands, but the case of the infant left to die her by mother in the initial adventure of don Fadrique, the protagonist, is exceptional: conceived in secret to an unmarried woman who appears only at the liminal space of balcony or window, she begins life as an abandoned "criatura" in a delapidated "corraliza" with no doors (298). Don Fadrique, who witnesses the delivery, rescues the baby, transports her to the house of a relative, and has her baptized "Gracia," perhaps an allusion to the wife's explanation of the "coustume des clercs" in *Les Cent nouvelles nouvelles* 41. The abandoned girl's benefactor, who claims he is her father, stipulates that from the age of three she be raised in a convent; there she will spend the better part of fourteen years, the duration of don Fadrique's amorous wanderings through Spain and Italy. Both mother and daughter retire to nunneries where they live among women: their retreat reflects the trajectory of Zayas's oeuvre, which "proceeds from the house of the father to the house of God"; the convent is ultimately "in truth the house of the mother" (Greer, "MP" 110). But since she is "la persona más importante de esta historia" (299), Gracia will one day emerge from her retreat.

Virtual prisoners in architectural enclosures governed by men, the women don Fadrique encounters consistently subvert their confinement in order to assert their independence. Serafina and doña Beatriz defer marriage in order to maintain covert and forbidden liaisons: Serafina with the rival known to don Fadrique; Beatriz with a black slave. In both cases, chance allows the hero to gain knowledge of their duplicity. In Madrid, doña Violante has no interest in matrimony and carves out her own space of "libertad" within her cousin's house, maintaining a room of her own, a "cuarto aparte" (327) that allows her to meet secretly with don Fadrique, but from which she ejects him in "la burla del zapato" (328). In all three cases, the clever women, or *discretas*, with whom don Fadrique becomes enamored profit from enclosure in order to create a domestic space that sustains their own freedom

as well as their provisional or permanent aversion to matrimony. Don
Fadrique remains on the margins of feminine enclosure, never able to
master the denizens of those unruly households. Like the husband of
Les Cent nouvelles nouvelles 41 who perceives only his wife's "parde-
hors" and has no access to her "pardedans" (180), or Arnolphe who
tries in vain to "mettre un ordre et dedans et dehors" (l. 1010), don
Fadrique is barred from mastery of what lies within the spaces which
enclose women. It is perhaps no accident that this "inside" or "dedans"
is also the space of example (Lyons 28) and "fermeture," whereas the
"outside" or "dehors," where the hero remains, is associated with
movement (Zumthor 59).

Unlike the women he pursues first in his hometown of Granada, and then in Seville and Madrid, don Fadrique moves freely
through geographical space. Hailing from one of the richest and most
noble families of Granada, upon the untimely death of his parents, he
seeks only to wed the beautiful Serafina, whose heart he aims to win
before he asks her parents for her hand in marriage. When he inadvertently learns the secret of her illicit liaison and pregnancy, he sets off
on "a sexual and emotional odyssey" (Brownlee 171) that takes him
throughout Spain and finally to Italy, where he intends to follow the
Duke of Osuna to Sicily, though he is sidetracked by "varios y diversos
casos" (329) in Naples and Rome, including an incident in which his
paramour tosses her murdered husband in a sack into the river.[7] His
initial experience leaves him "escarmentado en Serafina" and leads him
to conclude through inductive fallacy that all *discretas* will use their
wiles to deceive him: "por ella ultrajaba a todas las demás mujeres, no
haciendo excepción de ninguna, cosa contraria a su entendimiento,
pues para una mala hay ciento buenas, y no todas lo son, ni es justo,
mezclando unas con otras, culparlas a todas" (300).[8] If "repetition (or
the detection of repetition), comparison, and generalization" (Lyons
15) are requisite components for induction, then don Fadrique makes
an immediate generalization on women's treachery, without evidence
of repetition, with no basis for comparison and which is ultimately discordant with his innate sound judgment. His recurrent *tema* – "no había
de fiar en [las mujeres], y más de la discretas, porque de muy sabias y
entendidas daban en traviesas y viciosas, y que con sus astucias
engañaban a los hombres" (Zayas 300-1) – provides a shaky framework for interpretation of the misfortunes soon to befall him, which
allow him to validate through his own perception of repetition and subsequent comparison the fundamental truth of his original generaliza-

tion. It is thus that the hero's error engenders a kind of latter-day *errance* through space and time.[9]

If don Fadrique's wanderings in Spain are characterized by repetition, his travels in Italy constitute a textual iterativity, wherein "an example that explicitly points to an event that happened once actually stands for many similar events occurring through time" (Lyons 27). The "varios y diversos casos" that befall him in Naples and Rome serve only to strengthen his "opinión" (Zayas 329) that clever women undermine the authority of men, but don Alonso devotes fewer than two paragraphs to their description. This elision elicits a jab from Scarron's intrusive narrator in *La Précaution inutile*, at the critical moment when his hero, Dom Pèdre, recounts to the Catalan duchess, who joins him in his final tryst before his return home to Granada, his adventures thus far: "Là le Grenadin luy conta ses avantures de Grenade, de Seville et de Madrid, et celles aussi d'Italie, qui ne sont pas venuës à ma connaissance" (74). When Scarron performs a gesture of textual excision by removing Zayas's novella from the context of frame tale, he replaces the commentary of the frame-narrator, don Alonso, with critical salvos and digressions that at once reconfigure the absent frame and counter in mocking tones the faulty impressions of Dom Pèdre as "internal interpreter" (Lyons 24) of his own misfortunes.[10] In Zayas's novella, the practices of guarding secrets and of recounting stories reprise the embedded structure of domestic spaces which confine women: don Fadrique conceals the story of Gracia's illegitimate conception and birth by claiming her as his daughter (299), and he keeps to himself the spectacle of doña Beatriz's sexual predation of her black slave (311). On the other hand, once he arrives in Madrid, don Fadrique gives an account "de su vida y sucesos, sin nombrar partes" (313) to don Juan in order to encourage his cousin to follow his example and to confide in him the reasons for his melancholy mood; his cousin's confidence leads ultimately to don Fadrique's liaison with doña Violante. Likewise, before his hasty departure for Italy, don Fadrique recounts to his cousin "lo que había pasado" (329) in his ill-fated last rendezvous with doña Violante. In the tale's epilogue, don Alonso reiterates don Juan's role as confidant and intermediary: shortly before his death, don Fadrique consigns his story to writing and sends it to his cousin as don Alonso has just told it, "de la manera que aquí va" (340). Don Alonso's *maravilla* is thus a quotation of a written text that becomes confused with both oralization and example,[11] and a framed tale that itself contains a *mise en abyme* of the act of storytelling, which enacts the tenuous demarcation between *nouvelle* as "true story" and *conte* as oralized narration.[12]

As a result of its status as "a unit of discourse...fashioned from a mass of text that is not retained" (Lyons 18), Scarron's "Version" (32) of the Spanish novella puts into play the etymology of example in *eximere*, even as he omits or modifies the numerous links between frame and tale in the Spanish original, particularly with regard to don Juan's role as his cousin's sole confidant and publisher of the protagonist's secrets.[13] Through the detachment of example from maxim implicit in the operation of excision, the role of example in the construction of the hero's error is diminished, since Dom Pèdre's calamitous encounters with women fail to adhere to an overarching maxim that remains "external to discourse" and constitutes "possible common ground" between speaker and listeners (Lyons 28); Scarron highlights instead the conflict between Dom Pèdre as "internal interpreter" (Lyons 24) and the intrusive narrator who through his knowledge of the original text in Spanish is already apprised of the protagonist's foolish stratagems. Scarron's title thus centers on the uselessness of Dom Pèdre's precautions against cuckoldry, given the inherent inconstancy of women; Zayas's title, on the other hand, concerns the protagonist himself and his ultimate chastening not by a *discreta* but by a *boba* (340). The shift in the title's focus reflects Dom Pèdre's appropriation of the aversion to marriage characteristic of Zayas's Serafina, Beatriz and Violante: whereas don Fadrique's "escarmiento" (300) subsequent to his nearly disastrous marriage to the duplicitous Serafina causes him to generalize a single incidence of betrayal to distrust of all women, particularly those who put too much faith in their own wit (Zayas 300-1), Dom Pèdre is "fort dégousté du mariage, apres avoir eu si grande envie d'en taster" (Scarron 42). In addition to his fear of all women, the error of Scarron's hero implies a supplemental critique of matrimony bolstered by his mistrust of *femmes spirituelles*. It is thus that Scarron's near-translation of Zayas's story of the *discreto* led astray becomes a cautionary tale on the perils men face in marriage and the implicit menace of cuckoldry.

In both the Spanish and French versions of this variant on the theme of the absent husband cuckolded by a crafty and unfaithful wife, example and storytelling converge in the episodes of the Catalan duchess and the hero's subsequent marriage to the girl he had raised in the convent. Don Fadrique wastes fourteen years in Italy, always embroiled in deadly and deceptive amorous intrigues; Dom Pèdre spends fourteen or fifteen years abroad, and Scarron adds that after the time elapsed, his protagonist is "tousjours amoureux, ou si vous voulez débauché, toûjours grand avanturier et toûjours se confirmant dans son opinion qu'on ne pouvoit estre seurement marié avec une femme d'esprit" (72). In Scarron's version, Dom Pèdre's years in Italy transform him into a Don Juan whose initiation into love becomes an apprenticeship in debauchery: his serial misfortunes in Spain convert him to a serial seducer of women.[14] Moreover, his distrust of clever women is couched in terms of marriage, the problem he will soon discuss with the duchess. Scarron's conversion of poet to philanderer frames the episode of his encounter with the duchess and serves to augment his error.

Whereas the hero remains on the margins of enclosed feminine space in his first three encounters in Spain, upon his return, tired of the road and out of money, as he heads home for Granada, he sees the young duchess at the balcony of her country house, where she has been left alone by her old husband who has gone hunting. Through the intertermediary of a servant, she invites the passing stranger inside. The protagonist's previous trysts, tricks and deceptions take place at night; on this occasion he enters the duchess's château in broad daylight, around nine o'clock in the morning (Zayas 329-30; Scarron 72). In *El prevenido*, he tells her his entire story, including his resolution to return home in order to marry (330); she thus appropriates the role of confidant he assigned previously to don Juan. She offers sensible advice on don Fadrique's foolhardy intention to marry a woman who thinks only of loving her husband, maintaining his honor and caring for his children. They then retire to her bedroom in order to dine and to play (331). In *La Précaution*, the hero's principal motive in recounting his travels is to entertain the duchess; "curieuse de son naturel," she asks questions that indicate to Dom Pèdre her probable willingness to throw herself "à corps perdu dans la galanterie" (73). Unlike Zayas, Scarron has Dom Pèdre tell his adventures to the duchess inside "un grand cabinet fort frais," whose decorations, including a "lict de repos couvert de matelas de satin" (74) make clear that it is a lady's boudoir. Dom Pèdre's *récit* thus becomes part of his seduction of the duchess, and is included in Scarron's amplification of the pair's afternoon together, the object of a discreet ellipsis in the Spanish original: "convidándoles la soledad y el tiempo caluroso, pasaron con much gusto la fiesta, tan enamorado don Fadrique de las gracias y hermosura de de la duquesa que ya se quedara de asiento en aquel lugar, si fuera cosa que sin escándalo pudiera hacer" (331). In both versions, the conventional time of day set aside for storytelling in the *Decameron* and *Heptaméron* – the hours of afternoon heat – are devoted to the hero's and the duchess's adulterous frolicking.[15]

Just as Molière will stage his protagonist's verbal seduction of Charlotte in II.2 of *Dom Juan*, Scarron lays bare not only the potential scandal elided in the Spanish version, but the components and "Hypocrisie" of Dom Pèdre's skill at sexual conquest, in a new twist on the iterativity of example. His tryst with the duchess clearly stands in for his machinations with the previous objects of his desire: "Il estoit hardy comme un Lion et ne se trouvoit jamais seul avec une femme qu'il ne luy presentast son service" (76); he takes what he can and resorts to apologies to obtain the rest. The duchess's sage advice on Dom Pèdre's "grande erreur" of preferring a nitwit to a "femme spirituelle" in his choice of bride is profferred in her boudoir, and serves as the basis for Chrysalde's famous counsel to Arnolphe in I.1 of *L'École des femmes*.

> «Et comment sera-t-elle honneste femme...si elle ne sçait pas ce que c'est que l'honnesteté et n'est pas mesme capable de l'apprendre? Comment une sotte vous pourra-t-elle aymer, n'estant pas capable de vous connoistre? Elle manquera à son devoir sans sçavoir ce qu'elle fait, au lieu qu'une femme d'esprit, quand mesme elle se deffieroit de sa vertu, sçaura éviter les occasions où elle sera en danger de la perdre.» (75)

Dom Pèdre's error is amplified by his mendacious reprisal of the duchess's own warnings on his "grande erreur" in his seductive "Hypocrisie": he claims that the force of her charms has refuted the conclusions he drew from "tant d'experiences" (76). According to his discourse, she would be the "single counterexample" (Lyons 33) that undermines the validity of example based on repetition or iterativity. Dom Pèdre repeats the Duchess's evocation of *erreur* only in order to juxtapose it with his pressing malady: "Vous m'avez guery d'une erreur,...mais vous me laissez malade d'un mal qui est d'autant plus dangereux et difficile à guérir que je suis ravy de l'avoir et que je contente, en le souffrant, la plus noble ambition dont un homme puisse estre capable" (76). His words remain empty, since he has not in fact abandoned his error.

When night falls, the Duchess demands that her servants bring "lumières" (77); the candles that illuminate the reddened complexions of the new lovers reprise the role of night as harbinger of the hero's enlightenment, and signal moreover its falseness: it was at night that he discovered the clandestine pregnancy of Serafina/Séraphine, watched the spectacle of doña Beatriz/Elvire's forbidden love for a black slave, was the victim of Violante's tricks and infidelities. In their iterativity, these *expériences* form the foundation of his *opinion* that the only women fit for marriage are those who are stupid. The light in the night indicates that the hero will have one more chance to see the light, from the inside of architectural space rather than the outside, when the duke returns home unexpectedly.

Learning from her servants that her husband is on the point of entering her room, the duchess hurriedly ensconces her new lover in "une grande Armoire dorée où elle serroit ses eaux de senteur" (78); she locks him in, takes the key and throws herself back on the bed. By locking him in her closet with the "eaux de senteur" that as an aristocratic woman of the world she shares with nuns in the cloister, the duchess subjects the hero to the imbricated confinement characteristic of both worldly women and sisters in a convent, including his first paramour and her daughter: rather than engaging in his usual picaresque wanderings, he is inside a closet located in the duchess's bedroom, which in turn is inside the duke's country house.[16] By its embedded nature, the imprisonment of don Fadrique provides a fitting backdrop for storytelling by recalling the frame characters' situation in Lisis's bedroom. The hero's confinement inspires the duchess's subsequent *burla* which aims at both cuckolded husband and closeted lover: after he has dined, and in *La Précaution inutile*, laughed heartily at her "cent contes agreables" (78), the duchess makes a wager of "cent pistoles" (79) with her husband that he cannot name all the household objects made of iron; her luck has it that he fails to include the keys in his list.[17] In Scarron, the sum of one hundred *pistoles* correlates with the number of funny stories told by the duchess, an obvious allusion to collections of tales such as the *Decameron* or *Les Cent nouvelles nouvelles*. Storytelling is both the consequence and the object of the wager: in Zayas's novella, the duchess states explicitly, in the second person, her intention to "contar un cuento" (332) to her husband; in Scarron's version, the narrator transforms *cuento* into *avanture*: "elle luy vouloit apprendre une avanture, qui estoit une des plus plaisantes dont il eust oüy parler" (79).[18]

Like a character in a frame tale, then, Scarron's duchess tells Dom Pèdre's "avantures," which were "tres-rares" and "tres-divertissantes," as he related them to her; as *devisante*, she thus appropriates his voice, and in so doing enacts the passage from first to third person necessary for the "[movement] out of discourse and into history" char-

acteristic of example (Lyons 93): "jamais recit ne m'a plus diverty; et
je veux...qu'il vous divertisse vous-mesme" (80). Unlike in *El prevenido engañado*, where Zayas devotes much less space to the wife's
retelling of don Fadrique's travels, the duchess tells the hero's story
before not only her husband, but a crowd of servants, who reprise the
role of the auditors of frame tales; all those listening, including Dom
Pèdre in his closet, have a good laugh at the expense of the hero, who
entertains all through the intermediary of the duchess's voice. But his
story does not end there, since she subsequently violates the conventions of storytelling by including herself in the *avanture*: she relates in
the first person her tryst of that very afternoon and informs her husband
that her lover is in the closet, where he acts as auditor of her *récit*.[19]
Like the Renaissance novella, her tale is framed as a "recit veritable"
imbued with a "vray-semblance" (82) that makes it believable to the
listener.[20] The duke's suspicions are thus roused and he demands the
keys in a fit of jealousy, but his wife's remonstrances remind him that
he has forgotten to include those keys in his list of objects made of
iron. He thus owes her the "cent pistoles" they wagered; the sum in
question becomes her compensation for telling stories. Her
conte/compte becomes the occasion for the avaricious Duke to send his
"Argentier" to count the hundred *pistoles* and to give them to his wife
(83); *compte* as number or account and *conte* as fictitious tale thus converge in her account of Dom Pèdre's life.[21]

At the same time, by passing from Dom Pèdre's first person to
the third person and then to her own first person, the duchess stages the
distinction between novella as "recit veritable" (82) distinguished by its
novelty and rarity (Cotgrave) and *conte* as an oralized work of fiction,
an "histoire inventée," or as Cotgrave puts it, "an unlikelie tale, historie, relation."

> Faites les moy payer, comme vostre parole vous y oblige, et sçachez que je
> ne vous ay fait un si beau conte que pour vous faire remarquer que vous avez
> perdu et pour vous divertir, afin que vous ayez moins de regret en vos cent
> pistolles. Une autre fois ne soyez pas d'assez facile croyance pour recevoir
> pour vraye une histoire inventée. Il n'est pas vray-semblable que tant
> d'avantures extraordinaires soient arrivées à un homme seul, et il l'est encore
> moins que j'eusse fait ce compte-là, s'il eust esté veritable. (82)

The duchess at once converts novella into *conte* and makes the implausible story of Dom Pèdre's life a fictitious yarn destined to inspire the
laughter of its auditors. Cowering in the closet, the hero knows his
story is only too true. Besides handing over the hundred *pistoles* he

risked in the bet, the husband lauds his wife's "esprit merveilleux" (83), and all have a hearty laugh; in this variant of the "cocu battu et content" of medieval fabliaux, the clinking of coins and the laughter of the contented cuckold replace the key that would have made the duke privy to the duchess's duplicity and infidelity.

Now, Dom Pèdre's stance in the closet ensures that the duchess's *compte/conte* is also a spectacle, or "a significant appearance enacted outside or at the very frontier of language" (Lyons 29); the hero becomes a witness of what I designate as an unseen spectacle, an act of storytelling that is also a dramatic performance in which the play between first and third person allows the duchess first to play the role of stupid wife who retells to her husband her own peccadillos with no omissions, and then that of the *femme spirituelle* who knows enough to cleverly conceal her transgression so that her husband laughs at his own cuckolding, without perceiving his own role implied in the story she tells. In order to shed light on the lesson he should have learned on the road, the duchess locks Dom Pèdre in the dark closet, where he relies on his senses of hearing and smell, to the exclusion of sight, in order better to seize the message the duchess tries to convey. His enclosure is a kind of spectacle that he cannot see because of his own experience as roving blade; he suffers from a "blind spot," or an "invisibility of self to self" (Lyons 91) that prevents him from perceiving himself in the old cuckold and his choice of bride in the successive roles played by the duchess, who conceives example not as the iterative domain of experience but as a clear delimitation between "inside" and "outside," in which spectacle ought to serve a corrective end.[22] The darkness of the closet underscores the hero's blindness: he perceives himself as auditor rather than actor, and considers that he is the butt of one joke rather than two. His time in the closet ought to provide him access to self-knowledge, since according to Lyons, "if a person can learn about himself or herself, such learning has to pass through a representation from the outside" (89). It turns out, however, that Dom Pèdre believes only that he has again gained access to the intimate reaches of feminine duplicity, represented by the "eaux de senteur" kept in the closet; he cannot perceive that time spent on his travels and trysts has made him part of the spectacle he witnesses.

After the duke retires to his room and his *Argentier* counts out the hundred *pistoles* and hands them over to the duchess, she reveals to her trembling lover the lesson he ought to have learned from the wager: "elle essaya de luy faire avoüer qu'une femme d'esprit peut se tirer à son honneur d'un mauvais pas, dont la seule pensée peut faire mourir de peur une sotte" (84). He seeks only to beat a hasty retreat, but before he leaves she transfers to him the hundred *pistoles* she won in the wager, along with her portrait on a gold chain, and in the Spanish version, an extra hundred "ducados" (333). Dom Pèdre thus receives monetary compensation for the "service" (76) he rendered, at once sexual satisfaction and genial storytelling. In the Spanish novella, the duchess cajoles him to write to her; in the French version, she asks him to remember her and "de luy faire sçavoir de ses nouvelles" (84): the rest of the story will indeed contain the continuing unfolding of his novelistic life. At any rate, the unseen example enacted in the duchess's chamber misses the mark: rather than showing Dom Pèdre the choice he faces as an experienced – and therefore old – *avanturier*, it serves only to reinforce his initial error. He is in awe of the duchess's skill in transforming the true story of his life into fiction – "un conte si délicat" (84) – and pities the old duke and his trusting gullibility. Instead of enlightening the hero, his last tryst plunges him further into the darkened space of misunderstanding by reinforcing his "opinion qu'une femme d'esprit est d'une dangereuse garde, et [il] ne douta point que, si la Duchesse ne se fust trop fiée en son bon esprit, elle n'eust pas si-tost executé ce qu'elle avoit eu envie de faire et n'eust pas eu la hardiesse de le déclarer à son mary mesme" (85). He thus resolves to avoid the status of "mal marié" (85) by choosing a wife without the wiles to discern love from repugnance. But as Zayas's duchess tells the stranger in her house, "Mala opinión es la vuestra, que a toda ley una mujer bien entendida es gusto para no olvidarse jamás, y alguna vez os acordaréis de mí" (331). One day the hero will learn the lesson of the closet, but not before other objects made of metal take the place of the key which neither old duke nor seasoned wanderer are able to seize.

Just as the wager prevents the old duke from using the key to open the *Armoire* and know the truth of what his wife calls an "histoire inventée," Dom Pèdre lacks access to the key that would provide him with self-knowledge and allow him to understand his error. The key to the closet remains in the duchess's possession throughout the story she tells to her husband and the simultaneous spectacle she stages for Dom Pèdre; by its association with other objects made of iron, such as armor or swords, it becomes a sign of masculine potency that she appropriates – just as she claimed as the product of her own invention the true story of Dom Pèdre's life – and subsequently circulates. The iron of the key is in effect supplanted by the gold of the hundred *pistoles* that pass from cuckolded husband to wily wife to stunned philanderer. The laughing cuckold thus pays for his own horning, while the key becomes lost in a process of deferral, exchange and dissipation based on an alchemical operation through which the words of the duchess's story convert iron to gold. Having spent the money he took with him to Italy, Dom Pèdre returns home on a mule rather than a horse and can no longer afford a servant. The money and material favors that the duchess exchanges with Dom Pèdre for his "service" allow the itinerant knight to make his way back to Granada via Madrid.

Once in Granada, the hero first pays a visit to his aunt and learns that Serafina/Séraphine has remained in the nunnery and driven to death her erstwhile suitor. He is apprised also of the fate of Gracia/Laure, who in accordance with his wishes has been raised in a convent since the age of four. Now sixteen or seventeen, the girl is strikingly beautiful but according to Scarron, "sotte comme toutes les Religieuses qui sont venuës au monde sans esprit et en ont esté tirées dès l'enfance pour estre enfermées dans un Convent" (85-86). His characterization of the convent differs markedly from Zayas's: don Alonso remarks that Gracia is "figura hermosa, mas sin alma" and that her stupidity makes her an exceptional case among nuns, "que no ignoran nada" (334). The Spanish version's implicit praise of the convent is in harmony not only with the frame, in which a contagion of withdrawal inspires Lisis, her women friends and her mother to retire to the convent instead of choosing marriage, but with the representation of enclosures designated as feminine in don Fadrique's earlier adventures: those spaces allow women's cleverness to flourish behind closed doors to which the hero is denied the key.[23] Gracia's innate stupidity is an accident of her birth – she is "naturalmente boba" (334) – rather than the result of her education in the convent; Laure's dim wits, on the other hand, are the consequence of her education by nuns.[24] Scarron's sarcastic depreciation of the convent clashes with his own depiction of women confined in Dom Pèdre's wanderings across space and time, and lends plausibility to the hero's persistent error: he has found "ce qu'il cherchoit" not only because Laure is stupid, but because she strongly resembles her mother, a woman with whom he was "fort amoureux" (86), and he does not hesitate to marry her, after informing his aunt that he is not in fact the girl's father. The hero thus returns to his point of departure: he moves into his late parents' house – Zayas states explicitly that it is "herencia de su mayorazgo" (334) – and has it furnished for his new bride, who reprises the physical beauty of her mother, minus Serafina's duplicitous ways. His marriage to a simpleton seems to provide him the perfect opportunity to rectify a history gone awry, but his apparent return to previous circumstances denies the passage of time, which makes the new match unfeasible; in Scarron, whereas Séraphine was "aussi bonne pour femme qu'il estoit bon pour mary" (36), her daughter can only make a series of "grandes reverences" (87) when confronted with Dom Pèdre's verbal appropriation of her on their wedding night. If he is "plus sot que sa femme" (87), then the result of his travels is decomposition of the "beaucoup d'esprit" (35) he possessed before his amorous odyssey; at any rate, the fundamental inequality between husband and a wife who has passed for his own daughter portends his ruin.[25]

The hero's principal duty in taking a wife is to consummate his marriage in order to beget heirs to whom he would pass on his estate, just as upon his death his own father left to his son the house that the latter currently possesses and has lavishly furnished. But on his wedding night, Dom Pèdre seeks instead to test his wife's "simplicité": after seating himself in a pedant's "chaire" and having Laure stand before him, he claims her as his own: "Vous estes ma femme" (87), he intones. His time on the road has eroded the incongruous wisdom and prudence he displayed as a young man, but the new bride's tender age and her evident simplicity authorize him to play a paternalistic and professorial role. He then asks her if she knows "la vie que doivent mener les personnes mariées" (87); unlike the Spanish version, where don Fadrique asks Gracia if she knows "la vida de los casados" (335), the French adaptation inserts the verb "devoir," underscoring Dom Pèdre's own duty, which he will soon shirk. The new bride professes her ignorance of the life to which her husband refers, but promises to learn it as she would the "Ave Maria" (Scarron 87; Zayas 335); just as she learned her prayers in the convent, she will assimilate the mindless mechanics of her husband's dictates.[26] The bridegroom's discreet periphrasis, which ensures his bride's persistent ignorance, soon leads to concrete demonstration: he fetches his own suit of armor, complete with feathered headpiece, lance and sword, and has her suit up. Unlike the husband of *Les Cent nouvelles nouvelles* 41, who uses armor as an encumbrance to the fatiguing "amoureux jeu" in which he does engage, however unwillingly, the husband here has the wife patrol his room while he sleeps; night as a moment of enlightenment missed becomes finally a time for peaceful slumber. In the meantime, and in his haste to ensure his wife's fidelity, he forgets to consummate his marriage.

Now, the hero's transmission of his armor to his wife is a misallocation: as an "[inscription] of aristocratic genealogy" (Jones and Stallybrass 256), armor ought to be passed on from father to son, like the estate of which he has become master. Instead, by having his wife don his armor, he forgoes the pleasures of the flesh that would produce an heir in favor of the tenuous assurance that his wife is faithful to him; instead of genealogical heritage, the armor functions as a kind of chastity belt and birth control device that prevent Laure's impregnation and preserve her virginity. Moreover, the wife's wearing of a man's suit of arms constitutes an instance of cross-dressing that at the same time ironically likens her to Pallas.[27] Soon after the wedding, the bridegroom is called away on business at court, and the five or six days he was to be away turn into so many months. During the first days of his absence, Gracia/Laure dutifully performs "la vie des personnes mariées," according to her husband's instructions, but this lapse of time also permits the *clef* to the duchess's closet to lead directly to what Scarron calls the "clef maistresse," which unlocks all the doors to Dom Pèdre's newly-acquired house.[28] Predictably, during the new husband's absence, a gentleman from Córdoba passes through Granada, spies Laure at her balcony, and her beauty causes him to become enamored of her; like Dom Pèdre in his own earlier efforts at seduction, he passes back and forth beneath her window. The enterprising rake enlists the services of an old "conciliatrice des volontez" (89), who proposes to Laure that she grant him a private interview. The "vieille damnée" (90) enters the house by claiming she has "hardes" to sell; among her many talents at concocting beauty secrets, she manufactures the kind of perfumed waters the Duchess kept in her closet. Like Dom Pèdre, who offered his "service" (76) to the Duchess, the old lady claims that the Cordoban seeks to render "service" (90) to Laure, which she at first rejects by claiming she has more than enough servants. Despite the new bride's inability to comprehend figural language, the *entremetteuse* arranges a nocturnal meeting between the stranger and Laure; she hands over the "clef, qui ouvre toutes celles de la maison" (91).[29] The "clef maistresse" opens the space of feminine enclosure previously off limits to Dom Pèdre in his earlier adventures, as well as in his misbegotten precaution with his new bride, and at the same time, through the gendering of "clef," the object itself transfers household dominion from husband to wife, from master to mistress. By passing on the key to *entremetteuse* and then seducer, the wife gives away her husband's rule over the roost, leaving feminine enclosure – which is also the space of the husband's honor – open to seduction, in the word's etymological sense: the house always on the margins of the philanderer's road is incorporated into the road itself.[30]

Dom Pèdre's open house is clearly akin to the unfaithful wife's spread legs; through exchange and unlocking, he has become a cuckold by "[losing] control of what is 'his'" (Lyons 106). Like the *clerc* of *Les Cent nouvelles nouvelles* 41, the interloper beats a hasty retreat at the sight of the sentry he takes for an armed man, but apprised by the old lady of the husband's "extravagante precaution" (94) to guard his own honor, during a second rendezvous, the galant succeeds in teaching his new pupil "preceptes de mariage" (95) quite different from those of her husband. For her part, Laure never grows weary of learning, until she receives a letter from Dom Pèdre announcing his return from the court. According to the stranger's pedagogy, undressing replaces cross-dressing, just as he takes the husband's place in the marital bed; he is Dom Pèdre's "Lieutenant" (96). Through undressing as a stand-in for cross-dressing, the key also opens the enclosure of armor. The "detach-ability of armor" ought to permit genealogical continuity by "join[ing] father to son"; here its "alienable" nature (Jones and Stallybrass 257), accentuated by the hero's misplaced gesture of dubbing his wife, makes it an instrument of cuckolding, sterility and consequent genea-logical rupture.

On the night of Dom Pèdre's homecoming Laure disrobes and hops into bed with her husband, who is stunned that she is not in armor. She then explains that she has had "un autre mary" (96), and offers to pass on his teachings to Dom Pèdre, who in Scarron's version feigns illness and continues to do so until he is certain that his wife has not been impregnated by his rival. He realizes that Laure has compromised his honor and does not even have the presence of mind to conceal her transgression; he remembers at that moment the sage advice of the duchess: "[il] détesta son erreur et reconnut, mais trop tard, qu'une honneste femme sçait garder les loix de l'honneur, et si par fragilité elle y manque, qu'elle sçait cacher sa faute" (96). In Zayas's version, the hero's recognition of his error is even clearer: he spends the rest of his days lauding *discretas* who are also virtuous while keeping a tight rein on his wife in order to prevent further falls from grace. Dom Pèdre is cognizant of his error and has learned the lesson of the unseen spec-tacle staged during his time in the duchess's closet, "mais trop tard" (96). Only after he has been deceived by a *sotte*, through his own experience, does Dom Pèdre fully grasp the example provided by the duchess, who first told her husband all and then invented an ingenious cover by appropriating the traveler's own history and converting the events of his life into fiction. In so doing, she highlighted the fictitious nature of experience itself by transforming her own and the hero's experience into narration (Lyons 83-84).

The key to the closet, which the duchess never turns over to her husband, locks and opens only one door; the "mistress-key," on the other hand, opens all the doors to the hero's house, and is passed on to the serial seducer. Just as Dom Pèdre takes the key to the closet as a lesson intended only for the duke and fails to see himself in the old cuckold, he does not realize that the first passing stranger is interchangeable with himself as errant philanderer; his experience as maker of cuckolds blinds him to his status as cuckold once he risks taking a bride. Because the hero did not use the wager of the key to gain enlightenment, the "mistress-key" becomes the instrument of his own downfall. Through enclosure and spectacle, the structure of example is effective in both French and Spanish novellas, though the hero attains understanding too late to alter his fate. It is only at the moment of his chastening by a stupid woman that he gains "a consciousness of the succession of events through which [he] has passed" (Lyons 84) and is able to connect those events to the maxims proposed by the duchess.

Just as in his marriage, Dom Pèdre shirks his duty to create an heir to whom he would leave his armor, in death, he fails to follow the example of his own father, who bequeathed to his son the land and house that make him a rich young man and one of the most sought-after "partis" in Granada (36). Since Dom Pèdre's marriage remains sterile and childless, instead of leaving his lands to an heir, he transfers all his wealth to Laure, on the condition that she become a nun in the convent where her mother has resided since her daughter's birth, kept secret thanks to Dom Pèdre's complicity (97). Apprised of the "grand bien" (97) bequeathed to Laure by Dom Pèdre, Séraphine seizes that fortune and uses it to found a convent.[31] Through the intermediary of his will, then, Dom Pèdre becomes "fondateur [de] [monastère]," though ironically, "le droit d'entrée dans la clôture" (Reynes 214) accorded such benefactors is obviously beyond his reach. The amorous wanderer who so often was enticed by feminine enclosure and who learned its lesson only after his own house and prized possession – his stupid and virtuous wife – were cordoned off and then easily violated, leaves as his legacy another kind of feminine enclosure, the nunnery. His passing coincides with the reunion of mother and daughter in a space that serves as both prison and refuge for fallen women, and which excludes, in principle, the entry of men.[32] Dom Pèdre makes Laure's taking of the veil the condition of her inheritance in order to control from beyond the grave his wife's chastity, but the convent itself is nearly as permeable as the homes of worldly women.[33] Armor, keys and coins – both the hundred *pistoles* of the wager and the hero's immense fortune – lead to the ostensibly impregnable fortress of the convent; all become signs of the hero's impotence and sterile stratagems. At the conclusion of *El prevenido*, don Alonso implies that his *maravilla* has been an anti-Griselda, in which the husband who seeks to test his wife is punished for his temerity rather than rewarded with his spouse's gratitude and a family reunited and recomposed: "Y adviertan los que prueban a las mujeres al peligro que se ponen" (340).

While Zayas crafts her novella as an implicit response to the *Decameron*'s open-ended conclusion, both Spanish and French authors make the duchess's closet the site of both spectacle and exemplarity. They provide the hero with a belated enlightenment operative only in hindsight, after he has joined the confraternity of cuckolds created by his own amorous wanderings across space and time. His time in the closet functions as corollary to the enclosures which necessitate the development of women's wiles and wit, and which reflect the practices of both revealing and guarding secrets. By excising Zayas's novella from its context of frame tale, Scarron puts into play a concomitant diminution of the force of example, but retains Zayas's lesson of the duchess's closet. In this privileged space, storytelling and example converge in the young noblewoman's joke on both hero and husband, a trick that results in an alchemical transformation of the iron of keys to the gold of coins. Contrary to the duchess's intentions, the itinerant seducer's error – that marriage to a stupid woman will guarantee that his forehead will never be decorated with horns – is only reinforced by her alternate acting-out of dimwit and then witty woman, until he himself joins the ranks of cuckolded husbands. The crucial episode of unseen spectacle enacted outside the duchess's closet leads in both Zayas and Scarron to a genealogical deadend that inspires Molière to offer to his audience an analogous lesson in *L'École des femmes*.

Molière: Fragmented Exemplarity

If *La Précaution inutile* serves as Molière's primary source for *L'École des femmes*, how does he adapt story to stage? I contend that both armor and keys are central to his project of fragmenting the exemplary structure of the novella in order to render unfeasible the adherence of maxim to experience in Arnolphe's quest to preserve virtue in his choice of bride, and of transforming for the stage the novella hero's tardiness and concomitant forgetfulness regarding the passage of time. As Jones and Stallybrass point out, despite its apparent superiority to cloth because of its resistance to decay, Renaissance armor is "always already belated." It fails to keep "its promise of material preservation in the age of gunpowder"; what it contains is no longer safe, and its assurance of protection from harm is mere "fantasy." The propensity of armor to rust and its transferability undermine further its pretensions to durability (256). These traits of armor clearly apply to Dom Pèdre's foolish and fruitless precaution designed to maintain his ignorant bride's fidelity and virginity: it protects neither her chastity nor his honor; his improper dubbing of his wife only transfers his own legacy to the infertile domain of the convent. The belatedness of armor makes it a fitting icon for Dom Pèdre's tardy assimilation of the lesson of the closet.

Like Dom Pèdre, the aging Arnolphe is also too late, since Agnès's marriage to Horace has already been arranged before the play's opening scene. Through conversion of the "protective carapace" (Jones and Stallybrass 256) of armor to printed text read aloud – "Les Maximes du mariage ou les devoirs de la femme mariée, avec son exercice journalier" – Molière highlights the futility of his own hero's efforts to immure and appropriate Agnès in order to mold her as if she were "un morceau de cire" (l. 810). His presentation of the "Maximes" – which would rectify the interloper's "préceptes de mariage" (95) in *La Précaution* – clearly recalls Dom Pèdre's stance on his wedding night as he claims ownership of his new bride: he sits in a "chaire" and has Laure stand before him; for her part, "elle regardoit son mary aussi timidement qu'un escolier nouveau fait un Pedant imperieux" (87). Arnolphe has Agnès adopt the same posture and instructs her, "Là, regardez-moi là pendant cet entretien" (l. 677).[34] Just as Laure promises to learn "la vie que doivent mener les personnes mariées" as she would the Ave Maria, Arnolphe specifies as he presents Agnès with the "Maximes": "Ainsi qu'une novice / Par coeur dans le couvent doit savoir son office, / Entrant au mariage il en faut faire autant" (ll. 739-41). Unlike her counterpart in the novella, Agnès makes no promise to memorize; nevertheless, the equivalent of Laure's iterative parade across the bedroom floor is Agnès's recitation, as armor and the acting out of Dom Pèdre's sterile directives are transformed into a text that is, like armor, apparently resistant to the ravages of time. Moreover, like the suit of arms, it seems to serve a protective end that will result in continuation of the pedagogue's lineage: if Agnès follows their dictates, particularly the first maxim, she will enter the marriage bed, and once Arnolphe explains to her "ce que cela veut dire," she will produce heirs. But for the moment, the earnest husband-to-be intones, "il ne faut rien que lire" (ll. 747-53). In the same way in which Dom Pèdre neglects to consummate his marriage by having his wife patrol the bedroom, Arnolphe has Agnès read on, in an iterative, mechanical gesture that stands in for the numerous later readings that will presumably leave an imprint in her mind, like his discourse on the duties of married women: "Et jusqu'au moindre mot imprimez-le-vous bien" (l. 678). Arnolphe anticipates that his charge's reading of the "Maximes" will serve an exemplary function that is also utilitarian, resulting in a "direct behavioral modification" (Lyons 13) that will make Agnès an exception among the corrupt "femmes d'aujourd'hui" (l. 717). "Mais ne vous gâtez pas sur l'exemple d'autrui" (l. 718), Arnolphe continues: his text will replace the bad examples Agnès would find among worldly women and at the same time prevent him from joining the ranks of those whom he has mocked. Arnolphe seeks an anachronism, a woman who will be out of time and characterized by her belatedness. But above all, the little book and its contents arrive in Agnès's hands too late to take effect: not only have Horace and Agnès had their marriage arranged without their knowledge, but Love has already intervened to make Horace the object of her affection. Agnès has already permitted his visits, just as Laure allowed the Cordoban rake entry into her husband's house. Before leaving on his "voyage malheureux" (l. 385) that gave the new lovers time to meet, Arnolphe told his charge only that she was to see no one (l. 480); his textual intervention thus follows rather than precedes his "éloignement fatal" (l. 385). Dom Pèdre's time in the closet where the duchess stores her "eaux de senteur" is alluded to obliquely in the third maxim, which forbids the use of cosmetics: "Loin ces études d'oeillades, / Ces eaux, ces blancs, ces pommades, / Et mille ingrédients qui font des teints fleuris" (ll. 760-62); Arnolphe would clearly rank the duchess among the perverted "femmes d'aujourd'hui."

Just as he converts the iron of armor to useless text, Molière repeats the duchess's alchemical operation by transforming the iron of keys to the gold of the "cent pistoles" (l. 284) Arnolphe hands over to

Horace in order to finance his own rival's amorous enterprise; the same sum is transferred from Spanish to French novella, where *cien escudos* become *cent pistoles*, from old Duke to Duchess to novella hero, and from Arnolphe to Horace, in an exchange of money that makes plain the numerous connections between novella and play, particularly the ties between both Arnolphe and Horace and Scarron's Dom Pèdre. Moreover, in *L'École des femmes*, gold is also silver, or "argent," and in a gesture that recalls don Fadrique's nearly empty "bolsa" in *El prevenido engañado* (328), Arnolphe tells Horace he can keep the money and the "bourse" (l. 287) that holds it.[35] After confiding in Arnolphe his designs on Agnès, Horace exclaims famously,

> Vous savez mieux que moi, quels que soient nos efforts,
> Que l'argent est la clef de tous les grands ressorts,
> Et que ce doux métal qui frappe tant de têtes,
> En amour, comme en guerre, avance les conquêtes. (ll. 345-48)

Just as surely as the "mistress-key" leaves wide open the novella hero's house, so the money Arnolphe donates to Horace breaches the obstacles surrounding Monsieur de la Souche's "autre maison" (l. 146) and provides easy access to Agnès, the "joli bijou" (l. 338) encased, as it were, in the house's window that faces the street. Moreover, the object hidden in the Duchess's skirts becomes metaphor in Horace's discourse: the key is transformed finally into words that combine with money in order to allow Horace to storm the fortress of Arnolphe's "autre maison."

In the process of fragmentation that constitutes his staging of the novella hero's chastening, Molière doubles Arnolphe's residence: he has one dwelling that "[à] cent sortes de monde est ouverte à toute heure" (l. 144), and another that is ostensibly closed to the outside world, "où nul ne me vient voir" (l. 146); it is in the latter enclosure that he places for safekeeping the girl he plans to marry. His new name, Monsieur de la Souche, corresponds to Arnolphe's doubling of residence and promotes Horace's blind confidence in the man he takes for his best friend and "véritable père" (l. 1649). When Chrysalde chides Arnolphe for choosing such a ridiculous name at his age, his friend retorts that "la maison par ce nom se connoît" (l. 173); house and name converge to prevent Horace from detecting his rival in his friend. The novella hero's lack of progeniture and his concomitant breaking of genealogical ties is reprised in Arnolphe's double name; his vanity causes him to abandon "le vrai nom de ses pères" (l. 174) in order to found a lineage without succession. Dom Pèdre's open house is reiterated in the play's very setting, "une place de ville" (Molière l. 408) that renders open and public the private domain of the newly married protagonist of the novella; Arnolphe's other house, which correlates with his other name, is the home base of his "précaution" (l. 150).[36] Arnolphe's efforts to enclose Agnès take place off stage, and are relegated to the numerous recitals that make clear the play's debt to the embedded storytelling that plays such a central in both the Spanish and French novellas.

Molière's repetitive insistence on Arnolphe's "precautions" and his shift from man (*El prevenido engañado*) to maneuver (*La Précaution inutile*) clearly belie his debt to Scarron, but in my view, the central episodes of the novellas – the hero's stint in the closet, its reinforcement of his error and his foolhardy project to arm his wife – serve as foundation for Molière's version of failed exemplarity.[37] The play begins with Chrysalde's well-known advice on the risks incurred in Arnolphe's decision to marry after he has done no more than to observe and mock the poor cuckolded husbands who proliferate in their town; Arnolphe's status as bemused "spectateur" (l. 44) reprises at once Dom Pèdre's fourteen or fifteen years on the road of love and debauchery and his role as auditor of the unseen spectacle mounted by the duchess.[38] It is no accident, then, that Chrysalde repeats the duchess's counsel on the capacity of "femmes d'esprit" to distinguish right from wrong.

> Une femme d'esprit peut trahir son devoir;
> Mais il faut pour le moins qu'elle ose le vouloir;
> Et la stupide au sien peut manquer d'ordinaire,
> Sans en avoir l'envie et sans penser le faire. (ll. 113-16)

Through a process of excision analogous to Scarron's near-translation of Zayas's *maravilla*, Chrysalde echoes the duchess in a radically different context, that of Arnolphe's obsession with avoiding the horns of cuckoldry and his mocking observation of the misfortunes of others. Whereas the Duchess's unseen spectacle encourages Dom Pèdre to "see for himself" the truth of her example, Chrysalde relies only on a "direct affirmation" that is ineffective because it is not connected to tangible "evidence" (Lyons 28). Moreover, whereas Dom Pèdre's error is based on his own experience with women who are smart and mistresses of trickery, Arnolphe has no such experience; the story of his precocious love for the young, destitute, and helpless Agnès, which parallels Dom Pèdre's project to have Laure raised at a convent as his daughter, is also the story of his waiting for a bride and his investment of both time and money in the outcome.[39] Arnolphe's error is based on a mockery that depends on a third-person "raillerie" (l. 15) that allows him to claim with self-reflexive hilarity: "Souvent je me donne la comédie à moi-même" (l. 298); like the Duchess who tells "cent contes agreables" (l. 78) that cause her old husband to choke on his food, Arnolphe targets "cent pauvres maris" (l. 16) and broadcasts their secrets in "cent éclats" (l. 20). Molière's fracturing of example is thus linked implicitly not only to the sum exchanged across language and genre, but to collections of novellas in which cuckoldry is a banality (Lyons 106).

Arnolphe's steadfast belief that he is only *spectateur* of others' mishaps constitutes his blindness to his concurrent status as *acteur*; if indeed he marries, he risks joining the confraternity of horned husbands who have provided for so many years material for his "tablettes" (l. 307).[40] Molière stages the novella hero's blind spot by deconstructing the enclosed space of lady's *Armoire*, where Dom Pèdre found himself immured. Arnolphe is a mocker rather than a maker of cuckolds; Chrysalde is not a woman with whom he has just had a tryst, but a peer who tells without showing and who through "direct assertion" (Lyons 28) avoids the use of example. Despite his claims to knowledge of women (ll. 75-77) and to the "lumières" provided by "experience" (l. 1200), Arnolphe has neither; static observation of horned husbands and reiterative mockery take the place of Dom Pèdre's travels.[41] Finally, Arnolphe has not been walled in, as has Dom Pèdre, and made to witness the difference between stupid and smart woman; instead, he scurries about in vain efforts to impose order "dedans et dehors" (l. 1010), even as his struggles take place in the open "place de ville." It is not surprising, then, given the lack of exemplary structure evident in *La Précaution*, that Chrysalde's efforts at persuasion are in vain. Arnolphe counters his friend's advice by retorting: "Vous serez ébahi, quand vous serez au bout, / Que vous ne m'aurez rien persuadé du tout" (ll. 121-22). Will Arnolphe learn later – too late – the lesson of the closet, as did his analogue, Dom Pèdre?

As if to underscore his hero's belatedness, at the conclusion of *La Précaution*, Scarron proffers the lesson of his novella by omitting Zayas's overt allusions to an anti-Griselda: Dom Pèdre's story teaches that "sans le bon sens, la vertu ne peut estre parfaite, qu'une spirituelle peut estre honneste femme d'elle-mesme, et qu'une sotte ne le peut estre sans le secours d'autrui et sans estre bien conduite" (97). While excluding the third part – Agnès is no *sotte*, but a newly initiated *femme habile* by play's end – Molière seeks to enact the first two components of the novella's moral through a kind of disjunction that splits the "Gentil-homme Grenadin" (81) in the closet into two characters: Arnolphe, the middle-aged fool set to take a young simpleton as his bride, and Horace, the young rake who has his own "aventure" (l. 304). In the episode of the closet, Dom Pèdre's error, we may recall, is threefold: he fails to remember the passage of time that has put him on a par with the old duke duped by his cunning wife; he neglects to recall that his own philandering makes him equivalent to the first stranger who rides through town; he fails to see his own choice of bride in the two roles the Duchess plays before her guffawing husband. Molière's genius is to convert for the stage, through Arnolphe and Horace, the time of Dom Pèdre's travels to rivalry with himself: the old bridegroom-to-be vies with the young blade who rhymes "écus" with "cocus" (ll. 301-2).[42] At the same time, the duchess's dual roles as *sotte* and *femme spirituelle* become Agnès's apprenticeship under the aegis of Love, who causes her to evolve from naïve storyteller who reveals all (II,5) to adept dissembler who arranges a nocturnal rendezvous with her lover (IV,6) to frank truth teller (V,4).

It is noteworthy that the novellas' scene of enclosure is far removed from Chrysalde's sage remarks in I,1 and is reenacted instead in IV,6: Horace describes to Arnolphe his ensconcement in "une grande armoire" (l. 1153), while his "jaloux inquiet" (l. 1166) goes on a ridiculous and mute rant, breaking vases, throwing clothes and kicking a dog. Like Dom Pèdre in the duchess's *Armoire*, Horace hears without seeing and thus cannot recognize his rival.[43] This scene makes clear Arnolphe's affiliation with the old duke as well as the aging Dom Pèdre, and suggests that Arnolphe will not learn the lesson of the closet, whose space he never penetrates. Horace's *récit* underscores the separation in *L'École des femmes* of spectacle and exemplary lesson: what was outside the closet for Dom Pèdre – the duchess's wager and its corrective lesson on stupid and smart women – becomes out-of-bounds for Arnolphe, who will never learn the lesson of *La Précaution*, not even too late, since Molière's hero is already too late and always "outside." His error consists not only in believing that he must marry a *sotte* in order to avoid the cuckold's horns, but of basing his stratagems on his insistence that Agnès is "mariée à demi" (l. 1034) to him, and that his honor thus depends on her virtue. But the duties of a married woman cannot apply to a girl who is not yet married. A lesson implicit in the Catalan duchess's first role as stupid woman who tells all is that only a *sotte* would speak frankly; the *femme d'esprit* necessarily has the guile to hide her transgressions and maintain the status quo: peace and even laughter in her marriage to an older man whom she does not love, like the wife of *Les Cent nouvelles nouvelles* 41. Through her education at the convent and her liberation from enclosure, Agnès becomes a *femme habile* who speaks "franchement" (l. 1515) to her benefactor, but who does so without being stupid. At the same time, she evolves into a "belle raisonneuse" (l. 1546) who refuses to lie, anticipating the singularity of the Princesse de Clèves.

For his part, Arnolphe seeks to craft a quite different exception to the rule of feminine duplicity and *esprit*. Throughout the play, he endeavors to direct a drama whose outcome he will hear in subsequent *récits* proffered by his confidant and rival, Horace. Through theater, he seeks to repair damage already done and thereby to change fate.[44] But *L'École des femmes* is above all a play about storytelling, whose past tense counters the present of the stage. Horace's "trop de caquet" (l. 834) makes him exemplary of all Frenchmen, who are so vain "[q]u'ils se pendroient plutôt que de ne causer pas" (l. 839), according to Arnolphe, who hopes to extricate his rival's plans for the future from his accounts of his thwarted rendezvous with Agnès. The young innocent is also storyteller: she recounts the story of Horace's visits, which parallels the Cordoban stranger's easy entry into Dom Pèdre's house; like the duchess's story after she wins the wager, Agnès's account is "fort étonnante, et difficile à croire" (l. 484). Her *récit* is also the consequence of a wager, aborted in this case: in an effort to have her deny what he has already learned about her distractions during his time away, Arnolphe counters: "Et j'ai voulu gager que c'étoit faussement...." Agnès interrupts him by replying: "Mon Dieu, ne gagez pas: vous perdriez vraiment" (ll. 473-74). Her imperative and its conditional consequence highlight the ties between the duke's forgetfulness and Arnolphe's belatedness: both are too late to prevent the events to be recounted by their interlocutor, and the key of understanding eludes both.

Though he spends most of the play trying in vain to hear his own stage directions recited back to him, it is Arnolphe's ultimate refusal of story that reveals to him the vanity of his plot to marry Agnès. Upon Oronte's arrival with Enrique, since Arnolphe believes Horace's father has arrived in order to force his son into an arranged marriage with a stranger, leaving Agnès to her benefactor, he cuts short his friend's relation of his reasons for coming: "Sans m'en faire récit /

Je sais ce qui vous mène" (ll. 1674-75). Arnolphe thus betrays Horace by supporting "l'autorité de père" (l. 1682) in Oronte's efforts to bring his son's actions into line with his wishes. Only in the last act do Chrysalde and Oronte engage in a duet of rhyming alexandrine couplets to tell the story of Angélique, Chrysalde's sister, her love for Enrique, their clandestine marriage and its fruit, their daughter, who has been Arnolphe's ward. The child's illicit birth was covered "sous de feints noms" (l. 1742); manipulator of names, Arnolphe himself is in the end fooled by onomastics. It was Arnolphe's charity that saved the child and prepared her for impending reunion with her long-lost father. The story told at the end reprises the beginning of the French and Spanish novellas: the hidden pregnancy, illicit childbirth, the ostensibly charitable but self-interested motivations of the spectator of an unfortunate woman's shame all recall the hero's first ill-fated encounter with Serafina/Séraphine. Through the coincidence of paternal "sagesse" (l. 1767) and youthful "ardeur mutuelle" (l. 1768), Horace is able to accomplish what the novella hero could not: his arranged marriage will also be one based on the mutual love to which Dom Pèdre aspired; he avoids don Fadrique's initial fault in loving "donde tenga otro tomada la posesión" (Zayas 295). For his part, after Chrysalde's reiteration of Pantagruel's advice to Panurge in the *Tiers Livre* – "Si n'être point cocu vous semble un si grand bien, / Ne vous point marier en est le vrai moyen" (ll. 1762-63) – Arnolphe leaves the stage in a gesture of mute impotence, in which language itself decomposes into an inarticulate "Oh!" (l. 1764) that constitutes the ultimate disjunction of example and lesson, as he retreats to the house he will never share with Agnès; like Dom Pèdre's itinerary, Arnolphe's path from *place* to home is marked by sterility and genealogical closure.[45]

Conclusion: Griselda's Revenge

The last story of the *Decameron* ends with Dioneo's reflections on an alternate conclusion to the story of Gualtieri and Griselda: once he had expelled her from their house in a simple shift to cover the belly which bore his children, in one of his last capricious tests of his wife's patience and virtue, it might have been just if she had found another man to replace her rags with a "bella roba" (669), and in the process, implicitly, to make her husband a cuckold. At the same time, the tale's conclusion confirms Gualtieri's reputation for wisdom already established before his marriage to Griselda: he was "da reputar molto savio"

(660); after he relegitimizes their marriage and reunites Griselda with the children she believed he had murdered, his subjects deem him "savissimo," although they find reprehensible the "esperienze" he forced his wife to endure (668). But the people esteem Griselda "sopra tutti savissima" (668), that is, wiser than her husband. The conclusion of the *Decameron*'s final novella is a clear invitation to reconfigure the Griselda story – constructed around Gualtieri's efforts to "provare la pazienza" (663) of his new bride – as one in which the husband who tests his wife is chastised rather than compensated by a wife whose wisdom surpasses his own. By her use of the cognate "probar" in don Alonso's maxims which frame *El prevenido engañado*, and in the scene of the hero's wedding-night foolishness (293; 340; 335), María de Zayas takes up Boccaccio's challenge by making the noble *discreto* inferior in wit even to his *boba* wife: after her she relates her iterative romps with "el otro marido," don Fadrique is "desesperado y necio" (340). Though his *Version* omits the frame narrator's reflections on the hero's folly in probing his wife's innocence, Scarron retains the essential elements of Zayas's plot that make Dom Pèdre "[p]lus sot encore que sa femme" (87). By fracturing the exemplary structure of novella into a drama of belatedness, futility and the initiation of a *femme habile*, in which Arnolphe as "sage philosophe" (l. 1188) is chastened through storytelling by his ostensibly simple-minded ward, Molière stages through Agnès Boccaccio's ultimate fantasy of Griselda's revenge.

Notes

[1] The first proverb may be found in Cotgrave, "sot"; the second in Furetière, "clef." The latter specifies that it applies to "ceux qui ont des lieux mal fermez, ou...ceux qui ont pris des precautions inutiles pour quelque chose."

[2] Zayas's *Novelas amorosas y ejemplares* were first published together with the *Desengaños amorosos* (1647) in 1659 (Olivares 133). The frame characters speak of "maravillas" rather than "novelas," título tan enfadoso que ya en todas partes le aborrecen" (168). Larson notes that like Dom Pèdre of *La Précaution inutile* who puts his wife's innocence to the test, Arnolphe "decides to test the extent of [Agnès's] ignorance. This is the moment that Molière will reproduce; it is also the moment where the two plots diverge" (507). I contend that the two plots do not diverge so neatly. For *La Précaution* as the primary source of *L'École des femmes*, see Guichemerre: "Les protagonistes et l'intrigue de *l'École des femmes* (1662) viennent directement de la dernière mésaventure de Dom Pèdre" (28).

³ For the incompatibility of "le statut de personnage et celui de spectateur," see Force 31.

⁴ The palace in the Tuscan countryside where the storytellers of the *Decameron* gather is surrounded by "vari albuscelli e piante tutte di verdi fronde ripiene" and "pratelli dattorno e con giardini maravigliosi e con pozzi d'acque freschissime" (42). Likewise, the *devisants* of the *Heptaméron* tell their "veritable[s] histoire[s]" (9) in "ce beau pré le long de la riviere du Gave, où les arbres sont si foeillez que le soleil ne sçauroit percer l'ombre ny eschauffer la frescheur" (10). The setting of Plato's *Phaedrus* also contains shady trees and a stream (230c).

⁵ The reference to Babylon recalls Ninus's tomb, the ill-fated meeting place of Pyramus and Thisbe in Ovid's *Metamorphoses*, where there is also a fruit-laden tree and a cool spring (4: 88-90).

⁶ Lyons notes an analogous framework of enclosure in the *Heptaméron* (78). I would note that even though the *devisants* are guests at the monastery, since they tell their stories outdoors, they are less rigidly enclosed than Zayas's storytellers. For Zayas's use of the frame as a "narrative containing act, a fictional device designed to focus the exemplary power of her twenty tales toward the delivery of her primary explicit message" (women should avoid succumbing to desire), see Greer, *BT* 320 ff.

⁷ This is a likely reference to the story of the tour de Nesle, alluded to in Villon's "Ballade des dames du temps jadis": "Semblablement ou est la roine / Qui commanda que Buridan / Fût jeté en un sac en Seine?" (ll. 13-15). In the "Deuxième Discours" of *Les Dames galantes*, Brantôme describes the misdeeds of "cette reine qui se tenoit à l'hostel de Nesle à Paris: faisant le guet aux passans, et ceux qui luy renvoyent et agreoient le plus, de quelques sortes de gens que ce fussent, les faisoit appeller et venir à soy; et aprés en avoir tiré ce qu'elle en vouloit, les faisoit precipiter du haut de la tour, qui paroist encores, en bas en l'eau, et les faisoit noyer" (150).

⁸ Cocozella defines "escarmiento" as "the ability to learn from past experience" (197).

⁹ For the medieval notion of *errance*, see Zumthor 201-16. Unlike the medieval knight errant, Zayas's hero is also "le *type* de la ville"; he depends on cities as destinations rather eliminating them from "l'espace vrai" (204). His peregrinations constitute "un déplacement sans but" (206) rather than an unfinished trajectory; his story is a "reworking" of the picaresque model (Greer, *BT* 196), or "l'errance dans l'espace improbable d'une anti-aventure" (Zumthor 215).

¹⁰ Lyons notes the etymology of example "in the gesture of cutting – *eximere* – by which the unit of discourse is fashioned by its excision from a mass of text that is not retained" (18).

¹¹ Throughout his *maravilla*, it seems that don Alonso is conveying his own version of the story of don Fadrique, and thus making use of example, but the explicit reference to the hero's own account of his life makes don Alonso's tale an instance of quotation, which "allows the speaker/writer to distance what he is saying whereas example requires the speaker/writer to adopt or bring closer something that may come from far away" (Lyons 31).

[12] For an overview of the terminological confusion between *nouvelle* and *conte*, see Souiller 33-37.

[13] For some of Scarron's omissions and additons to Zayas's novella, see Meding 101-7. Scarron renames don Mateo, the relative with whom don Fadrique stays in Seville, Dom Juan; the don Juan of Madrid in *El prevenido* becomes Dom Rodrigue in *La Précaution*.

[14] Furetière defines "adventurier" as "un jeune homme galant, & entreprenant, qui cherche quelque heureuse fortune. Les *aventuriers* amoureux s'attachent à toutes les femmes, seulement pour l'honneur de les seduire."

[15] The stories begin at the stroke of nones ("nona") in the *Decameron* (43); in the *Heptaméron*, the *devisants* spend between noon and four telling stories (10).

[16] Reynes notes the official prohibition of "eaux de senteur" (to mask body odor), as well as their persistent use, in the early modern convent (100).

[17] In Zayas, the sum is "cien escudos" (332).

[18] Furetière's second definition of "adventure" is: "Intrigue d'amour, galanterie, bonne fortune."

[19] This part of the duchess's account would correspond to Souiller's parameters for "récit autobiographique" (279).

[20] For "histoire véritable" as a defining characteristic of novella, see Souiller 33 and Lyons 79-80.

[21] Cotgrave gives two spellings for the homophones *compte* and *conte*, but the definition of the latter is included in the former: "An account, a reckoning; a computation, or calculation; a number; also, a respect had, regard made of; also, the reason or cause of a matter; also, a fib, gull, tale; an idle, or unlikelie tale, historie, relation."

[22] The duchess's scheme corresponds to example as a "closed entity" outside the 'inside' constituted by the discourse of direct assertion" (Lyons 28), or her own attempts to point out directly Dom Pèdre's error to him.

[23] *Desengaños amorosos* 500-11. All other parenthetical references to Zayas are to the *Novelas amorosas y ejemplares*.

[24] Scarron may be echoing here the bitter remembrances of his wife, Françoise d'Aubigné (the future Madame de Maintenon), and her own education at an Ursuline convent (Reynes 248).

[25] At this point in *El prevenido*, don Alonso intervenes in order to question don Fadrique's status as *discreto*: "Y para mí, él no debía de ser muy cuerdo, pues tal sustentaba, aunque al principio de su historia dije diferente, porque no sé qué discreto puede apetecer a su contrario" (335).

[26] For "récitation de formules" in the convent, see Reynes 65.

[27] In Zayas, Gracia is "una imagen de la diosa Palas" (336); in Scarron, she wears an "habit de Pallas" (88). For the representation of *Pallas armata*, see Larson 508.

[28] In Zayas, Gracia hands over to her neighbor the "llave...maestra" to her husband's house. This expression in Spanish prompts one of the author's digressions in *La Pré-caution*, in which he anticipates the reader's criticism that he has included "la fable" in his novella by depicting an enchanted key. He retorts by citing his superior knowledge of Spanish language and culture: "Mais qu'il sçache de la part de son tres-humble ser-viteur que les Maistres, en Espagne, ont de pareilles clefs, qu'ils appellent maistresses et, qu'une autre fois il ne reprenne pas ce qu'il ignore" (92). In his 1683 English trans-lation of *La Précaution inutile*, John Davies renders "clef maistresse" as "Mistress-key" (57); I will use his expression when referring to the pass key.

[29] Guichemerre notes that "celles" refers to "toutes les chambres" (91 n. 119).

[30] For masculine honor and the inherent danger of slipping from "contrat de mariage" to "contrat de prostitution," see Force 77.

[31] In Zayas, Gracia's mother takes advantage of her daughter's stupidity in order to build the convent: "como [Gracia] era boba, fácil halló el consuelo, gastando la gruesa hacienda que le quedó en labrar un grandioso convento, donde vivió con much gusto" (340).

[32] For the reunion of mother and daughter at the conclusion of *El prevenido* as a "darker, still submerged tale of female suffering at the hands of patriarchy, with its resultant discovery of a female utopia outside the bounds of male-female intercourse," see El Saffar 24. According to Reynes, one of the convent's many functions was to serve as a prison for women guilty of adultery (225).

[33] For closure as a condition of conventual life, see Reynes 126-27.

[34] For the "didactic digit" and its role in Dom Pèdre's and Arnolphe's pedagogy, see Larson 507; 514-15. Zayas has her hero sit on the bed in this scene (335).

[35] Force notes that by refusing to allow Horace to pay his debt to him, Arnolphe main-tains the younger man in the position of *obligé*: "Horace doit à Arnolphe non seulement cent pistoles, mais une certaine qualité d'admiration proportionnelle à la générosité qu'Arnolphe a montrée en n'acceptant pas de remerciements" (90).

[36] For Arnolphe's "fantasy of enclosure" and the confusion of public and private domains in *L'École des femmes*, see Steinberger, particularly 133-34.

[37] Arnolphe cites explicitly at least five times his "précautions" (ll. 150; 1027; 1042; 1203). He rhymes the word with both "éducation" and "méditation."

[38] In his *Poëtique*, La Mesnardière designates spectators as "Auditeurs," an indication of the conflation of hearing and seeing in the seventeenth century (135).

[39] Harrison notes that "[a]n investment implies a willingness to wait for profit" (138).

[40] For the blindness of spectator to his status as actor, see Force 39-45.

[41] Force remarks that "Les personnages philosophes de Molière ont, comme Descartes, roulé çà et là dans le monde," and that Arnolphe's lengthy "méditations" (l. 1202) put him on a par with Molière's travelers. But it is worth noting that Arnolphe himself has stayed put; the passage of time ("vingt ans et plus") is not the equivalent of a life lived.

[42] Molière's staging of Dom Pèdre's blind spot and his fashioning of two stage characters from a single novella character lend credence to Michael Koppisch's contention that "[t]he two rivals are brothers under skin" (53), that they are "indistinguishable" (49).

[43] Clearly, Horace does not "see" Arnolphe here, as Koppisch claims (46), since if he did, he would recognize his rival and the gamble of confidence would come to an end.

[44] For Agnès as embodiment of the inconstant Fortuna, the play's "retroactive operations of fate," and Arnolphe's "displacement from spectator to director-producer as well as to object of ridicule," see Lalande 94-98.

[45] Martha Houle designates Arnolphe's inarticulate exit from the stage as "an ejaculation" (51); I characterize it rather as a sign of impotence. Pierre Force seems to adopt Arnolphe's persepctive on Agnès's status as "mariée à demi" when he observes that Arnolphe is "cocu moralement" (23), though not in fact. I would contend that just as Agnès cannot be only half-married, neither can Arnolphe be considered cuckold before matrimony.

Works Cited

Boccaccio, Giovanni. *Decameron*. Ed. Cesare Segre. Milan: Mursia, 1966.

Brantôme. *Les Dames galantes*. Ed. Maurice Rat. Paris: Garnier, 1967.

Brownlee, Marina S. "Elusive Subjectivity in María de Zayas." *Journal of Interdisciplinary Studies* 6.2 (1994): 166-83.

Les Cent nouvelles nouvelles. In *Conteurs français du XVIe siècle*. Ed. Pierre Jourda. Bibliothèque de la Pléïade. Paris: Gallimard, 1965: 1-385.

Cocozella, Peter. "María de Zayas y Sotomayor: Writer of the Baroque 'Novela ejemplar.'" *Women Writers of the Seventeenth Century*. Eds. Katharina M. Wilson and Frank J. Warnke. Athens: University of Georgia Press, 1989: 189-227.

Cotgrave, Randle. *A Dictionarie of the French and English Tongues*. London, 1611. Columbia: University of South Carolina Press, 1950.

El Saffar, Ruth. "Ana/Lysis/Zayas: Reflections on Courtship and Literary Women in María de Zayas's *Enchantments of Love*." *Indiana Journal of Hispanic Literatures* 2.1 (1993): 7-28.

Force, Pierre. *Molière ou le prix des choses: Morale, économie et comédie*. Paris: Nathan, 1994.

Furetière, Antoine. *Dictionnaire universel contenant généralement tous les mots françois. Corrigé et augmenté par Henri Basnage de Beauval. Nouvelle édition revû, corrigé et considerablement augmenté par Jean Baptiste de la Rivière*. 4 vols. The Hague, 1727. Hildesheim-New York: Georg Olms, 1972.

Greer, Margaret R. *María de Zayas Tells Baroque Tales of Love and the Cruelty of Men*. University Park: Pennsylvania State University Press, 2000.

_____. "The M(Other) Plot: Psychoanalytic Theory and Narrative Structure in María de Zayas." *María de Zayas: The Dynamics of Discourse*. Eds. Amy R. Williamsen and Judith A. Whitenack. Madison, N.J.: Fairleigh Dickinson University Press, 1995.

Guichemerre, Roger. "Introduction." *La Précaution inutile. Les Nouvelles tragi-comiques*. By Paul Scarron. Paris: Nizet, 1986. 19-30.

Harrison, Helen. Pistoles/Paroles: *Money and Language in Seventeenth-Century French Comedy*. Charlottesville: Rookwood Press, 1996.

Houle, Martha M. "The Marriage Question, or, the *Querelle des hommes* in Rabelais, Molière and Boileau." *Dalhousie French Studies* 56 (2001): 46-54.

Koppisch, Michael. *Rivalry and the Disruption of Order in Molière's Theater*. Madison, N.J.: Fairleigh Dickinson University Press, 2004.

Jones, Ann Rosalind and Peter Stallybrass. *Renaissance Clothing and the Materials of Memory*. Cambridge, U.K.: Cambridge University Press, 2000.

Lalande, Roxanne Decker. *Intruders in the Play World: The Dynamics of Gender in Molière's Comedies*. Madison, N.J.: Fairleigh Dickinson University Press, 1996.

La Mesnardiere, H.-J. Pilet de. *a Poëtique*. 1640. Geneva: Slatkine, 1972.

Larson, Ruth. "The Iconography of Feminine Sexual Education in the 17th Century: Molière, Scarron, Chauveau." *Papers on French Seventeenth-Century Literature* 20 (1993): 499-516.

Lyons, John D. *Exemplum: The Rhetoric of Example in Early Modern France and Italy*. Princeton: Princeton University Press, 1989.

Marguerite de Navarre. *L'Heptaméron*. Ed. Michel François. Paris: Bordas/Classiques Garnier, 1991.

Meding, Twyla. "Translation as Appropriation: The Case of María de Zayas's *El prevenido engañado* and Paul Scarron's *La Précaution inutile*." In *The Shape of Change: Essays in Early Modern Literature and La Fontaine in Honor of David Lee Rubin*. Eds. Anne L. Birberick and Russell Ganim. Amsterdam & New York: Rodopi, 2001. 91-118.

Molière. *Oeuvres complètes*. 2 vols. Ed. Robert Jouanny. Paris: Garnier, 1962.

Montaigne, Michel de. *Oeuvres complètes*. Ed. Maurice Rat. Bibliothèque de la Pléïade. Paris: Gallimard, 1962.

Olivares, Julián. "Introducción." *Novelas amorosas y ejemplares*. By María de Zayas y Sotomayor. Madrid: Cátedra, 2000. 11-147.

Ovid. *Metamorphoses*. 2 vols. Trans. Frank Justus Miller. 2nd edition. Cambridge: Harvard University Press, 1984.

Plato. *Phaedrus*. Trans. R. Hackforth. *The Collected Dialogues of Plato, Including the Letters*. Eds. Edith Hamilton and Huntington Cairns. Princeton: Princeton University Press, 1961. 475-525.

Reynes, Geneviève. *Couvents de femmes: La vie des religieuses contemplatives dans la France des XVIIe et XVIIIe siècles.* Paris: Fayard, 1987.

Scarron, Paul. *La Précaution inutile.* In *Les Nouvelles tragi-comiques.* Ed. Roger Guichemerre. Paris: Nizet, 1986. 31-97.

_____. *The Fruitless Precaution.* In *Scarron's Novels.* Trans. John Davies. London, 1683. 1-62.

Souiller, Didier. *La Nouvelle en Europe de Boccace à Sade.* Paris: Presses Universitaires de France, 2004.

Steinberger, Deborah. "Molière and the Domestication of French Comedy: Public and Private Space in *L'École des femmes.*" *Cahiers du dix-septième* 6.2 (1992): 131-39.

Villon, François. *Oeuvres.* Ed. André Mary. Paris: Garnier, 1962.

Zayas y Sotomayor, María. *Desengaños amorosos.* Ed. Alicia Yllera. Madrid: Cátedra, 1983.

_____. *Novelas amorosas y ejemplares.* Ed. Julián Olivares. Madrid: Cátedra, 2000.

Zumthor, Paul. *La Mesure du monde: Représentation de l'espace au moyen âge.* Paris: Seuil, 1993.

Prudes, Précieux *and Patriarchs:*
Pedagogies of Paranoia and Repression

Larry Riggs

It was the *values* associated with women that were suffering a further beating as the modern world dawned.
— Robert S. McElvaine, *Eve's Seed: Biology, the Sexes, and the Course of History*

Are the final words of *La Princesse de Clèves* – "et sa vie, qui fut assez courte, laissa des exemples de vertu inimitables" (395) – best read as the last in a long litany of hyperbolic superlatives? Or can they be interpreted more fruitfully as an ironical comment on the sterility and inhumanity of Mademoiselle de Chartres's/Madame de Clèves's fate? Is the ending a surprise, or is it the completion of a destiny set in motion by the Princess's mother's will to make her daughter exceptional? Is that exceptionalism, itself, a kind of trap?[1] Of what use are *inimitable* examples? Are they not prospective elements in what would amount to a pedagogy of frustrating futility and repression? Does the heroine attain transcendence of disorder and anxiety, achieving a state like the *précieux* ideal of high status through indefinite suspension, or does the process begun by her mother's pedagogy consign her to a space of repression essentially like the one constructed for Agnès by the paranoiac Arnolphe, in *L'École des femmes*?[2] Is her withdrawal to be understood as a positive assertion of an independent identity, or is it the end of a process whereby an identity has been constructed for her by a powerful pedagogy? In my view, the situation wherein Madame de Clèves winds up has much in common with what Molière's tyranni-cal, patriarchal buffoons threaten to impose on the young women they seek to control.[3]

It seems obvious that Madame de Lafayette is not proposing her heroine as an example to be imitated. She evokes an education based on a curriculum of stories intended to constitute a culturally appropriate and socially *valuable* subjectivity.[4] The implicit message of this pedagogical enterprise seems to be "do not be a woman in such a story."[5] What, then, is the *novel's* pedagogical purpose? What is the relation of the story Madame de Lafayette tells us to the orthodoxy defined by the stories told to her heroine? What sort of story is the young woman actually *in*? Is it, in the final analysis, a story that questions the value of stories? In one way or another, some of these questions have been asked, or at least implied, by other critics. As I will indicate in the notes here, several specific articles have been particularly useful to me. Feminist critics, such as Donna Kuizinga, Jane Marie Todd and Nancy K. Miller, have helped me to define my approach, which I believe to be, overall, a new one. I hope to go beyond what has already been said about Madame de Lafayette's novel. More importantly, I hope to begin, convincingly, to elucidate thematic connections among a wide range of seventeenth-century treatments of patriarchal culture.[6] Within the confines of this essay, I will limit this exploration to *La Princesse de Clèves* and Molière.

In dealing with this novel and two of Molière's plays, I propose to explore the relation of pedagogies, and therefore of "knowledge" and the making of meanings, to regulation of desires.[7] Pursuing and expanding my approach to pedagogy in Molière, I will show that Madame de Lafayette, like Molière, is aware that desire can be domesticated, or made convenient to prevailing values, through projection and substitution.[8] This is the case even – or especially – when male desire is represented as threatening or monstrous. Patriarchal regulation of female desire may well function by setting up a system of projections, in which desire not structured by orthodox social forms is made fearsome, and fascinating, to both sexes. It also seeks to force young women to internalize, to mistake for their own, an identity actually composed of the essential strictures of paranoiac patriarchal pedagogy. This process amounts to a second, culturally determined, *birth*, a masculine birth regarded as superior to the first, "merely" biological birth.[9] The virtuous, desirable, economically and socially valuable woman is the product of a process of manufacture. Both authors also suggest that such paranoiac pedagogy is a self-fulfilling prophecy.

First, though, what, in fact, *is* pedagogy? Ursula A. Kelly, in *Schooling Desire: Literacy, Cultural Politics, and Pedagogy*, provides an answer to this question that goes well beyond our usual, more or less unreflective definitions. In focusing particularly on the early modern and modern education of young women, Kelly argues that schooling is a "mode of social control" designed to produce particular forms of subjectivity and to elicit certain kinds of participation in social life (1).[10] Education constructs desire, forming subjectivities that substitute

for "natural" objects of desire those that it is convenient for the given
social order to provide. It is selective socialization into a certain version of the world.[11] Kelly pays special attention to pedagogies of literacy as means of forming socially convenient, self-disciplining subjects,
arguing that the stories we read and hear, the uses made of our literacy
and of our culture's archive of stories, are fundamental to systems of
social control. Pedagogy, then, is akin to a second, cultural birth, a
masculine birth, in that culture has long been regarded as a masculine
process of creation, and biological birth as a "merely" natural event.
The product of this pedagogy is an artifact shaped by the set of
imperatives, the desire, institutionalized in and by social norms.[12]

Other commentators supply complementary information and
analysis. Carolyn Merchant, for example, shows that early modern
education worked directly to disempower women.[13] According to Merchant, women ceased to be trained for business and other economically
significant activities, thus becoming more dependent on men (151). At
the same time, "feminine" forms of knowledge were being defined as
"witchcraft," and were being eradicated as part of the effort to profes-
sionalize knowledge and make it a masculine monopoly (140). The
structure of desire was explicitly influenced by the Neo-platonic ideology of love, which in effect defined the "ideal" woman as a chaste and
passive subordinate (Merchant 150).[14] The "work" of "perfecting" both
men and women required substituting culturally produced artifacts for
bodies as both subjects and objects of desire. Julie Hardwick documents the ways in which political and legal developments reflected and
reinforced this patriarchalist turn. Peggy Phelan and David Le Breton,
among many others, study the repression of the body in favor of "high"
cultural artifacts as a fundamental aspect of early modern culture.

Control of young women's access to information, management
of their literacy and especially of their use of writing, was a key means
of limiting their subjective sense of possibility, as well as their objec-
tive options. The issue of pedagogy is explicitly raised, in *La Princesse
de Clèves*, when, the "framing" evocation of the Court being finished,
Mademoiselle de Chartres and her mother are introduced. The paragraph in which we learn about *l'éducation* that Madame de Chartres
has given her daughter (248) speaks of the latter as both beautiful and
rich, and thus as one of the most desirable objects of attention and
ambition in France. That this education's purpose has been to accultur-
ate the young woman to what Kelly calls cultural embodiment, social
practice and regulated desire (3) is obvious. Madame de Chartres has

used tendentious representations to make a certain version of virtue the object of her daughter's desire: "elle faisait souvent à sa fille des *peintures* de l'amour...elle lui *contait* le peu de sincérité des hommes, leurs tromperies et leur infidélité..." (248, *my emphasis*). This "phallic mother," who must play the role of her daughter's dead father, encloses her daughter in a tradition of tendentious representations that delivers an essentially patriarchal message about female, as well as male, desire.[15] It is as if Madame de Chartres wanted to give her daughter a cultural rebirth as a being convenient to patriarchal designs and to make oneness with an idealized being, who is actually *not* herself, the object of the young woman's deepest desire. Mademoiselle de Chartres's education has placed her in a mental and emotional environment that reminds us of certain stories from the *Decameron* and *Heptaméron* and of "Le Petit Chaperon rouge." Her subjectivity is, to a significant degree, an internalized archive of stories to which she eventually refers all of her experiences at Court. This archive constitutes a set of defining delimitations, and, after her marriage, Madame de Clèves literally vacillates between more or less spontaneous experiences and the self-critique resulting from belatedly "recognizing" the relation of those experiences to her mother's lessons.

Having shown us that stories are elements in a curriculum, and that pedagogies are methods for managing desire, does Madame de Lafayette challenge us to wonder just what, if anything, the story of the Princesse is teaching? Can the novel be taken as an example of what Kelly means by "critical literacy"? I will argue here that it can. Critical literacy is the production and use of stories to expose, analyze and subvert the orthodox narratives that make us culturally literate (Kelly 10), which "sculpt" our minds and bodies for conformity and obedience. Before giving her account of Mademoiselle de Chartres's education, Madame de Lafayette evokes the Court from which the young girl has been isolated and for which she is being formed. We learn first, then, what Mademoiselle de Chartres has *not* learned.

This "frame story" about the Court has great significance for my reading of the novel. Superficially, the Court and its denizens are described in conventional superlatives. The King and his courtiers are all that is most beautiful, witty, graceful and noble in France. At the same time, Madame de Lafayette makes it clear that ambition, intrigue and deep enmities dominate the Court. Most significantly, I would argue, she informs us that this is a closed world presided over by a relationship that is both adulterous and *Oedipal*. Dead Fathers, transcendentally powerful patriarchs, most importantly François I, haunt the Court. Henri II is dominated by slavish passion for an older woman who was his father's mistress and who set out to seduce Henri in order to make a better man of him. She thereby made herself both his mother, in a sense, and the object of an actual father-son rivalry. Further insight into the motives underlying this world of superficial superlatives is provided when Madame de Lafayette informs us that François I preferred both of Henri's brothers to the son who actually became king.

Wounds and jealousies even deeper than those that beset lovers formed the authority-figure who rules this Court, which thus has something in common with Thebes under Oedipus: it is ruled by a perverse desire. Henri II himself embodies two of desire's most dangerous forms, and he presides, as "legitimate" authority, over a hungry society haunted by loss and lack. This is an intensely illuminated, paranoiac world of rivalries, triangular desire, and endless series of temporary objects for an insatiable sense of lack.[16] The story of La Princesse de Clèves is framed by this devastating evocation of a wounded boy-king who is manipulated by a mistress/mother figure and who is the forever unsuccessful rival of his dead father and brothers. If we read carefully, we are prepared to understand the life of tension and contradiction that begins for Mademoiselle de Chartres when she arrives at Court. We are acutely aware of the motives of those who will gaze upon "un des grands partis qu'il y eût en France" (248).[17] Madame de Chartres's isolation of her daughter has intensified the power of the pedagogy whose effect has been to sculpt her for greatest appeal to the very predatory Gaze whose terrible dangers are recounted in the stories the young woman has heard. It has simultaneously increased the danger she will face.

Mademoiselle de Chartres's father, like François I, is dead. Her mother must therefore both educate her and represent the family's interests in the competitive marketplace of aristocratic marriage. She must first protect her daughter and then throw her to the wolves. Moreover, the protection, in the form of devotion to virtue, makes Mademoiselle de Chartres more appetizing. As we find out when she first encounters Monsieur de Clèves, her sudden appearance as a marriageable woman produces surprise, and thus intensifies her desirability. Isolated in an enclosure of tendentious stories about predatory male desire, agonizing jealousy and disgraced women, Mademoiselle de Chartres has been sculpted for appeal to the very Gaze whose rapacity we have learned of in the "frame story." We are told, literally, that

Madame de Chartres's pedagogy has had as its purpose constructing her daughter's desire with virtue as its object: "...elle songea aussi à lui donner de la vertu et à la lui rendre aimable" (248). The goal of this education, then, has been to represent both male and female erotic desire as fearsome and to make virtue and reputation the objects of Mademoiselle de Chartres's "own" desire. Mademoiselle de Chartres *is* an artifact made to be perceived as socially and economically valuable. Her education has just the intention and effect elucidated by Kelly. That these lessons will place her in a tense, conflicted situation is made clear by the fact that virtue is represented by the mother as both a defense and, in effect, an attraction. As she adds to her daughter's value on the market, Madame de Chartres also increases her vulnerability, from within and without. Mademoiselle de Chartres desires unity with a being – an artifact – whose embodiment of virtue defines her vulnerability.[18]

What, in fact, makes virtue valuable? As a form of ornamentation, giving *éclat* and *élévation* (248) to a woman, virtue works to intensify the very desire it is supposed to protect against. It is analogous to the jewels that Mademoiselle de Chartres is selecting when Monsieur de Clèves first sees her. Virtue is, ultimately, the most appetizing of the attributes that draw the predatory male Gaze. It thus increases the power of that against which it is supposed to protect. Moreover, virtue's value depends on the fear associated with competitive male desire. Virtue is a prize and a prospective guarantee in a context defined by pervasive infidelity and unending rivalry. If a virtuous woman is "won," her value immediately decreases. Virtue is, therefore, incompatible with any form of consummated love; and yet, its value also depends on the belief that the woman may be accessible. This, then, motivates the indefinite suspension I have mentioned.

It is clear that Madame de Chartres has isolated her daughter from the predatory, patriarchal Court in order to make her a more *desirable* object there. The paragraph evoking Mademoiselle de Chartres's education tells us that she will be in a state of tense conflict with *herself*: "elle lui faisait voir aussi combien il était difficile de conserver cette vertu, *que par une extrême défiance de soi-même*" (248, *my emphasis*). The paragraph ends by preparing us to see that Madame de Chartres, herself, will be unable to remain faithful to her own pedagogy. According to Madame de Chartres, along with self-abnegation, loving and being loved by her husband makes preserving virtue possible for a woman. When we learn, later, that the mother "ne craignit point de donner à sa fille un mari qu'elle ne put aimer" (258), we see one of the dimensions of contradiction at the heart of Madame de Chartres's project. She is, in the end, both a prude and a patriarch: she condemns youthful passion, encloses her daughter in a paranoiac world of fearsome stories, and uses her as an item of exchange to form an alliance with another family without regard for her emotions. Are we to conclude that Madame de Chartres has complete confidence in the subjectivity she has made for her daughter, or that her arrogance amounts to hubris, or both?

Madame de Chartres's ambition and pride – she is "extrême-ment glorieuse" (248) – thus lead her, when the personal and political dynamics of the Court have blocked several possible glorious matches, to place her daughter in precisely the circumstances that will maximize the difficulty of her remaining virtuous. Madame de Clèves is now in the very situation for which her education has not prepared her, except by making her fearful of the male desire she has been formed to attract, and by putting her at odds with herself. Her situation has also made this predicament virtually inevitable. Does not virtue, as Madame de Lafayette has elucidated it for us, imply the woman's internalizing male desire and male rivalry/jealousy as, in effect, the objects of both *her* fear and *her* desire? Virtue has meaning and value only as a quality that awakens and resists male desire, and thereby both assuages and exacerbates male fear of rivals. A woman must want to be desired by more than one man if she wants to be known as virtuous. The issue of what her own desire might be focused on, other than the reputation for virtue that depends on others, cannot arise. Madame de Clèves's marriage to a man she cannot love can only intensify her need for that which is condemned and excluded by the essentially patriarchal curriculum that has shaped her.

Because she has been bombarded with precepts and deprived of experiences, Madame de Clèves is acutely vulnerable to the influences that surround her. In fact, here as in the Molière plays I will look at later, deprivation serves to intensify appetite. It is important, I think, to notice that Madame de Chartres's pedagogy is essentially negative: she relentlessly represents love as a pervasive motivation that causes only disasters. The hunger for experiences and knowledge that Mademoiselle de Chartres's education has, both deliberately and inadvertently, created in her interacts powerfully with the sense of lack dominating the Court. She comes to desire the Duc de Nemours principally because she has *learned* that he is *desirable*.[19] Her long isolation from the world she now inhabits makes her avid to learn about it in order to belong in it, and she has learned that Nemours is the most desirable man at Court. At the same time, her own belated arrival on the scene has made her an archetypal Object.

Ironically, Nemours also represents, too late, the very possibility that would have put Madame de Clèves in the situation her mother defined as happiest for a woman: loving a husband and being loved by him. Moreover, as the man desired by Queen Elizabeth I, Nemours would also have been the perfect realization of Madame de Chartres's own enormous ambition. Her innocent, sincere daughter is about to become the successful rival of a queen.[20] In a fit of wounded pride, Madame de Chartres has confronted her daughter with a choice: she can be a typical woman in a typical story of jealousy and domestic disaster, or she can be "inimitable." In fact, however, Madame de Lafayette's account has already taught us that life is not a story, not a *récit*, nor is it the illustration of a list of precepts; it is a *drama*. Madame de Clèves is not a listener or reader observing narrated events from outside; she is *surrounded*. The only way for her to escape the drama wherein she finds herself is to return to isolation.[21] Exceptionalism – inimitability – can be realized only in a *désert*; it is incompatible with human relationships.

When she realizes that her daughter is becoming passionately attached to Nemours, Madame de Chartres can only work to intensify the sense of guilt and fear – the *défiance de soi-même* – that have always been the core of what she has taught her daughter. By managing her own death as she does, Madame de Chartres makes grief and lack, abandonment and loneliness, the essential motives of her daughter's resistance to love.[22] In her last and most effective act of pedagogy, Madame de Chartres tells Madame de Clèves that her love for Nemours puts her "sur le bord du précipice" (277-78), evokes her daughter's duty to her husband, and asserts that her only hope lies in "de grands efforts et de grandes violences" (278) against her emotions. She tells her daughter that she is about to become the main character in yet another story of lost virtue. Madame de Chartres guarantees that this will be the *last word*, and that it will have all the authority conferred by death, by refusing to see her daughter again. She thus joins the dead fathers and insures that reunification with her, and thus death itself, will become objects of Madame de Clèves's deepest desire. Thanks to Madame de Chartres's managing her death for greatest pedagogical effect, her teaching becomes transcendental Law. At the same time, her death consummates Madame de Clèves's education to be in a state of tension and, by making her the embodiment of suspense and delay, makes her an even better archetype of the Object of desire. She has been taught to value a "self" that is not a living person, but an extremely desirable *parti* whose "own" desire is to resist that desirability, and thereby perpetuate it.

Madame de Clèves remains hungry for stories that will both teach her about the mysteries of the Court and give her a sense of belonging there.[23] After Madame de Chartres's death, Monsieur de Clèves replaces her, in a sense. His wife asks him to teach her about the corruption of Madame de Tournon, for example: "*Apprenez-moi*, je vous en supplie, ce qui vous a détrompé de Madame de Tournon" (280 *my emphasis*). Monsieur de Clèves obliges by telling her the story of Madame de Tournon, which seems another confirmation of Madame de Clèves's mother's lessons. After hearing about Madame de Tournon's disgraceful behavior, Madame de Clèves begins to live experiences that further confirm Madame de Chartres's teachings. She comes to know both euphoric moments of love and the despair of jealousy. Her "recognition" of what she experiences as what she has learned of in stories, combined with her hearing herself spoken of, though not named, in gossip, is what convinces her that a return to isolation is the only way to avoid becoming another all-too-imitable example in a story of amorous disgrace. Moreover, the fact that her husband's death is the result of a male rivalry, that the man to whom she owes and has sworn and avowed loyalty has died because of the love of another man, puts her in a situation somewhat analogous to that of Chimène, in *Le Cid*. To marry Nemours would, in a sense, make her a *prize or trophy* in a masculine contest, the approximate equivalent of a medieval widow seized on the field of battle where her husband has just been killed. So, Madame de Clèves's moral conscience, made up in significant part of the patriarchal condemnation of woman as temptress, combines with her desire to be more than an object and something other than a "typical" character in a story of disastrous love, to make marriage to Nemours impossible.[24]

In the end, our reading of the novel's final words depends on our assessment of the role of Madame de Clèves's education, of the stories she has learned, in her life. Is her return to isolation the appropriate response to the correspondence between what she has encountered at Court and what she was taught to fear, or have her induced fears distorted her perception of her experiences? Does her retirement from the Court represent the attainment of a relative independence, or is it the ultimate triumph of patriarchal repression, the ultimate infantilization? Is it a languishing anticipation of death, or an instance of *précieux* suspension? Is there a difference? Does she merely impose on herself the spatial and psychological enclosure that a paranoiac patriarchal tyrant like Arnolphe would see as the proper situation of a virtuous woman? Is her subjectivity itself a cloister? Does she return to the condition of her childhood? Has the Princesse internalized and thus come to embody the essence of patriarchy, itself? My critical reading, in Kelly's sense, suggests that Madame de Lafayette has written a novel that demands such a critical reading of a story of cultural embodiment.

Arnolphe, in *L'École des femmes*, has a project that is remarkably similar to that of Madame de Chartres: he wants to *form* a woman to specifications that are appropriate to his purposes.[25] Like Madame de Chartres, Arnolphe intends to shape a subjectivity that will make an ideal marriage-commodity, in this case, for himself.[26] Fear of both male and female erotic desire and pervasive male rivalry are as important in this play as they are in Madame de Lafayette's novel.[27] Arnolphe associates independent female subjectivity, or the relative freedom enjoyed by *femmes habiles,* with disorder and chance. His methodical repression of Agnès exemplifies the paranoiac intensification of patriarchal control of women and families that characterized early-modern France (see Hardwick). Molière here explicitly associates convent education with both stupefying ignorance and the perpetuation of abusive patriarchal power. Allen Kanner and Mary Gomes speak appositely of the "engulfing and dominating" tendencies of the patriarchal mind (117). Arnolphe's architectural and pedagogical engulfing of Agnès reflects his desire to incorporate her into his self. Arnolphe's ideal woman seems an evident parody of the neo-Platonic chaste and passive subordinate.[28]

A number of recent commentators have elucidated the motives of this mania for patriarchal control. E. Michael Zimmerman emphasizes the patriarchal fear that women will form identities other than those prescribed for them by patriarchy. He links this fear of women with the larger yearning to escape mortality and dependence, which are identified with nature and woman (248). Zimmerman also characterizes patriarchy as a system of would-be stable, clear boundaries *patrolled* by paranoiac men (257). Arnolphe's recruitment of spies to reinforce his vigilance certainly amounts to a patrolling of the architectural and pedagogical boundaries that he has placed around Agnès. Paul Shepard, too, sees the fear of death as a fundamental motivation of modern "Faustian Historical Man" (7), who fears biological nature, gendered as feminine, and consoles himself with fantasies of conquest. Finally, Bill Devall and George Sessions hypothesize that modern, urban men are afraid of being "recaptured" by the "charms" of women and nature (165).[29] Every woman is perceived as a threat to re-submerge the male's laboriously differentiated identity (Badinter 46). Arnolphe wants to produce, or manufacture, a dependably faithful wife, and his method relies heavily on pedagogical means. Like Mademoiselle de Chartres/Madame de Clèves, Arnolphe lives, and forces Agnès to live, in a world haunted by jealousy, predatory desire and disgrace. Here, as in my critical reading of Madame de Lafayette's novel, it seems that "virtue" in a woman means, in effect, that she must embody, must literally have a subjectivity made from, the essential tenets and injunctions of the patriarchal order.

Arnolphe's expectation that he can observe, understand, and control events without becoming entangled in them – "Enfin ce sont partout des sujets de satire; / Et, comme spectateur, ne puis-je pas en rire?" (ll. 43-44) – has something in common with Madame de Chartres's effort to wrap her daughter in a protective carapace of stories. In the play, as in the novel, however, the hope of occupying a point of view that comprehends what is happening from outside is chimerical. Arnolphe is determined not to be a character in a story of cuckoldry of the kind that he loves to hear about others, but, like that of Madame de Chartres, his method for avoiding what he fears increases the likelihood that it will happen. Like Madame de Chartres, he isolates his charge – of whom he has made, in a sense, a *daughter* – from the world in which what he hopes to teach her will have to be put into practice. His pedagogy will have the effect of increasing Agnès's vulnerability to, and her appetite for, the kind of learning – of experiences – of which his pedagogy deprives her. Arnolphe's enclosure of Agnès, both architecturally and pedagogically, exacerbates his insecurity and increases her incentive to escape. Arnolphe's method echoes the recommendation, in marriage manuals of the time written by Church officials, that domestic space be made a cloister. At the same time, as Chrysalde tries to show him in the play's opening scene, Arnolphe's systematic manufacture of a *sotte* will deprive *him* of pleasure, too. His control over Agnès deprives him of any pleasurable connection with her.[30]

Cloistering is the essence of Arnolphe's pedagogy. Having identified Agnès "dès quatre ans" (l. 130) as a malleable child, Arnolphe acquired her from her poverty-stricken "mother" and had her reared in a convent, "Pour la rendre idiote autant qu'il se pourrait" (l. 138). Acquisition of Agnès from the woman whom he took to be her mother, and his plan to determine the form and content of her identity, along with his ultimate intention to make her his perfectly obedient, childlike sexual object and the mother of his children, authorize us to see overtones of incest in his plan. Infantilization of women and usurpation of motherhood reflect the modern masculine project of taking control of all natural processes by subjecting them to the cultural work of making a Man. Arnolphe goes beyond the ethos of patriarchy by wanting to keep for himself a female who has been reared as his daughter. Agnès's convent education is thus linked to the essential motive of incest: complete control, extending to the scope of possibility represented by the future. This is another negative pedagogy, another pedagogy of deprivation.

That Arnolphe's larger purpose is to make himself into a *new man* is clear. Acquiring – buying – a wife who, even more than was normally the case at the time, will be an item of property, complements Arnolphe's adoption of a new name. By calling himself Monsieur de la Souche, he reveals his ambition to be the founding father of a new lineage. Taking a wife who can contribute nothing to the marriage – not even intelligent conversation, much less wealth and social status of her own – assures Arnolphe that he will stand alone as the origin of the new family. The name itself – *souche* – suggests, simultaneously, that Arnolphe wants to be the trunk of a new family tree and that his ambition will be sterile, or cut off. He will not be the trunk, but rather the *stump*, of the new family. Arnolphe's overweening desire will, in effect, leave him impotent and sterile, castrated. His ambition is related to the old dream of a masculine birth, of an exclusively male supplanting of female, natural reproduction. His *formation* of Agnès will make her the creature of a reproductive process entirely controlled by and identified with him. Like Madame de Chartres, Arnolphe intends to produce an ideal *parti*, but he will "exchange" this commodity with himself, thus short-circuiting even the confining pattern of patriarchy. This rejection of both generational succession and marriage as exchange is a sign of the excessiveness of Arnolphe's desire.

Like the Court in *La Princesse de Clèves*, the domestic world in which Arnolphe has imprisoned Agnès is saturated with desire and haunted by the sense of lack. Like Madame de Chartres, Arnolphe is intensely fearful of this desire, which, in his case, is his own. He, too, is *extrêmement glorieux*, and he is able to imagine isolating Agnès permanently by giving her to himself. Arnolphe feels surrounded by rivals – he *is* surrounded by rivals – for two principal reasons: first, he has loudly enjoyed and repeated stories of other men whose wives have been said to be unfaithful, thus giving them an incentive to wish him cuckolded; secondly, he fears his own desire, which, as we have seen, is excessive, and which he projects onto his surroundings. That education, or pedagogy, is a key to his plan, and that his conception of education, like that of Madame de Chartres, is relentlessly negative, is shown in the use he makes of the literacy that Agnès has acquired at the convent. *Les Maximes du mariage*, Arnolphe's domestic Bible, serves as the equivalent of Madame de Chartres's stories of disastrous love. Arnolphe exemplifies the controlled exploitation of literacy as a means of disempowering women and strengthening patriarchy.[31] He sees the disciplined absorption of moralistic texts as the next-best thing to total ignorance. His version of what Kelly calls cultural literacy is obviously intended to create a convenient subjectivity in Agnès.[32] The *Maximes du mariage* are a litany of negative injunctions. His awareness of the power of such manipulated literacy and his desire that Agnès internalize the injunctions as *self-discipline* are made evident when he says, "Imprimez-le-vous bien" (l. 678). One of the rules, of course, is against women's using their literacy – especially their ability to write – for their own purposes. This is just what Agnès will eventually do. The play thus seems to encourage, in us, a kind of critical literacy *about literacy*, an awareness of the oppressive power of something that is too often taken, uncritically, to be a means of liberation.

The remainder of the play adumbrates the ways in which Arnolphe's repressive, paranoiac pedagogy is worse than futile. Like Mademoiselle de Chartres, Agnès has been made more vulnerable by isolation. Her appetite for interaction, for experiential learning, is intensified by deprivation. Once again, the attempt to substitute precepts for experiences backfires, and the laboriously formed subjectivity, the valuable commodity, turns out to be vulnerable to the first serious assault by masculine desire. Moreover, Arnolphe's illusory position as a spectator separated from the drama dissolves. Far from achieving masterful, safe independence, he winds up not only involved in, but *financing* the comic story of his discomfiture. Here, as in the case of *La Princesse de Clèves*, it seems appropriate to pose some questions about the ending, and thus to open, again, the issue of critical literacy. Although she will marry Horace, whose principal real virtue is that he is not Arnolphe, is her "choice" not, in fact, an illusion? Is she attracted to Horace because he has qualities, or merely because he has served as the occasion for her emergence from the cloister? Although Arnolphe, himself, is defeated, does Agnès not continue to be delimited by the surrounding milieu of male desire and rivalry? Her fate seems the "opposite" of that of Madame de Clèves, but is it really that? Do the distorting effects of a pedagogy of repressive negativity persist? Molière invites us to read critically, in Kelly's sense, not only the repressive pedagogy represented by marriage manuals, but also the conventionally "happy" ending of his comedy.

The themes I have seen in *La Princesse de Clèves* and *L'École des femmes* are present, in highly concentrated form, in *Les Femmes savantes*. Here, too, the atmosphere is defined by a kind of pedagogy that reflects and serves ambition. Social ambition is once again linked to a conception of education. The play's main character, Philaminte, is obviously *extrêmenent glorieuse*. The learned ladies want to become socially prestigious subjectivities and, further, to dominate the cultural process whereby other subjectivities will be produced. Grammar, mind, poetry, ostensible transcendence of sex and the body, and an aggressively therapeutic pedagogy are tightly connected with law, sovereignty and high social status.[33] In fact, as Armande makes clear in her debate with her sister, Henriette, in the play's first scene, she sees the hierarchical distinction of mind and body as a key instrument of her social ambition.[34] *Titre, vulgaire, étage bas, petit personnage, nobles plaisirs, mépris, encens* and *pauvretés* are among the words and phrases used by Armande to distinguish what she regards as a new aristocracy from what is low and common. As in Madame de Lafayette's novel, education is taken to create what amounts to socially valuable, exploitable capital. As in *L'École des femmes*, the desire to found a new, "noble" lineage is in play. Here, another phallic mother will impose chastity on one daughter and attempt to use the other as an exchange commodity to form an alliance with a man whom she takes to be powerfully prestigious. A "philosophy," and the pedagogy that reflects and imposes it, play in this work the role of the tendentious stories in the novel and of the marriage manual in Molière's earlier play. The "philosophical" denigration of the body is the basis of the ladies' repressive pedagogy. Their *jargon* depends on the use of metaphors and other forms of abstraction to create the illusion of transcendence.

Their pedagogical imperative is so pervasive that their entire environment is "institutionalized." They imagine fully implementing this imperative by establishing an *Académie* – a pedagogical institution and enclosure – where everything will be taught.

The ladies' enterprise reflects the *précieux* practice of erasing the body from "refined" speech, of replacing the world of concrete experiences with abstractions. Such idealization of discourse, which is also a self-idealization by the speaker or writer of the discourse, is a fantasy of final, definitive meaning (Cottom 34). It also, like the pedagogical systems of Madame de Chartres and Arnolphe, attempts to substitute precepts for experiences. The former's curriculum of stories and the latter's effort to imprint on Agnès the injunctions in the *Maximes du mariage* prepare us to understand Molière's critique of the learned ladies' bookish speech and mentalist pedagogy. *Les Femmes savantes* shows that personal motives and physical desires are disguised, disfigured, and, ultimately, intensified by transforming them into normative language, by identifying them with a purportedly transcendent good Order.[35] Philaminte, the phallic mother who dominates the household, invokes Plato as an example whom she intends to outdo in founding a comprehensive pedagogical regime (l. 847). We will see that privileging signs over experiences can appear possible only in language and has the effect of disconnecting "reason" from reality.[36] At the same time, Molière argues that speaking and thinking in abstractions is actually impossible, since the "repressed" returns, or rather never leaves. The *savantes'* discourse constantly reveals the sub-text of desire that underlies and, in fact, motivates their abstractionism. In the opening scene, Armande's language shows that nature and the body are, in fact, the only real motives, sources, and referents of speech, however "refined."[37] Her metaphors would be entirely meaningless without their concrete terms. The play's very first line, in which Armande calls unmarried status a *titre*, shows that desire for higher social status motivates her speech and her thinking. Later, we will learn that other thinly disguised desires are in play, too. Her denunciation as *vulgaire* of the coupling of bodies in marriage – an intensely physical experience which obviously preoccupies her – shows that she understands denigration of the body to be a precondition for belonging to an elite. Molière also suggests, I would argue, that the desire to belong to an elite is itself already an unsatisfactory substitute for more physical desires. Armande's language, then, links her to Mademoiselle de Chartres and Agnès. All three have been taught to regard concrete desires and experiences as dangerous and unworthy. Once again, virtue requires internalizing male desire and resistance to it as the objects of the woman's "own" desire. To be educated, then, is to denigrate the body and the physical world. Investment in social power and transcendentalism is substitute gratification, which distorts and intensifies desire – makes it truly dangerous – by repressing it.

In fact, as Henriette sanely points out in her debate with Armande, their mother is actually an example of the compatibility, the *complementarity*, of mind and body, since she is both a mother and an intellectual. It is the hierarchical binary separating mind and body and making the former superior that places them in conflict. Philaminte is a *prude*, as well as a *précieuse* and a female patriarch: she would proscribe for her daughters pleasurable experiences which she has enjoyed, she preaches refinement and suspension at the expense of consummation, and she intends to have her daughters pay the price of her self-glorification. Philaminte's ascetic, tyrannical, pedagogical regime is not significantly different from Arnolphe's. We understand that adherence to her mother's philosophy is literally a sacrifice for Armande when we learn that Henriette is planning to marry Clitandre, who was Armande's suitor until he grew tired of being an unrewarded worshiper.

Armande has paid a high price for her ambition. She says that refusing to marry does not mean that one rejects being courted and adored. Armande thus idealizes a state much like that in which Madame de Chartres's conception of virtue places the Princesse de Clèves: needing to be desired but enjoined not to desire, except by desiring to be desired and to resist. Clearly, this form of self-idealization has cost Armande dearly. Clitandre would have been a confirming "mirror" for her idealized self, and his continued devotion would have enabled her to avoid giving up all of what she recalls, perhaps only vaguely, as the desire for which she has substituted ambition and refinement. Clitandre would then have functioned in the same way that her metaphors do: seemingly confirming the transcendence that she has invested in so heavily, but preserving the memory and the possibility of what has been lost through the substitution. Armande is in a situation much like that in which we saw the Princesse de Clèves: her value depends on both attracting and resisting men's desire. Paradoxically, her sense of having a virtuous subjectivity is entirely based on being an object. The *précieuse*, then, who is finally difficult to distinguish from a coquette, must, in effect, substitute a male's desire for her own by

identifying her ideal self with unsatisfied, but somehow still permanent, male desire. Armande is motivated, in large part, by the loss of
what her mother's philosophy both denigrates and idealizes: desire.
There is a double repression here, since it is, in fact, *male* desire with
which Armande "unconsciously" identifies. By affecting a lack of
interest in pleasure, Armande cooperates in the denial to the female of
the right to be a subject of desire and pleasure. As Henriette seems
intuitively to recognize, self-abnegation, however it is sweetened by
pretensions, accomplishes nothing. It can produce only sterility, only
inimitable examples. Armande has substituted an idealized, and sterile,
conception of herself for the other with whom she originally desired a
physical connection. Clitandre's imminent consummation of a physical
relationship with Henriette threatens Armande's pretense of existing
suspended between the terms of a metaphor.

The effects of the *savantes'* pedagogy are incisively analyzed
in the scenes involving Bélise, Martine and Trissotin. Bélise,
Philaminte's sister-in-law, has so entirely substituted stories for her
subjectivity that she is a female Don Quixote. She is able to live the
précieux fantasy of indefinite suspension because she never experiences contact with any actual man. She "lives" in the Utopia implied
by the ladies' rhetoric, truly disabled by the substitution of signs for
experiences. Representations have replaced the real world of bodies
and relationships. The learned ladies' grammatocentric regime is a
systematic violation of Molière's advice, in the *Préface* to *Tartuffe*, that
we speak of things, not of words. Their interaction with the cook, Martine, emphatically confirms this. When Martine hears *grammaire* as
grand-mère (l. 492*)*, she brilliantly, though unconsciously, parodies the
ladies' substitution of words and concepts for people. Martine correctly
calls the *savantes'* "prestige dialect" (Cottom 4) a *jargon,* thereby
implicitly undermining their pretension to make it universal.[38] Martine
is banished from the household for being unschooled, for resisting
Philaminte's imperialistic pedagogy. This is, of course, an example of
the self-abnegating substitution of words for bodily pleasures, since
Martine is the cook.[39]

The unsatisfactoriness and incompleteness of this substitution
are clearest in the *savantes'* relations with Trissotin, the hack *précieux*
poet. Act III, scenes 1 and 2 explore, in explosively concentrated form,
what I see as the themes of all three of the works I am reading, here.
Trissotin makes clear his intention to use the ladies as cultural breed-
ing-stock, saying, in scene 1, his poem is an "enfant tout nouveau né"

(l. 720) and that their approval "lui peut servir de mère" (l. 724). Substitution of signs for experiences and the colonization of female subjectivity by masculine desire could hardly be more powerfully evoked.
"Ne faites point languir de si pressants désirs" (l. 717), says Philaminte,
and Bélise echoes her: "Faites tôt et hâtez nos plaisirs" (l. 718). The
sexual subtext that has haunted the ladies' discourse from the beginning is very close to the surface here. Moreover, what is going on is literally sexual, since Philaminte intends to marry Henriette to Trissotin
in order to cement her relationship with the man whom she takes to be
a member of the new, bookish "aristocracy."[40] Like Madame de
Chartres, Philaminte is extremely proud and ambitious, and her project
is almost as abusively patriarchal as that of Arnolphe. She plans to sacrifice her daughter's desire and pleasure to her own, to make of her
daughter's body and subjectivity an offering to a *précieux* god. As in
the other two works, a pedagogical enterprise has as its purpose the
production of a disciplined subjectivity and a valuable marriage-commodity. The hierarchical separation of body and mind, and the
attempted substitution of the latter for the former, are epitomized by
Philaminte's assertion that marriage to – and therefore sex with – Trissotin will make Henriette more intelligent (ll. 1050-52). Here, in fact,
sex itself is being assigned a pedagogical purpose. Philaminte is both
hostile to her own femaleness and that of her daughters and determined
to exploit theirs to further her ambitions and inflate her pride.[41] The
repression of the body in favor of "high" cultural products is clearly
exemplified. Grammar and "philosophy" turn out to be delimitations
analogous to Mademe de Chartres's stories and Arnolphe's maxims.[42]

I hope that I have persuaded my readers by juxtaposing these
three canonical works that there is a level of interpretation on which
patriarchy, preciosity and prudery converge. Education, or pedagogy,
as an expression of paranoiac fear of desire and as a means of forming
and disciplining "convenient" subjectivities is explored – and, I have
argued, deplored – in all three works. Moreover, the canonical, definitive readings of texts that confine readers within the pedagogy of cultural literacy are analogous to the disciplining of desire, which I have
looked at here. The panic-stricken rage often expressed by those who
have committed themselves to such readings when truly critical readings are proposed must be taken to resemble Arnolphe's paranoiac
sermonizing. A fascinating issue for discussion elsewhere is the fact
that, in these works, distorted or disempowered motherhood is a
theme.[43] Madame de Chartres is obliged by her husband's death to

function as a patriarch as well as a mother. Agnès's real mother is dead, and Arnolphe is able to exploit the desperate poverty of the substitute "mother" to whom she has been given. Philaminte's ambition for cultural influence, with which we may well have some sympathy, induces her to substitute "masculine" traits for "feminine" ones and to subscribe to the prevailing denigration of femaleness as "merely" biological. Her pedagogy amounts to a masculine birth, through which her daughters will be re-produced as artifacts sculpted by patriarchal imperatives. All three works, I believe, encourage us to read critically some of the fundamental cultural precepts that continue to form us.

Notes

[1] Pierre Force explicitly compares the Princesse to the Molière characters whose fundamental error is regarding themselves as exceptions to some general rule about humanity (49-50).

[2] As I have argued elsewhere, in studying *Le Misanthrope*, the desire for distinction makes sense only within the social context, and therefore makes the would-be exception the creature of his or her spectators/partners (see my "Convergence"). Inevitably, society pressures all of its members to resemble one another. Does the Princesse de Clèves ultimately opt out of courtly society because she feels the pull of this logic of convergence? Is distinction or exceptionalism whose price is withdrawal to a *désert* – another reason for "speaking" of *Le Misanthrope* and *La Princesse de Clèves* in the same breath– meaningless? In any case, the ending is implicit in the beginning, since the Princesse has been taught that to be an example – an instance of a generalization about women – is to be disgraced.

[3] The fact that the Princesse, after her definitive departure from the Court, spends one half of each year in a "maison religieuse" (395) is one of several reasons to link her with *L'École des femmes* and with Agnès, whom Arnolphe threatens to send to a convent. To me, the most interesting of these reasons is that the grief that causes the death of Monsieur de Clèves is a result of his spying on his wife. In this, he resembles Arnolphe, for whom panoptical control is an obsession. Arnolphe speaks of recruiting spies all over the neighborhood. Monsieur de Clèves also reminds us of Alceste, who believes dubious evidence of Célimène's perfidy, evidence given to him by a kind of spy, and who thereby finds the unhappiness *he has sought*.

[4] These stories resemble, in interesting ways, the tales of women's nefarious influence during the Fronde that Domna Stanton refers to in her "The Fiction of *Préciosité* and the Fear of Women" (see especially 120-22). This supports my suggestion that Madame de Chartres has formed her daughter to be a valuable commodity within the patrarchal order, indeed, to serve as a support for that order. Her pedagogy, in other words, actually makes it impossible for her daughter to be truly exceptional. Mademoiselle de Chartres is formed by the sort of stories that Stanton associates with the cultural and political castration of women.

[5] Again, we encounter the paradox of distinction. Madame de Chartres intends to make her daughter a creature whose superior virtue and value will be evident to all, but, at the same time, she fears most of all that her daughter will become an example, an instance of a generalization. Is it, in fact, possible for a society to perceive value in what truly lies outside its lexicon of generalizations?

[6] I have referred to Stanton's excellent essay on the issue of *préciosité*. My use of the term here does not reflect agreement with the facile, sexist seventeenth-century inventions of ridiculous straw-women for the purpose of dismissing serious interventions by women in culture and politics. I am arguing, in part, that Madame de Chartres's pedagogy, and, to a degree, *préciosité*, reiterate and inculcate in women the same fear of the female that Stanton rightly identifies in "phallocratic" dismissals of serious, knowledgeable women.

[7] In a previous note, I have already mentioned *Le Misanthrope*, so I will, at least peripherally, be evoking more than two of Molière's plays. I must, now, also mention *Les Femmes savantes* and point out that Madame de Chartres resembles Philaminte in teaching her daughter to associate high status with repression of her own body and also, perhaps, in working to deprive her daughter of experiences that she, herself, has enjoyed. I will explore this play later in the essay.

[8] See, for example, my "Pedagogy, Power, and Pluralism in Molière."

[9] It can be argued that the formation of "character," for both men and women, entails internalizing patriarchy, itself.

[10] In making what I think is a closely related point, Jane Marie Todd refers to Michel Foucault's contention that the modern subject, characterized by introspection and self-criticism, is formed by internalizing power (226). It seems to me, then, that the famous *aveu* – which is both a confession and a kind of oath – can be interpreted as a proclamation by the Princesse of both her subjective depth and her commitment to know that depth. The "depths," of course, must be shameful. Internalizing her mother's powerful lessons, then, has linked her pride inextricably to her self-distrust. Here again, we have something very much like what Arnolphe wants to impose on Agnès: he wants Agnès literally to internalize the strictures of the *Maximes du mariage* – "Imprimez-le-vous-bien" (l. 678) – as her subjectivity. Madame de Chartres's lessons similarly make up the fund of examples which amount to internalized proscriptions for her daughter.

[11] Robert S. McElvaine gives a definition of culture that, in my view, complements what Kelly says about teaching: "[Culture] refers to a human practice that intervenes in nature in order to promote certain ends" (85). This definition prompts us to ask, "what is the operative conception of 'nature'?" and "whose ends are to be promoted?"

[12] I believe it is legitimate and instructive to suggest that education, itself, is a kind of seduction. Pedagogy, after all, is persuasion, and, as Kelly argues, persuasion with a view to structuring desire. John D. Lyons's "Epilogue" to Patrick Henry's volume of criticism on the novel includes a passage that is apposite here (239).

[13] Among the other feminist commentators on patriarchy and early modernity in general whose work I have found useful are Val Plumwood and Evelyn Fox Keller. The most persuasive account of patriarchy's origin and evolution that I know is McElvaine's *Eve's Seed: Biology, the Sexes, and the Course of History*.

[14] Here is another dimension of paradox: the virtuous woman must, in effect, desire to be desired, but must not positively desire. She must – like the Princesse – internalize as her "own" subjectivity an imperative to attract male desire and, at the same time, assuage male fears of rivalry by resisting that desire.

[15] Interestingly, and despite her mother's desire to make her exceptional, the Princesse will become the incarnation of a cliché when she accepts moral responsibility for her husband's death, which is really the result of paranoiac male rivalry and of her mother's decision to marry her to a man she cannot love. The rhetoric of seventeenth-century gallantry makes the woman the cause of male love and, therefore, of potentially deadly male rivalries. Steven Rendall's article is useful in this connection. I believe that it is important to point out, too, that Madame de Chartres sets her daughter up to accept moral responsibility for her husband's death by making Madame de Clèves, in a way, responsible for *her* death: she says that she prefers to die rather than to see her daughter fall. This projection onto women of responsibility for men's dangerous desire is, of course, in keeping with much Judeo-Christian theology, notably that of Tertullian (see McElvaine 196-97).

[16] Philippe Desan's superb article on the economy of love in the novel is helpful here, though I do not completely agree with his neat separation of an aristocratic and a bourgeois erotic economics. Desan is right, of course, to argue that the shift to an economy of market relations and endless transactions was a major preoccupation in Madame de Lafayette's time and circle. The relation of this shift to the idea of personal identity is described best, I think, in La Rochefoucauld's *maxime supprimée* 603: "Les rois font des hommes comme des pièces de monnaie: ils les font valoir ce qu'ils veulent, et l'on est forcé de les recevoir selon leur cours, et non pas selon leur véritable prix." The corrosion of virtue and identity by circulation is certainly a theme in the novel. However, the relation between desire and a sense of lack goes beyond market economics. In his analysis of Charles Perrault's "Peau d'âne," Louis Marin says that the proliferation of exchange values concentrates and increases power (187). Thus, it is true that, for a time, the expanding economy of exchange values worked to the advantage of monarchical power.

[17] The first thing that we are told about Mademoiselle de Chartres is that she "attira les yeux de tout le monde" (247). She emerges from isolation directly into the brilliantly lit arena of desire and rivalry.

[18] It is worth remembering that, in its etymology, virtue is closely associated with masculinity.

[19] This, it seems, is what links desire/love tightly to jealousy: insofar as desire in general and desire for a particular person are learned or imitative, it – like virtue – depends on the certainty that the object is also desired by others, was *first* desired by others. Neither the object nor the desire can be entirely one's own.

[20] We should remember that, in *L'École des femmes* and *Le Misanthrope*, sincérité is associated with ignorance and/or malleability in women. In the case of Alceste, it is also associated with rejection of corrupt social communication and flight to a *désert*, just what the Princesse will choose as her last recourse.

[21] Force's *Molière ou le prix des choses* is useful here. Force analyzes both the illusion of spectatorship in Molière and the fact that vision is inescapably an exchange (see especially 52). In this connection, I believe that Arnolphe's desire to tell and to be told

stories of cuckoldry is especially apposite as we examine the issue of stories in *La Princesse de Clèves*.

[22] I agree with Todd, here, up to a point. Todd says that the mother's power is greatly enhanced – made absolute – by her death (229). However, Todd contends that the mother-daughter relationship is portrayed as "pre- or extrasocial...specular communication" (229). It seems clear to me that the relationship is completely conditioned by the social, insofar as Madame de Chartres intends to make her daughter a supremely desirable and valuable object within the social. Here, yet again, we encounter the paradox of distinction. I cannot agree with Todd that Madame de Lafayette is proposing this relationship as an ideal alternative to the social. Perhaps the key point is that Madame de Chartres is, in significant part, playing the role of a father. Her daughter is, in fact, deprived of her mother.

[23] The theme of economy seems relevant again. Madame de Chartres's formation of her daughter in isolation from the Court and on a regime of stories, combined with the intention to make the young woman, thereby, a more spectacular personage at the Court, has produced a double hunger, a double sense of lack: a hunger for stories and a hunger for more knowledge, in the form of stories, of that of which she is ignorant – the Court.

[24] Constant Venesoen draws a connection between the novel and Molière's *Dom Juan*: "Dans *Dom Juan* il [Molière] donne d'avance raison à la Princesse de Clèves qui refuse d'épouser un homme qui, selon elle, ne serait bientôt qu'un mari infidèle" (5). Insofar as this is her motivation, Madame de Clèves seems trapped in the confines of a pedagogy that defines both male and female desire as corrosive, impermanent, and disgraceful. Since her mother has, apparently, succeeded in substituting virtue itself for all other possible objects of Madame de Clèves's desire, withdrawal from relationships is her only option. Again, she winds up in the same "space" to which tyrannical patriarchs consign disobedient wives and daughters. Virtue depends on desire that is permanent only because it is separated from any human object.

[25] Richard Sörman's analysis of Arnolphe's project is very acute. He points out that, in order to control an other's desire, the would-be dominant subject must snuff it out or prevent it from arising, at all. Sörman connects this idea explicitly with pedagogy: "De fait, il est clair qu'Arnolphe s'efforce d'annihiler chez sa pupille tout ce qui èchappe normalement au contrôle des éducateurs – désir, sexualité, pensée, liberté" (59). I would add that Arnolphe's paranoiac fear of cuckoldry is a manifestation of what I have called the paradox of virtue. In order to believe that he has a virtuous wife, he must believe that she is desired by others. Indeed, like Harpagon in *L'Avare*, his sense of the value of his property depends on assuming that others want to steal it. Arnolphe is, like all of Molière's narcissistic solipsists, at odds with himself. If he succeeds, he fails. If Agnès cannot desire, then she cannot desire him. If she is not desirable to others, she cannot be desirable to him. As Chrysalde tells him, there is no love or pleasure without risk and trust. I would also suggest that Sörman may be wrong to think that desire, sexuality, thought and liberty are really inaccessible to ordinary educators.

[26] Mary E. Hawkesworth usefully links the advent of an economy based on commodity production and exchange with hostility to the body and to sensuality, particularly to women's bodies and senses (160). This idea that the regime of exchange requires repression of the body of the person to be exchanged illuminates the pedagogy of Madame de Chartres, as well as that of Arnolphe. Moreover, it supports my suggestion,

in responding to Desan, that this process does not begin with the coming of a specifically bourgeois economy. Under patriarchy, women have always been proto-commodities.

[27] Michael S. Koppisch's analysis of male rivalry in this play is useful. Koppisch argues persuasively that Arnolphe and the young galant, Horace, like all rivals, converge and that Agnès may have less to gain than we may think by choosing to marry Horace (see Chapter 2).

[28] Again, it is interesting to note the similarities between Arnolphe's paranoia and that of both Monsieur de Clèves and Alceste. They are all made incapable of perceiving women clearly, or interpreting correctly what they experience, by pervasive fear. As I have mentioned, they all have recourse to spies, and they all seek confirmation of their worst suspicions.

[29] One must think here of Arnolphe's calling women "animaux" (l. 1579).

[30] Should we ask whether Madame de Clèves is, in any sense, a *sotte*? Has early isolation disabled her for life in society? Does she perceive and come to love real qualities in Nemours, or is he, as Horace is for Agnès, merely the first man to make skillful overtures to her?

[31] Arnolphe reminds us of both Madame de Chartres and Monsieur de Clèves when he invites Agnès to confess to him, as if he were a parodic *Directeur de Conscience*. This is actually the role the Princesse virtually asks her husband to play, after her mother's death. Foucault's idea that confession is integral to modern subjectivity as internalized power surely illuminates the context of Arnolphe's method (Todd 226-28).

[32] Sörman points out that Arnolphe's intention is no less than to have Agnès internalize, through his pedagogy, a conception of what a woman/wife – and therefore she – is (60).

[33] I cannot agree with Venesoen that, in this play, Molière attacks "la femme qui refuse de 'jouer le jeu' du mariage" (46). In order to impute bad motives to Molière, Venesoen has to attribute to Philaminte good motives for which I see no evidence in the play. If, as Venesoen asserts, Philaminte's love of philosophy is an example of "compensations culturelles à un mariage miné," then we must conclude that she is dissatisfied with her husband's weakness. The idea that she becomes "phallic" in order to fill a void left by her husband undermines any contention that she and her disciples are trying to escape the bounds of patriarchal ideology. Indeed, the mind/body distinction that the *savantes* endorse so energetically is the very basis of the worldview that elevates "masculinity" over "femininity."

[34] This distinction, of course, is itself what creates the possibility of hierarchization and thus serves as an instrument of patriarchal denigration of women.

[35] Sörman's study of the links between love and knowledge, and his suggestion that the search for each is a quest for certainty, is particularly apt in his treatment of this play. I would argue that the learned ladies are precisely like Descartes in seeking to find in the mental realm the certainty – and the control – that can never be found or achieved in the natural, bodily, social, erotic realm. This is another reason for seeing similarities among Philaminte, Arnolphe and Madame de Chartres.

[36] Philaminte and her disciples exemplify what Margot Norris calls "pornology": the anti-natural, anti-corporeal bias that mandates investment of libidinal energy in supposedly high cultural artifacts or activities, or in abstract visions of order (11).

[37] See my "Reason's Text as Palimpsest: Sensuality Subverts 'Sense' in Molière's *Les Femmes savantes*."

[38] Daniel Cottom usefully refers to Nietzsche, who called grammar a metaphysical discipline comparable to the reign of God (4).

[39] George Lakoff and Mark Johnson argue persuasively that there is really no such thing as entirely abstract, "disembodied" thought.

[40] Sörman compares the reading – the consumption, as Molière clearly realizes – of literary texts to the familiar desire to know and dominate an object: "Le lecteur désire la consommation du texte et le dévoilement de sa signification, et toute lecture est à ce titre à comprendre comme une espèce de recherche" (74). The illusion of definitive reading of texts is, then, a result of misguided substitution of literature for stubbornly ambiguous human objects of desire.

[41] Descendants of the seventeenth-century women who struggled for cultural influence, the *salonnières*, most notable among whom was Madame de Pompadour, generally achieved influence by sponsoring the careers of male writers and artists (see Goodman).

[42] According to Stanton, "repression and regression set in" under Louis XIV, and women lost what they had gained under his mother's regency (124). The works I have looked at here seem to train a pitiless lucidity on the question of what it means or would mean for women to "gain" in the context of a phallocratic society. If, as Stanton argues, fear of women is connected with the primal fear of losing the mother – the primal love-object – then it is interesting to reflect on the fact that Madame de Clèves, Agnès and Philaminte's daughters are all, in one way or another, deprived of their mothers.

[43] This is a principal focus of my new book, *Molière and Modernity: Absent Mothers and Masculine Births*.

Works Cited

Badinter, Elisabeth. *XY: On Masculine Identity*. Trans. Lydia Davis. New York: Columbia University Press, 1995.

Cottom, Daniel. *Text and Culture: The Politics of Interpretation*. Minneapolis: University of Minnesota Press, 1989.

Desan, Philippe. "The Economy of Love in *La Princesse de Clèves*. In *An Inimitable Example: The Case for The Princesse de Clèves*. Ed. Patrick Henry. Washington, D.C.: The Catholic University Press of America, 1992. 104-24.

Devall, Bill and George Sessions. *Deep Ecology: Living as if Nature Mattered*. Salt Lake City: Gibbs Smith/Peregrine Smith Books, 1986.

Force, Pierre. *Molière ou le prix des choses: Morale, économie et comédie*. Paris: Editions Nathan, 1994.

Gaines, James F., and Michael S. Koppisch, eds. *Approaches to Teaching Molière's* Tartuffe *and Other Plays*. New York: Modern Language Association of America, 1995.

Goodman, Elise. *The Portraits of Madame de Pompadour: Celebrating the Femme Savante*. Berkeley: University of California Press, 2000.

Hardwick, Julie. *The Practice of Patriarchy: Gender and the Politics of Household Authority in Early Modern France*. University Park, P.A: The Pennsylvania State University Press, 1998.

Hawkesworth, Mary E. "From Objectivity to Objectification: Feminist Objections." In *Rethinking Objectivity*. Ed. Allan Megill. Durham: Duke University Press, 1994. 151-77.

Henry, Patrick, ed. *An Inimitable Example: The Case for The Princesse de Clèves*. Washington, D.C.: The Catholic University of America Press, 1992.

Kanner, Allen D. and Mary E. Gomes. "The Rape of the Well-Maidens: Feminist Psychology and the Environmental Crisis." In *Ecopsychology: Restoring the Earth, Healing the Mind*. Eds. Theodore Roszak, *et al*. San Francisco: Sierra Club Books, 1995. 111-21.

Keller, Evelyn Fox. "The Paradox of Scientific Subjectivity." In *Rethinking Objectivity*. Ed. Allan Megill. Durham: Duke University Press, 1994. 313-31.

Kelly, Ursula A. *Schooling Desire: Literacy, Cultural Politics, and Pedagogy*. London: Routledge, 1997.

Koppisch, Michael S. *Rivalry and the Disruption of Order in Molière's Theater*. Madison, N.J.: Fairleigh Dickinson University Press, 2004.

Kuizenga, Donna. "The Princesse de Clèves: An Inimitable Model?" In *An Inimitable Example: The Case for The Princesse de*

Clèves. Ed. Patrick Henry. Washington, D.C.: The Catholic University of America Press, 1992. 71-83.

Lafayette, Madame de. *Romans et Nouvelles.* Paris: Garnier Frères, 1961.

Lakoff, George and Mark Johnson. *Philosophy in the Flesh: The Embodied Mind and Its Challenges to Western Thought.* New York: Basic Books, 1999.

Le Breton, David. *Anthropologie du corps et modernité.* Paris: Presses Universitaires de France, 1990.

Lyons, John D. "Epilogue." In *An Inimitable Example: The Case for The Princesse de Clèves.* Ed. Patrick Henry. Washington, D.C.: The Catholic University of America Press, 1992. 235-55.

McElvaine, Robert S. *Eve's Seed: Biology, the Sexes, and the Course of History.* New York: McGraw-Hill, 2001.

Merchant, Carolyn. *The Death of Nature: Women, Ecology, and the Scientific Revolution.* San Francisco: Harper, 1989.

Miller, Nancy K. "Emphasis Added: Plots and Plausibilities in Women's Fiction." In *An Inimitable Example: The Case for The Princesse de Clèves.* Ed. Patrick Henry. Washington, D.C.: The Catholic University of America Press, 1992.15-38.

Molière, Jean-Baptiste Poquelin. *Oeuvres Complètes,* Paris: Editions du Seuil and The Macmillan Company, 1962.

Norris, Margot. *Beasts of the Modern Imagination: Darwin, Nietzsche, Kafka, Ernst, and Lawrence.* Baltimore: The Johns Hopkins University Press, 1985.

Phelan, Peggy. *Unmarked: The Politics of Performance.* London: Routledge, 1993.

Plumwood, Val. *Feminism and the Mastery of Nature.* London: Routledge, 1993.

Riggs, Larry. "Context and Convergence in the Comedy of Le Misanthrope.*" Romance Notes* 25.1 (1984): 1-5.

_____. *Molière and Modernity: Absent Mothers and Masculine Births.* Charlottesville: Rookwood Press, 2005.

_____. "Pedagogy, Power, and Pluralism in Molière." In *Approaches to Teaching Molière's* Tartuffe *and Other Plays.* Eds. James

Gaines and Michael Koppisch. New York: Modern Language Association of America, 1995. 74-82.

_____. "Reason's Text as Palimpsest: Sensuality Subverts 'Sense' in Molière's *Les Femmes savantes.*" *Papers on French Seventeenth-Century Literature* 54 (2001): 93-103.

Roszak, Theodore, Mary E. Gomes, and Allen D. Kanner, eds. *Ecopsychology: Restoring the Earth, Healing the Mind.* San Francisco: Sierra Club Books, 1995.

Shepard, Paul. *The Others: How Animals Made Us Human.* Washington, D.C.: Island Press/Shearwater Books, 1996.

Sörman, Richard. *Savoir et économie dans l'oeuvre de Molière.* Acta Universitatis Upsaliensis. *Studia Romanica Upsaliensa 62.* Stockholm: Elanders Gotab. 2001.

Todd, Jane Marie. "The Power of Confession: The Ideology of Love in *La Princesse de Clèves.* In *An Inimitable Example: The Case for The Princesse de Clèves.* Ed. Patrick Henry. Washington, D.C.: The Catholic University of America Press, 1992. 225-34.

Venesoen, Constant. *La relation matrimoniale dans l'oeuvre de Molière.* Paris: Lettres Modernes, 1989.

Zimmerman, E. Michael. "The Blessing of Otherness: Wilderness and the Human Condition." In *The Wilderness Condition: Essays on Environment and Civilization.* Ed. Max Oelschlaeger. San Francisco: Sierra Club Books. 245-70.

Didactic Strategies in French Classical Comedy

Perry J. Gethner

Late in the seventeenth century the Italian troupe based in Paris commissioned a motto from the noted neo-Latin poet Jean de Santeul. The result, "Castigat ridendo mores" (It [comedy] corrects manners through laughing), became the best-known formulation of the doctrine that comedy teaches moral lessons and is therefore beneficial to the audience. In the course of the frequent quarrels over the morality of the stage, or lack thereof, which raged throughout much of the seventeenth and eighteenth centuries, many defenders of comedy subscribed to Santeul's claim.[1] Their position may be summarized as follows: comedies accurately portray the vices and follies of current society and hold them up to ridicule; spectators guilty of such behavior can easily recognize themselves in the characters and will be shamed into reforming. It is quite likely that some of the comic playwrights gave mere lip service to the notion that their plays should instruct as well as entertain. After all, financial and popular (as opposed to critical) success depended on giving audiences works that they could enjoy. However, in certain cases playwrights seem to have been quite sincere in their desire to combine utility with delight. This study will examine some of the techniques they used to inculcate moral lessons and try to gauge the success of their comedies as genuine works of art.

The term "didactic strategy" was, of course, not part of the critical vocabulary of the time. I am here using it to designate self-conscious attempts to present a moral lesson either through the plot as a whole or through prominent characters or episodes. I will focus on didacticism that affects the play as a whole, rather than on isolated speeches. As a result, I will pass over such standard conventions as *sententiae* (traditional maxims, deemed universally valid), widely used in sixteenth-century humanist drama and considered so effective as moral lessons that printed editions often directed the reader's attention to them with quotation marks in the margin.[2] However, theorists of the following century criticized the overuse of this convention on aesthetic grounds and sometimes even questioned its moral effectiveness. In any case, these rhetorical ornaments were far more prominent in tragedy than in comedy, where they tended to become trivialized when placed in the mouths of foolish characters, such as pompous pedants.

I

Those who wrote plays for use in schools were the most obviously preoccupied with immediate moral utility and explicit didacticism. Although most school plays were tragedies and those composed for boys were often in Latin, there is one known example of comedies specifically intended for school use: the collection of forty short dramatic proverbs by Françoise d'Aubigné, better known as Mme de Maintenon. As one of the foremost educators of girls in the seventeenth century, the second wife of King Louis XIV was fully convinced of the value of dramatic performances to develop public speaking skills, as well as instilling religious lessons. She commissioned tragedies based on the Old Testament from three professional playwrights, although after things got out of hand with the first production, Racine's *Esther*, she kept the performances private and banned elaborate costumes and scenery. However, she eventually came to realize that a very different type of drama was needed to inculcate specific moral lessons in a manner that would be both engaging and meaningful for her charges. For her older students, she composed a number of conversations that analyzed specific good or bad moral traits, beginning with concrete examples and leading to a general definition of the trait and an explanation of its significance. These dialogues, intended to be read aloud, are not dramatic in any way, and the characters are apparently the very students who were intended to recite them. However, realizing that such conversations were too abstract for younger students, who would also wish for something more entertaining, she borrowed the form of dramatic proverbs.[3]

In this parlor game akin to charades, the plot illustrates a well-known proverb, but the proverb itself is never stated within the text, requiring the audience to guess it.[4] Although the majority of the dramatic proverbs that were eventually published emphasize humor or satire, the fact that they tend to provide concrete demonstrations of good advice meant that the form could lend itself easily to explicit moralizing. Not surprisingly, Maintenon went farther than any other practitioner in emphasizing the didactic function. In fact, she eschewed all the traditional dramatic conventions to focus on the moral issues. As a result, the playlets are closer to moral dialogue than to drama, containing little or no action, and no real character development. In many of them Maintenon treats questions of direct personal interest to her students, such as what life will be like after they leave school, how much liberty (the word occurs with great frequency in the playlets) they can expect in the future, what obligations they will have to their parents, husbands and society at large, and how one needs to behave in order to keep one's reputation. She does not shy away from mentioning potential dangers, and explicitly warns about such unpleasant fates as seduction, domestic abuse, separation, divorce, bankruptcy and social rejection. In addition, she directly addresses a variety of issues connected with money, including the importance of staying within one's budget and the dangers connected with gambling and ostentation; she insists that it is no shame to live in peasant-like simplicity if one cannot afford the trappings of the standard aristocratic life style.

Because of her willingness to sacrifice aesthetic considerations to moral utility, Maintenon jettisons the celebrated three unities. Instead of limiting a playlet to a single action, she often jumps back and forth between two or more contrasting plots that exemplify different aspects of the moral issue at hand. For example, in number 39 ("L'occasion fait le larron") we get three vignettes that illustrate the situation from different angles. A woman who knows that gambling is dangerous is finally pressured to participate in a game and loses a huge sum; another woman, who entrusts to a male friend a large sum that she has won at cards but does not want her husband to find out about, suddenly dies and the friend decides to tell no one and keep the money; an unscrupulous young man (probably a servant) arrives by chance at the preliminary stage of an abduction and appropriates the casket with jewels that the woman lowers out the window. None of these episodes is developed in depth, and there is no epilogue to draw them together, although, to be sure, the moral lesson speaks for itself. Even when there is a more linear plot, Maintenon often juxtaposes, without warning, commentaries on the issue from different groups of people. In the final playlet, "Les femmes font et défont les maisons," which consists of discussions of the contrasting behavior of two noblewomen, neither ever appears on stage. Instead, we hear about their personalities and activities from two perspectives: that of their servants (two maids who are friends discuss the contrasts between their mistresses), and that of their husbands (with the husband of the bad wife represented by a friend). Maintenon also ignores the unity of time, frequently dividing a playlet into two segments, a before and an after. A typical example is number 37 ("Qui compte sans son hôte, compte deux fois"), where a girl is eager to get married in order to escape from her mother, who is very austere and keeps her locked up. She anticipates a life of luxury, pleasure and freedom once she is united to her wealthy fiancé, but soon discovers that he is even stricter and more austere than her mother. The author does not specify how much time has passed, but it is at least several months. As usual, the time of the action is however much is required for her to make her point effectively.

One of the main lessons in Maintenon's proverbs is that people must learn to accept life as it is, not as we would like it to be. In particular, girls must not indulge in daydreams about their future, since most of what happens to us in life is beyond our control and since contentment comes from accepting our obligations gracefully. A particularly direct example of this is number 27, illustrating the proverb "Se disputer de la chape à l'Evêque." Three girls, presumably students at Saint-Cyr, discuss what they plan to do upon leaving school. Mlle Vaudreuil, whose mother plans to place her with a princess, is pleased because she will be at court, where she can enjoy grandeur and honors. Mlle Maisonneuve finds dependence on powerful protectors demeaning, and looks forward to returning home to live with her mother, who will indulge her. Mlle Marville wants to live in a convent but without taking vows, which will allow her to do good works and be respected, while enjoying full liberty. Two older ladies, hearing them argue, intervene and inform the girls that none of the three will get her wish, owing to the dire financial problems facing each of their families. The playlet ends abruptly, without allowing the girls to give vent to their disappointment. A similar warning delivered by the older generation to the younger occurs in number 33, "Toujours pèche qui en prend un." Here a wise middle-aged woman from the provinces, staying temporarily in Paris because of a lawsuit, is introduced to a group of girls, each of whom embodies a kind of wrong thinking. One girl is frivolous and lacks common sense; a second is convinced that life at court is the only worthwhile existence; a third is kind, pious and reasonable, but determined to become a recognized scholar; a fourth esteems only riches. Mme Duceaux patiently explains the flaw in each girl's views. Particularly surprising is the claim that reading can be dangerous unless the book leads to our salvation or our happiness; indeed, the pursuit of knowledge is not inherently good for women, who are required by social convention to keep such talents hidden. Mme Duceaux also debunks the notion that life at court is ideal. Echoing Maintenon's own views on the subject, she declares that life at court is a constant constraint, since one must always disguise one's true feelings, adapt oneself to one's superiors, and sacrifice rest, health and often conscience in order to please them.

I have referred to the dramatic proverbs as comedies, but to what degree are they genuinely comic? Apart from the obvious fact that they deal with non-heroic characters engaged in day-to-day activities, many of them employ devices borrowed from traditional comedy. For instance, there are several examples of tricksters tricked. Perhaps the most startling is in number 32 ("La tricherie en revient toujours à son maître"), where a mother, convinced that male friends, if carefully chosen, are better for a young girl than female friends, especially those of her own age, arranges for her daughter to have private conversations with a respectable middle-aged gentleman. The man turns out to be a hypocrite, who proceeds to fill the girl's head with irreverent and anti-religious ideas. However, his plan to turn the naive girl into a libertine backfires: pressured to take a wife, he has entrusted a friend to choose his bride, with the sole stipulation that she be "sage," and the bride whom the friend eventually selects is none other than his protégée. People who make exaggerated boasts of their abilities or plans are invariably humiliated. A young military officer, a snobbish spendthrift who is unwilling to face serious hardships, returns home in disgrace without making it to the battlefield (number 15). A shrewish wife who, assisted by her temperamental mother, vehemently announces her refusal to accompany her husband to his official post in the provinces, is at the last moment physically dragged into the carriage (number 7). A girl who proposes to engage in a program of extreme austerity, hoping to impress the world with her piety, quickly gives up on it and goes to the opposite extreme, embracing a life of wild pleasure (number 38). People who believe themselves to be safe from misadventure because of confidence in their basic goodness and rationality are ruined by a single imprudent decision, as in the case of a respectable young man who is pressured to accompany a dissolute friend to a gambling den, which is promptly raided by the police (number 25), or a young woman who is persuaded by an unscrupulous friend to accept a box of jewelry and ribbons from a male admirer, who then feels authorized to break into her house and demand an assignation (number 10). There are cases of swindling, theft, fraud and manipulation, some of which go unpunished. In short, although few passages in the playlets could be called funny and the punishments of some of the characters are very harsh, the extensive use of ironic reversals and the constant deflating of characters' expectations definitely link these works to the world of comedy.

One of Maintenon's basic principles is to keep the spectators from empathizing with the characters, whose conduct needs to be judged calmly and objectively. That explains why most of the scenes are so short, and why we constantly skip from one group of characters to another. This technique, however, detracts from aesthetic satisfaction, since Maintenon does not always make it clear from the start who the characters are, and the extremely disjointed nature of many of the playlets can make them confusing at first reading. In addition, the one-dimensional characters are often so colorless that they fail to hold our interest. Few of the characters possess genuine self-knowledge, and most of the foolish ones seem incapable of learning from their mistakes. In many cases, instead of seeing the characters themselves in action, we witness other characters discussing and judging them. In short, it is a type of drama that forces us to focus on the general rather than on the particular and that de-emphasizes its own theatrical character. All in all, though, as pedagogical devices for young students who are intended to develop critical judgment, Maintenon's proverbs seem quite effective.

II

It goes without saying that plays destined for the public stage would employ less obtrusive methods of teaching moral lessons. Playwrights who intended their works to be both staged and published would need to keep a different balance between entertainment and instruction and to avoid overt preaching. They would also feel compelled to observe the three unities and the other main conventions of French classical dramaturgy. As a result, the didactic strategies they tended to adopt restricted the moralistic dimension to specific characters or scenes, while leaving ample room for comic characters and situations.

Perhaps the most obvious technique for introducing moral instruction into a play is to make one of the characters a wise teacher who dispenses good advice. The problem from the comic playwright's perspective is that, even though the recipients of sage advice tend to be foolish, the sages themselves are either totally serious, in which case the scenes in which they appear tend not to be funny, or else they are silly, in which case their advice is discredited, both with the other characters and the audience. Molière, as the pioneer of *comédie de caractère*, a type of comedy dominated by a powerful and incurable maniac, often included a character that later generations have termed the *raisonneur*, whose voice of good sense contrasts with the main character's irrationality. However, as recent scholarship has increasingly emphasized, these characters do not really function as mouthpieces for the author's views or as the voice of absolute wisdom.[5] For one thing, the *raisonneur*, as a descendant of the traditional type character of the pedant or *docteur*, tends to be a pompous and self-impressed individual who speaks at enormous length and fails utterly to convince his interlocutor. In certain instances the character defending good sense or conventional morality actually provokes laughter: Sganarelle in *Dom Juan* is a buffoon who trips over his words and literally falls on his face, while Chrysalde in *L'École des femmes* is a cynic who pushes his arguments to farcical extremes. Even scenes featuring a highly articulate and sensible orator, like Cléante in *Tartuffe*, may generate laughter because of the maniac's hostile or bored response to him. If Molière did indeed believe that his plays were vehicles of moral utility – a view that is not universally held today or in the playwright's own day – then the lessons he intended were neither explicit nor simplistic and would require individual reflection after the performance, rather than rote retention of moral pronouncements made within the text.

It would never have occurred to Molière to make the *raisonneur* into the central character of a comedy, but that is precisely what his one-time enemy Edme Boursault did at the end of the century with a pair of explicitly moralistic plays featuring the fabulist Aesop. In *Les Fables d'Esope* (1690) the title character, who has become chief minister of King Crésus, is sent into the countryside to dispense homespun wisdom and practical advice, while in the sequel, *Esope à la cour* (1701), he counsels mainly the king and his nobles.[6] Esope's principal method is a combination of bluntness and story telling. The goal of introducing a fable into every conversation (and Boursault creates the impression that his hero improvises them to suit the situation), is twofold: to link the specific case to a general principle, and to make the lesson more palatable to the listener, owing to the power of art. The allegory in Esope's tales is so transparent that only the most obtuse listener could fail to make the necessary connection. Admittedly, only those who are already predisposed to virtue embrace his teachings eagerly; those who are hardened in their vices recognize themselves in the fables but get angry at him, rather than agreeing to mend their ways. One example should suffice: when (in the second play) Iphis, the disgraced chief minister, appeals to Esope for assistance and admits to the imprudence of his past behavior, which caused his fall from favor, the fabulist reinforces the lesson with a tale entitled "La Guenon et son maître." In this fable a powerful nobleman allowed all kinds of freedom to a pet ape, whose antics he found amusing, until one day she became too proud and thought she could rip off his mustache, whereupon he beat her and kicked her out of his house. This is a minimally disguised account of the minister's real story: in the course of a feast the king encouraged the guests to name his faults, Iphis was overly frank in his response, and the king banished him from court. However, because the minister displays sufficient contrition, Esope persuades the king to reinstate him, arguing that people who are given a second chance tend to perform better.

There are several additional reasons for Esope's relative success as a moral instructor. First of all, far from being an academic, he is an ordinary person, indeed an ex-slave, and he never allows his new position as royal advisor to cloud his judgment. Moreover, there is no classroom. Those whom Esope counsels tend to be either prior acquaintances who like him, or strangers who come to seek his advice. Although in the first play he often appears harsh and insensitive, in the sequel he is usually more compassionate, and in some cases his kindness is even more persuasive than his fables. The best example of this is the conversion (in the second play) of the envious ministers Trasibule and Tirrène. After their slanders and schemes against Esope have been unmasked and the king has sentenced them to forfeit their goods to their intended victim, Esope startles everyone by forgiving them, restoring their wealth, and requesting a different sentence: they should be made to love him as much as they have hated him. The ministers are so deeply moved that they admit their guilt, declare their admiration of Esope's generosity, and presumably turn into good people.

The closest Boursault gets to a classroom scene is when Esope tries to convert Iphicrate, a retired army general who is genuinely virtuous but does not believe in the gods, accepting instead a version of Epicureanism à la Gassendi (*Esope à la cour*, III, 3). Although the king has urged Esope to work on this esteemed nobleman, it is Iphicrate who takes the initiative in seeking him out, having heard people praise the fabulist's wisdom. Esope combats the general with two arguments: causality (someone must have created the first humans and the whole universe) and fear of the hereafter (if you knew you were going to die within one hour, would you still disbelieve?). Iphicrate is shaken by this reasoning, though not fully persuaded. However, he thinks highly enough of Esope and is sufficiently worried about theology that he sets up a second meeting.[7] It should be obvious that this episode, like many other sections of the play, is far from comic. The more serious tone testifies to Boursault's place in a new generation of comic playwrights who were more concerned with sentiment and moralizing than with laughter and who believed in the possibility of reclaiming or even converting foolish or misguided characters. It also testifies to the author's increasing concern in his later years with trying to reconcile drama and religion. Indeed, he went so far as to consult a theologian, the Theatin priest Caffaro, on the question of whether a playwright could still be a good Christian.[8] There can be no doubt that he wanted his comedies to be genuine vehicles of edification.

Needless to say, the dramatic model that Boursault chose for his Aesop plays contains several serious problems: they are *pièces à tiroirs*, consisting mostly of unrelated episodes tied together only by the presence of the title character; also, it is difficult to make the sage a genuinely interesting figure, rather than a mere spouter of moral platitudes. Feeling it important to show that the sage's good sense also governs his private life, Boursault chose to make Esope's matrimonial prospects his frame in both plays. In the first the provincial governor Léarque, hoping to benefit from Esope's influence with the king, tries to force his daughter to wed the fabulist. Esope pretends to agree to the betrothal, but once he has satisfied himself that the love between the girl and her original fiancé is genuine, he convinces the father to consent to their union. In *Esope à la cour* the title character really does plan to marry: he has found a pretty young fiancée who genuinely loves him and whom he genuinely wants as his wife, but first he needs to cure her of several flaws. Fortunately, because of her reasonable nature and her great respect for him, as well as his preference for persuasion over coercion, she is willing to heed his criticisms, and they are united.

The popularity of Boursault's two plays, which long remained in the repertory, inspired a handful of imitations at rival theaters. The prolific scholar Eustache Le Noble composed a version of his own for the Italian company, entitled simply *Esope* (1691), that retains all the main features of the original (episodic structure, Esope's habit of

improvising a fable to suit every situation).[9] He altered the protagonist's job title from royal minister to judge, though Esope appears in
his professional capacity for less than half of the play. Where Le
Noble's version most conspicuously fails is in the fact that Esope plays
two clashing roles in his private life and handles them both badly. He
has a teenage daughter, Colombine, whose wishes he totally ignores
and whom he betroths to an elderly doctor, simply because that man,
like himself, is a hunchback. At the same time, he has a young and
pretty fiancée, Rodope, an ex-prostitute who has tired of her old life
and now seeks respectability. But instead of treating her with respect,
he is domineering and even forces her to accept a list of marital rules
that accord the wife almost no freedom. By acting like the stereotypical
tyrant, both as father and as fiancé, and by evoking memories of such
irrational Molière characters as Arnolphe and Argan, Esope forfeits our
esteem, revealing how little he is able to incorporate his wise advice
into his private life. Le Noble, eager to include as much farce as possible in order to satisfy the Italian troupe, even arranges to have Esope
outwitted by the two women, culminating in a silly masquerade where
Colombine, pretending to be a rival hunchback doctor, persuades her
father to break his promise to the other doctor and give "him" the
power to choose the girl's husband. Curiously, the comedy also contains a piece of literary satire: Esope, responding to a tasteless sonnet
that a silly poet has composed in honor of his upcoming marriage, tells
a fable to show that all parents, even monkeys, are so blinded by self-
love that they regard their offspring as beautiful.

The only imitation of Boursault to achieve popular success was
Louis Fuzelier's *Momus fabuliste, ou les noces de Vulcain* (1719). Here
the improviser of fables is the jester god, Momus, whose habit of
frankly telling all the other gods, to their face, the truth about their
character and conduct is a constant source of irritation to them. He has
finally provoked the wrath of Jupiter, who threatens to banish him from
Olympus forever unless he stops making satirical comments. Fright-
ened by this threat but unwilling to keep his views to himself, Momus
realizes that he can achieve the same result by using thinly disguised
allegories. He admits that his fables will not change anyone's behavior,
but at least they will allow truths, both general and particular, to get
told. The gods do, in fact, recognize themselves in the fables Momus
devises, though, predictably, their response is to get angry, rather than
thinking of changing their ways. The only character to profit from his
advice is an inexperienced nymph who needs to learn how to be coy

and seductive if she wishes to keep the interest of her fickle lover. Nonetheless, Momus, by explicitly differentiating between satire and moral edification, admits that the primary goal of telling fables is entertainment, not instruction: "on dira peut-être que mes fables ne sont que satiriques...eh! mais, la satire n'est-elle pas instructive & de plus réjoüissante? ma foi fasse des fables purement morales qui le jugera à propos, pour moi, je me garderai bien de prendre ce ton-là, il ne réüssit pas" (sc. 7). The plot, which is, as usual, little more than a pretext for the fables, arises from Destiny's decree that Vénus must choose a husband that day, and each of the male gods shows an interest in her, while all the goddesses are jealous. Vénus finally chooses Vulcain, and Jupiter, after learning that Junon has retired to her room with the vapors after hearing one of Momus's fables, pardons his jester. Fuzelier's comedy could be viewed as more subversive than the earlier fable plays if the satire of the gods was actually intended as a critique of the French aristocracy and even of the royal family – something that would have been too dangerous to present during the Sun King's reign, but was allowable during the more relaxed atmosphere of the Regency.

If the highest success rate for moral instruction is found among moralistic poets, it must be readily admitted that professional philosophers invariably fail as purveyors of wisdom. Indeed, the vast majority of professional teachers found in plays are descended from the stock figure of the pedant, a fixture of medieval and Renaissance comic literature. The majority of these characters possess abundant knowledge that turns out to be mere trivia, have no practical sense, are utterly self-absorbed, constantly mingle Latin words and phrases with their French, and quote classical authors at unnecessary length. Leaving aside episodes where the pedant functions in his standard capacity as teacher of rudimentary subjects, such as Latin grammar, there are a few cases where the teacher tries to counsel an adult on serious matters. The most famous examples are the two philosophers whose advice Sganarelle in Molière's *Le Mariage forcé* (1664) solicits about his proposed marriage. Neither scholar ever addresses the issue, since each quickly gets bogged down in abstract matters unrelated to Sganarelle's problem. The frustrated protagonist finally exacts his revenge for the pomposity, long-windedness and insensitivity of the pedants by administering a sound thrashing to one of them. At the same time, Molière evokes no sympathy for Sganarelle, who refuses to take sound practical advice until it is too late. Not all pedants go to such extremes of self-absorption. But even in a parallel episode in Dorimond's *L'École des cocus*

(1659), when the Docteur really pays attention and gives correct advice, plainly stated, to a fool, the scene retains such stock *lazzi* as having the pedant speak at interminable length and indulge in endless explanations of scholastic terminology. In this play also the interlocutor refuses to heed the sound warning (sc. 2). To the extent that these comedies contain a didactic strategy at all, the lessons would seem to be the need to be a good listener and to apply one's knowledge to the needs of real people in the real world.

A more unusual technique is to have a foolish character read a book by a real philosopher whose wisdom is universally recognized. The incorrigible gambler Valère in Jean-François Regnard's *Le Joueur* (1696) is so distraught over a prolonged losing streak that he orders his valet to grab a book – any book – from his library and read to him in order to calm his nerves. The book chosen, Seneca's treatise on the worthlessness of riches, fits Valère's situation perfectly, but, of course, the young man is completely incapable of profiting from the wise advice it contains; indeed, he is unable to pay attention for more than a few moments at a time. On the other hand, the valuable moral lesson is lost neither on the valet, who explicitly draws the connection between the book and his master's situation, nor on the audience, who get yet another laugh at the title character's expense.

III

The didactic technique most often discussed by theorists of the drama was poetic justice, although curiously the French, unlike the English, never developed a formal name to attach to it. By showing the rewarding of virtuous characters and the punishment of evil characters in the final scenes, playwrights were deemed to convey a suitable moral lesson, indicating how they felt about such types of behavior. Virtually every theoretical defense of drama written in the seventeenth and eighteenth centuries insisted on the key role of the denouement in guaranteeing the moral legitimacy of that art form. The major problem with applying poetic justice to comedy, as opposed to tragedy or tragi-comedy, is that genuinely evil characters are not funny and that to apply severe punishments to them would detract from the light-hearted mood of the comic finale. Nevertheless, poetic justice can apply to comedy in a less extreme form, in that the behavior of ridiculous char-acters exposes them to the scorn of the saner characters (and of the audience) and that they often encounter some form of public humilia-

tion at the play's conclusion. At the same time, the comedies employing this convention tend to be reticent about mentioning its religious
underpinning. Unlike tragicomedies from the first half of the seventeenth century, in many of which the distribution of rewards and punishments is explicitly ascribed to divine providence, the comedies do
not mention God at all at the denouement, in part because of the
increasingly strict code of theatrical *bienséances,* and also because the
comic genre presents an unheroic and less serious picture of humanity.

While reward in comedy typically consists of achieving a
desired marriage or being reintegrated into family or community, it is
not immediately apparent which types of punishments such a play can
administer. Certainly, to condemn a bad character to death would be
inappropriate for the genre. Don Juan is the obvious exception, but
Molière was the only French dramatist to label his treatment of that
subject a comedy. His contemporaries, Dorimond, Villiers and Rosi-
mond, all labeled their versions tragicomedies, no doubt because of the
fact that one or more characters die on stage and because the plot has
so little in common with standard scenarios for comedy.

For the majority of writers, who continued to endorse the
Aristotelian principle that comedy should focus on characters who are
more silly than wicked, the preferred formula for the denouement
involved reconciliation and forgiveness, rather than punishment. Disobedient children and wily servants are typically pardoned, especially
if their misconduct was undertaken in order to advance the cause of
young love. Even unscrupulous rivals may share in the final festivities.
Moreover, most comic playwrights believed that punishments, when
they do occur, must be either humorous (beatings, public humiliation)
or at least involve no lasting physical harm. As the critic Geoffroy
expressed it, "Manquer un mariage, être chassé d'une maison, essuyer
une petite humiliation, voilà les plus grands châtimens que puisse
infliger la folâtre *Thalie.*"[10]

Since, as already noted, the typical reward of the sympathetic
characters in a classical comedy is marriage to one's beloved, failure to
make a desired marriage is indeed a logical punishment. If the eccentric
is young but has a flaw so uncontrollable as to render him or her a
hopeless social misfit, that person is excluded from matrimony and
often banished from the social group. The character's reaction to the
reversal may range from shocked speechlessness to insouciance or
defiance. In some cases, the eccentric is judged insane and confined to
his or her own private dream world. In the most extreme example,

Desmarets de Saint-Sorlin's *Les Visionnaires* (1637), such is the fate of
the entire cast, and no marriages take place. An older man or woman
seeking a much younger partner is almost invariably foiled, forced to
yield to a younger and more suitable rival. Those who accept defeat
gracefully can be integrated into the concluding celebration, whereas
those who find their comeuppance too painful are either driven from
the stage or rush off uttering cries of rage or frustration. An eccentric
who is so imprisoned in his comic personality that he cannot properly
interact with others is likely to become the victim of a practical joke,
which may also constitute a public humiliation. The public disgrace
may even include some physical abuse, especially in the case of brag-
gart soldiers, who ever since the time of Plautus have tended to receive
a thrashing, thus openly revealing their inability to put their protestations of valor into practice. A more severe punishment, used very
rarely, is banishment to a convent. This is invoked only when girls
have disobeyed their parents, or wives have flouted their husbands'
authority, in such a serious way that pardon is deemed to be impossible.

      The most innovative technique of punishment introduced in
seventeenth-century comedy is expulsion from the house, and it was
the brainchild of Molière.[11] By presenting an impostor who succeeds in
entering the home of a well-to-do family and making himself indispensable, in hopes of dispossessing the owners, he allowed for a denouement related to poetic justice: unmasking is now linked to eviction,
which entails the utter collapse of the villain's plans. This denouement
can be perceived as a consequence of another of Molière's innovations:
the explicit link between comedy of character and an indoor setting, as
opposed to the standard outdoor decor of Latin comedy. While Molière
was not the first French playwright to move comedy indoors, he was
the first to grasp its symbolic value. The house becomes a microcosm
of upright, middle-class society, and the malefactor becomes a kind of
housebreaker, aiming to disrupt the lives of the inhabitants, and at
worst, to dispossess and banish them. His expulsion is thus tantamount
to excluding him from the company of all *honnêtes gens*. Tartuffe is
the blackest of these intruders, but Trissotin in *Les Femmes savantes*
and Béline in *Le Malade imaginaire* also plot the domination of their
respective households and the confiscation of all assets, only to be
foiled at the end. The expulsion of the impostors is the immediate
result of a charade in which they are tricked into revealing their true
motives. In those cases where the impostors practice a two-fold decep-

tion (claiming to possess an esteemed trait, such as great piety or erudition, and to feel strong affection for their hosts), the unmasking occurs in two stages. First, they are shown to be a sham in their alleged field of expertise, and only later are their mercenary motives exposed. Moreover, whereas the learned ladies lack the erudition to pierce Trissotin's veneer of learning and poetic skill and Orgon fails to perceive the difference between religious devotion and hypocrisy, they need only their bourgeois common sense to comprehend the personal betrayal.

To be sure, Molière introduced a stricter version of poetic justice into *Tartuffe*, where the title character is sent off to prison. In this case, however, the impostor has run afoul of the king himself: Louis, who, needless to say, never appears on the stage, understands at once that Tartuffe is trying to manipulate him in order to pursue his sinister designs against Orgon, and he quickly recognizes Tartuffe as a man guilty of unspecified but serious criminal behavior in the past. Tartuffe's combined defiance of religious and political authority, combined with transparently insincere protestations of loyalty to both, is certainly one of the reasons why Molière chose such an unusually harsh fate for him.

The majority of the comic characters who go beyond mere silliness into serious immorality are impostors and troublemakers of various kinds, who need to be neutralized, and often expelled, as well. There are, in addition, several other categories of comic characters who are automatically excluded from the concluding marriages and reconciliations of comedy, such as fops, financiers and gamblers; in other words, those who take money too seriously and/or do not take true love seriously enough. The reasons are not hard to find. The comic denouement reinforces the middle-class principles of a stable and faithful marriage based on love and compatibility (hence the need to pair off young people who are "meant for one another") and a proper, but not excessive, regard for money and the material comforts it can provide. The male who views the opposite sex merely as objects of dalliance or exploitation cannot make a suitable husband and father. The same is true of those whose attachment to money is so extreme that it precludes any genuine attachments to other people.

Of the categories listed above, that of fop, also known as *homme à bonnes fortunes* or *petit-maître*, is the least serious and the only one capable, in certain plays, of changing his ways. Marivaux's *Le Petit-maître corrigé* (1734), which gives a succinct statement of their creed: "on nous aime beaucoup, mais nous n'aimons point: c'est notre usage" (I, 3), is also one of the plays where the basic emotion of love, felt for the first time, makes the male coquette turn serious. But even those who do not reform merely undergo the typical unmasking and lose the esteem of a small group of admirers. They may also miss the chance to make an advantageous marriage with a wealthy heiress and may occasionally lose some of their own money in the process. Nevertheless, since dashing young men still maintain their good looks and their attractiveness to women, their careers are presumably far from over. The reaction of the title character of Anne de La Roche-Guilhen's *Rare-en-tout* (1677) is typical. Undaunted by the loss of both of the women he has been courting and by the revelation of his duplicity, he vows to keep traveling from one city to the next, assured that he is irresistible. Even if their motives are strictly mercenary, fops experience no greater punishment than the foiling of their current plans. For example, the adventurer of Dancourt and Saint-Yon's *Le Chevalier à la mode* (1687), who chases after older women in order to wheedle money from them, is totally undismayed to lose the two women with whom he was on the verge of contracting matrimony, fully aware that Paris is filled with gullible women waiting to be deceived. Unless he happens to fall in love for real, there is no reason for him to settle down and join the bourgeois social order. The same is true for female coquettes, who must usually learn to place true love and sincerity above affectation and ephemeral "conquests" before the comic poet will grant them a husband.

The insatiable financier typically receives a severe, but singularly appropriate retribution: having amassed a huge fortune by cheating others, he is himself cheated and loses everything. The punishment is compounded by a two-fold humiliation: he will no longer be able to afford the luxurious lifestyle that he has previously enjoyed, and his lowly social origins, which he has taken great pains to conceal, are made public. His marital plans are foiled, as well, though this setback is less painful to him than the others since he is incapable of genuine love. However, his punishment does not necessarily lead to the reestablishment of a stable moral order. Alain-René Lesage's *Turcaret* (1709), the greatest of the comedies of finance, presents a world where all the characters are dishonest and opportunistic, if in varying degrees, and the audience suspects that the financier's competitors and successors will eventually share his fate.

Florent Dancourt's *Les Agioteurs* (1710) is probably the financier comedy that best fulfils the criteria of poetic justice, in that most of
the other main characters are honest and are allowed to triumph at the
expense of the malefactor. The speculator Trapolin is so devious and
unethical that his godfather, the usurer Zacharie, who originally set him
up in business, looks honest by comparison. Imagining himself to be
attractive to women, Trapolin has accepted a sizable loan from the
wealthy Mme Sara as surety that he will marry her, while at the same
time he has proposed marriage to her beautiful young niece Suzon.
Since the girl seems willing to accept him, he entrusts to her care the
money that he has swindled from his associates. Suzon uses this money
to compensate her beloved Clitandre, whose notes Trapolin has cal-
lously refused to repay. In the final act Trapolin is completely ruined,
undone by overconfidence both in his superior business acumen and in
his personal charm, which prove equally illusory. Even his godfather,
who assumes the promise to wed Mme Sara, is content to let him
flounder. Dancourt arranges the presence of honest characters in this
play through the coincidence of Trapolin's lodging in the same building as Mme Sara, presumably an *hôtel garni*, which might also explain
how her late husband came to be a business partner of Zacharie. The
hôtel lacks the social and moral cohesiveness of a home, since it allows
a wide variety of people to meet under the same roof. Significantly, at
the end of *Les Agioteurs* all the residents move out: Mme Sara and
Suzon will, of course, go with their husbands, and Trapolin will probably have to return to the country.

Misers, unlike financiers, devote all their energies to hoarding
money, rather than to accumulating more of it. Their stinginess has a
harmful effect only on themselves and their families, which means that
they do not constitute a serious threat to society as a whole. Provided
that their power over the family is neutralized at the end, thus allowing
the children to marry suitable partners and lead normal lives, no punishment need be inflicted upon them. In fact, Harpagon in Molière's
L'Avare (1668), the most famous of dramatic misers, is so close to
insanity and so incapable of affection for others that he accepts with
complete indifference the multiple defeats he experiences at the play's
end: the frustrating of his grotesque plan to remarry, the fact that his
children have lost all respect for him, and the probability that they will
have little to do with him in the future now that a new and more suitable father figure (Anselme, the long-lost father of Valère and Mari-
ane) has been found. Even the theft of his treasure, which drives him

into a horrifying frenzy at the end of the fourth act, is never perceived by him as a punishment, although the audience might well consider it as a symbolic retribution for his idolatrous worship of a material object. Instead, he views himself as a victim of cosmic injustice, for which the appropriate solution is to call out for an army of executioners to hang the entire city! Once he recovers his "chère cassette," he permanently withdraws into the world of his private mania.

Compulsive gamblers, another group that places inappropriate value on money, resemble the characters of tragedy in that gambling is presented as a fatal, uncontrollable passion.[12] However, it is also an unheroic, petty, contemptible passion, which disqualifies it from tragic status. It is equally alien to the happy ending of comedy, for gambling, when it becomes a mania, is in total opposition to the virtues of ordered society, with its emphasis on close family ties, moderation and stability. Unlike the impostor and the seducer, the gambler is not interested in scheming or, for that matter, in any kind of planning ahead. He believes in luck, convinced that it is on his side – if not now, then at some future time. This self-delusion encourages selfishness, even insolence when luck favors him, whereas a losing streak induces indignation against fortune or insincere promises to reform. The gambler is not, of course, concerned with money for its own sake, as are the misers or financiers: it is the game itself that fascinates him to the point of monopolizing his whole life. While this makes him rather unstable psychologically and blatantly irresponsible morally, it is not the chief reason for his exclusion from the standard comic denouement. Like the fop, but out of reflex rather than calculation, the young male gambler toys with women and with love, and because of his lack of seriousness he will lose the girl in the end. Regnard's *Le Joueur*, the most famous of the gambler plays, ends in a singular way: Angélique, though madly in love with the title character Valère, finally realizes that he is incapable of any genuine affection, dismisses him and agrees to marry his middle-aged uncle. The young man has seemed, at least some of the time, to be very fond of Angélique, but he loses her without the slightest regret and leaves the stage with an expression of hope that his luck at cards will change. This suggests that he will probably never reform and deserves to rank with the many other comic characters too obsessed with their own private manias to be concerned about their exclusion from ordinary society.

As in the case of impostors, the treatment accorded to gamblers varies with their sex and age. The older fanatics of gambling are shown as grotesque and practically insane, neglecting not only their basic responsibilities but even such physical needs as food and sleep. A long-term veteran of the gambling tables will sometimes turn into a card-sharper: such characters, like the impostor, are invariably unmasked and expelled, losing their money in the process. The type of gambler singled out for unusually drastic punishment is the married woman. Her husband has the right to repudiate her for disrupting the household and its finances, and for neglecting her basic responsibilities to spouse and children. This special vindictiveness can be justified in part by the somewhat disreputable company that tended to frequent the private "Académies" and by the risk of adultery. No cases of conjugal cheating are shown in these comedies, but there are occasional allusions to that danger as early as Molière's *L'École des femmes* (I. 1). One of the characters in Dancourt's *La Désolation des joueuses* (1687) insists that the officials responsible for the newly enacted ban on lansquenet have acted too hastily, and lists the following among the unfortunate consequences which have not been properly considered: "Une dame recevait-elle un bijou considérable de quelque amant, le mari n'avait rien à dire, sa femme l'avait gagné au lansquenet" (sc. 10).

The penalties are stiffest in Raymond Poisson's *Les Femmes coquettes* (1671), where the women are shipped off to a convent by their irate husbands. The main character, Flavie, while not guilty of any crime, has been shrewish to her long-suffering husband, has obtained a large amount of money from her wealthy uncle by pretending that she delights in making frequent charitable donations, spends huge sums on frivolous pursuits, especially gambling, and enjoys indulging in malicious little games with her friends. In the last act the men hide in a closet in order to overhear the proceedings at her all-female dinner party, for which she has prepared a "mets exquis" - in fact, a plate filled with gold coins for the guests to take and spend. It is a perfect symbol of Flavie's indifference to social norms and even to religion, since she has been pretending to be a kind of saint. The husband's vengeance (a word that rarely occurs in comic denouements) does contain an element of poetic justice, since her deportation to a remote and austere cloister will turn her unscrupulous sham of religiosity into a reality.

What distinguishes the married female gamblers from the handsome young men like Valère is, as already noted, the fact that the comic ending consecrates marriage and the family as a stable social institution. Valère, by remaining celibate, harms only himself by gambling and cannot interfere with the institution, whereas Flavie the home-wrecker must be dealt with in a more severe way. Unless she is able to reform, the marriage must be dissolved. A third possibility of harm is when a parent's gambling threatens to ruin the child's future. Thus, Mme Orgon, the title character of Charles Rivière Dufresny's *La Joueuse* (1709), gambles away her daughter's dowry, but in a delightfully improbable twist, the girl's clever fiancé, knowing her to be an inept player, manages to win the entire sum from her at cards and then restores it to the daughter. Although Mme Orgon goes unpunished at the end, her marriage to M. Orgon is unalterably shattered: the two already inhabit separate parts of the house and, because of the different hours they keep, they almost never meet. It is also true that she has intermittent periods of sanity, when her conduct is reasonable and her maternal instincts revive, but the arrival of a gambling partner suffices to dispel those moments.

If comedy is the genre of laughter and levity, there are things nonetheless that it holds sacred and cannot allow to be flouted with impunity. Especially in an absolutist age, there could be no tolerance for those who failed to respect the basic social, moral, political and religious conventions. Violators are (in most cases literally) shown the door, and those with power must be stripped of it, with those posing the greatest threat suffering the most spectacular reversals. This phenomenon would become more accentuated during the eighteenth century, as a shift occurred in the conceptualization of comedy. A number of playwrights and theorists, including such influential figures as Destouches, Mercier and Restif de la Bretonne, would in fact propose that the genre move away from ridiculous characters and focus instead on those who are odious and even depraved. The aesthetic danger, as they failed to perceive, was that plays whose bad characters pose a genuine challenge to the basic norms of society are not comic and bear a greater resemblance to the villains of the emerging genre of melodrama.

It should be noted that, although in the vast majority of cases the punishment of the incorrigible eccentric or villain is deemed self-sufficient as a moral lesson, there are occasional instances where the characters explicitly proclaim the moral in the final lines, either to one another or to the audience. Condemnation when placed in the mouths of servants risks appearing tongue-in-cheek, as in the concluding lines of Pierre Corneille's *Le Menteur* (1644), which betray the playwright's own ambivalence toward his protagonist: "Comme en sa propre fourbe un menteur s'embarrasse! / Peu sauraient comme lui s'en tirer avec grâce. / Vous autres qui doutiez s'il en pourrait sortir, / Par un si rare exemple apprenez à mentir" (ll.1801-4). Admission of one's own folly tends to sound more convincing, as in the final speech of Catherine Durand's fourth dramatic proverb (1699), where a pair of coquettes and a pair of fops discover that each has been playing the same game against all the others: "Juste retour des choses d'ici-bas! chacun de nous voulait tromper, et a été trompé à son tour. Adieu, Messieurs; allez essayer si la fidélité vous réussira mieux, et nous ferons la même épreuve" (sc. 12). An unusually dark self-critique occurs in the final speech of Molière's *George Dandin* (1668), where the title character admits both his own folly and the likelihood that his life is irretrievably ruined: "Ah! je le quitte maintenant, et je n'y vois plus de remède; lorsqu'on a, comme moi, épousé une méchante femme, le meilleur parti qu'on puisse prendre, c'est de s'aller jeter dans l'eau la tête la première" (III, 8).

IV

Another possible approach to the staging of moral edification is to show foolish characters enlightened or even reformed by watching the bad examples set by others, depicting mimetically the effect that the play is supposed to exert on the thoughtful viewer. The internal spectacle may take the form of a stratagem or of a play-within-a-play. The former technique is a mainstay of comic plots and was especially beloved of Molière. In its most common form the sane characters arrange for the foolish character to overhear a compromising conversation, or else the deceiver is manipulated into betraying his or her true feelings or motives by a character that arrives in disguise or tells a deliberate falsehood. Stratagems never work as a device of moral reform, since the internal spectators learn to recognize other people's faults, but not their own. The other technique, however, is extremely rare. Indeed, the only play of the seventeenth century in which an on-stage spectator reforms as the direct result of watching a play is a tragicomedy, Gillet de la Tessonerie's *Le Triomphe des cinq passions* (1642). In this intriguing baroque work, a young Athenian, admitting at the outset that he is guilty of five serious vices, goes to a magician to request a cure. The latter obliges by summoning up the spirits of historical figures who embodied each of those vices and who in each case perished miserably because of them. After viewing the five intercalated tragedies, the hero announces that he is cured, and presumably goes on to become a paragon of virtue. Gillet would go on to write a second tragicomedy along the same lines, *L'Art de régner* (1645), where a wise governor, entrusted with the education of a young prince, shows his charge five playlets demonstrating the good or bad behavior of kings of yesteryear. However, since the prince appears to be virtuous already, the purpose seems to be more reinforcement than conversion.

Of course, reform is possible only when the person is willing to admit to his or her shortcomings and wishes to do something about them. Such is emphatically not the case in the satirical comedy *Elomire hypocondre* (1670) by Le Boulanger de Chalussay. This scathing attack against Molière shows the great playwright, renamed Elomire (an anagram of his real name) seeking medical attention for his physical and mental disorders. Among the remedies prescribed by the physicians is viewing a comic play, and the work Elomire is made to watch, "Le Divorce comique," dramatizes his problems directly. In this intercalated playlet Elomire confronts a mutiny by the members of his troupe, who force him to own his faults as man, as director, and as playwright, and to agree to reform in all three areas (IV, 4). Some of those failings are ethical in nature: his arrogant treatment of his colleagues, his hypocritical refusal to acknowledge his lowly origins and unsavory past, and his use of indecent language and immoral situations in his plays. But Elomire the spectator is infuriated rather than chastened; instead of taking the lessons to heart, he vows revenge against the doctors. Significantly, he denies none of the charges leveled against him, but neither will he openly admit them. In fact, throughout the entire play he refuses to reveal his real identity, although the doctors know it from the outset. As a technique of persuasion for characters on the stage, the play-within-a-play achieves its sole successes in comedies where older men who object to the acting profession find that they have misjudged it and become reconciled to family members who have embraced it. However, the changes of heart found in Corneille's *L'Illusion comique*, Georges de Scudéry's *La Comédie des comédiens* and Philippe Quinault's *La Comédie sans comédie* have little in common with moral reformation.

Not until 1737 will a French playwright attempt to dramatize the motto "Castigat ridendo mores" by means of an intercalated spectacle. In Barthélemy Fagan's *Les Originaux*, the last in a set of three one-act comedies collectively entitled *Les Caractères de Thalie*, we see a character who recognizes his own faults after observing them in a group of his acquaintances and agrees to reform. Fagan does not actually use the play-within-a-play technique, which had fallen out of favor by the end of the seventeenth century, but his plot bears an unmistakable resemblance to it. When the widowed Marquise expresses concern about the degree to which her son, the Marquis, has been recently corrupted by the vices of elegant society, her close friend and soon-to-be fiancé, the Chevalier, undertakes to cure the young man. The plan is to have him meet with five visitors, each of whom embodies one of the Marquis's vices, but carried to an extreme. Not only does the Chevalier believe that his method will be more effective than a direct rebuke; he also explicitly compares his stratagem to a play, with the further comment that he finds little difference between the stage and real life.

The exposition provides several reasons why this effort at reformation is likely to succeed. Firstly, the young man's vices are completely artificial: far from representing his true nature, they were adopted under peer pressure. This fundamental change in the nature of the comic protagonist is one of the hallmarks of eighteenth-century sentimental comedy. No longer a prisoner of a dominant "humeur" or "caractère," he or she has become foolish by subscribing to the mores of a foolish and corrupt society. Similarly, it is not surprising that by Fagan's generation the majority of comic protagonists come from the aristocracy, rather than from the upper middle class, as was the norm in previous centuries. Because of his inherent nobility, the aristocrat was thought to possess both the innate virtue and the strong will to acknowledge faults and to change.

Secondly, the Marquis is genuinely in love with Hortense, the beautiful young woman whom his mother has selected as his bride, although he has recently, under the influence of court foppery, begun to treat his fiancée with coldness and to affect disdain for marriage. The final realization of his deep love for Hortense is indispensable to his ultimate reformation. Indeed, as has already been shown, it is precisely the triumph of true love over such artificial snobbery that allows for the conversion of the *petit-maître* or coquette in a number of comedies by Fagan's contemporaries, whereas those characters whose fickleness and selfishness are so ingrained that they are incapable of genuine love and commitment are prevented from marrying and banished from the comedy's final reconciliation. It is significant that even in the so-called Age of Reason only a blend of reason and sensibility could effect a genuine moral conversion that audiences could take seriously.

Each of the five vices needing to be corrected (ignorance, carousing, malicious gossip, dueling, callous treatment of women) is exemplified by an eccentric who makes a single appearance and then disappears from the play; none of these two-dimensional figures elicits the slightest sympathy from the other characters or the audience. The interviews form a loose type of progression, starting with a man whom the Marquis knows only slightly, continuing with three people whom he knows reasonably well but whose faults he has failed to notice before, and ending with a good friend whom he has greatly admired in the past, only to be undeceived now. The young man never suspects that the procession of "originaux" has been carefully arranged, since all the visitors have perfectly plausible reasons for their arrival. Moreover, none of the visitors is aware of being used by the Chevalier as part of a scheme to reform the Marquis. The result is that, with no thought of role-playing, they act in the most natural (that is, the most foolish) manner.

The first visitor should suffice as an example of Fagan's method. The Sénéchal, who is in the service of the Marquise, arrives to compliment the young man on his impending marriage. Upon noticing a copy of *Télémaque* in the room, he admits to being puzzled by the strange name, having heard of neither the novel nor the mythological character. He then proceeds to relate how, when he was received into his position, he made a mess of the learned discourse he was required to deliver, filled with fancy words and Latin phrases. At first the Marquis, who prides himself on never having learned Latin either, is merely amused. But he is shocked when the older man makes a conspicuous error in a verb conjugation, exhibits faulty knowledge of French geography and history, and wishes for the revival of polygamy, which in his account existed only two or three centuries earlier. At the end of the scene the Marquis, appalled by such total ignorance on so many subjects, is forced to conclude: "Il est certain que l'ignorance, poussée à cet excès, a quelque chose de honteux" (sc. 5). After the fourth visit he begins to make the connection with his own behavior: "Seroit-il possible que j'eusse quelque ressemblance à ce que je viens de voir, et à tout ce que j'ai vu aujourd'hui? Si cela étoit, en vérité, je serois bien haïssable" (sc. 14). By the end of the final visit he openly acknowledges his faults to his mother and fiancée, promises to mend his ways, and blames his unworthy behavior on "faux airs" that have turned him away from his true nature (sc. 17).

The incompatibility between *comédie de caractère* and sentimental comedy begs a crucial question: if the essence of someone's
personality is an all-consuming vice, in what sense does he remain the
same person if he reforms? Can the leopard change its spots and remain
a leopard? The answer that Fagan seems to give in his play is that once
the comic protagonist becomes a three-dimensional human being with
a wide variety of traits, the process of reformation requires not a total
metamorphosis, which audiences tend to find unbelievable, but rather a
modification of only certain parts of that person's conduct. The essence
can remain the same, provided that the individual has enough common
sense to recognize that some specific areas need improvement. One
might even argue that the more foolish traits a character possesses, the
easier it is to recognize them as such and to correct them. It can hardly
be a coincidence that in Fagan's day the great masterpieces of Molière
were falling out of favor with audiences, just as the theory of *caractères* on which they were based was losing its appeal for dramatists.

How seriously did eighteenth-century spectators take the moral
conversion shown in this comedy, especially the highly optimistic doctrine of human perfectibility that provides the moral underpinning for
it? At least some of them appear to have been convinced, judging from
this statement from the theater historians La Porte and Clément:
Fagan's play was well received, in large part "grâce à ses excellents
traits de morale, ingénieusement accommodés au Théâtre, et exposés
tantôt avec une sérieuse et aimable élégance, tantôt avec des agréments
satiriques."[13] Others accepted the basic premise of the play but faulted
the execution, on the grounds that a person with so many vices to correct would need far more time and serious reflection to cure himself
fully of them.[14] Still others delighted in the witty dialogue and the
procession of droll caricatures, but rejected the moralistic focus. Such
an attitude must have inspired Dugazon, a leading actor at the
Comédie-Française, when he undertook to revise the play in 1802,
adding three new scenes, radically rewriting others, and totally eliminating the moral lessons. Perhaps after the upheavals of the French
Revolution Paris audiences could no longer be expected to identify
with aristocratic libertines or to care whether they could be reclaimed.
On the other hand, it is possible that even in previous generations the
play's popularity depended solely on the procession of "originaux" and
not on the moral dimension, and that Dugazon, realizing this, was simply making more explicit the comedy's chief asset. Furthermore, it

suggests that by 1800 the mode of tearful comedy, with its overt moralizing and unabashed display of sensibility, was falling out of favor.

The foregoing discussion suggests that during the course of the seventeenth and eighteenth centuries the notion of didacticism in comedy underwent repeated modifications. If in Molière's day the presentation of moral issues was generally nuanced and discreet, Boursault helped lead the way toward a more preachy type of play, allowing both for increased pathos and for Enlightenment-inspired optimism about human perfectibility. During the early decades of the eighteenth century there was an unstable situation as playwrights tried to find a middle ground that would sacrifice neither amusement nor explicit moralizing, but by mid-century tearful comedy, often including general comments about virtue and vice, had begun to supplant laughing comedy in popularity. During the latter part of that century there was likewise an increasing belief in the didactic powers of literature, and authors such as Mme de Genlis would write collections of plays aimed specifically at promoting the moral education of the young. (Unlike Mme de Maintenon, however, Genlis destined her moralistic comedies and works of fiction for a wide audience and published them.) It is far from clear how many dramatists took seriously the view that they had a mission as moral teachers, and how many were merely following shifts in popular taste.[15] In any case, apart from Boursault and the authors of school plays, comic playwrights, even the most moralistic of them, seem not to have felt much concern about the relationship between art and religion and approached morality from a purely secular angle. At the very least, all the authors discussed here shared one fundamental belief: if comedies could, whether by explicit preaching or by social satire, force audiences to think seriously about flaws in themselves and the world around them, then the genre had to have a beneficial effect on society.

Notes

[1] For an overall history of the objections to the stage from Plato to the present day, see Barish. For a detailed history of the quarrels over drama in France in the early modern period, see Barras and Thirouin.

[2] On the history of the *sententia* as a dramatic device, see Scherer. More recent studies include Garofalo.

[3] Maintenon never intended these works for publication. They survived in manuscript and were printed in 1829 by L.-J. Monmerqué. The date of composition cannot be established with precision. References to them in her letters and in the memoirs of former students of Saint-Cyr suggest that she began writing the proverbs prior to 1703, and several passages in the playlets apparently allude to events in 1701 and 1708. It is possible, however, that they were composed gradually over a long period, extending from around 1695 to 1715. Four of the proverbs were reprinted by Gréard in his collection of Maintenon's writings on education. See also Brown and Plagnol-Diéval.

[4] For a history of this subgenre, see Brenner. I agree with Brenner that Maintenon is unlikely to have known the very first collection of dramatic proverbs to be printed, that of Catherine Durand in 1699. I have reedited Durand's playlets in volume 2 of my anthology.

[5] See, most notably, Herzel and Peacock.

[6] Following the appearance of the sequel, the first play became popularly known as *Esope à la ville*. There is a modern edition of it by Terence Allott. For a useful analysis, see Ravel.

[7] This scene was suppressed in performance, apparently out of concern that church officials would object to letting such a sensitive subject be publicly discussed.

[8] Even though Caffaro's reply provided only a lukewarm endorsement of the theater (overtly didactic plays are allowable for Christians, but only if they are read and not seen staged), the publication of his letter in 1694 (which Boursault apparently did without obtaining his permission) touched off a firestorm that resulted in a vehement rebuttal by Bossuet and harsh punishment of the priest from Church officials.

[9] On this author, see the articles by Hourcade. Le Noble had a genuine fascination with Aesop and would reuse him as a character in some of his satirical and moralistic works. He would also compose fables throughout his career.

[10] Lettre 21 in the periodical *L'Année littéraire*, 1784, I: 305.

[11] For a fuller treatment of Molière's innovative treatment of stage settings, see my article in *Theatre Journal*.

[12] For a detailed treatment of gamblers in French comedy, see Alvarez-Detrell and Paulson. This volume also includes an edition of Poisson's *Les Femmes coquettes*.

[13] Quoted in Clerc, 21.

[14] This was the judgment of the translator of the 1799 Venice edition of the comedy. In addition to criticizing the unnatural rapidity of the foolish characters' arrival and of the Marquis's conversion, he faulted the conception of several of the fools, found Hortense boring, and considered the whole idea of episodic comedy to be a mistake. Clerc reprints this essay (211-14).

[15] One of the main reasons why it is so difficult to assess the sincerity behind the rhetoric of dramatic didacticism is the way the debate was framed at the time. The most

extreme of the theologians who attacked the stage claimed that all worldly entertainments were inherently immoral and constituted a danger to proper Christian life. This meant that all plays were wicked, regardless of their content. Thus, playwrights who presumably would have preferred to argue merely that plays are innocent recreation found themselves pressured into claiming that their works genuinely taught moral lessons and could make the spectators into better people. They may have felt uncomfortable with such a position, but the alternative would have been to let their critics go unanswered.

Works Cited

Primary Sources

Boursault, Edme. *Théâtre de feu Monsieur Boursault.* 3 vols. Paris: Compagnie des Libraires, 1746.

_____. *Les Fables d'Esope.* Ed. Terence Allott. Exeter: University of Exeter Press, 1988.

Corneille, Pierre. *Le Menteur.* In *Œuvres complètes.* Vol. 2. Ed. Georges Couton. Paris: Gallimard, 1984.

Dancourt, Florent, *La Désolation des joueuses, Le Chevalier à la mode, Les Agioteurs.* In *Théâtre du XVIIe siècle.* Vol. 3. Ed. Jacques Truchet and André Blanc. Paris: Gallimard, 1992.

Desmarets de Saint-Sorlin, Jean. *Les Visionnaires.* In *Théâtre du XVIIe siècle.* Ed. Jacques Scherer and Jacques Truchet. Vol. 2. Paris: Gallimard, 1986.

Destouches, Philippe Néricault. *Œuvres de théâtre.* 5 vols. Paris: Prault père, 1745.

Dorimond [Nicolas Drouin]. *L'École des cocus.* In *Farces du Grand Siècle.* Ed. Charles Mazouer. Paris: Librairie Générale Française (Livre de Poche), 1992.

Dufresny, Charles Rivière. *La Joueuse.* In *Œuvres.* 4 vols. Paris: Briasson, 1747.

Durand, Catherine. *Comédies en proverbes.* In *Femmes dramaturges en France (1650-1750), Pièces choisies.* Vol. 2. Ed. Perry Gethner. Tübingen: Gunter Narr, 2002.

Fagan, Barthélémy. *Théâtre de M. Fagan, et autres œuvres du mesme auteur.* Paris: N. B. Duchesne, 1760.

Fuzelier, Louis. *Momus fabuliste, ou les noces de Vulcain.* Paris: Pierre Simon, 1719.

Genlis, Stéphanie-Félicité. *Théâtre à l'usage des jeunes personnes.* 5 vols. Paris: M. Lambert, 1785.

Gillet de la Tessonerie. *L'Art de régner.* Ed. P. E. Chaplin. Exeter: University of Exeter Press, 1993.

_____. *Le Triomphe des cinq passions.* Paris: Quinet, 1642.

La Roche-Guilhen, Anne, *Rare-en-tout.* In *Femmes dramaturges en France (1650-1750), Pièces choisies.* Ed. Perry Gethner. Vol. 1. Paris, Seattle, Tübingen: Biblio 17, 1993.

Le Boulanger de Chalussay. *Elomire hypocondre.* In *Œuvres complètes* by Molière. Vol. 2. Ed. Georges Couton. Paris: Gallimard, 1971. 1231-86.

Le Noble, Eustache. *Esope.* Paris: G. de Luynes, 1691.

Lesage, Alain-René. *Turcaret.* In *Théâtre du XVIIIe siècle.* Ed. Jacques Truchet. Vol. 1. Paris: Gallimard, 1972.

Maintenon, Françoise d'Aubigné de. *Extraits de ses lettres, avis, entretiens, conversations, et proverbes sur l'éducation.* Ed. Octave Gréard. Paris: Hachette, 1885.

_____. *Proverbes inédits.* Ed. M. de Monmerqué. Paris: J.-J. Blaise, 1829.

Marivaux, *Le Petit-maître corrigé.* Ed. Frédéric Deloffre. Geneva: Droz, 1955.

Mercier, Louis-Sébastien. *Du Théâtre ou nouvel essai sur l'art dramatique.* Geneva: Slatkine, 1970. (Original edition: Amsterdam, 1773)

Molière, Jean-Baptiste Poquelin de. *Œuvres complètes.* 2 vols. Ed. Georges Couton. Paris: Gallimard, 1971.

Regnard, Jean-François. *Le Joueur*. In *Théâtre du XVIIe siècle*. Vol. 3. Ed. Jacques Truchet and André Blanc. Paris: Gallimard, 1992.

Restif de la Bretonne, Nicolas. *La Mimographe, ou Idées d'une honnête femme pour la réformation du théâtre national*. Amsterdam: Chamguion, 1770.

Secondary Sources

Alvarez-Detrell, Tamara and Michael G. Paulson. *The Gambling Mania on and off the Stage in Pre-revolutionary France*. Washington, D.C.: University Press of America, 1982.

Barish, Jonas. *The Anti-theatrical Prejudice*. Berkeley and Los Angeles: University of California Press, 1981.

Barras, Moses. *The Stage Controversy in France from Corneille to Rousseau*. New York: Institute of French Studies, 1933.

Brenner, Clarence D. *Le Développement du proverbe dramatique en France et sa vogue au XVIIIe siècle*. Berkeley: University of California Press, 1937.

Brown, Penny. "Rehearsing the Future: Madame de Maintenon's *Proverbes dramatiques* for the Demoiselles at Saint-Cyr." *Seventeenth-Century French Studies* 26 (2004): 209-18.

Clerc, Albert. *Barthélemi-Christophe Fagan, auteur comique 1702-1755: Contribution à l'histoire de la comédie en France au XVIIIe siècle*. Paris: E. de Boccard, 1933.

Garofalo, Elena. "Forme majeure et forme mineure de l'écriture tragique: Le raisonnement sententieux chez Corneille et Racine." *Littératures classiques* 51 (2004): 91-103.

Gethner, Perry. "The Role of Decor in French Classical Comedy." *Theatre Journal* 36 (1984): 383-99.

Grégoire, Vincent. "Avatars de la pratique théâtrale adoptée par Mme de Maintenon à Saint-Cyr." *Papers on French Seventeenth-Century Literature* 46 (1997): 35-52.

Herzel, Roger. "The Function of the Raisonneur in Molière's Comedies." *MLN* 90 (1975): 564-75.

Hourcade, Philippe. "Eustache Le Noble, au(x) hasard(s) de la polygraphie." *Littératures classiques* 49 (2003): 265-80.

_____. "Esope à la scène." In *Hommage à Jean-Pierre Collinet*. Ed. Jean Foyard and Gabriel Taverdet. Dijon: Association bourguignonne de dialectologie et d'onomastique, 1992. 185-92.

Peacock, Noël A. "The Comic Role of the Raisonneur." *Modern Language Review* 76:2 (1981): 298-310.

Plagnol-Diéval, Marie-Emanuelle. *Madame de Genlis et le théâtre d'éducation au XVIIIe siècle*. Oxford: Voltaire Foundation, 1997.

Ravel, Jeffrey. "Language and Authority in the Comedies of Edme Boursault." *Papers on French Seventeenth-Century Literature* 28 (1988): 177-99.

Scherer, Jacques. *La Dramaturgie classique en France*. Paris, Nizet, 1950.

Thirouin, Laurent. *L'Aveuglement salutaire. Le réquisitoire contre le théâtre dans la France classique*. Paris: Champion, 1997.

Behind Closed Doors:
Theater, Pedagogy and the *"Crisis"* of Esther

Anne L. Birberick

In 1686, the institution of Saint-Cyr opened its doors to the first class of *demoiselles*, leading *Le Mercure galant* to comment in its pages,

> Quel bonheur, pour nous aussi bien que pour les Français qui nous suivront, que Dieu nous ait donné un monarque qui, outre le nombre infini de grandes choses qu'il a faites pour la gloire des peuples et pour leur utilité, en a fait trois dignes de sa grandeur [...]. Vous les trouverez dans l'établissement des Invalides, dans celui des compagnies de jeunes gentilhommes [...] et dans celui de Saint-Cyr [...]. Quant à l'établissement de la maison de Saint-Cyr, il donne aussi lieu à la noblesse de servir le roi pusique les pères qui auront les filles dans cette communauté, étant déchargés de la dépense à laquelle les engagerait l'obligation de les faire instruire selon leur naissance, seront plus en pouvoir de servir le roi avec leurs fils.[1]

Always astute in the politics of flattery, it is not surprising *Le Mercure galant* should praise the king for the establishment of the new school and his financial support of its 250 students. Yet the driving force behind the institution was not Louis XIV but Mme de Maintenon. For her, the dream of founding a school for the daughters of impoverished nobles first took shape in 1684 when her boarding school for young bourgeois girls moved from Rueil to Noisy-le-Sec. Dismayed by what she considered to be the commonness of her pupils, Maintenon believed the daughters of the aristocracy, even if poor, had an innate sense of dignity and good taste that protected them from a multitude of bad habits. What they lacked was a place where these worthy qualities could be cultivated through proper instruction. The Maison de Saint-Cyr would provide them with just such a place.

In discussing Saint-Cyr, scholars traditionally divide the early history of the school into three periods: the "worldly" (1686-89), a period that represents the formative years of the school; the "mystical" (1690-97), a period that encompasses Maintenon's fascination with the

Quietist movement; and the "normal," starting in 1698 and continuing over the next century.[2] It is the worldly period that will be of primary concern to us, since Racine's biblical play, *Esther*, was first performed on January 26, 1689, and may be understood as marking the end of this period. Until *Esther* and the "crisis" that followed the play's production, a quiet secularism pervaded all aspects of the school as Maintenon sought to render her pupils good Christians while avoiding "les misères et les petitesses de certains couvents" (cited in Hepp 8). Toward that end, she launched an educational program that broke with the long-standing tradition that all secondary schools, as well as the university, remain under church control. To instruct her students, Maintenon established a community of laywomen, the Dames de Saint-Louis who, although bound by a vow of celibacy, did not belong to any religious order. Moreover, the students worked, studied and slept in rooms whose cheerful décor created an atmosphere far removed from monastic austerity. Within this inviting space, the *demoiselles* pursued a course of study that included French literature, history, geography, arithmetic and the natural sciences. The school was even more pioneering in the field of women's education, for in addition to promoting academic achievement, it also promoted correct French usage and an appreciation for culture; thus, the students studied music and painting as well as performed in short morality plays, short humorous skits and full-length plays such as *Esther*.[3]

The present essay seeks to examine *Esther* within its pedagogical context. Recent criticism has examined the changes that occurred at Saint-Cyr following the performance of Racine's play. François H. Girard, Vincent Grégoire, Noémi Hepp and Carolyn Lougee, for example, have pointed to some of the ways in which Maintenon restructured the school's curriculum in response to the "crisis of *Esther*," whereas Raymond Picard and Jean Dubu have focused on Racine's artistic evolution, exploring the dramatist's return to a more classical form of tragedy in his subsequent biblical play, *Athalie*. Although I draw upon these scholarly findings, I would like to approach the "crisis of *Esther*" from another perspective, that of spatial relations. This approach also departs from the critical tendency exemplified by the work of René Jasinski, Jean Orcibal, Georges Forestier and Lucien-Gilles Benguigui to view *Esther* as a sacred drama. In focusing on the question of space both inside and outside the discursive boundaries of the play, I will argue that Racine's tragedy foreshadows the crisis to come. Toward that end, I begin by discussing the genesis of *Esther* as well as the circumstances surrounding its production. That the play was to be a most private affaire afforded Racine a certain artistic freedom; hence, I touch upon the dramatist's decision to disregard the unity of place. The decision not to respect this unity leads, within the context of the play itself, to a discussion of the notion of *secret* in its double meaning as hidden knowledge and private space. The essay closes with a return to pedagogical issues as I discuss briefly the ties among Fénelon, Maintenon and Saint-Cyr and the way in which *Esther* unintentionally undercuts the role of domesticity for women that Fénelon envisions in his treatise *De l'éducation des filles*.

* * *

In having her students perform plays, Maintenon was drawing upon an established practice in the *collèges* where "comédies de dévotion" were one of the pedagogical tools used to help young men develop the oral skills necessary to speak expressively in public. For the *st-cyriennes* this practice was, however, intended to serve another purpose. The young ladies attending Saint-Cyr, unlike the students of the *collèges*, came from all the provinces of France. While they shared certain traits – for example, nobility of birth – they did not share a common French language, since their geographical diversity reflected regional differences in expression and accent. As a result, Maintenon saw the teaching of proper French, especially with respect to the spoken language, as one of the school's primary objectives. To achieve this goal, she employed a variety of oral exercises that brought together linguistic and moral instruction: short morality plays (*Conversations*), humorous skits (*Proverbes*) and theatrical productions. Racine himself addresses Maintenon's innovative instructional program in the preface to *Esther*.

> On leur fait faire entre elles sur leurs principaux devoirs des Conversations ingénieuses, qu'on leur a composées exprès, ou qu'elles-mêmes composent sur-le-champ. On les fait parler sur les histoires qu'on leur a lues, ou sur les importantes vérités qu'on leur a enseignées. On leur fait réciter par coeur et déclamer les plus beaux endroits des meilleurs Poètes. Et cela leur sert surtout à les défaire de quantité de mauvaises prononciations, qu'elles pourraient avoir apportées de leurs Provinces.[4]

The theater represented, then, another means by which Maintenon and her staff could cultivate good pronunciation as outlined in Vaugelas's *Remarques sur l'art de bien prononcer*.[5]

Interestingly, the promotion of theatrical exercises during this worldly period of Saint-Cyr reflects less the influence of the school's founder than it does the influence of Mme de Brinon, an Ursuline nun whom Maintenon first met when visiting her friends the Montchevreuils at their country estate. Mme de Maintenon took an immediate liking to Brinon, and since the Ursuline's convent had been closed owing to poverty, she engaged her as an instructress first at Rueil and, then later, at Noisy-le-Sec. Having worked under Maintenon's supervision at these two earlier schools, Brinon was a logical choice to serve as the directress of the newly established Maison royale de Saint Louis. Yet Maintenon was soon to regret her decision. Described as having "une sensiblité au plaisir et à la diversité" (cited in Danielou 87) Brinon was a *précieuse réligieuse* who enjoyed far too much the visits to Saint-Cyr paid by the ladies of the court as she dreamed of turning the school into a center of conversation and influence. Her desire for worldly pleasures extended into the realm of the material, for she was considered a spendthrift prone to extravagances. Such behavior troubled Maintenon and, in a letter to the abbot Gobelin dated 10 November 1688, she expressed her concern.

> Je voudrois que Mme de Brinon fût moins éloquente et plus régulière, qu'elle connût moins le monde et mieux les devoirs de son état, qu'elle fût moins visitée au dehors et plus accessible au dedans, qu'elle usât de plus de sévérité à l'égard d'elle-même et de plus d'indulgence à l'égard des autres. (cited in Danielou 88)

The situation did not, however, ameliorate itself. On 10 December 1688 Mme de Brinon was abruptly whisked away by the marquise de Montchevreuil who came for her armed with a *lettre de cachet*. It appears that Mme de Brinon's decision to have his Majesty's officers serve her dinner at Marly was one extravagant act that could not be tolerated.

Although Brinon was no longer present at Saint-Cyr when *Esther* was first performed in 1689, she had nonetheless instilled in the *demoiselles* a taste for lavish theatrical productions. Under her guidance, the young ladies presented not only the old sacred dramas used by other *collèges* at the time but also new and original plays that she had composed herself. Finding the Ursuline's original compositions to be of poor quality, Maintenon authorized students to perform select works from established dramatists. *Marianne* by Tristan L'Hermite, *Polyeucte* and *Cinna* by Corneille, and *Alexandre* and *Andromaque* by Racine were all staged by the students. However, *Andromaque*'s rheto-

ric of love and passion, along with its portrayal of a pagan, heroic virtue, finally proved to be an inappropriate subject matter as well as a
dangerous influence, leading Maintenon to announce to Racine, "Nos
petites filles viennent de jouer hier *Andromaque*, et l'ont jouée si bien
qu'elles ne la joueront plus, ni aucune de vos pièces" (*Œuvres complètes* 1677). As it turned out, she was to change her mind.

The solution, Mme de Maintenon believed, was to commission
Racine to write "quelque poème moral et historique dont l'amour fût
entièrement banni" (*Œuvres complètes* 1673). The dramatist proposed
the subject of Esther which, as he was later to explain in his preface, is
"[une] histoire...pleine de grandes leçons d'amour de Dieu, et de
détachement du monde au milieu du monde même" (*Œuvres complètes*
946). While this remark addresses Maintenon's concerns, it is revealing in two other respects. First, Racine calls attention to the importance
of place or space ("au milieu du monde"); second, he suggests that
boundaries can exist ("détachement") even when piety is surrounded
by worldliness. But for the young performers of *Esther* was this distance between the sacred and the profane actually respected? Or were
boundaries blurred, and even erased?

From its inception, *Esther* was intended to be a private affair,
not a public event. The royal privilege, signed by Louis XIV himself,
forbad public performances and it was not until 1721, after the death of
Maintenon, that the actors of the Comédie Française were granted the
right to stage the play. Nonetheless, the amateur production of *Esther*
turned out to be quite a professional undertaking.[6] Racine himself
rehearsed with the *st-cyriennes* in much the same way as he had
rehearsed the actresses in his earlier secular plays. Berain, the official
set designer for all courtly spectacles, created the décor for each of the
three acts while Louis XIV furnished tapestries in addition to pearls
and diamonds from the royal guard-robe – jewels that had served
twenty years earlier as accessories in the great court ballets – to adorn
the costumes of the novice actresses. Yet even more interesting than
this infusion of worldliness into a sacred drama is the space in which
the play was staged.

Although two rehearsals took place in Mme de Maintenon's
private rooms at Versailles, it was never an issue that *Esther* would be
performed anywhere else than inside the walls of Saint-Cyr. The large
vestibule located on the third floor of the girls' dormitory was selected
as the site and transformed into a theater. The area was divided into
two sections: one for the stage and one for the audience. The space for

the audience was further divided into two amphitheaters; the smaller one would accommodate the faculty who oversaw the programs of the Maison royale de Saint Louis while the larger one would receive the students themselves. This seating would be assigned according to rank, with the older girls, "les bleues," occupying the benches nearest the stage and the youngest girls, "les rouges," filling the benches higher up and in the back. Chairs were also set up between the two amphitheaters for members of the public attending from the outside. What is striking about this seating arrangement is the way in which a courtly presence inserts itself between the young pupils and their teachers. On a symbolic level, we may understand this arrangement as another example, set forth in spatial terms, of the blurring between piety and worldliness.

The fact that *Esther* was to be performed only at Saint-Cyr afforded Racine a certain artistic freedom he had heretofore not experienced.[7] Unlike his previous tragedies, this new play only had three acts, used a chorus and disregarded one of the unities. The unexpected success of the play, however, opened its author up to criticism, making it necessary for him to justify his artistic choices in terms of a pedagogical imperative based on the notion of "plaire et instruire"; hence, Racine claims he does not respect the unity of place out of deference to his students' need for enjoyment: "Cependant comme on voulait rendre ce divertissement plus agréable à des Enfants, en jetant quelque variété dans les décorations, cela a été cause que je n'ai pas gardé cette unité avec la même rigueur que j'ai fait autrefois dans mes Tragédies" (*Œuvres complètes* 947). Whether or not we accept Racine's explanation, the need for a justification signals yet another way in which courtly society – here, represented by public opinion – penetrated the secluded world of the *st-cyriennes*.

One final aspect of the staging is also worth discussing. Since *Esther* responded to a didactic imperative, the *st-cyriennes* were not only assigned the principal roles but also the secondary roles as well as those of the chorus. Yet there was a notable exception: Mme de Caylus, the niece of Mme de Maintenon. It is for this *précieuse* that Racine added a prologue to his play, and it is she, as Piety, who speaks the opening lines in praise of the Maison de Saint Louis. While it is understandable that Racine would use this occasion to pay homage to his patrons, it is also ironic that a member of the court – not a member of the school – should be chosen to rhapsodize about Saint-Cyr, this "lieu par la Grâce habité" (l. 2), this "aisile plus fidèle" (l. 4) where "loin du tumulte, aux devoirs les plus saints / Tout un peuple naissant est formé par mes mains" (ll. 5-6), this "Palais" where "tout respire ici Dieu, la paix, la vérité" (l. 70). The public responded enthusiastically to the performance, even comparing her to the famous actress la Champmeslé.[8] At the second performance, Mme de Caylus played the role of Esther, a role that she assumed again on the 5th of February when the king and queen of England were in attendance. Once again, the reviews of her performance were most flattering, so much so that Maintenon decided it would be in the best interests of the school if her niece no longer performed. Nonetheless, with the appearance of Mme de Caylus, we may see the detachment of Piety from the world being subtly called into question.

Word of Racine's new play spread quickly, so that almost overnight members of the court were petitioning to be placed on the guest list. Entrance into the production was exclusive and, as a result, closely guarded. Even Louis XIV personally took part in monitoring admission; he would place himself at the interior door, raise his cane to serve as a barrier, wait until those who had been invited were seated, and then close the door. Among the last of those granted the privilege to attend *Esther* was Mme de Sévigné, who commented upon the uniqueness of the event in a letter to her daughter: "[...] Je ne puis vous dire l'excès de l'agrément de cette pièce. C'est une chose qui n'est pas aisée à représenter et qui ne sera jamais imitée" (cited in *Œuvres complètes* 1679).

There were those, however, who did not share Sévigné's or the court's enthusiasm. One such individual was François Hébert, Curé de Versailles. Already known as a staunch critic of the theater, Hébert refused the invitation personally extended by Maintenon to attend a performance of *Esther*; instead, he offered a lengthy critique that outlined the pernicious effects of such a theatrical performance on the *demoiselles*. For him, acting exposed the young girls not only to the sins common of their sex – vanity, pride, curiosity – but also to a courtly presence that would ultimately destroy their modesty and obedience.[9] Hébert explains it as follows in his *Mémoires*.

> On détruit donc ce qu'on veut faire en elles d'un autre côté quand on les fait monter sur un théâtre à la vue de toute sorte de personnes de la Cour. On leur ôte par ce moyen cette honte modeste qui les retient dans leur devoir, car une fille qui a fait un personnage dans une comédie aura beaucoup moins de peine de parler tête à tête à un homme, ayant pris sur elle de paraître tête levée devant plusieurs. [...] J'ajoute que, si on peut permettre à de jeunes garçons dans le collège de s'exercer dans les tragédies à la déclamation, on ne doit pas se servir de cet exemple pour l'autoriser parmi les jeunes filles

[...] les filles, devant pour être sages aimer la retraite et leurs maisons, doivent éviter de se faire voir et demeurer cachées. (124-25)

His fears, it would turn out, were well founded. With all the
attention coming from the king and his court, how could a young girl's
head *not* be turned? I would like to suggest, however, that in addition
to these external forces there are, inscribed within *Esther* itself, elements that foreshadow the unruliness that was to follow.

* * *

Drawn from the Book of Esther, Racine's play follows fairly
closely its source.[10] An orphan, Esther is raised by her uncle Mardochée in the hope that she will one day become the salvation of the
Jewish nation. He maneuvers her to marry Assuérus, the king of Persia,
but instructs Esther to hide her true identity. When Assuérus, at the
urging of his minister Aman, plans to have all the Jews killed, Mardochée commands his niece to reveal her secret. Esther initially hesitates
because she risks death if she enters the king's throne room without his
express permission. Nonetheless, she accepts her mission. Once across
the threshold, Esther's emotions overwhelm her and she faints, only to
be raised up and pardoned by Assuérus for her transgression. The king
accepts Esther's offer to dine in her private chambers later that day,
and it is at this banquet that she discloses the secret of her birth and
denounces Aman as an enemy of the king. Persuaded by Esther,
Assuérus spares the Jews and, in a reversal of fortune, Aman suffers
the fate he had destined for Mardochée, while Mardochée accepts the
court position once held by Aman.

Racine's play revolves around two crucial acts: Esther's
entrance into the throne room and the revelation of her birth. These
acts share a common thread, for both draw upon the notion of *secret*. In
its principal use, *secret* indicates the idea of hidden knowledge: "Ce
qui doit être tenu caché, ce qu'il ne faut dire à personne" (*Larousse*). In
the seventeenth century, *secret* was also commonly used to describe
private space; hence, Furetière offers the following example in his dictionary: "Un lieu secret, c'est le privé." In other words, we may understand *secret* in spatial terms as well, for it describes "[un] Lieu situé à
l'écart, retiré ou loin de la vue d'autrui" (*Larousse*). Racine implicitly
evokes both senses of the word when, in his preface, he speaks about
the unexpected public success his play had, arguing that the performance by the *st-cyriennes* was so remarkable that it could not have been
kept hidden: "ces jeunes Demoiselles ont déclamé et chanté cet

Ouvrage avec tant de grâce, tant de modestie, et tant de piété, qu'il n'a pas été possible qu'il demeurât *renfermé dans le secret* de leur Maison" (*Œuvres complètes* 946, *my emphasis*).

Racine also plays upon the double meaning of *secret* in *Esther*. In Act I, which takes place in the private apartments of Esther, the word itself appears six times (ll. 29, 53, 82, 92, 98 and 280) even as its significance resonates semantically through other word clusters: "caché" / "obscurité" or "solitaire" / "seule" / "séparée" / "renfermé." If we examine the opening exchange between Esther and Élise, her confidant, we discover that secret knowledge and private space are closely intertwined.

> On m'élevait alors solitaire, et cachée,
> Sous les yeux vigilants du sage Mardochée.
> Tu sais combien je dois à ses heureux secours.
> La mort m'avait ravi les auteurs de mes jours.
> Mais lui, voyant en moi la fille de son frère,
> Me tint lieu, chère Élise, et de père, et de mère.
> Du triste état des Juifs jour et nuit agité,
> Il me tira du sein de mon obscurité,
> Et sur mes faibles mains fondant leur délivrance,
> Il me fit d'un Empire accepter l'espérance.
> A ses desseins secrets tremblante j'obéis.
> Je vins. Mais je cachai ma race et mon pays. (ll. 43-54)

This description of how Esther became queen of Persia is significant in two respects. First, Esther is clearly associated with both notions of *secret*, for not only does Mardochée sequester her from the world, he also instructs her to hide her true identity. In other words, up until her marriage to Assuérus, she inhabits a space far removed from the public gaze and, once married, she carefully guards the secret of her Judaism. However, the new position as queen causes personal grief, since Esther must also conceal her true feelings: "Hélas! Durant ces jours de joie et de festins, / Quelle était en secret ma honte, et mes chagrins!" (ll. 81-82). She emphasizes again her disdain for royal power by distinguishing between public and private space: "Ce bandeau, dont il faut que je paraisse ornée, / Dans ces jours solennels à l'Orgueil dédiés, / Seule, et dans le secret je le foule à mes pieds" (ll. 278-80). The conflict between Esther's public and private personae is again expressed in spatial terms when she explains, in language evocative of Mme de Maintenon's undertaking at Saint-Cyr, the need for a secluded place in which to educate young Israelites.

> Jeunes et tendres fleurs, par le sort agitées,

Sous un ciel étranger comme moi transplantées.
Dans un lieu séparé de profanes témoins,
Je mets à les former mon étude et mes soins. (ll. 103-06)

Second, the description is significant in that Racine associates Mardochée with the idea of *secret* as well. We are first introduced to Esther's uncle through the terminal rhyme of "caché" / "Mardochée" (ll. 43-44), which is appropriate since he is responsible for Esther's seclusion as a child. Yet Mardochée himself represents a hidden presence. Although he is physically absent throughout most of the play, he nonetheless exerts a tremendous influence over his niece; indeed, he compels her to carry out his "desseins secrets," and Esther herself remarks, "Absent je le consulte. Et ses réponses sages / Pour venir jusqu'à moi trouvent mille passages" (ll. 95-96). Moreover, it is Mardochée who has already instructed Esther to reveal one complot to her husband: "Déjà même, déjà par ses secrets avis / J'ai découvert au Roi les sanglantes pratiques / Que formaient contre lui deux ingrats Domestiques" (ll. 98-100). Clearly, Mardochée has access to secret information and is in a position to use this knowledge to further his agenda. Within the political arena, then, he functions as a marginal but powerful figure, a role which is fittingly represented in spatial terms by his having taken up a position outside the palace doors ("Du Palais cependant il assiège la porte," l. 433; see also ll. 459, 560 and 617-18). By the play's end he will have crossed this threshold and openly assumed power.

The sacred space of Esther's chamber in Act I has its mirror image in the profane space of Assuérus's throne room in Act II. Although one promises safety while the other evokes danger, both are depicted as secluded locations with restricted access. Esther herself is acutely aware of the price exacted on those who enter the throne room without permission. As she explains the royal interdiction to Mardochée, we find again the idea of concealment.

Hélas! Ignorez-vous quelles sévères lois
Aux timides mortels cachent ici les Rois?
Au fond de leur Palais leur majesté terrible
Affecte à leurs Sujets de se rendre invisible.
Et la mort est le prix de tout Audacieux,
Qui sans être appelé se présente à leurs yeux: (ll. 191-96)

Even Aman, Assuérus's most trusted advisor, is observant of this space's singular nature, for he exclaims to Hydaspe in Act II's opening scene, "Dans ce lieu redoubtable oses-tu m'introduire?" (l.

373). We may understand, then, both Esther's chambers and Assuérus's throne room as private or "secret" places.

As I indicated earlier, Racine chose to disregard the unity of place in *Esther*. Act I takes place in Esther's private apartments; Act II unfolds in Assuérus's throne room; and Act III is set in Esther's salon and personal gardens. The change in setting underscores the notion of *secret*, for it calls attention to the fact that Esther and Assuérus inhabit distinct personal spaces in which each one enjoys a certain freedom. When Esther penetrates the inner sanctum of Assuérus in Act II, she breaks down the physical boundaries that had heretofore separated them and, in doing so, sets into motion what is to become the physical intrusion of Assuérus's secular world, with its politics and court intrigues, into her pious world. We witness this event in Act III when Esther willingly opens her doors to the king and the court. The act begins with Zarès warning her husband, Aman, as they wait outside the closed doors to Esther's chambers.

C'est donc ici d'Esther le superb Jardin,
Et ce Salon pompeux est le lieu du festin.
Mais tandis que la porte est encore fermée,
Écoutez les conseils d'une Épouse alarmée. (ll. 826-29)

Zarès's fears are well founded because with the opening of these doors Esther will not only reveal the secret of her birth but also step into the public spotlight. In other words, she will assume a more active and, by extension, more political role as she influences state policy, saves the Jewish nation and brings about the downfall of Aman. The transformation of Esther from a passive and compliant young woman to an active and rebellious one parallels the shift in décor as private spaces become increasingly public.

In revealing the secret of her birth, Esther brings to a close her personal metamorphosis into *une femme forte*. However, it is with her entry into the throne room that the process begins. Supported by her attendants, Esther crosses the threshold of Assuérus's private chambers, speaks one and a half lines to her attendants, and then faints: "Mes filles, soutenez votre Reine éperdue / Je me meurs" (ll. 634-35). Racine sets the stage for this dramatically charged moment in Act I, scene 3. In this earlier scene, Mardochée informs his niece of the plot against the Jews and commands her to reveal immediately the secret of her birth to the king, "Allez, osez au Roi déclarer qui vous êtes" (l. 190). For Mardochée, what is of the utmost importance is a verbal act, since Esther must first confess her origins and then plead her people's cause; for Esther, what is of the utmost importance is a physical act, since she must enter Assuérus's throne room uninvited and risk death. Undoubtedly, what Mardochée instructs Esther to do is dangerous but in responding to her uncle, Esther shifts the danger inherent in his command from her speech (the confession) to her actions (entrance into the throne room).

The shift in emphasis from a verbal act to a physical act is reversed in the swoon scene itself (Act II, sc. 7). Infuriated by the intrusion into his chamber, Assuérus's anger turns to surprise upon recognizing that the intruder is his beloved wife. His surprise quickly changes to concern when she faints, and this concern soon becomes encouragement, for after holding out his scepter to pardon Esther her transgression, he urges Esther to reveal the reason behind the visit.

> Osez donc me répondre, et ne me cachez pas
> Quel sujet important conduit ici vos pas.
> Quel intérêt, quels soins vous agitent, vous pressent?
> Je vois qu'en m'écoutant vos yeux aux Ciel s'adressent.
> Parlez. (ll. 679-83)

Empowered to speak, Esther remains nonetheless reluctant to do so at this particular moment, and her cryptic reply ("J'attends ou mon malheur, ou ma félicité," l. 687) only inflames her husband's curiosity. As Assuérus's response to Esther moves from anger to curiosity, the scene's action progresses from physical acts – Esther fainting, Assuérus extending the scepter – to verbal acts represented by the king's injunction to speak. In one sense, then, we may understand this scene as not only preparing the way for Esther's revelation but also as signaling the movement from Assuérus's voice, and the power it holds, to Esther's voice, and the power it will come to have.

From the beginning of the revelation scene (Act III, sc. 4), it is apparent that the balance of power between Assuérus and Esther has undergone a change. As we have seen, the action no longer unfolds in the king's throne room but in the queen's private gardens, which have now been opened up to select members of the court. Moreover, the focus is on Esther's ability to speak, for as Assuérus states in the scene's opening line, "Oui, vos moindres discours ont des grâces secrètes" (l. 1016).[11] The primacy given to speech is further underscored when the king enjoins Esther to articulate her desires (l. 1022) and she responds, "Mais puisqu'il faut enfin expliquer mes soupirs, / Puisque mon Roi lui-même à parler me convie" (ll. 1027-28). Although her reply suggests an obedient and deferential attitude, the *récit* following Esther's shocking disclosure of her Jewish origin suggests the opposite; indeed, she reveals herself to be a consummate orator through her ability to combine verbal eloquence and rhetorical shrewdness.

Esther's *récit* comprises 97 lines and its length signals a departure from the swoon scene in which she spoke, in dialog with Assuérus, a total of 37 lines. Esther now holds center stage. In recounting her story, she seeks to accomplish three goals. The first of these is to convince her husband that the Jewish people are good, loyal subjects. Esther begins by explaining the reason behind their enslavement (ll. 1058-77) but while doing so, she also emphasizes that the Jews remain devoted to their God despite the harsh punishment He has inflicted upon them. Such obedience on their part extends to the temporal realm, for they believe Assuérus to be a benevolent ruler (ll. 1078-82) whom God has chosen to reign over them (l. 1077). It is because the Jewish people see in Assuérus a king who is worthy of their respect, esteem and allegiance that Mardochée refuses to acknowledge Aman's power as legitimate: "Il [Mardochée] n'a, devant Aman, pu fléchir les genoux / Ni lui rendre un honneur qu'il ne croit dû qu'à vous" (ll. 1126-27). The depiction of the Jewish people as good citizens stands in stark contrast to the depiction of Aman as a corrupt citizen. Esther's second goal, then, is to discredit the king's minister. In fact, it is he – not the Jews – who is responsible for undermining the "bonheur public." To make her case, Esther employs a series of ad hominem attacks that reduce Aman to the fearful and evil Other; he becomes "un Barbare," "Ennemi cruel," "Ministre infidèle et barbare," "un Scythe impitoyable" and "un perfide Etranger." Yet even more importantly, she depicts this "Etranger" as Assuérus's rival, one who, under the guise of offering counsel, is aspiring to undermine the king's own authority. By calling into question Aman's motives, Esther successfully touches a nerve in Assuérus, since the possibility of having been the dupe of a trusted minister strikes a blow to royal vanity.

Once she has shaken her husband's confidence in Aman, Esther is better positioned to achieve her final goal, which is to persuade Assuérus to countermand the order to massacre all his Jewish subjects. Here, Esther suggests that the king would be better served if he were to ally himself openly with the God of the Jews and to make her point, she enumerates all the instances in which their God had ensured Assuérus's military victories and protected him from harm. In other words, it would be more politically savvy for the king to align himself with a powerful god than with a scheming minister. By appealing to Assuérus's vanity, by playing upon his insecurities and by proposing an alternate ally, Esther persuades the king first to question the foundation of his beliefs – "J'étais donc le jouet...Ciel, daigne m'éclairer"(l. 1138) – and then later embrace Mardochée as his new minister, "Mortel, chéri du Ciel, mon salut, et ma joie, / Aux conseils des méchants ton Roi n'est plus en proie" (ll. 1176-77). Through the revelation of her secret, Esther has discovered the power of her own voice, allowing her to overthrow the current political power and save the Chosen People from genocide.

With Act III, secrets – in both senses of the term – are made public. Not only does Racine have his heroine disclose the secret of her birth but he also has Esther open up her private apartments to the court. But what might this revelation of secrets intimate about the "crisis" of *Esther* that was to follow? And what might Esther's discovery of her own voice suggest to the young girls of Saint-Cyr who performed the play? I would like to suggest an answer to these questions by looking briefly at the connection between Fénelon and Saint-Cyr.

* * *

In 1687, a year after Mme de Maintenon first opened the doors of the Maison royale de Saint Louis, François de Salignac de la Mothe-Fénelon published his *De l'éducation des filles*, one of the most coherent and complete statements from that period on the education of women. In this treatise, Fénelon outlined an educational program designed to produce hard-working, dutiful and virtuous noble women whose primary concern would be taking care of household affairs. As he explains it in Chapter I,

> [u]ne femme judicieuse, appliquée et pleine de religion, est l'âme de toute une grande maison, elle y met l'ordre pour les biens temporels et pour le salut. [...]Le monde n'est point un fantôme, c'est l'assemblage de toutes les familles; et qui est-ce qui peut les policier avec un soin plus exacte que les femmes, qui, outré leur autorité naturelle et leur assiduité dans leurs maisons, ont encore l'avantage d'être nées soigneuses, attentives au detail, industrieuses, insinuantes et persuasives? [...] Voilà donc les occupations des femmes, qui ne sont guère moins importantes au public que celles des hommes, puisqu'elles ont un maison à régler, un mari à rendre heureux, des enfants à bien élever. (92-93)

While women are destined to hold center stage in the domestic arena, they are not, however, meant to participate in the public arena; hence, Fénelon asserts that women "ne doivent ni gouverner l'Etat, ni faire la guerre, ni entrer dans le ministère des choses sacrées; ainsi elles peuvent se passer de certaines connaissances étendues, qui appartiennent à la politique, à l'art militaire, à la jurisprudence, à la philosophie et à la théologie" (92). This celebration of the domestic woman has at its heart, as Carolyn Lougee has argued, an implicit proscription against a *mondain* education and, with it, the culture of polite society.[12] By examining Fénelon's views on female education within the context of his socio-political views, Lougee shows that his emphasis on simplicity and frugality serve, in part, as a counter to what he perceived as one of the pernicious effects of polite society: luxury. Luxury, especially with respect to women, promoted ambition, vanity, the corruption of manners, and most importantly, the disruption of the social hierarchy; in other words, preparing young women to become ladies of the court (or *salonnières*) – not mothers of noble families – would bring about the further degeneration of French society. As a result, Fénelon strongly cautions educators to protect young girls from the corrupting influence of *le bel esprit* (152-53) and provide them, instead, with a program of study that is commensurate with their socioeconomic position: "On doit considérer, pour l'éducation d'une jeune fille, sa condition, les lieux où elle doit passer sa vie, et la profession qu'elle embrassera selon des apparences; prenez garde qu'elle ne conçoive des espérances au-dessus de son bien et de sa condition" (165).

Given Mme de Maintenon's desire to produce at her institution noble girls who are dutiful, industrious, filled with piety and prepared to return to domestic life in the provinces, it is not surprising to find certain affinities between Fénelon's pedagogical program and the curriculum established at Saint-Cyr.[13] The connection between the two becomes even stronger when we consider that Fénelon was one of the school's confessors as well as Maintenon's spiritual advisor from 1689 to 1694 and that he often preached at Saint-Cyr. Moreover, he was consulted on the school's *Constitution*, co-authored with Godet des Marias the *Esprit de l'Institut* and wrote a significant part of his *Instructions et avis sur divers points de la morale et de la perfection chrétienne* for Maintenon's pupils. The affinity extends into instructional methodology as well, since both Fénelon and Maintenon embraced the notion that education should combine the useful with the agreeable. As one means of achieving this goal, Fénelon cites the value of teaching "les histoires saintes" as well as having students act out the stories: "ces représentations les charmeront plus que d'autres jeux, les accoutumeront à penser et à dire des choses sérieuses avec plaisir, et rendront ces histoires ineffacables dans leur mémoire" (120). Ostensibly, then, having the *st-cyriennes* perform *Esther* should have represented the ideal lesson plan for Maintenon and Fénelon.

History has, however, shown us otherwise. As Hébert de Versailles had predicted, the quasi-public production emboldened the young performers and, rather than inspire piety, promoted unruliness. By 1691 order and discipline still had not been fully restored to the school, leading Mme de Maintenon to rue, in a letter to Mme de Fontaines, the unexpected results of her pedagogical practices.

> La peine que j'ai sur les filles de Saint-Cyr ne se peut réparer que par le temps, et par un changement entier de l'éducation que nous leur avons donnée jusques à cette heure. [...] J'ai voulu que les filles eussent de l'esprit, qu'on élevât leur coeur, qu'on formât leur raison; j'ai réussi ce dessein; elles ont de l'esprit, et s'en servent contre nous; elles ont le coeur élevé, et sont plus fières et plus hautaines qu'il ne conviendroit de l'être aux plus grandes princesses. A parler même selon le monde, nous avons formé leur raison, et fait des discoureuses présomptueuses, curieuses, etc. [...] Mais, madame, il ne faut point en beaucoup discourir avec elles; tout, à Saint-Cyr, se tourne en discours; [...] Il faut encore défaire nos filles de ce tour d'esprit railleur que je leur ai donné [...] Le silence et l'humilité seront les meilleurs moyens, on parle trop chez nous. (cited in Danielou 94-95)

Although Maintenon sought to mold young women in the fashion of Fénelon's educational program, *Esther* opened up, however unintentionally, the possibility of a different life through its interaction, both on and off stage, between court society and pious society. Thus, while Racine avoided in his play the problem of love and the passions this emotion inspires, he ended up kindling in the *demoiselles* the desire to participate in the public sphere. The seeds of this desire, I would like to suggest, are contained within the play itself through the notion of *secret*.

As we have seen, the idea of *secret* reveals itself in two significant ways. In spatial terms, the boundary between private and public space is dissolved as Esther first penetrates the private – although politically charged – throne room of Assuérus and, then in turn, opens up her own secluded gardens to members of Assuérus's court. In both instances, the crossing of thresholds marks Esther's passage into the political arena as she engages in courtly intrigue as well as influences public policy. Interestingly, just as Esther is thrust into the public spotlight, so too are the *demoiselles* of Saint-Cyr who perform in the play. In staging *Esther*, the young girls find themselves unexpectedly coming into contact not only with courtly, or polite, society but also with many of the luxurious elements that Fénelon associates with it. Hence, it is not surprising to find, in the post-*Esther* reforms instituted by Maintenon, that the limited performances of Racine's second biblical play, *Athalie*, were without elaborate sets or bejeweled costumes. Retrospectively, then, we may discern a touch of irony in Racine's prefatory assertion that Esther's story is full of "grandes leçons d'amour de Dieu, et de détachement du monde au milieu du monde même," since a desire for greater worldly attachments appears to be one of the unintentional lessons it imparted to the young students of Saint-Cyr.

The use of *secret*, in the sense of hidden knowledge, foreshadows another unexpected lesson. Esther's transformation from hesitant and silent women (the swoon scene in Act II) to a confident and vocal one (the revelation scene in Act III) exemplifies not only the allure but also the power of speech. In finding her own voice, Esther enters into the political arena with the delivery of a passionate – and rhetorically astute – plea on behalf of the Jewish people. In other words, Esther leaves the domestic sphere, which is represented in the play by her instruction of the young Israelites within her private chambers, to enter the public sphere. For the *demoiselles*, Esther's discovery of her voice appears to announce the discovery of their own, a discovery Mme de Maintenon laments in her September letter to Mme de Fontaines.

Although Racine's *Esther* figures as a symbol of Mme de Maintenon's innovative pedagogical approach, the play's subject matter as well as its staging opened up to the *demoiselles* the possibility of participating in the world of polite society. For it to be the pedagogical success truly desired by Maintenon, *Esther* and its young performers should have remained hidden in "le secret de leur Maison."

Notes

[1] Cited in Milhiet 26. His essay offers an excellent over view of the history of Saint-Cyr, including materials taken from the archives.

[2] In addition to Milhiet, see the biographies of Mme de Maintenon by Danielou, Prevot and Haldane. Danielou, in particular, offers a good account of Maintenon's earlier educational endeavors as well as the different periods of Saint-Cyr.

[3] Recently, scholarly attention has turned to the role that music played in *Esther* as a pedagogical tool and in the creation of a new theatrical genre. See Gormley for a discussion of the former and Piejus for a discussion of the latter.

[4] *Œuvres complètes*, Vol. 1 edited by Georges Forestier 945. All further references are to this edition and cited within the text.

[5] For discussion of the pedagogical value of drama with respect to Saint-Cyr, see Hammond 153-69; Dubu's "Les 'Comédies de dévotion'"; and Girard 160-61.

[6] In discussing the staging of *Esther*, I have relied on Forestier's account as it appears in his "Notice" to the play in *Œuvres complètes* 1678-81 and on Dubu's essay "Mme de Maintenon and Racine."

[7] In his chapter devoted to *Esther*, Raymond Picard suggests that the play's success allowed Racine to glimpse a new kind of tragedy of which he would be the master. Picard also argues against the view that the play was suppressed because it was a political allegory (that is, condemnation of the enemies of Port-Royal or a Jacobite drama about the Restoration of England). I am in agreement with Picard on both accounts.

[8] In the introduction to their edition of the correspondence among Mme de Maintenon, Mme de Caylus and Mme de Dangeau, the editors discuss Caylus's connection to Saint-Cyr and, in particular, her performance as Piety in *Esther*. See *L'Estime et la tendresse* 47-49.

[9] Hébert's condemnation of the theater is part of a long tradition. For an overall history of the objections to theater from Plato to the present, see Barish.

[10] For comparisons between Racine's *Esther* and its biblical sources, see Orcibal, Benguigui and Jasinski.

[11] Richard Scholar picks up on Assuérus's exclamation to argue that *Esther* is "a drama about radically different conceptions of grace" (318). In doing so, he offers an illuminating reading of the transgression scene as well as reveals the subtle ways in which Racine plays on the word *grace*.

[12] See, in particular, chapters 11 and 12 of *Le Paradis des femmes*.

[13] Fénelon's educational program for young girls and its relation to that of Saint-Cyr has been studied as well by Snyders (154-70); Girard (159-63); Danielou (115-27).

Works Cited

Barish, Jonas. *The Anti-theatrical Prejudice*. Berkley and Los Angeles: University of California Press, 1981.

Benguigui, Lucien-Gilles. *Racine et les sources juives d'*Esther *et* Athalie. Paris: L'Harmattan, 1995.

Borota, Franck et al. *Les Demoiselles de Saint-Cyr. Maison royale d'éducation 1686-1793.* Archives départmentales des Yvelines. Azzano-San-Paolo, Italy: Grafedit, 1999.

Danielou, Madeleine. *Madame de Maintenon, éducatrice.* Paris: Bloud & Gay, 1946.

Davis Jr., James Herbert. *Fénelon.* Twayne World Author Series 542. Boston: G. K. Hall & Co., 1979.

Dubu, Jean. "Les 'Comédies de dévotion': Genre dramatique ou mode?" *Revue de l'Histoire de Versailles et des Yvelines.* 75 (1991): 21-31.

_____. "Madame de Maintenon et Racine." In *Les Demoiselles de Saint-Cyr: Maison royale d'éducation 1686-1793.* Archives départementales des Yvelines. Azzano-San-Paolo, Italy: Grafedit, 1999. 115-29.

Fénelon, François de Salignac de la Mothe-. *De l'éducation des filles.* In *Œuvres.* Vol. 1. Ed. Jacques Le Brun. Bibliothèque de La Pléïade. Paris: Gallimard, 1983.

Furetière, Antoine. *Le Dictionnaire universel.* Paris: Le Robert, 1978.

Girard, Françoise. "Le système éducatif à Saint-Cyr." In *Les Demoiselles de Saint-Cyr: Maison royale d'éducation 1686-1793.* Archives départementales des Yvelines. Azzano-San-Paolo, Italy: Grafedit, 1999. 150-67.

Gormley, Gráinne. "Moreau as Teacher: The Impact of his Vocation on the Composition of *Esther.*" In *Racine: The Power and the Pleasure.* Eds. Edric Caldicott and Derval Conroy. Dublin: University College Dublin Press, 2001.

Grand Larousse de la langue française. Vol. 6. Paris: Librairie Larousse.

Grégoire, Vincent. "Avatars de la pratique théâtrale adoptée par Mme de Maintenon à Saint-Cyr." *Papers French Seventeenth-Century Literature* 24.46 (1997): 35-52.

_____. "La Femme et la loi dans la perspective des pièces bibliques raciniennes représentées à Saint-Cyr." *XVIIe Siècle* 179.2 (1993): 323-36.

Haldane, Charlotte. *Madame de Maintenon: Uncrowned Queen of France*. Indianapolis and New York: The Bobbs-Merrill Company, Inc., 1970.

Hammond, Nicholas. *Fragmentary Voices: Memory and Education at Port-Royal*. Biblio 17-152. Tübingen: Gunter Narr Verlag, 2004.

Hébert, François [Curé de Versailles]. *Mémoires du Curé de Versailles: François Hébert 1686-1704*. Intro. Georges Girard. Paris: Les Éditions de France, 1927.

Hepp, Noémi. "L'univers feminine de Saint-Cyr: L'idéal et le reel." *Revue de l'Histoire de Versailles et des Yvelines*. 75 (1991): 7-20.

Jasinski, René. *Autour de l'Esther racinienne*. Paris: A.-G. Nizet, 1985.

LeRoy, Pierre-E and Marcel Loyau, eds. *L'Estime et la tendresse. Correspondances intimes de Mme de Maintenon, Mme de Caylus et Mme de Dangeau*. Paris: Albin Michel, 1998.

Lougee, Carolyn C. *Le Paradis des Femmes: Women, Salons, and Social Stratification in Seventeenth-Century France*. Princeton: Princeton University Press, 1976.

Maintenon, Madame de [Françoise d'Aubigné]. *Conseils et instructions aux demoiselles pour leur conduite dans le monde*. Vols. 1 and 2. Ed. M. Th. Lavallée. Paris: Charpentier, 1857.

_____. *Dialogues and Addresses*. Ed. and trans. John J. Conley, S. J. Chicago: University of Chicago Press, 2004.

_____. *Recueil des instructions que Madame de Maintenon a données aux demoiselles de St-Cyr. D'après un manuscript original et inédit appartenant à la Comtesse de Gramont d'Aster*. Paris: J. Dumoulin, 1908.

Milhiet, Jean-Joseph. "Historique de la maison royale de Saint-Louis." In *Les Demoiselles de Saint-Cyr: Maison royale d'éducation 1686-1793*. Archives départementales des Yvelines. Azzano-San-Paolo, Italy: Grafedit, 1999. 11-110.

Orcibal, Jean. *La Genèse d'*Esther *et d'*Athalie. Paris: Vrin, 1950.

Piejus, Anne. "*Esther*, un modèle paradoxal de théâtre musical pour Saint-Cyr." *Papers French Seventeenth-Century Literature* 24.47 (1997): 395-420.

Picard, Raymond. *La Carrière de Jean Racine*. 2nd ed. Paris: Gallimard, 1961.

Prevot, Jean. *La première institutrice de France. Madame de Maintenon*. Paris: Belin, 1981.

Racine, Jean. *Œuvres complètes*. Vol. 1. Ed. Georges Forestier. "Bibliothèque de La Pléïade." Paris: Gallimard, 1999.

Reynes, Geneviève. *Couvents de femmes. La vie des religieuses cloîtrées dans la France des XVIIe et XVIIIe siècles*. Paris: Fayard, 1987.

Scholar, Richard. "'Je ne sais quelle grâce': Esther before Assuerus." *French Studies* 56.3 (July 2002): 317-27.

Snyders, Georges. *La pédagogie en France aux XVIIe et XVIIIe siècles*. Paris: Presses Universitaires de France, 1965.

Perfect Harmony:
Love and Marriage in Early Modern Pedagogy

Claire Carlin

In societies where formalized conjugal union exists, its social, religious and political ramifications make it a fundamental institution. The right to marry or to refuse marriage is a preoccupation of twenty-first century Western society that finds echoes in the early modern upheavals of the Renaissance and the Reformation. In sixteenth-century France, the role of the family, the celibacy of priests, and increased State intervention in marriage law became topics of intense debate that continue today, paralleled then and now by discussion of the relationship between spouses.[1]

The exchange among Renaissance writers on all aspects of marriage took place in the context of humanist scholarship that would give new perspective on accepted practices. Guided by the dictum of pleasure and instruction so essential to their Greco-Roman models, the textual production of the humanists links moral treatises, social relations and art (literature, music and the plastic arts). In *Littérature et politesse*, Emmanuel Bury demonstrates how the revival of the *paideia*, or sum of textual knowledge, led authors to mine the texts of Antiquity for lessons in both morality and mores: in order to live well in the here and now, we must behave in a manner respectful of others and that promotes action in the community, action underpinned by graceful rhetoric that assures successful communication. The need for skilled expression highlights the aesthetic dimension of social contact.[2] Conduct manuals, books of moral teaching and literary texts all imagined a society improved by reading, and since marriage was an institution many believed sorely in need of improvement, treatises on the subject flourished. To the dominant representations of the Middle Ages (quarrelsome couples in popular literature, adultery in courtly texts), new models of marriage would be added, with communication skills at the forefront. These secular, didactic, yet entertaining treatises are the focus of this study.

Inspired by neo-Platonism, humanists tended to insist upon the plasticity and perfectibility of human nature with a view to counteract the Reformation (and Augustinian) view of our weakness and its inherent misery (Bury 14, 19-20). The notion that the individual could be molded (or form herself or himself) into a successful actor on the social stage thanks to contact with the Ancients signals the beginnings of the modern concept of subjectivity (Vizier 66-72): self-management, self-control, self-consciousness all evolved as part of the "civilizing process" described by Norbert Elias. In the wake of the humanists, seventeenth-century authors developed the doctrine of *honnêteté*, which emphasizes enjoyable conversation in a salon setting with women playing a key role, as well as a new *savoir mondain* disseminated more in collections (*florilèges*, *polyantheae*, commonplace books) than through original texts in their entirety, as Bernard Beugnot has shown (257-79). The content of the seventeenth-century *paideia* shifted away from Antique and Italian models without abandoning them entirely; contemporary writers and fragmentary forms took precedence. The ideal of flexibility, the key to graceful behavior, is suggested in the preference for compendia. Alongside them were born treatises on sociability published by the dozens in the seventeenth century: reading continued to gain legitimacy as a method for acquiring the capacity to converse in society. Indeed, *honnêteté* could be acquired through self-instruction. As Bury puts it, in these treatises "il s'agit d'ouvrir la voie d'un univers clos à des hommes qui ne lui appartiennent pas," professional men and their sons, *roturiers* rather than aristocrats (62).

But what of bourgeois women? Carolyn Lougee points out that noblewomen dominated the salons (113-37), yet we know that the non-aristocratic *honnête femme* existed as an ideal alongside her male counterpart. Jean Mesnard traces the parallel development of the *honnête homme* and the *honnête femme* and sees no difference between the descriptions furnished in two early treatises on *honnêteté*, Faret's *L'Honneste homme ou l'art de plaire à la cour* (1630) and Jacques du Bosc's *L'Honneste femme* (1632). Both authors cite *l'art de plaire*, especially in conversation, as the most important characteristic of *honnêtes gens*. To please does not mean brilliance, it means the ability to adapt to any given situation (at court or in a salon) with grace, and without affectation of any sort; this is the foundation of decorum or *bienséance*. Modesty, an absence of pedantry, the simplicity that accompanies sincerity, self-knowledge, self-mastery and a lively, agreeable countenance are the virtues that produce ideal conduct in both sexes. The ethical and the aesthetic combine seamlessly in *honnêteté* (Mesnard 21-27). Although only a fraction of non-aristocratic women participated in salon culture before the *Fronde*, an elite minority was making its way into *la vie mondaine* (Lougee 51-54, 212-14; Timmermans 87-89).

Nonetheless, the home is where a married woman belongs most of the time, according to Du Bosc (III, 80-95). It is not surprising to find home and hearth emphasized in the texts by clergy (Du Bosc was a Franciscan). In the more than twenty ecclesiastical marriage treatises that I have examined, restricting female movement is absolutely necessary to ensure domestic harmony. Secular writers of the sixteenth century often agree with the religious manuals born of the Catholic Reformation's efforts to renew and "purify" the institution of marriage, whereas seventeenth-century non-religious treatises are anchored in a worldly vision of polite society which extends boundaries for women. The didactic marriage manual as a genre had its roots in the humanist movement of the Renaissance, and evolved along with it to produce a revolution – in the nuptial imaginary, if not in the reality of married life.

Marriage Manuals of the Renaissance

Any consideration of writings on early modern marriage should begin with Erasmus, who initiated the questioning of certain tenets of Catholic marriage from within the Church. As early as 1497, even before Martin Luther's earliest pronouncements denying marriage was a sacrament and promoting marriage for priests, Erasmus was composing his *Encomium Matrimonii*, translated into French by the Chevalier de Berquin and published in 1525 as the *Déclamation des louenges de mariage*.[3] The fact that Berquin was burned at the stake in 1529 largely as a result of this translation illustrates the seriousness with which Erasmus's views were received in France.[4] His most controversial proposal puts marriage and virginity on an equal plane, thus launching the revalorization of marriage that would preoccupy the Counter-Reformation. He also posits the possibility of marriage for priests, as well as the idea that conjugal relations are not sinful: although they should not be pursued for pleasure but rather to satisfy natural bodily needs, sex in marriage provides the peace of mind necessary for spiritual growth.[5] Orthodox in his comments on the goals of marriage (procreation, licit satisfaction of physical desire, mutual aid and comfort), Erasmus nonetheless opens a breach in Catholic theology that had repercussions throughout the sixteenth century, as the Church struggled to combat challenges not only from the Protestants but also from Christian humanists.[6]

The rulings of the Council of Trent and the resulting crop of Catholic Reformation marriage treatises authored by priests created the textual landscape in which other genres of texts on marriage were able to flourish, among them Erasmus's own *Colloquia*. These conversations are usually light and comical in tone; one of interest to this study appeared in French translation in 1707, as *La femme mécontente de son mari*; its original title is *Conjugium*. In it, two wives argue over the best way to influence husbands into providing more freedom of movement and action. The portrait of shrewish Xantippe recalls misogynist and misogamist medieval *fabliaux*. Her method is constant harassment of her husband, whereas Eulalie is the model wife, agreeable and submissive to her husband's wishes, with the result that she has a great deal of autonomy thanks to his trust in her. Eulalie is obviously a cultured woman, citing sources from mythology and history to make her points, reinforcing the notion that Erasmus promulgates elsewhere that women should be educated, for ignorance will only lead to misbehavior and error. Molière's Agnès is, of course, a case in point. Évelyne Berriot-Salvadore and Linda Timmermans have underscored the Erasmian belief in education as the guarantor of fidelity in women, thus potentially repressive rather than liberating (Berriot 52-60; Timmermans 31-36). But by the time *L'École des femmes* appears in 1662, educated women had increasing opportunities to exercise their minds outside the domestic sphere, as salon culture expanded to include more members of the bourgeoisie – and as the debates about marriage continued. The characteristics of the ideal marriage and the role of marriage in society are topics that reoccur in the several genres of texts, including religious treatises, polemical misogamist satire, legal and medical documents, fiction, poetry and theatre. In 1523, *Conjugium* launched the genre studied here, that is, texts on marriage containing advice on conduct in which the focus is not religion and which may take a variety of forms, including allegory, dialogue, anecdotes, and description or prescription interspersed with verse. These documents seek to instruct, artfully. Unlike the didactic religious treatises, no one formula determines the presentation of material and the reader's pleasure is considered the primary tool of persuasion.

Secular marriage treatises of the sixteenth century all copiously cite a diversity of religious and secular authorities, but one classical source dominates: Plutarch's *Préceptes conjugales*, which appeared in seven different French translations between 1535 and 1572.[7] The version cited here will be the first, Jean Lodé's, in its 1536 printing. Despite the liberties taken with Plutarch's text, it reflects accurately the preoccupations of sixteenth-century France: the principles put forth appealed to humanists seeking to participate in the renewal of Christian marriage, since traditional values could be upheld alongside some progressive views. The influence of Plutarch on the *Conjugium* of Erasmus is evident: the patient, caring, joyful wife is able to control her temperamental or wayward husband, but overtly domineering women (often unfaithful to boot) deserve punishment (Precepts ii, iv, vi, ix-xii, xviii, xlv, xlix). The necessary subordination of wives to husbands is repeated in several passages, but so is the idea that shared responsibility and mutual respect make for successful marriage (Precepts vii, viii, xiv, xxiv, xlvi, lviii). In social life, the wife's role is to stay home, and to let her husband speak for her when others are present (Precepts xix, xxii, xxv, xxxvii-xl), and yet Plutarch's first precept suggests the importance of communication and the aesthetic dimension of seventeenth-century *honnêteté*: the three most important things in marriage are "Eloquence, persuasion & grace mutuelle." Although a wife's sphere of influence is severely limited in all of the sixteenth-century moralizing marriage treatises, there is an opening toward a more pleasurable idea of marriage accompanied by the true balance of power proposed in many seventeenth-century texts.

Plutarch did not neglect the pleasure associated with conjugal relations, but Jean Lodé made sure to frame his discussion of the body and eroticism in terms of the Christian doctrine of "conjugal chastity" or restraint during sex, which should take place "avecque tout honneur, et reverence en soy presentant lung a laultre" (Precept li). For each spouse, it is essential that "le lict nuptial luy soit comme une escolle & exercice de toute honnestete & continence" (Precept lvi; see also xxxvi and l). Religious marriage manuals of both centuries emphasized that sex was meant for procreation and not for pleasure, but the majority of secular writers, even the most moralistic, took Erasmus's separation of sex and sin as a step toward a communion of bodies that could complement the communion of souls in marriage (an idea further developed in the early seventeenth century by François de Sales). Nevertheless, even the most facetious observations on marital sex included the notion of conjugal chastity alongside the possiblility of physical pleasure.

The dialectical structure of the *Préceptes conjugales* appealed to Renaissance humanists: in all of the secular didactic treatises, the enjoyable rhetorical game of illustrating the pros and cons of marriage always resulted in a synthesis praising the institution. Four examples have been chosen to illustrate the variety of approaches taken by sixteenth-century commentators on marriage. The authors aim to entertain as they instruct, and though the same can be said of the century's well-known literary texts that address marriage such as Rabelais's *Tiers Livre*, several stories in Marguerite de Navarre's *Heptaméron* and the debate in verse between Philippe Desportes and Nicole Estienne, much less critical attention has been paid to the work of Jean Bouchet, Pierre Boaistuau de Launay, Pierre de La Primaudaye and François Tillier and their collective role in the evolving discourse about marriage in the early modern period.[8]

Jean Bouchet belonged to the school of *Grands Rhétoriqueurs*, known for their brilliant, elaborate and sometimes provocative stylistic effects. In *Les Triomphes de la Noble et amoureuse Dame: Et l'art d'honnestement aymer / Composé par le Traverseur des Nopces perilleuses*, first published in 1536, Bouchet developed rules for harmonious marriage based on civility between man and wife, followed by debates among allegorical figures such as Prudence, Theology and the Soul, who introduce Biblical references to the situations described by Plutarch. The Christian setting is maintained in long passages about sex, body parts (in great detail), healthy eating (complete with recipes), and ending with advice on sleep habits and dream interpretation. In the second part of *Les Triomphes de la Noble et amoureuse Dame*, the Lady is tempted by the Prince of Sensual Delights and his minions, Lewdness and Youth. Luckily for the Lady, Divine Grace, a priest, and Jesus himself intervene to save her from mortal sin. The remainder of the story chronicles her continuing struggle and eventual victory over many sorts of temptation before a peaceful death. Although marriage only occupies the first third of Bouchet's text, it is the basis of the Lady's earthly happiness and the place from which sin, in the form of adultery, attracts her.

The tension between peaceful contentment and conjugal agitation of various sorts characterizes all four documents under consideration. In Pierre de Boaistuau de Launay's *De l'excellence et dignité de Mariage* (1567), the agitation is once again primarily sexual in nature.

Boaistuau's treatise follows his translation from the Latin of *L'Histoire de Chelidonius Tigurinus, sur l'institution des Princes Chrestiens & origine des Royaumes*; in the context of advice to princes, marriage is suggested as the best remedy for lust, a vice particularly damaging to royalty since impure bloodlines can endanger a monarchy. From there, Boaistuau continues with a discussion of the weakness of the flesh that affects us all, citing Aristotle, the Old and New Testaments and Saint Augustine. Wives are his next target: they must be obedient because of their intellectual inferiority. Nonetheless, the dialectic takes over: wives should be treated well, as faithful friends and companions for life. With their special, natural graces and sweetness, women are a gift from God to men; to prove his point, Boaistuau cites authorities including Plutarch, the Church Fathers, Boccacio, and even Christine de Pisan. Marriage accumulates positive attributes as an institution essential to nature, religion, and the growth of the State. The ideal marriage means complete communion between husband and wife. And yet – the distance is great between the ideal marriage and the typical one characterized by adultery and ungrateful, greedy children. Husbands bear the brunt of the blame, in Boaistuau's view, as power engenders responsibility. He ends with an enumeration of the positive aspects of marriage, noting that Christian tolerance and forgiveness should govern the behavior of spouses. Happy marriage is portrayed as a most laudable goal, very difficult to attain.

The difficulty of reaching that utopian space of marital bliss is a view shared by Pierre de La Primaudaye. His *Académie françoise* (1577) takes the form of a conversation among four young gentlemen of his native Anjou who expose diverse views on a number of topics. A Protestant, La Primaudaye's text stands out for its defense of female education, not just in the repressive sense of instruction in modesty and obedience, but in a full range of studies, with an emphasis on classical philosophy. True companionship in marriage is once again the ideal, and La Primaudaye suggests a practical means to achieve it. Like the other sixteenth-century moralists cited here, he exposes the negative along with the positive aspects of marriage and relations with women, instable creatures that they are. He, too, castigates lust and the adultery it all too often provokes. Like the others, La Primaudaye comes down on the side of marriage despite its disadvantages and the relative rarity of a truly happy union. Although he repeats themes already familiar to readers of the time, his advice is forward looking in its emphasis on female achievement. Besides the education of women and the reiteration of the notion of friendship between spouses, civility, mutual respect and the absence of lustful passion are the secrets to marital success.

An attack on passionate love launches François Tillier's *Livre du Philogame ou amy des nopces* (1586). Jealousy and the fear of cuckoldry prevent many men from marrying, according to Tillier. Nonetheless, a wise, modest wife who will be a comfort and a helpmate is held out as such a pleasurable possibility that it only makes sense to attempt married life, to say nothing of the importance of progeny. This contrast continues throughout the treatise, as Tillier explores the problematic nature of desire. With constant references to Plato, he lauds the physical beauty as the starting point for conjugal communion, and yet warns that the inclination toward a beautiful woman carries the danger of bewitchment, moral blindness, slavery and the fever associated with erotic love. Tillier intermingles the verse of different classical and contemporary authors in each of his chapters; in Chapter 5 we find Ronsard's observations on passion.

> Injuste amour fusil de toute rage,
> Que peut un cœur soubmis à ton pouvoir,
> Quant il te plaist par les sens emouvoir
> Nostre raison qui preside au courage? (35)

Reason should be our guide in choosing a spouse, and not "ce fils de putain Cupidon" (39). Easier said than done, Tillier admits, especially when money is almost as attractive as good looks; a marriage based on greed can be as disastrous as a marriage based on ephemeral physical attributes. The permanence of marriage makes the choice of utmost importance, and the risks laid out by Tillier would appear to outweigh the benefits he mentions in Book One.

In Book Two, however, like his compatriots earlier in the century, Tillier offers some practical solutions to the marriage dilemma. He aims his remarks at husbands, who have more power to create the conditions for domestic peace. They should treat their wives well, but not watch them too closely (ignorance is bliss). Moderation in household life is the key: along with an attitude of tolerance, modesty in dress, ornamentation, diet and entertainment for both spouses will foster the kind of conjugal friendship that all of the writers cited here promote.

Over the course of the century, the ideal of reciprocity and harmony in marriage appears increasingly attainable, laying the groundwork for its seventeenth-century manifestations. All four of the exemplary authors cited here place marriage in its social and political context, agreeing with Michel de Montaigne in his Essay III, 5 (*Sur des vers de Virgile*) that "On ne se marie pas pour soi, quoi qu'on dise: on se marie autant ou plus, pour sa postérité, pour sa famille: L'usage et l'interêt du mariage touche notre race, bien loin par-delà nous" (1328). Political order relies in turn upon the stability of families. A look at royal decrees from the reigns of Henri II through Louis XIV clearly demonstrates how important marriage practices were considered by the monarchy, which entered into a power struggle with the Catholic Church for authority over the institution – a contest the Crown eventually won.[9] In this context, secular marriage manuals distanced themselves further from Catholic doctrine, and especially from its determination to keep women in their place, at home and silent.

Marriage in Seventeenth-Century Salon Culture

When François de Grenaille published *L'Honneste mariage* in 1640, he made explicit the union between marriage and *honnêteté*, thus placing his discussion of marriage in the context of salon culture by making it clear that social interaction outside the home was expected of his female readers. This is his only innovation, albeit an important one. The themes prevalent in sixteenth-century marriage treatises reappear in Grenaille's work, and his constant allusions to Christian virtue give his moral directives a rather severe tone, reminiscent of Du Bosc's *Honneste femme* in its opinions on the limited social role women should play. Grenaille is not the only secular author to adopt a vision closer to the one promulgated by priests in the many religious marriage manuals published during the century.[10] In an era when several treatises on conjugal life were being produced each decade by clergy and laity alike, tendencies emerged among the secular authors that suggest subgenres. It is possible to divide the non-religious manuals into three categories: moralizing, facetious and, for want of a better term, *galant*.

A well-ordered household based on Christian tolerance and understanding is the dominant theme of the work of the "moralizers" such as Antoine Courtin (1674), le Sieur de Mainville (1683), Jacques Chaussé de la Terrière (1685) and the anonymous author of *La Félicité du mariage* (1702). Like Grenaille, and unlike their sixteenth-century predecessors, these authors did consider socializing a duty, although in moderation. But in more ways than not, these texts of the final third of the century hark back about 100 to 150 years. They instructed women in particular on conduct in society, always emphasizing a self-effacing modesty as the premier virtue of the Christian wife: the clever conversation required for success in elite salons is superfluous to this vision of married life. Conservative in their social views, these writers were also in the end conservative in their reprise of the themes and dialectical structure of sixteenth-century didactic marriage manuals. Like Renaissance writers, they attempted to make moral lessons more appealing by using varied forms such as dialogues and letters. The style and tone have been updated, but the fundamental similarity of approach is striking.

Courtin's *Traité de la jalousie, ou moyens d'entretenir la paix dans le Mariage*, sufficiently popular to be republished in 1685, focuses on Christianity as a guide to moderating passions destructive of family stability. In *Du Bonheur et du malheur du mariage*, Mainville presents a series of letters between a young widow and her male advisor. The very first letter sets the tone: the advisor "luy fait craindre un mauvais choix, et l'avertit qu'elle n'en fera pas de bon, si elle ne préfere son salut et la gloire de Dieu aux interêts de la terre (1). When he begins to advise her niece, the emphasis on Christian virtue is maintained: "Que les Mécontents dans le Mariage n'ont point de meilleur remede à leurs maux, que de les souffrir en silence, ou de n'en parler qu'à Dieu" (168). Chaussé de la Terrière's preface sounds notes of salon society when he tells young men that in marriage, they can taste "des voluptés d'autant plus douces qu'elles sont pures et innocentes. Enfin il vous donne des préceptes pour apprendre à bien parler et bien juger des Dames; c'est à dire de ce que naturellement vous aimez le plus, et que les Loix mêmes de la civilité vous obligent de respecter." But the accent on piety and the Holy Scripture as the guide for married life place this treatise, along with the other post-1670 documents, into the "moralizing" category. In 1702, *La Félicité du mariage* demonstrates the predominance of such discourse through the end of the century. In a dialogue between Agaton, a single man, and Aristarque, who encourages his friend to marry, Christian duty remains the primary reason for taking a wife. Remarks such as "une femme est entre les mains d'un mary ce que l'argile est entre les mains d'un potier" (10) do not suggest the kind of reciprocity in male-female relations that we find in the *galant* texts of the 1650s and 1660s. Mutual obligation is framed from a perspective very similar to that of the sixteenth century when Agaton starts to accept his friend's lessons: "Vous m'avez fait comprendre que si une femme fait quelque faux pas contre son devoir, c'est que tres souvent nous sommes les premiers à trebucher, ou pour mieux dire, nous l'obligeons par nostre mauvaise conduite à se laisser entraîner à des passions ausquelles sans doute elle resisteroit si nous estions toujours dans nostre devoir" (36-37). The husband's responsibility implies a dominance that was absent from the earlier, more idealized *galant* sub-genre of marriage manuals.

In the first decades of the seventeenth century, the most prevalent sub-genre is composed of facetious texts such as the *Forest nuptiale* of Cholières, published in 1600, the article on marriage in La Mothe Le Vayer's *Dialogues faits à l'imitation des anciens* (1632 or 1633), and Paul Caillet's *Tableau du mariage représenté au naturel* (1635). Tongue firmly in cheek, they make light of the didacticism of the sixteenth-century manuals as well as the religious treatises that began to appear in the 1630s, but without descending into the misogynist and misogamist polemics so prevalent early in the century.[11] In length and structure, facetious treatises on marriage mirror the serious, moralizing secular texts that were to be published in greater numbers in the last third of the century, whereas the pre-1625 comic satirists stick to verse forms or short fiction.

Le Sieur de Cholières provides a cross-cultural panorama of marriage practices, drawn from historians and travel writers. This sort of survey was not uncommon in sixteenth-century treatises, and served to demonstrate the superiority of Christian marriage over pagan versions of the institution. Cholières sings the praises of marriage throughout *La Forest nuptiale*, contrasting the sacred union of the Christian couple with the desecration of marriage by the licentious, a group that includes Catholic priests and monks, whom he calls "Bramins" and "Brachmans."[12] Their sexual appetite resembles that of barbarous foreigners; unmasking these depraved sinners is the pretext for one hundred and fifty pages of exposition of the sexual mores of the "Romains, Babyloniens, Persans, Tartares, Chiots, Turcs, Thraciens, Moscovites, Gots & Suesses, Laponiens, Arabes, Senegheens, Aethiopiens, Calcutiens, Malabariens, Narsingueens, Campioniens, Camuliens, Tarnassariens, Thebetheins, Fezeens, Cubeens & Haitiés, Sauvages, Patagoneens & Yucateens, Prestres, Brahmins, Brachmans" (Avant propos, n.p.), with special attention to rituals at the time of loss of virginity. Occasionally, Cholières includes a digression on the loose morals of French women, but the thrust of *La Forest nuptiale* is titillation rather than misogyny.[13] The focus on sexual exoticism detracts from his celebration of the perfect harmony of the ideal couple, which the opening lines of the treatise claim as its principal topic.

Like *La Forest nuptiale*, Paul Caillet's *Tableau* praises marriage only to undermine the positive portrayal by proving that the institution is problematic across cultures. He, too, surveys exotic practices: his treatise is *"enrichi de plusieurs rares curiosités, figures, emblèmes, histoires, loyx, mœurs et coustumes de diverses nations"* which serve to illustrate the main points of his concluding chapter. Such blatant criticism as "…le Mariage a en toutes ses figures un si hideux aspect qu'il semble plus à fuir qu'à desirer" (226) is nonetheless counterbalanced by attenuating remarks: "C'est à la verité un grand mal qu'une femme, mais c'est encores un plus grand mal de n'en avoir point" (237). His final distinction between the ideal and a harsh reality presents the same kind of tension we see from Cholières.

> Nous concluons donques que le mariage, consideré *in abstracte*, est indefiniment bon, voire du tout necessaire; mais si nous venons à particulariser les hypotheses et les individus *in concreto*, nous advouërons volentiers *seculum quid, per accidens*, et par la corruption de la nature il est cause de tant de malheurs en beaucoup de familles, qu'il seroit plus expedient pour plusieurs de n'y avoir jamais pensé, que de gemir perpetuellement sous le joug d'un miserable servage. (242-43)

And yet the ideal exists and even dominates the final pages of the *Tableau du mariage* with examples of conjugal love and fidelity (256-64). All of the authors of "facetious" texts on marriage include the notion of perfect conjugal harmony, but they problematize it radically.

This is certainly the case with the last of the three considered here. A conversation among three friends is the form take by La Mothe Le Vayer's "Dialogue sur le mariage." Eleus is curious about the institution; Cassander is a bachelor who counsels him to marry; and Philocles is an apparently contented married man who warns against the tie that binds. The stage is set for over thirty pages of witty critique, based on problems frequently examined in writings on marriage from Antiquity onward. Philocles points out that passionate love is an unstable basis for marriage (473-74), that in any case a virtuous, intelligent woman is hard to find (476). Most wives will neglect their household and spend any money accorded them on clothing or outings, with a view to committing adultery (480-81). Laws in favor of marriage have been necessary throughout the ages in order to convince people to enter into this dreadful state (479). La Mothe Le Vayer's most important remark for situating the discussion in the context of *honnêteté* and the salon culture that were developing in the 1630s is that a husband can never win a wife's affection freely given, since she is constrained to have conjugal relations and to show a modicum of respect (475). Our author seems to announce, albeit back-handedly, the *galant* texts of the 1640s through the 1660s. In the elite salon world they depict, male-female affective ties based on courtship rituals and the woman's freedom to refuse a suitor create a stimulating tension that is absent from marriage. The marital status of the participants was irrelevant to most; whether sexual relations were involved or not, ostensible if not legal liberty from the prison of marriage made a new form of relationship imaginable.

The *galant* sub-genre belongs chronologically and thematically between the moralizing and facetious texts. Born in the salons at the same time that *galant* literature emerged (1640-1650), its apogee was in the 1660s (Denis, *Parnasse* 11). Delphine Denis defines *la galanterie* as "un art d'aimer et de vivre en société" (*Parnasse* 9); Antoine Courtin defined adultery as "ce crime qui se déguise à la vérité sous le nom de galanterie dans les païs corrompus" (296). Writing twenty years after the marriage texts in this sub-genre were published, Courtin exploits the erotic connotations of the words *galanterie* and *galant* for his didactic ends. But when the topic of marriage was first introduced into *galant* discourse, a new definition of the institution became possible.

It should be noted that *galanterie* and marriage were usually dissociated. Typical illustrations of this divorce appear in texts of the *galant* genre such as Charles Sorel's *Discours pour et contre l'Amitié Tendre, Hors le Mariage* (1663) and the Abbé de Pure's novel, *La Prétieuse* (1654). Sorel's dialogue promotes the ideal of *amitié tendre*, or "loving friendship," but insists that it can only exist outside marriage. As La Mothe Le Vayer had suggested in the 1630s, conjugal relations and the constraints of marriage for life destroy the conditions necessary for *amitié tendre*.[14] A neo-Platonic ideal of purity and freedom (reminiscent as well of the medieval courtly love tradition) situates *amitié tendre* in European literary and cultural history, and yet its manifestation in seventeenth-century France retains certain particularities associated with salon culture. Michel de Pure's four-volume novel depicts almost nothing but discussion in a Parisian salon whose social dynamic produces a theory of male-female relations heavily influenced by group interaction. Marriage is explicitly condemned as detrimental to healthy and happy union between the sexes (see II, 13-38, for example). As in Sorel's text, the constraints inherent in marriage are obstacles to the realization of perfect friendship. The more than one thousand pages of Pure's salon-centered novel make it clear that friends of the opposite sex can fully enjoy each other's company only in the presence of others, spectators of their performance of elegant, disincarnated intimacy.

Nevertheless, some writers chose to introduce *amitié tendre* into marriage, awkward though the fit might be. Louis Couvay begins *L'Honneste Maitresse ou le Pouvoir Legitime des Dames sur ceux qui les recherchent honnestement en Mariage* (1654) by exploring premarital courtship, during which women have real power, based on their natural "perfections," which include beauty, grace, a sweet disposition, a good mind, good morals, and, not least important, exemplary mores. Like royal power, women's power is God-given and ladies should be worshipped as God's ambassadresses on earth (293-95). Couvay distances himself from the moralizers when he explains that he has no intention of promulgating precepts for wives, as had been so common in the sixteenth century. Rather, he wants to inform women of their rights and powers, before and after marriage (Preface, n.p.). Couvay enters the realm of true *galanterie* when he defends love matches, noting that he is not supporting unruly passion governed by bodily impulses, but rather love based on reason, anchored in the merit of the potential wife (297-300).

Allegorical dialogue is the form chosen by F. Joyeux for his *Traité des Combats que l'Amour a eu contre la Raison et la Ialousie. Où il adjoute le duel innocent du corps & de l'ame de l'Apologie du Mariage, avec un petit discours sur l'élection que l'homme doit faire d'une femme* (1667). Unlike Jean Bouchet's allegorical work of 1536, however, this text proclaims its playfulness and its adherence to the world of the here and now. Situated in the salon of Scine, the author's love interest, the debate between Love and Reason is won handily by Love. His strategy is to enter into a truce with his traditional enemy: Love explains his antipathy to forced marriage by demonstrating that it is not he, but the authoritarian father who is unreasonable. The soul knows only unrest and discontent if one's spouse is not suited to one's taste – an important concept in salon aesthetics. Love considers living in an atmosphere of harmonious good taste a necessary condition for inner peace; morality meets aesthetics in choosing a marriage partner (11).

After Love has convinced both Reason and Jealousy to adopt his point of view, the scene is set for Joyeux's *Apologie du mariage*. The institution is based, as in Couvay's text, on loving friendship rather than unbridled passion. It is also rooted in a reciprocal pedagogy: a wife can study under her husband's tutelage (67), but she can also teach: "par la beauté de ses yeux, nous pouvons remarquer un rayon de la divinité, & nous eslever par les merveilles de la creature à l'admiration, & à la connoissance du Createur; quels Livres, quelle Philosophie, nous peut aussi parfaitement, & aussi utilement enseigner la temperance, la modestie, la pieté, la devotion, la charité, & la continence" (68).

With the end of Joyeux's treatise, we return explicitly to the subject of this volume, instruction. It is fitting to conclude with another text born of salon culture that communicates lessons in an artful way: Madeleine de Scudéry's *Clélie, Histoire romaine* (1654-1660). Although many novels, plays and poems of the period examine "the marriage question," the treatment in *Clélie* parallels the didactic marriage manuals: as in *La Prétieuse*, time is taken often during the ten volumes for group conversation, mirroring the discussions that took place in Scudéry's own very popular salon and reflected in the dialogues of Sorel and Joyeux. Famous works centered on marriage such as *L'École des femmes* and *La Princesse de Clèves* have been the object of massive amounts of scrutiny from critics, and the problematization of marriage in the adult fairytales so popular at the end of the century are currently the object of much critical attention. But aside from a 1979 article by Nicole Aronson and my recent contribution, the discussion of marriage in the salon scenes of *Clélie* has not been much developed.

Madeleine de Scudéry's characters criticize marriage more than they praise it, for the same reasons exposed in *La Prétieuse* and the "facetious" texts: the ideal of *amitié tendre* requires freedom in the choice of a love object, and freedom to develop the relationship according to the impetus of both reason and natural (physical) inclination, which come together in shared tastes. And yet, where other works of fiction denigrate marriage, *Clélie* furnishes additional, positive perspective.

In *La muse galante: poétique de la conversation dans l'œuvre de Madeleine de Scudéry*, Delphine Denis shows that the pedagogical function of the novel is closely linked to the art of conversation, which in turn is indispensable when learning polished, polite behavior and the capacity for pleasing one's interlocutors that is *honnêteté*. For success in the salons, it was necessary to exhibit good taste and to give pleasure by one's gracious demeanor and skills as a conversationalist (11-13). These aesthetic criteria gradually replaced traditional ethical ones as the basis for human relations, and Madeleine de Scudéry's novels, especially *Clélie*, demonstrate the shift. This declaration by one of the characters, Valérie, illustrates the challenge of placing marriage in the setting of salon culture and *honnêteté*.

> Je vous asseure, dit Valerie, qu'il est plus difficile que vous ne pensez, d'estre tout à la fois un bon mary, un agreable Amant, et un fort honneste homme, car pour estre Amant, il faut estre esclave; pour estre mary avec honneur, il faut estre maistre, & pour estre un fort honneste homme, il ne faut estre ny le tyran, ny l'esclave de sa femme. Je soutiens mesme qu'il y va de l'honneur de celles qui ont de bons maris, de leur laisser une authorité qui paroisse aux yeux du monde, quand mesme par excez d'amour, ou par quelque autre cause, ils n'en voudroient pas avoir; et qu'une fort honneste femme ne doit jamais souhaiter qu'on dise qu'elle soit la gouvernante de son mary; mais seulement qu'elle a du credit sur son esprit, qu'il l'estime, qu'il la croit, & qu'il l'ayme, & non pas qu'il luy obeït aveuglement, comme s'il estoit incapable de se conduire par luy mesme. (*Clélie*, III, 1, 334-36 [new edition, 130])

The way out of the dilemma is for the wife to take on the burden of performing perfect conjugal harmony very carefully, so as not to give the impression of female dominance.

In the next passage, the husband's public performance disguises *amitié tendre* in the married couple. As La Mothe Le Vayer, Sorel and Pure suggest, it was not fashionable to be in love with one's spouse,

> ...comme vous les sçavez, ce n'est guere la mode de voir des Maris amoureux de leurs femmes. Ie vous assure, reprit Plotine, que Persandre l'est tousiours de la sienne, qu'il le sera toute sa vie; et que toute la difference qu'il y a de ce qu'il estoit autrefois, à ce qu'il est aujourd'huy, c'est qu'il ne fait pas le galant en public: mais pour les sentimens de son cœur ils sont aussi tendres, aussi passionnez, et aussi pleins de respect, qu'ils l'estoient du temps qu'il n'estoit que le Rival de Turnus, Et pour moy ie ne sçache rien de plus injuste, que le procedé de ces gens qui sont cinq ou six ans à gemir, à soûpirer, et à faire toutes les choses imaginables pour venir à bout d'épouser une femme qu'ils aiment, et pour la mépriser le lendemain. (*Clélie*, II, 3, 1344-45 [new edition, 472])

The complaint of the last sentence opens the door to a more public disclosure of spousal affection.

Clélie builds on *galant* marriage discourse by initiating a new art of marriage based on pleasing one's spouse the way *honnêtes gens* please in society, with natural affability and the ability to communicate with graceful eloquence. Traces of this theory of marriage were present in the didactic works of the sixteenth century, but their moralizing, Christian perspective leaves little room for the aesthetic dimension of *amitié tendre*. The seventeenth-century moralizers carried the baggage of salon culture, even as they resisted its values by insisting upon the subservience of women. Grenaille, writing in the heyday of *honnêteté* in 1640, is the one "moralizer" linked, albeit tenuously, to salon culture, when he uses section titles such as "Que l'union des esprits est plus douce que toutes les satisfactions de la chair" (70) and "Que le mariage est le lien de la plus parfaite amitié" (83). Grenaille's emphasis on the superiority of spiritual love over physical love coincides with the *précieux* perspective enunciated by all of the *galant* authors cited here, as exemplified not only in *Clélie* but in the life of Madeleine de Scudéry.[15] The duty to have conjugal relations is a major factor in marital unhappiness in the facetious treatises; they all conclude that the truly harmonious couple is an unmarried one. It is only in the *galant* texts that *amitié tendre* exists as a successful model, based on respectful, elegant, pleasurable communication. At the midpoint of the *Grand Siècle*, instruction and art had become inseparable.

The sixteenth century laid the groundwork for the promise of *amitié tendre*, but its textual realization lasted only about twenty years. The disappearance of the ideal in marriage manuals (as in the novel) corresponds to the rise of moralizing texts on marriage after 1670 – and to a religious, moral and philosophical critique of *honnêteté* by Jansenist-leaning writers (Bury 129). If human virtue is illusory, how can *amitié tendre* sustain relationships? After all, assumptions about the virtue of "married friends" underpin it. In the 1680s, the court of Louis XIV became a more somber place with the King's marriage to Madame de Maintenon and "conversion" to a stricter religious practice. A pessimistic turn colored most textual production: anxiety penetrated writing about marriage for the rest of the century whether it be in religious treatises, moralizing secular manuals, medical and legal tracts or literary texts. Besides the novels and fairytales already mentioned, even comic theatre goes beyond the traditional happy ending of a wedding ceremony to portray the darker side of married life, as Guy Spielmann demonstrates in his masterful study, *Le jeu de l'ordre et du chaos: comédie et pouvoirs à la fin de règne, 1673-1715*.[16] Instruction meant lessons in life's harsh truths, leaving very little trace in the nuptial imaginary of the sweet conviviality and artful communication that had characterized *amitié tendre*.

Notes

[1] Research for this study was made possible by a grant from the Social Sciences and Humanities Research Council of Canada. In *Le mariage en Occident*, Jean Gaudemet describes "la crise du XVIe siècle" (275-95).

[2] Bury 9-13 and *passim*. Cicero of course furnishes the image of the public orator, the model citizen whose sense of decorum has both moral and rhetorical implications (22).

[3] Allan Reese suggests 1497 as the date of composition, on the occasion of the marriage of Erasmus's pupil and patron, Lord Mountjoy (552-53). When first published in Louvain in 1518, the title was *Declamatio in genere suasorio de laude matrimonii*; the Basel publisher Froben adopted the title *Encomium Matrimonii* in his edition the same year. Luther's first important publication on marriage did not appear until 1522 (Gaudemet 269-71).

[4] Émile Telle describes the circumstances of Berquin's condemnation in the introduction to his edition of the *Déclamation*; he notes that Berquin was "le premier humaniste, noble de naissance, qui périt pour ses convictions religieuses" (3).

[5] Jean-Claude Margolin edited the *Encomium Matrimonii* in 1975 for the complete works (ASD, I-5, 333-417; 333-82 for these points).

[6] A debate among students of Erasmus continues to this day as to the radical nature of Erasmus's positions: Reese sees Erasmus backing off from the ideas expressed in the *Encomium* when he publishes the *Institutio christiani matrimonii* in 1526, disagreeing with Telle's view of this texts as a reaffirmation of the *Encomium* (Reese 558-59; Telle edition of Berquin 60-61). The ambiguity of the *Institutio* may well be explained by Erasmus's strategies for self-protection in his volatile times.

[7] Robert Aulotte enumerates the Latin and the French translations, all of them problematic until Amyot's in 1572. The dates of the other French versions are 1535 (Jean Lodé), two in 1546 (one from the Italian of Sperone Speroni; the translator of the other is anonymous), 1558 (Jacques Grévin), 1559 (Jacques de la Tapie), 1564 (Jean de Marconville), 1571 (Étienne de la Boétie).

[8] Only scattered references to these treatises appear in the books by Maclean, Berriot-Salvadore, Timmermans and Jordan.

[9] The Council of Trent's most important ruling on marriage occurred in one of the last sessions of 1563: the *Tametsi* decree forbade clandestine marriages, as a result of pressure from the French king, thus paving the way for further State intervention in the institution. See Gaudemet, 288-91, and the *Recueil des Edits, Declarations, Ordonnances et Règlemens Des Rois Henry II. François II. Charles IX. Henry III. Henry IV. Louis XIII. Louis XIV. & Louis XV. Concernant les Mariages.*

[10] Grenaille had in fact been an ecclesiastic in his early adulthood (Vizier 8). For more on religious marriage manuals, see Agnès Walch, as well as my article, "Le mirioir du mariage."

[11] See the article by Gilles Banderier as well as my own "Misogamie et misogynie dans les complaintes des mal mariés au XVIIe siècle" for studies of the polemicists.

[12] The *Dictionnaire des lettres françaises* notes that Cholières may be the pen name for the Protestant author Jean Dagoneau (266, 317), which could explain the attack on priests.

[13] For example, "Il y a des femmes entre nous et trop plus qu'il ne seroit à souhaiter, qui encores qu'elles portent doüaire à leurs marys, se sont bien achepter: car sans tirer hors ligne de compte le temps, qu'elles font perdre à leurs mignons, pour estre courtisées, devant que leurs finacées puissent iouïr de l'ayse le plus souvent frauduleux, que l'on se promet devoir estre apporté la premiere nuict des nopces, faut despendre en ioyaux, affiquets, habits & festins plus que ne monte la dore, et en cas que restitution ait lieu par la mort du mary, il faut augmenter quelquesfois la somme de la moytié du doüaire...pour le droict de seure vie de la femme. Ie vous demande si la femme n'est pas bien acheptée" (4-5). And "Si toutes nos fringuantes, qui ont si grande envie de sçavoir aux despens de leur pucellage que c'est de s'acoupler avec le masle, estoient assubietties à la rigueur d'une telle loy...i'en tiens la plus-part si doüillettes qu'elles aimeroient mieux estre filles toute leur vie, qu'avec une si mal plaisante ceremonie commencer leurs nopçages..." (83).

[14] See my article, "Charles Sorel, arbitre de l'amitié tendre," for a detailed analysis of this text.

[15] See Nicole Aronson's biography for a description of the relationship between Scudéry and Paul Pellisson.

[16] Lewis Seifert discusses the dystopic endings of tales by female authors of the end of the century (129-32). See also my remarks on Madame d'Aulnoy's *L'Histoire d'Hypolite, comte de Duglas* and its intercalated fairy tale, "L'île de Félicité," in "La nuit du couple" (517-22).

Works Cited

Primary Sources
Sixteenth-century texts

Boaistuau de Launay, Pierre. *L'Histoire de Chelidonius Tigurinus, sur l'institution des Princes Chrestiens & origine des Royaumes, Traduit du Latin en Françoys par Pierre Bouaistuau, natif de Bretaigne des parties de Nantes, Avec un traité de paix & de guerre, & un autre de l'excellence & dignité de Mariage. Ensemble une autre histoire de la fausse religion de Mahemmet, & par quel moyen il a seduit tant de peuple, lesquelz sont de l'invention du translateur.* 1567; rpt. Lyon: Benoist Rigaud, 1576.

Bouchet, Jean. *Les Triomphes de la Noble et amoureuse Dame: Et l'art d'honnestement aymer / Composé par le Traverseur des Nop-ces*. Paris: n.p., 1536.

Érasme, D. *Déclamation des louenges de mariage (1525)*. Trans. le Chevalier de Berquin. Ed. Émile V. Telle. Geneva: Droz, 1976.

_____. *La femme mécontente de son mari, ou Entretien de deux dames sur les obligations & les peines du mariage. Traduit du latin d'Érasme*. Trans. Sieur de la Rivière. Paris: Veuve Clouzier, 1707.

Erasmus, Desiderus. *Opera Omnia Desiderii Erasmi Roterodami*. Amsterdam: Holland-North Publishing Co., 1969-.

La Primaudaye, Pierre. *L'Academie françoise. En laquelle est traitté de l'institution des Mœurs, & de ce qui concerne le bien & heu-reusement vivre en tous Estats & conditions: Par les Preceptes de la doctrine, & les exemples de la vie des anciens sages & hommes Illustres*. 1577; rpt. Paris: Jacques Chouet, 1598.

Montaigne, Michel de. *Les Essais* [1595 edition]. Ed. J. Céard *et al.* Paris: Librairie Générale (La Pochothèque), 2001.

Plutharque de Cherone Grec, Ancien Philosophe: historiographe, traictant entierement du gouvernement en mariage nouvelle-ment traduict de Grec en Latin & de latin en vulgaire francoys maistre Jehan Lode Licencier en Loix natif du diocese de Nantes au pays de Bretaigne à l'honneur & exaltation de toutes gens, conioingtz en mariage. Lequel traictye fut envoye par ledict Plutharque a deux excellens personnaiges Gregoys Sire Policianus & dame Euridice sa comgaigne & espouse. Paris: Denys Janot, 1536.

Tillier, François. *Le premier et second, livre du Philogame ou amy des nopces*. Paris: Guillaume Bichon, 1586.

Seventeenth-century texts

Caillet, Paul. *Le Tableau du mariage représenté au naturel, enrichi de plusieurs rares curiosités, figures, emblèmes, histoires, loyx, mœurs et coustumes de diverses nations, et illustré de fleurs poétiques et oratoires des plus célèbres auteurs anciens et modernes*. Orange: E. Voisin, 1635.

Chaussé de la Terrière, Jacques. *Traité de l'Excellence du Mariage; de sa Necessité, et des Moyens d'y Vivre Heureux. Où l'on fait l'Apologie des femmes; contre les calomnies des Hommes.* Amsterdam: Abraham Wolfgangh, 1685.

Cholières, le Sieur de. *La Forest nuptiale, où est representee une varieté bigarree, non moins emerveillable que plaisante, de divers mariages, selon qu'ils sont observez et practiquez par plusieurs peuples et nations estranges: Avec la maniere de policer, regir, gouverner et administrer leur famille.* Paris: Pierre Bertault, 1600.

Courtin, Antoine. *Traité de la jalousie, ou moyens d'entretenir la paix dans le Mariage.* 1674; rpt. Paris: Helie Josset, 1685.

Couvay, Louis, D. M. *L'Honneste Maitresse ou Le Pouvoir Legitime des Dames sur ceux qui les recherchent honnestement en Mariage.* Paris: Guillaume de Luyne, 1654.

Du Bosc, Jacques. *L'Honneste femme.* 3 vols. 1632; rpt. Yverdon: n.p., 1649-1650.

Faret, Nicolas. *L'Honnête homme ou l'art de plaire à la Cour* (1630). Ed. M. Magendie. Paris: Presses Universitaires de France, 1925.

La Félcité du mariage, ou les moyens d'y parvenir. Paris: Pierre Gissey, 1702.

Grenaille, François de. *L'Honneste mariage.* Paris: T. Quinet, 1640.

Joyeux, F. *Traité des Combats que l'Amour a eu contre la Raison et la Ialousie. Où il adjoute le duel innocent du corps & de l'ame de l'Apologie du Mariage, avec un petit discours sur l'élection que l'homme doit faire d'une femme.* Paris: Martin Hauteville, 1667.

La Mothe Le Vayer, François de. *Dialogues faits à l'imitation des anciens.* Corpus des Œuvres de Philosophie en Langue Française. Ed. André Pessel. Paris: Fayard, 1988.

Mainville, le Sieur de. *Du Bonheur et du malheur du mariage, et des considérations qu'il faut faire avant que de s'y engager, ouvrage moral et curieux.* Paris: Vve S. Huré, 1683.

Pure, Michel de. *La Prétieuse ou le mystère des Ruelles.* 2 vols. Ed. Émile Magne. 1654; rpt. Paris: Droz, 1938-1939.

Recueil des Edits, Declarations, Ordonnances et Règlemens Des Rois Henry II. François II. Charles IX. Henry III. Henry IV. Louis XIII. Louis XIV. & Louis XV. Concernant les Mariages. Avec plusieurs Arrests notables intervenus sur ce sujet. Nouvelle Edition Augmentée jusqu'à present. Paris: Henry Charpentier, 1724.

Sales, Francois de. *Introduction à la vie dévote* (1608). Paris: Nelson Éditeurs, 1900.

Scudéry, Madeleine de. *Clélie, Histoire romaine.* 10 vols. 1654-1660; rpt. Genève: Slatkine, 1972.

_____. *Clélie, Histoire romaine.* Seconde partie 1655. Ed. Chantal Morlet-Chantalat. Paris: Champion, 2002.

_____. *Clélie, Histoire romaine.* Troisième partie 1657. Ed. Chantal Morlet-Chantalat. Paris: Champion, 2003.

Sorel, Charles. *Œuvres Diverses, ou Discours Meslez.* Paris: Compagnie des Libraires au Palais, 1663.

Secondary Sources

Aronson, Nicole. "Amour et mariage dans les œuvres de Mlle de Scudéry." *L'Esprit Créateur* 19.1 (Spring 1979): 26-39.

_____. *Mademoiselle de Scudéry ou le voyage au pays de Tendre.* Paris: Fayard, 1986.

Aulotte, Robert. *Amyot et Plutarque. La tradition des Moralia au XVIe siècle.* Geneva: Droz, 1965.

Banderier, Gilles. "Le mariage au miroir des poètes satiriques français (1600-1650)." In *Le Mariage dans l'Europe des XVIe et XVIIe siècles.* Ed. Richard Crescenzo *et al.* Presses de l'Université Nancy II, 2003. 243-60.

Berriot-Salvadore, Évelyne. *Les femmes dans la société de la Renaissance.* Geneva: Droz, 1990.

Beugnot, Bernard. *La mémoire du texte. Essais de poétique classique.* Paris: Champion, 1994.

Bury, Emmanuel. *Littérature et politesse. L'invention de l'honnête homme (1580-1750).* Paris: Presses Universitaires de France, 1996.

Carlin, Claire. "Charles Sorel arbitre de l'amitié tendre." In *Charles Sorel polygraphe*. Eds. Emmanuel Bury and Éric Van der Schueren. Québec: Presses de l'université Laval (Les collections de la République des Lettres – Série Symposiums), 2006. 453-62.

―――. "Le Miroir du mariage: La métaphore dans quelques traités catholiques du XVIIe siècle." In *La Spiritualité/L'Épistolaire/ Le Merveilleux*. Eds. D. Wetsel and F. Canovas. *Biblio 17*. Vol. 145. Tübingen: Gunter Narr, 2003. 95-109.

―――. "Misogamie et misogynie dans les complaintes des mal mariés au XVIIe siècle." In *La Femme au XVIIe siècle*. Ed. Richard G. Hodgson. *Biblio 17*. Vol. 138. Tübingen: Gunter Narr Verlag, 2002. 365-78.

―――. "La nuit du couple: La dissolution du marriage dans l'imaginaire des XVIe et XVIIe siècles." In *Penser La Nuit (XVe-XVIIe siècle)*. Ed. Dominique Bertrand. Paris: Champion, 2003. 505- 23.

―――. "Préciosité et théologie: L'amour conjugal dans *Clélie* et dans quelques traités catholiques sur le mariage." In *Madeleine de Scudéry: Une femme de lettres au XVIIe siècle. Actes du colloque international de Paris (28-30 juin 2001)*. Eds. D. Denis et A.-E. Spica. Artois Presses Université, 2002. 141-53.

Denis, Delphine. *La muse galante. Poétique de la conversation dans l'œuvre de Madeleine de Scudéry*. Paris: Champion, 1997.

―――. *Le Parnasse galant. Institution d'une catégorie littéraire au XVIIe siècle*. Paris: Champion, 2001.

Dictionnaire des lettres françaises. Le XVIe siècle. Ed. Michel Simonin. Paris: Fayard (La Pochothèque), 2001.

Elias, Norbert. *The Civilizing Process*. Vol I. Trans. E. Jephcott. Oxford: Basil Blackwell, 1978.

Gaudemet, Jean. *Le mariage en Occident: Les mœurs et le droit*. Paris: Les Éditions du Cerf, 1989.

Jordan, Constance. *Renaissance Feminism: Literary Texts and Political Models*. Ithaca: Cornell University Press, 1990.

Lougee, Carolyn. *Le Paradis des Femmes. Women, Salons and Social Stratification in Seventeenth-Century France.* Princeton: Princeton University Press, 1976.

Maclean, Ian. *The Renaissance Notion of Woman. A Study in the Fortunes of Scholasticism and Medical Science in European Intellectual Life.* Cambridge, U.K.: Cambridge University Press, 1980.

Mesnard, Jean. "'Honnête homme' et 'honnête femme' dans la culture du XVIIe siècle." In *Présences féminines: Littérature et société au XVIIe siècle français. Actes de London, Canada (1985).* Eds. I. Richmond and C. Venesoen. *Biblio 17.* Vol. 36. Paris-Seattle-Tübingen: Papers on French Seventeenth Century Literature, 1987. 15-46.

Reese, Allan W. "Learning Virginity: Erasmus' Ideal of Christian Marriage." *Bibliothèque d'Humanisme et Renaissance,* LVII.3 (1995): 551-67.

Seifert, Lewis. *Fairy Tales, Sexuality and Gender in France, 1690-1715: Nostalgic Utopias.* Cambridge, U.K.: Cambridge University Press, 1996.

Spielmann, Guy. *Le jeu de l'ordre et du chaos: Comédie et pouvoirs à la fin de règne, 1673-1715.* Paris: Champion, 2002.

Timmermans, Linda. *L'acces des femmes à la culture (1598-1715). Un débat d'idées de Saint François de Sales à la Marquise de Lambert.* Paris: Champion, 1993.

Vizier, Alain. "Présentation" to *L'honnête fille,* by François de Grenaille. Paris: Champion, 2003. 7-107.

Walch, Agnès. La spiritualité conjugale dans le catholicisme français, XVIe-XXe siècle. Paris: Les Editions du Cerf, 2002.

Satirical Realia:
The Caractères' *Conversion of Royal Pedagogy to Social Critique*

Mark A. Cohen

The Discovery of the Author

The *Caractères* did not bear La Bruyère's name on its title page during his lifetime.[1] He did however insert it in a cryptic form within the text in a remark added for the 5th edition of 1690 (*"Geoffroy D***"*) and in its definitive form in the 6th edition of 1691 ("Geoffroy de La Bruyère"). Although by this time the author's identity was well known, withholding it in this ambivalent manner represented a complex moral gesture. The literary ethics he espoused deemed it essential that one not rely on one's name and status to promote one's book but instead leave it to succeed or fail on its own merits. It was in the energies and skill that went into the writing itself and not self-promotion that its success should lay. Yet one of the key aesthetic mechanisms that made the merit of the text was its playful suggestion that there might indeed be a real-life counterpart in contemporary Paris who embodied the apparently exaggerated forms of behavior exhibited by the Characters within it. A large part of the book's initial popularity derived from this mobilization of the reader's powers of recognition, hence the proliferation of the infamous *clés* that saw in the text a potent demand for matching up the ridiculous types with actual individuals. By the 5th edition La Bruyère was quite prepared to recognize *this* fact himself.

The text already contained a quite unproblematic self-identification of the anonymous author with Theophrastus by way of the Humanist ethos of imitation. There were numerous additions along the same lines.[2] These associations were in ideological terms nothing more than La Bruyère's alignment of his current textual activity with a venerable tradition of sages and scriptural models. It was essentially impersonal. However when it came to actually *naming* himself, as opposed to an idealized ancestry, function or style, he begins to look more like one of his own Characters. The *Caractères* occasionally names actual targets by giving them an exotic Greek or Roman title like the other Characters. Real names however are always adduced by way of praise.[3] "Geoffroy de la Bruyère" partakes of both naming regimes: it is and is not his name, an exact parallel and yet a fantastic attribution. In a chapter replete with attacks on the aristocracy's ridiculous naming practices and claims of venerable lineage, he seems to be aping their onomastic arrogance.

> Je le déclare nettement, afin que l'on s'y prépare et que personne un jour n'en soit surpris: s'il arrive jamais que quelque grand me trouve digne de ses soins, si je fais enfin une belle fortune, il y a un Geoffroy de la Bruyère, que toutes les chroniques rangent au nombre des plus grands seigneurs de France qui suivirent Godefroy de Bouillon à la conquête de la Terre-Sainte: voilà alors de qui je descends en ligne directe. (*De quelques Usages* 14, 417)

What is the precise meaning of this obvious piece of satiric self-humiliation and why does it have to bear the weight of his authorship? La Bruyère's family background was bourgeois; his claim to fame derived from quite different sources. The "ligne directe" from which La Bruyère was, in his own mind, descended, was utterly different, entirely literary and freely chosen, that of Theophrastus.

The following essay takes its bearings from the fact that while La Bruyère was writing the *Caractères* in the mid-1680s his actual profession was not that of the detached *moraliste* observer but of a mouthpiece for a very real aristocratic lineage, tutor to the grandson of the Grand Condé, and then a courtier in his house, ennobled by the family for his services. La Bruyère was indeed found 'worthy by someone' ("digne de...soins") and given a quite generous monetary 'fortune' but it was not for being a feudal hero. Instead it was for teaching someone else to be one with modern versions of the "chroniques...des plus grands seigneurs." His ultimate attitude to his aristocratic patrons can be gauged from the presentation of the text itself, which bears no dedication to the new Duke of Condé or his son.[4] The usurpation of a lineage that is not his in *De quelques Usages* 14 is a satiric reversal of his voicing of a heritage that was not his imposed on him by his preceptorship.

Before and After the *Caractères*

When critics consider the prehistory of the *Caractères* it is the difficulties and embarrassments the shy *philosophe* must have experienced in the hurly-burly of court life that have garnered most of their attention. Yet the only evidence for the supposed cause of the animus fueling chapters like *De la Cour* is either internal to the chapter itself or anecdotal and therefore ultimately unverifiable. On the other hand, shortly before the publication of the *Caractères* in 1688, from the autumn of 1684 to December 1686, La Bruyère acted as one of the preceptors of the sixteen-year-old Duke of Bourbon, grandson of Louis II de Bourbon, known to history as the Grand Condé, a scion of one of France's greatest families and a cousin of Louis XIV. La Bruyère taught the Duke primarily history, geography, genealogy and a Who's Who of Versailles. We possess reliable information about La Bruyère's activities from his own hand in the form of letters he wrote to Condé that describe the curriculum as well as voicing carefully worded complaints that express between the lines the difficulties of a dutiful tutor faced with a recalcitrant pupil. We also possess extensive contemporary documentation relating to his and others' preceptorships that can help us reconstruct the conditions in which he worked.

To be sure, pedagogical writing is not the most important influence on the *Caractères* as such. The primary sources of the text are to be found elsewhere, ranging from the ancient genres of the Theophrastan Character and Roman Satire to the *moraliste* tradition initiated by Erasmus with its characteristic *formes brèves*. The *Caractères* was no less a fully *contemporary* text, responding dialogically to contemporary French theater, philosophy and religious discourses through assimilation, parody or direct reference. Yet a good case can be made for the relevance of La Bruyère's preceptorship to understanding the genesis of the *Caractères* and its usefulness in assessing the work's much-debated political stance.

Firstly, La Bruyère does occasionally address the topic of education and childhood directly in the text.[5] His interest in the scene of education goes beyond the typical *classique* claim to be mixing instruction with delight. From the first lines of the initial preface to the *Caractères*, in the *Discours sur Théophraste*, he displays a heightened sensitivity to the reception and interpretation of didactic texts in the face of a varied and perhaps obtuse readership. He devoted the whole of what would have been his second publication, the *Dialogues sur le*

Quiétisme, to describing a religious *directeur* mis-directing a *pénitente* under his care. Secondly, an assessment of the preceptorship offers us a way of 'placing' La Bruyère in socio-political terms without risk of anachronism because the role of preceptor forced the individual involved to negotiate a conflict between caste and competence, aristocrat and Humanist, that was common to many of the great writers of the time who found themselves operating within the confines of the seventeenth-century court. Thirdly, La Bruyère's ideological mentors were *all* royal pedagogues, in particular Bossuet, who had held the most prominent preceptorship of all as the personal tutor of the Dauphin from 1670 to 1680.

Whatever the origins of La Bruyère's attitude to court life, it must have been inflected in some way by the activity that brought him into court in the first place. For us, La Bruyère is primarily a writer and *académicien*. But if his career post-1688 was lived in apparent separation from the Condé household it is nevertheless well to remember that from 1686 until his death in 1696 the author of the *Caractères* was, socially speaking, the Condés' 'man,' a courtier wholly reliant on them for his noble title, daily bread, lodgings, income and (if necessary) protection and that this enviable position was the direct result of his services to the family as preceptor. The desire on his part to occlude this fact governs the oddly inappropriate turn of *De quelques Usages* 14. The importance of merit in the *Caractères* as one of the principal virtues disdained by the Court is pertinent in this regard because La Bruyère's actual services and merit were in chronological terms linked with his preceptorship solely, not his writing or contributions to the *anciens* party during the *Querelle*. The merit he himself had exhibited in the world until the overnight success of the *Caractères* in 1688 could only have been the proper performance of his teaching duties.

In principle there was nothing to be ashamed of. The role of the royal preceptor was not a negligible one. There was no higher public calling for a Humanist in the *ancien régime*. It allowed the man of learning to imagine that he could have a direct impact on government without challenging the preexisting hierarchy in which his actual standing might be relatively low. Conversely, in the absolutist universe an enormous premium was placed on the monarch's education since there could be no other avenue for the promotion of good government than his personal knowledge and rectitude, effectively ignoring any possibility that the institution itself might need reform. Yet as La Bruyère was preparing his very first venture into the world of letters at a relatively late age he clearly chose not to declare himself to the world as a Humanist pedagogue.

In contrast, La Bruyère was able to express quite openly the place he occupied in relation to his literary forbears, ancient and modern (*Introduction* 15, *Préface* 65). The *Caractères* is pervaded by constantly sounded notes of connection and distancing. Although the earlier editions of the *Caractères* are less innovative than the later ones, it was in the mid-1680s that La Bruyère initiated the process of moving a more abstract, derivative ur-text to one increasingly favoring the detailed social descriptions that distinguish him from La Rochefoucauld and Pascal.[6] He recognized their importance to his writing and help in legitimating his moral-philosophical ambitions, even as he asserted his difference from them in a number of ways, in particular his stylistic differences. As soon as the preceptorship was over in 1686, La Bruyère added to his own work a translation of Theophrastus's *Characters* and redaction of *Discours sur Théophraste*, both composed sometime between late 1686 and May 1687, a humanist accretion quite foreign to them.[7] The fact that La Bruyère had been a preceptor marks yet another difference, though one La Bruyère preferred to ignore. La Rochefoucauld was an aristocrat himself whose major writing is not directly concerned with the practicalities of the classroom; Pascal apparently commented that there was no higher calling than the instruction of a Prince but he never got to undertake such a venture. La Bruyère, however, was writing and organizing his masterpiece at the same time that he was teaching. We now turn to a consideration of how these two activities might have influenced one another. It can be shown that the doubts La Bruyère came to harbor as to the significance and perhaps even the possibility of royal pedagogy helped shape his highly detailed form of social critique.

Joining the Condés

Condé was a cousin to the king, Louis XIV, and perhaps after Louis himself the most highly regarded figure in the land on account of his brilliant generalship in battle, exploits as legendary hero then daring rebel of the Fronde and finally as the most notable example of the high nobility's submission to the new monarchical order in the 1660s. Condé successfully managed to amass enormous wealth and influence after his return from exile, rebuilding his political base in his own region as well as serving the king again on the battlefield. He also strove successfully to create a court that did not seek to rival Louis's politically but managed to express Condé's own formidable, restless intellect by protecting prominent writers in need and entertaining intellectually advanced discussion with leading thinkers of the day. These certainly included free-thinkers but also leading churchmen such as Bossuet. As a result, Condé's court was one of the few official sites in louisquatorzian France where new ideas could be freely examined. La Bruyère came into contact with controversial opinions there, represented by the leading luminaries of Europe, the sort he criticizes in *Des Esprits forts*. He also witnessed the old libertine's Christian reform as he became increasingly pious in his waning years, welcoming figures like Bossuet and Bourdaloue to write for him. On a less intellectual level, La Bruyère would have also met in Condé's orbit another key figure pilloried in the *Caractères* in Gourville, the very type of the uncultured financier who manages to outdo his betters. He was a man of low birth who had very capably re-established Condé's finances in the 1660s, enriching himself mightily in the process while becoming Condé's most trusted confidant.

La Bruyère's position enabled him to experience life at the very highest reaches of French society for the first time in his life at Chantilly, Condé's refurbished and 'sublime' retreat, and at Versailles where La Bruyère's lessons with the Duke mostly took place. His employers gave him a fine example of the French aristocracy to study. Notoriously difficult and immensely powerful, sometimes brilliant and supportive of the arts but afflicted with mental instability, they were often cruel and arrogant to those who lived around them. However, he was neither part of their inner circle nor an especial target of their malice. Four years before the publication of the *Caractères* and the fame it brought, La Bruyère was not being summoned by them to display his wit or learning as an equal in the liberal atmosphere of the Condé court. In fact, his role was closer to that of an intellectual laborer or technician, called upon to salvage a potentially disastrous situation for the family, converting an immature and uncouth young prince into a model courtier.[8]

In the summer of 1684, the now sixteen-year-old Duke had finished his second year of philosophy and ended his studies at college but both his general comportment and mastery of certain forms of knowledge essential to shine at Court were sorely lacking. The family's fortunes now rested on his shoulders not (as had been the case for his grandfather) in the form of a military command or a great office of

State, but in that of marriage to the king's daughter, a change that was emblematic of the new relationship Louis XIV had established between himself and the great families who ruled in the provinces.

Condé had been in mid-century the very embodiment of the great aristocrats' claim to share in government with the king as semi-independent rulers, expressing the feudal ideal of the king's being merely the most powerful knight amongst equals. Louis XIV's administrative triumph over them in his assertion of a personal government in 1661 was not however a total repudiation of the aristocratic principle. He sought to master not destroy the hierarchy, a process abetted on both sides by a general desire for peace after the turbulence of the 1650s. He retained power wholly in his own hands by using only men of lower birth in government who were therefore reliant on him for whatever status they obtained, while keeping the hierarchy stable by lavishing favors on the existing aristocracy itself so long as it displayed loyalty and due deference. One expression of this double game of recognition and debasement was his attempt to legitimize his natural offspring by marrying them off to other members of the royal family. It was to further this policy that Louis agreed to permit the Duke to marry Louis XIV's natural daughter, the Duchess of Nantes. Condé readily went along with the plan. He was ailing and wanted to ensure his family's continuing influence after his death. Condé's son, the Duke of Enghien, a far lesser man in every respect, was desperate to become part of Louis XIV's intimate group and promoted the marriage in the hope that it would gain him the right to be present at the much coveted early morning *entrée* to the king's bedchamber.[9] Whatever their differences on the question of how to educate the Duke, Condé and his son agreed that in exchange for greater proximity to the numerous benefits the king might bestow it was worth compromising the purity of their caste.[10] La Bruyère, of course, never attacks this procedure directly. Despite this, it would be easy enough to draw the parallels between an aristocracy prepared to exchange pedigree for cash by marrying wealthy non-noble financiers so often pilloried in the *Caractères* and the maneuver involved in marrying the king's bastards.

La Bruyère had been recommended to the family by no lesser personage than Bishop Bossuet who had been meeting with Condé since the 1660s to discuss philosophy and theology and now could offer his advice with greater authority still because he had recently been the Dauphin's preceptor in the 1670s. Politically speaking, as Bossuet's trusted representative, La Bruyère embodied the sort of Gallican orthodoxy that would appeal to Louis XIV while retaining an uprightness and sharpness of intelligence Condé himself admired.

Until his employment with the Condés, La Bruyère had been associated with Bossuet's circle but otherwise enjoyed no more intimate connection to the great powers of the land. For his own part, he hailed from a solidly bourgeois background of Parisian lawyers, government officials and financiers. He had studied law and qualified for the Bar in 1665 though early on he chose to devote himself to letters and never seems to have practiced. An inheritance from his uncle allowed him to purchase the position of tax inspector in the *généralité* of Caen that secured him a comfortable yearly income and a non-hereditary title of nobility, but apart from his initial visit to prove he possessed the requisite legal knowledge he never went to Caen again and did not fulfill his duties. He had twice proven his qualifications for a given social position and then withdrawn from its actual exercise to the quiet of reading and contemplation, choosing to remain unmarried and live with his mother and then brother in a frugal, sedentary and unobtrusive manner. As far as we know during his lifetime he never traveled or desired to travel far beyond the gates of Paris. What originally drew him out of his perfect state of philosophic detachment is unclear. It has been suggested that he needed money after his savings were stolen. Most probably La Bruyère shared Bossuet's fundamental belief that it was his duty as a Christian and a Frenchman to school his princes in virtue and letters. In any case, the step was a decisive one. After the Great Condé's death in 1686, La Bruyère sold the last tie he possessed to his former independent life, the post of *trésorier*, to accept the generous offer of the Condé's to became their *gentilhomme*. Such largesse was not uncommon coming from great families. Whether it was simply thoughtless generosity or a mark of considered recognition is hard to gauge. For a moralist who tends to equate financial gain and courtly favors with abject groveling and injustice judging the true measure of his desert in this instance must have been the source of some anxiety. Moreover, the preceptorship was of brief duration and not a great success. The non-remunerative rewards of writing offered a much more desirable clarity.

The Course of the Preceptorship

In his role as royal preceptor La Bruyère was charged primarily with teaching the Duke what might be thought of as the aristocratic "humanities," subjects that were essential for a person of his high birth to function successfully at Versailles or in the army. They would not have been immediately familiar to someone like La Bruyère given his primarily bourgeois background, his legal training (still heavily imbued with scholasticism) or his literary tastes, which ran from the spiritual challenges of the Church Fathers to the theatrical exaggerations of the burlesque. This apparent mismatch of teacher and subject matter was quite common – preceptors were typically university men with little military experience or proximity to the court. The initial unfamiliarity was inevitable and most often in louisquatorzian France easily surmountable. Many contemporary bourgeois desired nothing better than to be competent in precisely those areas of social knowledge that were not theirs in order to facilitate social climbing. Tutors were indeed the most likely candidates for such caste reconciliation precisely because of their background. They were hired for their ability to teach noble pupils the rudiments of the classical curriculum and could be expected to exploit their scholarly abilities in the presentation of whatever materials were to be taught, even if it had little to do with the university curriculum in which they had been trained. Moreover, by La Bruyère's day many of the *robin* class, noble or not, who would have favored a more austere rhetoric back in mid-century, had come to accept the courtly mode of discourse, especially as it glorified the military exploits of the Sun King.

The preceptor to royalty or the higher nobility in seventeenth-century France often found himself in the strange position of being the representative of noble values even while he was transmitting the treasures of Humanistic letters, a mere intermediary among school, child and family. Hired for their mastery of higher learning, they were for all that nothing more than another *domestique* in a large household, filling in the gaps of their charge's education. In the seventeenth century the potentially troubling issue of the tutor's being more worthy and more knowledgeable than those who had employed him was never raised. In *Le Bourgeois gentilhomme*, for instance, the tutors are discarded after the first act and the question of *their* place in the hierarchy thereby finessed. Once such questions were considered seriously they contributed to the creation of the modern intellectual. It is here that assessing the position of the preceptor is important because we can see that La Bruyère's life from 1684 to his death was effectively split between the two roles. As preceptor he was wholly in thrall to his employers' sub-

ject matter and thereafter was one of their many clients; as a writer he
was an independent commentator on French society.[11]

As nobles became progressively concerned to give themselves
the basic foundations of a Humanist education they began to send their
children to the Jesuit schools as boarders instead of educating them at
home. Jesuit education was organized with quasi-military efficiency
and a level of social egalitarianism that was remarkable in its day.[12] But
it was also designed to propagate what Thomas Pavel has called an "art
d'éloignement," the creation of a hermetically sealed world in which
Latin grammar, rhetoric and performance were taught within a framework of complete immersion and intense competition over seven or
more years of rigorous instruction.[13] The intention was to give students
the ability to speak and write Latin as if it were their mother tongue.
Naturally this focus meant other subjects were neglected, virtually everything most useful for noble life at court or the army: French, military
sciences, social graces, recent history, including that of the pupil's
family history, and geography. The great families made up for these
omissions by employing a tutor to teach these subjects to their sons in
the private apartments where they lived apart from the non-noble
interns.

Nobles habitually did not pursue higher degrees. They needed
only the basics of letters – anything more would have bordered on
derogation, aping bourgeois earnestness or scholarly pedantry. However, the Condés realized belatedly that the Duke's education at the
prestigious Jesuit college of Clermont had been a failure and that his
schooling was not over. He had been treated in his college with indul-
gence by his Jesuit teachers, more concerned perhaps to garner the
prestige of having such a pupil than to undertake the difficult task of
reforming him. As a result, they never revealed the extent of his defi-
ciencies to his family. In class they placed him on a golden throne and
anointed him the leader of one team of students in their various competitive exercises. They, in turn, showered him with adulation. But to
the outside world he displayed childish rage, immaturity, high-handed
arrogance and lack of courtly graces. His live-in tutor, Deschamps,
thought little of the Jesuits and because he refused to pander to the
Duke, he naturally bore the brunt of his bad behavior. Unable to teach
the Duke the subjects he was responsible for and which were the most
crucial ones for his future, it was he who first urged that the Duke
should be sent home as soon as possible for remedial schooling. There
was no time to lose. If the king, notoriously punctilious as he was,

should be apprised of the Duke's unsuitability he was fully capable of choosing someone else for his daughter's hand.[14]

Deschamps quickly withdrew, probably worn out or unwilling to continue, and La Bruyère, who was originally to be his aide, was given full responsibility for the Duke's instruction. Condé did not live at Versailles and La Bruyère was expected to keep him abreast of his grandson's progress. La Bruyère was a reluctant courtier. He did not rush to write to Condé to assure him that all was going well nor did he enjoy following the Duke around in order to keep abreast of his every movement. Condé insisted on being kept informed, however, which is why we have seventeen letters written by La Bruyère to his employer reporting on the progress of his grandson, which are effectively the earliest writings of La Bruyère's that we possess.[15] They are letters written by a subordinate to a grandee and display little of the verbal skill that marks La Bruyère as one of the great stylists of the French language. Nevertheless they give us a good idea of La Bruyère's experience as a preceptor, outlining the details of the lessons' primary content as well as the framework in which they were carried out. In essence, La Bruyère's job was to drum facts and dates into the Duke so that he in turn could declaim them before assembled members of the family. La Bruyère never fails to assure Condé that he is performing these duties assiduously and brings to his attention everything preventing his pupil from studying properly like absences or, more often, lack of effort. However, the report is a dry one: sticking to the subjects taught, the speed at which they are being covered and general remarks about the quality of the Duke's application, whether improved or not fully satisfactory. The final letter we have, from May 1686 makes the same complaints about the Duke's lack of concentration as the previous ones, suggesting that there had been no great change in the Duke's lukewarm attitude to study over the course of the preceptorship.

Nothing is said about intellectual development or social graces, otherwise an essential component of an aristocratic education. This was taken care of by another instructor, the *gouverneur*, generally an impoverished but higher-caste aristocrat, often a former soldier. La Bruyère was restricted to relaying to his pupil the ability to perform the knowledge that had been learnt. The terms he used in the letters rely on a mirroring vocabulary in which ideally La Bruyère's action is met with and expresses its own answering action in the pupil. So he gives an account (*rendre compte*) to Condé of the Duke's ability to render an account (*rendre compte*) of his lessons. He assures Condé of his care and effort (*application*) and informs him as to whether the Duke has shown a sufficient level of it. He repeats (*redire*) to Condé how he has made the Duke repeat what has been explained. His language registers the fact that it is the duty of a servant to do this to prove he is doing as he ought to be: "Comme mon unique application est d'avancer les études de monsieur le duc de Bourbon, et que je travaille à cela à Versailles du matin au soir sans nul relâchement, ma plus grande joie aussi est d'en *rendre compte* à Votre Altesse Sérénissime"(9 January 1685, 633, *my emphasis*), or again, "C'est aujourd'hui un jour de géographie; nous en sommes encore à l'Italie; j'essayerai de la finir avec la Sicile cette après-dînée, et j'*espère qu'il en rendra un jour bon compte* à Votre Altesse Sérénissime, aussi bien que de la Flandre et du cours du Rhin, qu'il avait un peu oublié la dernière fois" (3 April 1685, 635, *my emphasis*). In the *Caractères*, Ménalque's valet uses the same expression when giving his manic master an account of where he has been in order to calm him down: "Le valet arrive, à qui il demande fièrement d'où il vient; il lui répond qu'il vient de l'endroit où il l'a envoyé, et *il lui rend un fidèle compte* de sa commission" *(De l'Homme 7, 303, my emphasis*). This mirroring of language between the letters and the *Caractères* is seen again with the reappearance of the word *application* in *Du Mérite personnel*.

> qu'un homme de cœur pense à remplir ses devoirs à peu près comme le couvreur songe à couvrir.... Ils ne sont tous deux appliqués qu'à bien faire, pendant que le fanfaron travaille à ce que l'on dise de lui qu'il a bien fait. (*Du Mérite personnel* 15)

In both letter and chapter the servant moves across a certain terrain at the behest of another, swallowed up in the simple purity of his action. The folding in (from *ad-plicare* 'to fold to') of self and task point to the dutiful performance carried out to the best of one's ability irrespective of whether or not it receives recognition or indeed success.

The Duke was a difficult, moody adolescent with a violent temper whose lack of concentration resulted in him being constantly distracted from his lessons by all the pleasures available to royalty such as hunting, horse-riding and balls. La Bruyère's task required patience and perseverance. On more than one occasion he had to ask Condé to exert his authority to keep the Duke in the classroom. He lacked any of his own. The tedium La Bruyère must have experienced in carrying out these thankless tasks can be gauged from his persistent recourse in the letters to the aforementioned expression *rendre compte* that, in the *Caractères*, often conveys unnecessary speech.[16] Because the Duke was having difficulty mastering the basics, there was little room for more expansive Humanist commentary in the form of moralizing examination of historical actions or interesting digressions on customs that formed the kernel of the Humanist exploitation of history to serve as an exemplary teacher of moral behavior (*historia magistra vitae*).[17]

La Bruyère's Pedagogical Background

La Bruyère's close friends and intellectual mentors Bossuet, Fénelon and Fleury were all, at one time or another, preceptors to royalty.[18] Bossuet had been the principal teacher of the Dauphin for ten years (1670-1680), while Fénelon was to fill the same role for the Dauphin's son, the Duke of Burgundy, ten years later from 1689 to 1694. Fleury had first been the preceptor for the Princes of Conti in the 1670s, then the king's natural son (until his death in 1683), and was to become sub-preceptor with Fénelon in 1689, taking over from him with his blessing when Fénelon was disgraced as a result of the Quietist controversy in 1696. These preceptorships were often onerous and drawn-out affairs with uncertain results, to be sure, but they were carried out in the best of conditions with all the resources and authority necessary. The preceptors ended their tenure with their prestige enhanced, substantial official rewards and the deep respect of their charges. Bossuet's followers from the Petit Concile took his materials (if not his methods) as a model, and the key members of the group provided each other mutual assistance in their tasks so it is more than likely that La Bruyère prepared his own courses by reading their pedagogical works, all of which pre-date his preceptorship.

It is possible that La Bruyère had first come into contact with Bossuet by helping in the preparation of the *Ad usum Delphini* edition of the classics.[19] We do know that La Bruyère participated in the Bible discussion group that met informally in the gardens of Versailles from 1673 to 1682, dubbed the Petit Concile by Fontenelle, where he became friends with Cordemoy, Fénelon and Fleury. However they met, Bossuet must have been impressed with La Bruyère's abilities to have recommended him to Condé. In turn, La Bruyère was a life-long devotee of Bossuet and must have been proud to have been chosen. Indeed, in all probability when La Bruyère was originally engaged by the Condés he planned to follow the curriculum Bossuet had created for the Dauphin over the decade of the 1670s, a comprehensive humanistic program aimed at creating the ideal humanist prince, proficient in the Latin classics, the Catholic creed, French history and government as well as logical argument. He further shared Bossuet's enthusiasm for Cartesianism as a model of clear thinking. The curriculum had garnered a high degree of prestige when full details were published for the world to see in Bossuet's 1679 "Letter to Innocent IX."[20] In February 1685, Bossuet observed a class La Bruyère gave to the Duke expounding Descartes's philosophy and pronounced himself well pleased with his candidate's performance.

However, circumstances dictated that La Bruyère had to be satisfied with a far reduced version of his master's example. Firstly, on Condé's insistence the curriculum came to focus primarily on the teaching of history and contemporary politics, which, given his glorious past and hopes for his grandson, was only natural. Secondly, the Duke was already fourteen years old when La Bruyère began to teach him and proved far less amenable to instruction than the Dauphin, who had been just seven. Lacking in his grandfather's exceptional talents, he does not seem to have been a particularly good student. In any case, the Duke married the Duchess of Nantes when he was fifteen in 1685 and was to be increasingly taken up by court life and royal amusements in the company of the Dauphin and his other royal cousins. As soon as Condé died in 1686 the Duke immediately moved to Court to attach himself closely to Louis as a member of the inner circle of the royal family. Studies were effectively set aside for more important matters.

All of the members of the Petit Concile prepared themselves intensively, devising rigorous, comprehensive curricula whose diversity was intended to give the Prince a full range of the essential 'sciences' that would enable him both to rule effectively as well as understand the nature and duties of the exalted place he was to occupy: history, logic, classical letters and religious doctrine. These curricula were then fully implemented in highly organized, full-time programs lasting many years. The Petit Concile's commitment to pedagogy was further reflected in pedagogical treatises of one kind or another written by them either as a suggested program (Fénelon's *De l'éducation des filles*; Fleury's *Traité des études*) or as the result of previous pedagogic experience (Bossuet's "Letter to Innocent 1X").[21] Although they were practicing priests and fully engaged participants in religious polemic and writing, they laid aside their other activities to devote their considerable talents to their preceptorships almost exclusively. It is a mark of the deep reflection and intense labor which they lavished on their pupils that the notes and classroom materials they prepared form the basis for their most highly significant works: *Discours sur l'histoire universelle*, *Télémaque* and the *Mœurs des Israélites*.

Such writing was a true expression of the tripartite influence of Christianity, Humanism and patriotism that had formed these men as it had so many others in the *officier* class of louisquatorzian France. Most often coming from relatively undistinguished backgrounds, they were ennobled and awarded choice living arrangements by the regime for their services and loyalty without ever feeling that they had to give up their higher Christian principles because nothing indeed answered their vocation to serve more clearly than the call to instruct the Prince.[22] As staunch supporters of absolutism they deployed classical letters in good Augustinian fashion to show the future king how to rule in a Christian manner. Their ideas, a sort of Christian primitivism that could often have (paradoxically) a reformist modernizing tendency, were aimed at effecting policy change from *within* the existing system. It was by the thorough education of the ruler and his servants that the hierarchy could best be preserved because if they could be taught to be upright, competent, charitable and thrifty the pedagogues firmly believed kings would definitely earn the people's trust and obedience. With respect to their original royalist pedagogic context and intentions Bossuet's *Politique tirée des propres paroles de l'écriture sainte* and Fénelon's *Télémaque* are largely comparable, although they are generically very different kinds of works and were shaped by no less different pedagogical methods. Above all, the members of the Petit Concile strongly believed in the role of historical example, whether of figures from antiquity, the Bible or the royal family itself, as the most effective means of teaching their charges. Only history preserved the traditionalist's desire to embed the present in the past in a seamless continuity while, in pedagogical terms, combining timeless moral lessons with striking images and an emphasis on the practical realities of governance.[23]

La Bruyère formed part of their circle and shared their most fundamental ideas. He was put forward by Bossuet to teach the Duke as a result of his deep commitment to the Petit Concile. Fleury had also been considered for the same post (he had tutored other members of Condé's family previously). Yet far from exhibiting the same direct continuity between pedagogical and scriptural practice as theirs, the book La Bruyère produced immediately following the end of his preceptorial tenure, the *Caractères*, is a repudiation of it. If the *Caractères* is instruction ("On ne doit parler, on ne doit écrire que pour l'instruction," 61) it is aimed not at a pupil but at the general public, bypassing its royal reader completely.[24] If it is a document framed by the same Humanist 'goals' of installing morality through example and the deployment of a large set of different kinds of knowledge (Greco-Roman letters, Cartesianism, the sublime, Pascalian 'proofs' of God and so on) no less politically conservative than theirs, its corrosive views of the ruling classes and acute observations of how court society was skewing social behavior ultimately served to undermine the current regime in a way that is utterly foreign to that of his friends. For all of its various distancing frames, whether of classical imitation, satiric moralism and Bossuetian sublime, the *Caractères'* creative energies are expended primarily on the *contemporary,* the middling ranks of society and backroom dynamics that were shaping France's daily life *in the present.* Indeed the Greek frame La Bruyère chose for his own work, unlike that of his churchmen friends, was not that of the divinely sanctioned paternalistic Hebrew Scriptures or its Greek counterparts but a frankly republican Athens and a clearly pagan philosopher, Theophrastus, with no potential for allegorical accretions. The stress was therefore placed implicitly on a comparison not of moralities but of *institutions.* There is obviously as much *vice* in ancient Athens as there is in seventeenth-century Paris. That is how the literary imitation of one epoch's Characters by another can work so successfully. The difference between the two locales lies elsewhere. As La Bruyère makes clear in the *Discours sur Théophraste,* Athens had avoided the worst of luxury and lack of public spirit not because its people were morally superior but because it did not have a Court and its people ruled themselves.

All the intra- and extra-textual evidence shows that this separation between pedagogy and text was not his overt intention. La Bruyère remained wedded to the essentially Bossuetian ideals of creating a Christian monarchy, using the purely moral authority of the classroom to inculcate good governmental principles or, later, the admonishments of the pulpit, to guide the king without challenging his monopoly of political power. The homiletic substructure of the *Caractères* was clearly demonstrated by Maurice Lange in his classic *La Bruyère, critique des conditions et des institutions sociales.* The use of pagan (Ancient Greek) literature to 'form' a king as carried out by Fénelon's *Télémaque* or his translations of La Fontaine's *Fables* was not alien to La Bruyère either as numerous remarks that rehearse "une image naive des peuples et du prince qui les gouverne" in *Du Souverain* readily attest. Furthermore, the explicit tendency of his politics can be gauged from what would have been his next publication, the *Dialogues sur le Quiétisme* on which he was working when he died suddenly in 1696. In the Pascalian mode of the *Provinciales,* this text lets the quietist priest reveal in his own words the narcissism and anarchy that would prevail if all the faithful were to ignore the existing traditions and authority of the Church and seek their own, spiritually haphazard path to God.

The Petit Concile's strong attack on aristocratic luxury was not intended to promote equality but instead to make the aristocracy capable of governing well by getting it to follow more farsighted economic practices, on the one hand, and to display self-control in a manner that would enhance its moral authority over inferiors, on the other. In the specific case of educational policy, Fleury's apparently modernizing desire to take the classics out of the general curriculum and replace them with useful knowledge such as French, mathematics and vocational training was designed to keep all the different social strata firmly in their place and thus better able to fulfill their specific tasks in the economy within the currently existing hierarchy. The Petit Concile's program for the royal children was far more exalted and traditional than anything they proposed for the lower orders. It included an intensive survey of classical literature – though here too their ultimate concern was not self-cultivation per se but moral instruction, which they effected by a careful choice of more practical classical texts, especially historical ones, full of rich examples of wise or foolish princely conduct.

Here we enter the realm of speculation, but it is fair to assert that the much reduced conditions of teaching that La Bruyère experienced in comparison with his friends led him to question the ultimate value of transmitting the humanities to one's betters. In *Des Grands,* one of the most significant criticisms of the aristocracy is that it is essentially *ineducable.* The grandees are presented as being so ignorant and yet so powerful that it seems virtually impossible to administer any correction to them. They literally cannot be addressed. Of those who might have been in a position to instruct these aristocrats, the educated and "habiles," the men of merit who happen to be on hand are not recognized for what they are, while the others, capable but mercenary, are busy ensuring they are well instructed so as to be able to take over everything from their dissolute, ignorant masters.[25] La Bruyere's pupil and his father the Duke of Enghien (on whom Ménalque was based) were obvious models for this fundamental worthlessness and complacency.

Even the Grand Condé himself, who was so unlike his progeny in every other respect, was still to La Bruyere's mind someone whom education cannot touch because he was "né ce que les plus grands hommes ne deviennent qu'à force de règles, de méditation et d'exercice" (Æmile *Du Mérite personnel* 32, 106). Whether the *grands* are supremely gifted or utterly incompetent, the mechanisms of French society ensure that hard work, forethought, and philosophical study will never be necessary or available to them.

Refusal of the Pedagogical Role

What place is left then for someone like La Bruyère, who is not a *grand*, a mercenary or a genuine educator? In these circumstances writing becomes for La Bruyère the carrier of the essentially bourgeois excellence of doing one's work well. It is not inserted in any actual economy and is therefore unthreatening as an activity. After all, if merit is not rewarded under the debased conditions of court life the logical step is to alter the system of distribution to ensure that it is. Yet La Bruyère holds back from suggesting a remedy. Aesthetically speaking, he judges good writing to be its own reward. The refusal of financial remuneration for the *Caractères* and the withholding of his name from the work's title-page display his desire to place transcendent standards of excellence over worldly measures of success or pragmatic reforms. His friends, on the other hand, were occasionally emboldened to exercise real power over the royalty they were instructing. In the mid-1670s, at the height of his preceptorship, Bossuet urged the king to reform his sexual life. In the 1690s, during his stewardship of the Dauphin's son, Fénelon passed on to Madame de Maintenon letters intended for the king's eyes that admonished the king for his ruinous warmongering. Throughout the first decade of the 1700s he gave the Duke of Burgundy direct political advice on current events in secret correspondence.

La Bruyère's move to assert his writing's value is predicated on his refusal after the fact of the position of preceptor. For a text that so obsessively and meticulously charts late seventeenth-century French social castes', figures', and functions' places in the hierarchy relative to one another, the *Caractères* is extraordinarily reticent about its author's own social position. All the self-identifications scattered throughout the *Caractères* are types of indirect social critique and not genuine representations of La Bruyère's social reality. What has been elided though in every case is his actual place in society in 1688, when the *Caractères* was first published: a "gentilhomme ordinaire" of the Condé household.

As Fontenelle noted, "Bossuet…fournissait ordinairement aux princes les gens de mérite dans les lettres" using the enormous prestige he had garnered from his own preceptorship of the Dauphin in the 1670s.[26] La Bruyère was one of these 'people of merit' and though the merit he refers to in *Du Mérite personnel* is defined in an ethereal manner as the combination of lack of recognition on the part of the powerful and the determination to be virtuous regardless, in actual fact La Bruyère's merit did not go unrewarded by the great. Only the merit concerned was not that of writing well or of instructing others in virtue as the *Caractères* would have it. Rather it was of a more down-to-earth kind, his diligence in fulfilling the *charge* of royal pedagogue to the satisfaction of his employers. In fact, to La Bruyère's mind merit and *fonction* are inherently opposed; there is no room for the exercise of a virtuous *charge*.

> Il faut en France beaucoup de fermeté et une grande étendue d'esprit pour se passer des charges et des emplois, et consentir ainsi à demeurer chez soi, et à ne rien faire. Personne presque n'a assez de mérite pour jouer ce rôle avec dignité, ni assez de fonds pour remplir le vide du temps, sans ce que le vulgaire appelle des affaires. Il ne manque cependant à l'oisiveté du sage qu'un meilleur nom, et que méditer, parler, lire, et être tranquille s'appelât travailler. *(Du Mérite personnel* 14, 100)

The activity of "enseigner" is conspicuously absent. This suggests that La Bruyère did not value his activity as preceptor. In effect, it did not display his virtue or merit. He prefers the risk of seeming lazy to that of what would have been an accurate and quite honorable identification.

If La Bruyère felt that pedagogy was so restrictive he would rather reduce it to nothingness than admit to his involvement; his view of writing is sometimes expressed in a similar fashion. The connection between these two activities for La Bruyère can be found in his sense that in neither case could he comfortably speak in the name of history. As a preceptor, his voice was ventriloquized by a discourse both ideologically alien to him and poorly received by its noble *destinataire*. As a writer, his explicit generic choice to write satire is framed as a retreat from saying anything of grand significance and an assertion of specifically aesthetic virtues. This conformed to Louis XIV's wish to remove politics from the public sphere.

Un homme né chrétien et Français se trouve contraint dans la satire; les grands sujets lui sont défendus; il les entame quelquefois, et se détourne ensuite sur de petites choses, qu'il relève par la beauté de son génie et de son style. *(Des Ouvrages de l'esprit* 65, 94)

But it also entailed recognition that perhaps "les grands sujets" had been fatally compromised by having been placed so out of bounds. One could no longer write history or praise one's betters in any meaningful sense under a regime of such sycophancy and rampant self-interest in which the arbitrary favor of the king decided everything. From La Bruyère's point of view, though, this fact confirmed the failure of noble pedagogy and energized him to make an artistic virtue of it. To conclude, we can look at the way certain passages of the *Caractères* show how La Bruyère's withdrawal from the grand language of history, so central to the aristocratic humanist classroom, emerges from his unsatisfactory engagement with just these materials in his teaching of the Duke.

The Demolition of Heroic Language

In the *Caractères* the language La Bruyère was transmitting in the classroom is sometimes *converted* into matter for ironical manipulation. A fine example of this process can be found in *Du Souverain* 11, which relies on a specific set of documents La Bruyère had first rehearsed in the history lessons he ran through with the Duke. In the famous parallel portrait Basilide and Démophile represent contrasting reactions to current reports of an on-going war.

Démophile, à ma droite, se lamente, et s'écrie: "Tout est perdu, c'est fait de l'Etat"...Basilide...à ma gauche.... "Voilà, s'écrie-t-il, une grande nouvelle; ils sont défaits, et à plate couture; le général, les chefs, du moins une bonne partie, tout est tué, tout a péri." (279-80)

The defeatist Démophile and optimist Basilide are both led to exaggerate or even invent events to suit their respective temperaments. The reactions, embellishments, over-interpretations, plans to flee or celebrate that La Bruyère lays out at length in all their frenzied delusion are normal functions of the public sphere. They are what happens when an enormous flow of information meets desires and firmly entrenched beliefs.

La Bruyère's response to them is not to assert his own opposing views on the actual course of events so much as to dampen and restrict their wild efflorescence. The extremes of the two characters' discourses point naturally to the right place of speech in the center.

> Réduisez-le...à dire simplement: Le Roi a beaucoup d'ennemis, ils sont puissants, ils sont unis, ils sont aigris: il les a vaincus, j'espère toujours qu'il les pourra vaincre. Ce style, trop ferme et trop décisif pour Démophile, n'est pour Basilide ni assez pompeux ni assez exagéré. (281)

La Bruyère's advice is rhetorical in nature. It is about preserving moral rectitude by purifying language while completely bracketing the issues and judgments themselves. Direct criticism of Louis's polices is simply out of the question. Yet the king's war is, nevertheless, not fully supported. The critique works by reducing the pressure of words on the will. The suggested response given above is, to be sure, patriotic but it undercuts itself by its very modesty. In the final, utterly simple hope whose simplicity is both touching and weak, the king and the I are, grammatically, in the singular and their reactions located in the past or future as against the enemies' triple hammer blows "ils sont puissants... unis...aigris" that occur and thus recur in the present tense. One cannot exert much patriotic *pressure* like this; the mediocre position in between extremes certainly manages to avoid the vices of mendacity or cowardice displayed by the Characters Basilide and Démophile. It is, though, not the stuff of victory. We are reduced to making no analytical statements at all about the situation but we have also withdrawn ourselves implicitly from out and out commitment. La Bruyère removes himself from political commentary, the grand events of the day, in order to criticize instead the minutiae of language through which character is revealed.

The withdrawal is the result of an unstated repugnance felt towards the grand language of royal history itself. Absolutism remains unchallenged but also starved of popular energy. Critics have generally understood La Bruyère's rhetoric in a passage like this within the wider context of the *Caractères'* decided preference for a mode of Christian simplicity in language that is expressed *in De la Chaire* or the clarity of quasi-Cartesian reasoning in *Des Esprits forts*. From the perspective of the preceptorship, however, these remarks can be seen as the result of something akin to an *Umfunktionierung* of preexisting materials.[27] In La Bruyère's first letter to Condé recounting the lessons his grandson was receiving, the passage from topic to topic is described as an energetic movement of rapid seeing and visiting,

> j'attends quelquefois que nous ayons passé à des choses nouvelles, afin qu'elle [son Altesse i.e. Condé] en soit exactement informée, et de tout le

chemin que nous faisons. J'entrerai demain dans l'histoire de Charles viii; la vie de Louis xi nous a menés au delà de ce que je pensais.... Je fais voir l' Italie à Son Altesse [the Duke], pour la mener de là en Hongrie, en Pologne et dans les États du Turc en Europe; je lui ai appris ces derniers jours la Suède, le Danemark, la Scandinavie, et l'Angleterre avec l'Ecosse et l'Irlande, assez scrupuleusement. J'ai rebattu les généalogies que je lui ai déjà enseignées, et vais entrer dans celles des maisons de Saxe, Lorraine, Holstein, Savoie, et peu d'autres qui sont entrées dans votre branche de Bourbon. (Letter 1, 9 February 1685, 633-34).

It is the same movement as that of the vainglorious Basilide who revels in his vision of the war's progress though he is sitting safely in Paris far from the front.

Basilide met tout d'un coup sur pied une armée de trois cent mille hommes; il n'en rabattrait pas une seule brigade: il a la liste des escadrons et des bataillons, des généraux et des officiers; il n'oublie pas l'artillerie ni le bagage. Il dispose absolument de toutes ces troupes: il en envoie tant en Allemagne et tant en Flandre, il réserve un certain nombre pour les Alpes, un peu moins pour les Pyrénées, et il fait passer la mer à ce qui lui reste. *(Du Souverain* 11, 280)

In the lesson La Bruyère is giving to the Duke he is not guilty of the same falsifying enthusiasm. It is the language itself that commits the fault. He is nonetheless being paid to run through the dynastic map of Europe and traverse it like a general with his pupil who might, unlike him, conceivably assume this role some day. It is perhaps meant to be exciting for the pupil, but for the instructor such rapidity bespeaks either superficiality or something worse. The discomfort La Bruyère might have felt at his unsuitability for this task can be gauged from the fact that in *Du Souverain* 11 Basilide replaces the La Bruyère of the letter as the anxious musterer of movement. Secondly, there is the moral emptiness of the list. The language of the history is supposedly neutral but what the satire of Basilide reveals is that it is a form of war-fare itself – or at least that the precondition of war is precisely to look at the map as if it were nothing but a set of names to be accumulated as thoroughly as possible.

La Bruyere's master Condé was thoroughly immersed in such language. He was one of France's greatest generals and bravest war heroes. All of the Condé men had or would fight campaigns.[28] The decidedly un-military La Bruyère cannot criticize Condé or the king directly so he does so by satirizing a smaller version of them in Basilide (from the Greek *basileus* meaning 'king'). Elsewhere in *Du Souverain* it is the horrors of war rather than its necessity that is stressed as the two remarks directly preceding *Du Souverain* 11 readily attest.[29] Across the chapter as a whole conquest is never celebrated. Both Démophile and Basilide are portrayed as equally self-interested. The former cares only about his sudden fears and his property, the latter seeks self-glorification in a vicarious exercise of power. Yet their names tell a different story. Démophile is the lover of the people (*demos-philein*); Basilide happily sends them off to their deaths. La Bruyère finds a way to retreat from the large issues of politics that enables him to find his own voice, the self-controlled reasoner. The satiric extremes portrayed demand not only that we reduce ourselves to avoid them but that we examine the sources of our hysteria as they emerge from within a specific kind of discourse. La Bruyère was an eyewitness to the aristocracy's decline, both the natural degeneration of a family (from the brilliance of the Grand Condé to the sullen torpor of his grandson) and its self-debasement before the tainted blandishments of Versailles. In moving from preceptorship to writing the *Caractères*, La Bruyère turns from the dynastic map of Europe, ripe for free-booting royal appropriation, to the claustrophobic moral cartography of Versailles in which, as the *Caractères* reveals, even royalty finds itself imprisoned.

Conclusion

La Bruyère concludes one of his letters to Condé with the words,

> Je ménage avec soin tout le temps qui m'est accordé sans en rien perdre, et profite le mieux que je puis de l'application de monsieur le duc de Bourbon, dont je suis assez content. Quand je le serai moins, je ne vous le dissimulerai pas: je le lui ai déclaré nettement et cela fait un très bon effet. (Letter 5, 7 July 1695, 639)

In the letter, La Bruyère must retail a vast panoply of facts that are not his own – "les pays héréditaires"; "[l]a vie de Louis xii;" "l'Italie…vue fort en détail" and so on – to a pupil for whom they had an intimate, feudal connection. When the pupil fails to master them La Bruyère must have recourse to Condé. His clear declaration is the mere transmission of someone else's authority whose voice passes through him. In *De quelques Usages* 14 La Bruyère says "[j]e le déclare nettement" about an invented feudal lineage that would justify his being rewarded by a sinecure or other monetary prize. It is an open lie of course, aimed at aristocrats who claim special privileges because of a real ancestry as well as bourgeois like La Bruyère himself who invent a bogus one. When seen in the light of the preceptorship, however, it can help us track the passage that took place in the intervening years as he went from preceptor to writer because it still bears the scars of his refusal to go along with a certain practice of language. It points to the emergence of La Bruyère's legitimate claim to a self made against the grain of a highly rewarding ideology that threatened to bury the self and indeed all of France in its fantasy of easily acquired dignity.

Notes

[1] The edition used is *Les Caractères,* ed. Robert Garapon. Chapter name, remark number and page number will be given in the body of the text.

[2] The 4th edition added an equally anonymous philosopher who observes the world in order to improve it (*Des Ouvrages de l'esprit* 34, 78) and an Erasmian *Socrate*, the sane chronicler of an insane world (*Des Jugements* 66, 372). In the 5th edition La Bruyère associates himself with the "peuple" in preference to the aristocracy because the former are simple, inoffensive and good while the latter are powerful and malignant (*Des Grands* 25); the worthy *philosophe* who turns no one away from his door (*Des Biens de fortune* 12, 182-83); and *Antisthène* (*Des Jugements* 21, 356), whose name and more dramatically rendered prose makes him into a Character himself, a writer-philosopher sickened by the world's vice.

[3] See *Du Mérite personnel* 26 where Erasmus is contrasted with *Trophime*, a veiled reference to a certain Cardinal Le Camus who had accepted his office without consulting the king or being truly worthy of the rank when others like Bossuet had been passed over.

[4] In the following essay Condé will refer to the Grand Condé, Duke to his grandson, Duke of Enghien to Condé's son, the Duke's father.

[5] See Mazaheri "Enfance et Utopie" and my article "La Bruyère and the 'Usage' of Childhood." The relevant passages can be found in *De l'Homme* 49-59, 314-17 and *De quelques Usages* 71, 438. La Bruyère's comments on the usefulness of learning languages and the impressionability of young minds draw on the pedagogical works of his friends Fleury and Fénelon in these passages. *De quelques Usages* 71 is quoting directly from Erasmus's widely read educational manual *De pueris*.

[6] For the dating of individual remarks see Garapon's judicious article, "La chronologie de la composition des 'Caractères'." He thinks that many of the remarks added to later editions had been written before 1687.

[7] Boileau spoke of a completed manuscript of the *Caractères* to Racine in a letter of 19 May 1687 in which he dubs La Bruyère 'Maximilien' and the book his 'Théophraste.' Cited in Garapon, *Les Caractères* (vi).

[8] Indeed he was really a third choice. The Duke's personal tutor unexpectedly retired and Fleury turned the post down.

[9] For information on the Condés, see: Allaire, *La Bruyère dans la maison de Condé*; Bannister, *Condé in Context*; and Béguin, *Les Princes de Condé*. Saint-Simon left devastating portraits of Condé's son and grandson; one slowly went mad, while the other grew into a bitter and lonely misanthrope of no accomplishments.

[10] The project of the marriage had been set in motion by Condé's son who thought there was nothing better in the world than the life of the favored courtier. Condé had higher ambitions for his grandson, military honors, high office, perhaps a kingdom. It was he and not his son who determined the curriculum La Bruyère was to follow.

[11] La Bruyère is often read in this dual fashion, at once republican and conservative, traditionalist and *écrivain*. Julien Benda nicely resolved the problem by suggesting that La Bruyère should not be defined by any particular position but rather according to "sa constante désir de parler [de la société de son temps], de faire des problèmes sociaux la substance de ses réflexions," thus preparing the way for the crucial role 'public opinion' would play in shaping French political life in the eighteenth century (xviii). The preceptorship helps us grasp the specificity of this turn to the public by seeing it as an ideological site in which La Bruyère turned away from an insider's discourse of which he was merely the relay to an outsider's one which, though far more limited in its critical scope than those of the eighteenth-century *philosophes*, was one that directly challenged the premises of the Humanist accommodation of noble superiority.

[12] The standard surveys of French seventeenth-century education are Snyders *La pédagogie en France aux XVIIe et XVIIIe siècles* and Roger Chartier et al. *L'éducation en France du XVIe au XVIIIe siècle*. An important corrective to Snyders' limited version of the Jesuits is to be found in Dainville, *L'éducation des jésuites*. The Duke's case, though, does happen to fall under Snyders' admonitions.

[13] For the role of the preceptor at this period see Chapter 2 of Motley *Becoming a French Aristocrat*.

[14] One of the only accounts we have of this whole episode is found in Allaire, Chapters 6-8, on which I have drawn heavily.

[15] They can be most easily consulted in *Œuvres complètes,* ed. Benda (633-53). Letter number, date and page number are given in the text. Another useful source for gleaning information about the preceptorship is historical records pertaining to the Condé family's day-to-day life at the time to be found in the Condé archives. Allaire cites these at length.

[16] In the *Caractères, rendre compte* is sometimes used pejoratively to convey a speech that is pedantic, small-minded or garrulous, sometimes in its primary sense of giving an accurate account. Pejorative uses: *Discours sur Théophraste* 17, *De la rusticité, De l'épargne sordide, De la sotte vanité, De l'ostentation.* In *Caractères de Théophraste,* see: *De la Cour 18, De la Ville 15; De l'Homme 66* (with *trouver*); *Des Jugements 99; De la Mode 24* (with *trouver*); *De quelques Usages 57; Des Esprits forts 3.* For positive uses, see: *Des Femmes 49; De la Société et de la Conversation* 11, 25; *Des Grands 13,* 15; *Des Jugements 28* (with *tenir*) and 77.

[17] La Bruyère mentions doing this only twice. The Duke seems to have enjoyed it but because he was not successfully memorizing the basic materials there was little time for more advanced types of discussion.

[18] For the ideas of the group as a whole the essential reference is Cuche, *Une pensée sociale catholique*. The bibliography on these authors is of course extensive. For Bossuet, see: A. Floquet, *Bossuet, précepteur du Daupin, fils de Louis XIV et évêque à la Cour*; Jean Meyer, *Bossuet* (141-200) and Chapter 3 of *L'éducation des princes en Europe du XVe au XIXe siècle*; Régine Pouzet, "Introduction," to *Charles IX*; Thérèse Goyet, *L'humanisme de Bossuet* (91-145). For Fénelon, see: Emmanuel Bury, "La paideia du *Télémaque*"; Charles Dedeyan, *Télémaque ou la liberté de l'esprit*; Françoise Gallouédec-Genuys, *Le prince selon Fénelon*; Jeanne-Lydie Goré, "Introduction," *Télémaque*; Marguerite Haillant, *Culture et imagination dans les œuvres de Fénelon "Ad usum Delphini,"* and Fénelon, *Les Aventures de Télémaque*; Volker Kapp, *Télémaque de Fénelon*; Jacques Le Brun's notes Fénelon; and "Du privé au public" (235-60). For Fleury, see: François Gaquère, *La vie et les oeuvres de Claude Fleury*; Bernard Jolibert's introduction to *Traité du choix et de la méthode des études*; and Raymond E. Wanner, *Claude Fleury*. La Bruyère's other closest friend, Géraud de Cordemoy, was yet one more prominent member of the group who became a royal preceptor. Bossuet shared his interest in Cartesianism and was instrumental in his appointment as *lecteur* of the Dauphin in 1673. Although his major works are primarily philosophical in nature, he also wrote a treatise on education as well as a history of the reign of Charlemagne, *Ad usum Delphini*, that remained unfinished at his death (see introduction to Géraud de Cordemoy *Œuvres philosophiques*). To indicate how close-knit the ties were in this milieu we can further note that at La Bruyère's side during the preceptorship was a certain Jacques Sauveur, who taught the Duke mathematics and the science of fortification. This mathematics prodigy had been discovered by Cordemoy living in very humble circumstances and then introduced to Condé by Bossuet.

[19] His collaboration would explain both his exemption from duties incurred as *trésorier* and his initial meeting with Bossuet who was nominally in charge of the whole undertaking. The propaedeutic employment of a classical text with a simplified, succinct commentary beneath may have suggested to him the use of Theophrastus for his own text. The connection between the Character and basic classroom materials is discussed at length in Vol. 2 in Marc Escola's *La Bruyère*, although he does not discuss La Bruyère's own pedagogical experience. The point here is that there is a complete disjunction between the pedagogic use of ancient texts and the materials La Bruyère was obligated to use in the classroom with his pupil.

[20] See *Correspondance*, Vol. 2 (112-61).

[21] Bossuet, see above n. 20; Fénelon *De l'éducation des filles* (91-171 [1696], 1201-30 [1687]); Fleury, *Traité du choix et de la méthode des études* (29-120).

[22] Fénelon was an exception, having been born into a noble though impoverished family.

[23] As Bossuet says in *Discours sur l'histoire universelle*, written expressly for the Dauphin: "Quand l'histoire seroit inutile aux autres hommes, il faudrait la faire lire aux princes. Il n'y a pas de meilleur moyen de leur découvrir ce que peuvent les passions et les interests, les temps et les conjonctures, les bons et les mauvais conseils. Les histoires ne sont composées que des actions qui les occupent, et tout semble y estre fait pour leur usage. Si l'expérience leur est necessaire pour aquerir cette prudence qui fait bien regner, il n'est rien de plus utile à leur instruction que de joindre aux exemples des siècles passez les experiences qu'ils font tous les jours. Au lieu qu'ordinairement ils n'apprennent qu'aux dépens de leurs sujets et de leur propre gloire, à juger des affaires

dangereuses qui leur arrivent: par le secours de l'histoire, ils forment leur jugement, sans rien hasarder, sur les évenemens passez" (1-2). The question cannot be discussed here but few of the commentators mentioned in note 18 consider whether the preceptorships they describe with such erudition were actually *successful*. There is some evidence, with the Dauphin certainly but even in the case of Fénelon's charge (who underwent with Fénelon's celebrated *douceur* a supposedly miraculous conversion from uncontrollable young boy into an extremely conscientious adolescent on whom the reformist movement could pin its hopes) that these preceptorships were not. In the Dauphin's case, we may surmise this was a result of the unrelieved, brutal rigor imposed upon him coupled with an impossibly ambitious curriculum; in the case of the Dauphin's son, it was unsuccessful, in part, because the child did not develop a fully-fledged personality of his own; Fénelon continued to exercise too great an authority over him until the Dauphin's death.

[24] Le Brun notes that though originally aimed at a royal reader, the lessons of *Télémaque* or *Politique tirée des propres paroles de l'écriture sainte* are enunciated in a recognizably general mode applicable to all readers. Nevertheless the original addressee was not a fiction in either case. (Louis XIV had the same eventual diffusion in mind when he wrote his *Mémoires pour l'instruction du dauphin*.) Bossuet retains the mystery of state apparatus and simply pronounces doctrine. *Télémaque*, for all its *mise en scène* of the relationship of teacher and pupil, keeps the reader at one remove by the clear hierarchy that underlies the world in which it takes place; Télémaque is still a prince and Mentor a divine authority in a way that the protagonists in Rousseau's *Emile* are not. Indeed, Fénelon implicitly assumes for himself an enormous amount of power in the *Télémaque* thus conveying a belief in the legitimate authority of adviser over prince. La Bruyère has completely removed the princely scene of instruction from his presentation.

[25] "Pendant que les grands négligent de rien connaître, je ne dis pas seulement aux intérêts des princes et aux affaires publiques, mais à leurs propres affaires; qu'ils ignorent l'économie et la science d'un père de famille, et qu'ils se louent eux-mêmes de cette ignorance...des citoyens s'instruisent du dedans et du dehors d'un royaume, étudient le gouvernement, deviennent fins et politiques, savent le fort et le faible de tout un Etat, songent à se mieux placer, se placent, s'élèvent, deviennent puissants, soulagent le prince d'une partie des soins publics" *(Des Grands* 24, 261).

[26] Cited in Allaire, 346.

[27] In *Du Souverain* 24 there is a similarly frenetic aping of the royal desire for rapid conquest conveyed by a syntax of accumulated clauses. The mode of critique is different though – it is not that of 'self-reduction' but the idealizing question and generalizing philosophic statement. It works not by saying directly that the king is not as he should be, but by setting up an ideal and asking rhetorically whether a good king conforms to it or not. This form of critique derives from the Petit Concile's use of the Greek past to shame the present in good Christian Humanist fashion.

[28] La Bruyère would soon serve as a mediator of military discourse not his own for Condé himself and there is some evidence that perhaps another reason he had been chosen as preceptor was his knowledge of foreign tongues. As the letter of 3 April 1685 records, Condé ordered La Bruyère to translate for him from German a summary of Hungarian history and royal genealogy, background for the contemporary war taking place between the Austro-Hungarian armies and the Turks. Condé's nephews had fled

Versailles, against the orders of the king, who was informally allied with the Turks, in order to participate in it in true crusader style against the infidel.

[29] For a convincing statement of La Bruyere's essential pacifism see Lafond, "De la guerre et de la paix, de la monarchie et de la république, dans 'Démophile et Basilide' ("Du Souverain ou de la République" 11)."

Works Cited

Primary Sources

Bossuet, *Correspondance*. Vol 2. Ed. Charles Urbain and Eugène Levesque. Paris: Hachette, 1909.

_____. *Discours sur l'Histoire Universelle*. Paris: S. Mabre-Cramoisy, 1681.

Fénelon, François de *Œuvres*. 2 vols. Ed. Jacques Le Brun. Paris: Gallimard, 1983.

_____. *Les Aventures de Télémaque. Fils d'Ulysse*. Ed. Marguerite Haillant. Paris: Nizet, 1993.

Fleury, Claude. *Traité du choix et de la méthode des études*. Ed. Bernard Jolibert. Paris: Harmattan, 1999.

_____. *Mœurs des Israelites*. Paris: Veuve G. Clouzier, 1681.

La Bruyère, Jean de. *Les Caractères*. Ed. Robert Garapon. Paris: Bordas, 1990.

_____. *Œuvres complètes*. Ed. Julien Benda. Bibliothèque de la Pléiade. Paris: Gallimard, 1951.

Secondary Sources

Allaire, Étienne *La Bruyère dans la maison de Condé*. 2 vols. Geneva: Slatkine Reprints, 1970.

Bannister, Mark. *Condé in Context: Ideological Change in Seventeenth-Century France*. Oxford: Legenda, 2000.

Béguin, Katia. *Les Princes de Condé. Rebelles, courtesans et mécènes dans la France du Grand siècle*. Paris: Champ Vallon, 1999.

Bury, Emmanuel. "La *paideia* du *Télémaque*: Miroir d'un prince chrétien et lettres profanes." *Littératures Classiques* 23 (1995): 69-78.

Chartier, Roger, Marie-Madeleine Compère and Dominique Julia. *L'éducation en France du XVIe au XVIIIe siècle.* Paris: SEDES, 1976.

Clair, Pierre and François Girbal. "Introduction." In *Oeuvres philosophiques* by Géraud de Cordemoy. Paris: Presses Universitaires France, 1968.

Cohen, Mark A. "La Bruyère and the 'Usage' of Childhood: The Idea of Pedagogy in the *Caractères*." *French Forum* 26.2 (Spring 2001): 23-42.

Dainville, François de. *L'éducation des jésuites: XVIe-XVIIIe siècles.* Ed. Marie-Madeleine Compère. Paris: Editions de Minuit, 1978.

Cuche, François-Xavier. *Une pensée sociale catholique: Les idées de Fleury, La Bruyère et Fénelon.* Paris: Le Cerf, 1991.

Dedeyan, Charles. *Télémaque ou la liberté de l'esprit.* Paris: Nizet, 1991.

Escola, Marc. *La Bruyère.* 2 vols. Vol. 2. *Rhétorique du discontinu.* Paris: Champion, 2001.

Floquet, Amable. *Bossuet, précepteur du Dauphin, fils de Louis XIV et évêque de la Cour: 1670-1682.* Paris: Firmin-Didot, 1864.

Garapon, Roger. "La chronologie de la composition des 'Caractères'." *Littératures classiques*, suppl. 13 (Jan. 1991): 43-50.

Goré, Jeanne-Lydie. "Introduction." *Télémaque.* Paris: Garnier-Flammarion, 1968.

Goyet, Thérèse. *L'humanisme de Bossuet.* 2 vols. Paris: Klincksieck, 1965.

Gaquère, François. *La vie et les oeuvres de Claude Fleury (1640-1723).* Paris: J. de Gigord, 1925.

Halévi, Ran, ed. *Le savoir du prince: Du moyen âge aux lumières.* Paris: Fayard, 2002.

Haillant, Marguerite. *Culture et imagination dans les oeuvres de Fénelon "Ad usum Delphini."* Paris: Les Belles Lettres, 1982-83.

Kapp, Volker. Télémaque *de Fénelon: La signification d'une oeuvre littéraire à la fin du siècle classique.* Tübingen: Narr; Paris: Place, 1982.

Lafond, Jean. "De la guerre et de la paix, de la monarchie et de la république dans 'Démophile et Basilide' (*Du Souverain ou de la République,* 11)." In *Diversité, c'est ma devise: Mélanges offerts à J. Grimm pour ses soixante ans.* Paris-Seattle-Tübingen: Papers of French Seventeenth-Century Literature, 1994. 281-99.

Lange, Maurice. *La Bruyère, critique des conditions et des institutions sociales.* Paris: Hachette, 1909.

LeBrun, Jacques. "Du privé au public: L'éducation du prince selon Fénelon." In *Le savoir du prince, du moyen âge aux lumières.* Ed. Ran Halévi. Paris: Fayard, 2002. 235-60.

Mazaheri, Homayoun. "Enfance et Utopie." In *La satire démystificatrice de La Bruyère: Essais sur* Les Caractères. New York: Peter Lang, 1995.

Meyer, Jean. *Bossuet.* Paris: Plon, 1993.

_____. *Éducation des princes en Europe du XVe au XIXe siècle.* Paris: Perrin, 2004.

Motley, Mark. *Becoming a French Artistocrat.* Princeton, N.J.: Princeton University Press, 1990.

Pavel, Thomas. *L'art de l'éloignement.* Paris: Gallimard, 1996.

Pouzet, Régine. "Introduction." In *Charles IX: Récit d'histoire.* Ed. Régine Pouzet. Adosa: Clermont-Ferrand, 1993.

Snyders, George. *La pédagogie en France aux XVIIe-XVIIIe siècles.* Paris: Presses Universitaires France, 1965.

Wanner, Raymond E. *Claude Fleury 1640-1723, as an Educational Historiographer and Thinker.* The Hague: Nijhof, 1975.

The Prince and the Subject
at the Intersection of Emblematic Poetry and Art:
Moral and Pragmatic Reflection in
Jean-Baptiste Chassignet's Poetry
and Pierre de Loysi's Engravings

Christine McCall Probes

Poetry is a speaking picture, and a picture is a silent poem.
— Simonides (in Plutarch, *De Gloria Atheniensium*, III, 346)

Critics of Jean-Baptiste Chassignet have focused on his *Mespris de la vie et consolation de la mort* (1594). The neglected *Sonnets franc-comtois*, composed 1612-1615, were published only in the late nineteenth century by Théodore Courtaux, who posited their authorship after comparing their themes and style with those of Chassignet's *Mespris*.[1] Raymond Ortali, who concurs with Courtaux, devoted a chapter of his seminal volume, *Un Poète de la mort: Jean-Baptiste Chassignet* (1968), to a consideration of the subjects, themes, and technique of the *Sonnets franc-comtois* (115-25).[2] Ortali argues that Chassignet wrote the sonnets guided by the emblematic engravings of Pierre de Loysi, rather than the inverse. Since an engraving may contain elements extraneous to its accompanying sonnet, Ortali holds that the engravings came first. Furthermore Chassignet had expressed some difficulty in composing *ex nihilo*; Ortali parallels this "guided composition" with that found in Chassignet's *Paraphrases sur les cent cinquante Psaumes de David* (1613) and explains, "C'est que les gravures en font une obligation au poète" (120-21). Daniel Russell in his authoritative *Emblematic Structures in Renaissance French Culture* has illuminated the general situation of the emblem's construction in the late Renaissance and early seventeenth century as, with the greater use of copperplate engraving, "increasingly the artist became the originator...of emblems [...and] the pictures increasingly became the starting-point of the emblem" (188).

The 89 *Sonnets franc-comtois* and their accompanying engravings by Pierre de Loysi are preceded by an encomiastic dedicatory quatrain to Clériadus de Vergy, governor of Franche Comté from 1602 to 1630. Elsewhere I have analyzed in detail the quatrain and the associated portrait of the dedicatee that features a myriad of elements imbued with both temporal and eternal significance.[3] Chassignet's previous literary creations included not only the *Mespris* but also the *Paraphrases sur les douze petis prophètes du viel testament* (1601) and the *Paraphrases sur les cent cinquante psaumes de David* (1613). Around the time of the composition of our *Sonnets franc-comtois*, Chassignet was also occupied with his legal and diplomatic career. Enjoying the esteem of his colleagues and the friendship of rulers Archduke Albert and Archduchess Isabelle, he was sent abroad on several diplomatic missions and was charged at home with fiscal, agricultural and civic duties. Municipal archives testify amply to Chassignet's devotion to the governance of his region and his own manuscripts from the first quarter of the seventeenth century include writings both historical and contemporary on the kings of France, the house of Savoie, the kingdom of Burgundy, the governor of Franche-Comté and the parliament of Dole as well as on the art of navigation.[4] It is hardly surprising then, given Chassignet's active dedication to citizenry and crown, to discover in the coetaneous *Sonnets franc-comtois* a similar compelling concern for subject and prince.

As I have investigated Chassignet's work and de Loisy's related engravings, I have become impressed with their prevalent pedagogical and didactic thrust.[5] The emblems address a large and diverse body of potential readers: "l'homme vicieux," "l'homme et la femme de bien," allegorical figures, personified material objects and, of special interest to the present examination, princes and subjects.

In his recent article "La *paideia* du *Télémaque*: miroir d'un prince chrétien et lettres profanes," Emmanuel Bury reminds us of the roots of the genre in pagan Antiquity, the Middle Ages and the Renaissance. Complementing the tradition of princely instruction found in the writings of Xenophon, Saint Thomas, Christine de Pisan, Erasmus, Budé and others (Bury 69-70) is the emblematic tradition from Alciati to contemporaries of Chassignet such as author/artist Jean-Jacques Boissard, whom Margaret McGowan believes the poet may have known personally (143). Within the ambitious scope of the emblem genre, which may comprise the entire world and its inhabitants, the instruction of both prince and subject or "grand citoyen" occupies a significant place.[6]

My present examination of the art of instruction chez Chassignet and de Loysi as it bears on princes and their subjects, focuses on the following points: the crucial role of images and historical examples as "preuves," the motif of woman as warrior and counselor, the sustained appeal to the five senses (yet a sonnet such as XXXVI may counsel: "Ce n'est pas assez d'adorer la peinteure / ...De parer de flambeaux toute une sepulture / ...Il faut... / Tenir ses sens reglés au veuil de la raison), the moral and political reflections, and the harmony (or rarely, disharmony) among the various components of the emblematic whole: engraving, *devise*, *distique* or couplet and sonnet.

Chassignet, who represented the throne in legal, military and fiscal duties both at home and in various dispatches abroad (Annexe IV in Ortali 169-77), dedicates his *recueil* to the valiant and prudent Clériadus de Vergy, governor of Franche-Comté.[7] A passion for peace and unity underlies the volume, inspiring the instruction directed to rulers and subjects. Russell places Chassignet among several poets, including d'Aubigné and Du Bartas, "all marked by the same mentality that spawned the immense popularity of emblems" (*Emblematic Structures in Renaissance French Culture* 225). The impact on royalty is clear; Russell reminds us of Henri de Navarre's appreciation: "[ces poètes] me laissent la teste pleine de pensees excellentes, d'images et d'amblemes, desquels ont prevalu les anciens."[8]

Instruction through Images as "Proofs"

In the "mirror for princes" found in the Chassignet/de Loisy volume, images such as the scepter and the lance, a magnet, a comet, a hand writing on a block of marble, among others, convey the attributes of a wise ruler. Admonitions may accompany exhortations as in sonnet LXXVIII where the accompanying engraving represents a crown supported by two columns symbolizing piety and justice. This anti-Machiavelli sonnet addresses the "Sectaires malheureux du Tuscan secretaire," cautioning, "Renversés ses pilliers, l'empire tombera." The succinct warning of possible disaster for the prince's kingdom contrasts with the highly developed description of personal loss to the prince. While he will gain wisdom as he is reminded "qu'il releve vassal d'un seul Dieu sa couronne," he will lose his kingdom.

[Dieu], pour felonnie envers sa majesté,

Retire à soy le fief, le chasse hors de son throne,
Et remet en son lieu justice et pieté.

Warnings to princes illustrated by images from the animal kingdom are disparate at times; an engraving may feature dogs and a wild boar while the corresponding sonnet in a mode of *amplificatio* heaps image upon image – a viper, a bull, a mongoose, a crocodile – to communicate a caution (XXIX). The engraving depicting a wild boar held in check by the smaller of two dogs establishes the concept while the sonnet with its several additional images elaborates the argument, intensifying its effect by gory detail. The mongoose buries himself in the crocodile's belly, and "d'une aspre morsure, / Luy rompe à belles dents les intestins fumeux." A double maxim effects the transition from animal to man as it confers authority on the warning to the "grand" and "puissant." The negative instruction conveyed by word and image is relieved only in the final two words of the sonnet, as the prince or other powerful person is reminded of help that can come from a friend of lower estate: "Toy donc qui des petits ne fais estat quelconcque, / Pour te voir hault monté, sache qu'il ne fut oncque / Ny ennemy leger, ny de petit amy." The inclusion of "petit amy" would indicate the poet's attentiveness to the considerable heritage of fables on the subject. The early modern reader/viewer of this emblematic composition could have been prompted to recall the lessons of fables from various *Ésopes* such as "Le Lion blessé à la patte par l'épine," "Le Lion sauvé par la souris," and the famous "Débat du ventre et des membres du corps," the latter also taken up by Rabelais in the *Tiers Livre.*[9]

A negative image in an engraving may contrast with a positive image or allusion in its accompanying poem. A wild boar in an artistic image may represent qualities to be avoided – avarice and cupidity, while a reference to Alexander the Great in the associated sonnet may incarnate bravery and courage (XLII). Seemingly disparate allusions may converge to extol a value essential to prince and subject alike. Sonnet XXXII praises work as the means to true glory and honor; the engraving featuring a helmet on a panoply suggests the prince's military prowess while the sonnet emphasizes the ruler's two-fold function as patron of the arts and sciences as well as leader of armies. References to "le labeur des neuf doctes pucelles" and to Alexander's conquests act as proofs. Orest Ranum has written authoritatively and at length on the important role of Alexander in the seventeenth-century cult of the hero, reminding us of the great interest in Amyot's translation of Plutarch's *Lives* (1559).[10] Perhaps in coupling the Muses and

Alexander, Chassignet had in mind their inspiration of the various poets and philosophers of Antiquity who celebrated the famed conqueror. Alternatively, Chassignet might be recalling Alexander's role as patron of the arts or his favorite reading, the *Iliad* (Curtius 80).

Occasionally an artistic depiction and its corresponding sonnet are entirely given over to a quality or conduct to be avoided. Chassignet's inspiration may derive from a complex scene of Antiquity. The image of the banquet given by Dionysius I for his courtier Damocles (Cicero, *Tusculanae Disputationes* 5, 61) depicted in detail in de Loysi's illustration accompanying sonnet LX, complete with sword hanging by a hair over the courtier's head, offers convincing proof of "le triste estat du tyran inhumain." The reader cannot miss the negative focus; the Latin maxim, "Nunquam bene tuta tyrannis" [The tyrant is never safe], provides the interpretive *devise*, while the French couplet with its repetitive negative particle, "Jamais, jamais la tyrannie / N'est d'asseurance assez munie," drives home the categorical emphasis. Not content with the descriptive mode of engraving, *devise* and couplet, Chassignet vivifies the emblem in his poetic discourse by a double interrogative; the sonnet's first tercet invites the prospective reader to contemplate the engraving and determine for himself a tyrant's happiness. The rhyme-words, pairing "haultain" with "incertain" and "table" with "redoutable," underscore both the qualities the prince must avoid as well as probable consequences.

> Juge-tu bien heureux le roy fier et haultain
> Sur qui pendille à nud, pendant qu'il est à table,
> Entre les mets friands, un glaive redoutable,
> Soustenu seulement d'un filet incertain?

The poet addresses the second interrogative specifically to the prince, then adopts a parenetic style as he delineates the behavior to be avoided.

> Prince, veux-tu regner sans soupçon et sans crainte,
> Ne donne à tes sujets occasion de plainte,
> Ne leurs oste leurs biens, leurs femmes, leurs honneur.

The final tercet's imperative and double maxim take up again the terror of the artistic rendering. The poetry thus intensifies the emblematic whole through powerful references to the concept of fear, reiterated by four verbal forms of "craindre" as well as by the substantive "peur."

> Crains sur tout d'estre craint; la peur sçait mieux esteindre
> L'amitié que la mort, et le fascheux seigneur

Qui de beaucoup est craint beaucoup de gents doit craindre.

Justice should characterize the prince's administration; as a magnet attracts iron, the subject of de Loisy's engraving accompanying sonnet L, justice will attract even the most "barbares." The hand portrayed in the illustration represents, as the sonnet clarifies, the government of princes who would do justly and listen to instruction, "Si vous faites justice et n'estes point ignores," while the iron represents the barbarous peoples who would respond favorably to a just administration. To convince the skeptical prince, Chassignet amplifies his argument, heaping upon each other as proofs the names of numerous recalcitrant tribes and nations whose barbarity would have been apparent to the Renaissance and early modern reader: "[les] Arabes felons,...les Turcz..., les Tartares, les Moscovites fiers et les Scythes avares,...les Gelons."[11] As a parallel construction to the enumeration of nationalities who if shown justice would follow obediently "l'ombre de[s] talons" of the ruler, the poet issues a series of imperatives to the prince: "Gouvernés, praesidés... / Dominés, commandés" and, finally, "notés." The last imperative introduces the final argument or "proof," formulated as a maxim.

Princes, notés cecy: l'homme est né raisonnable,
Fuyant l'oppression, comme estant compagnable,
Qui courbe voluntiers sous un juste seigneur.

The closing tercet unifies the emblematic whole as it reminds the prince/reader of the magnet's attraction, comparing it to the natural appeal that justice and honor would have for the "Romain" and the "Scythe."

Justice and military might are complementary; the design corresponding to sonnet LXX features a scepter and a lance. In an expository mode, the poet first interprets the lance, representing the prince's qualities of strength, valor and boldness, both in competitions and military engagements. If "fort" rhymes with "effort" (he repulses his enemy's efforts), it also rhymes with "accort" and "tort." The prince must be gracious and prudent, discerning right from wrong. This second interpretation of the engraving, focusing on the scepter, emphasizes the prince's rule of equity: "par loix, par droicture et justice." Whereas elsewhere Chassignet may develop one or more positive attributes of the prince or warn against a negative trait such as unbridled ambition in military conquests (in sonnet XI, for example), here he presents together the essential qualities of the perfect prince. It could be argued that the coordinate conjunction of the Latin *devise*, "Armis et legibus," provides the key to the emblem's interpretation. The balance suggested by "et" finds its counterpart in the sonnet's two parallel maxims whose terms are reversed: "La force sans justice en temerité passe, / La justice sans force est de peu d'efficace." To complete the picture of this "plus hault point de perfection," Chassignet reminds us of de Loisy's design and the qualities it symbolizes. Again, balance is essential; the verbs "accoupler" and "joindre" highlight this feature as do the adverb "ensemble" and the reiterated "et" and "avecque."

> Mais d'accoupler ensemble et le sceptre et la lance,
> Et joindre la justice avecque la vaillance,
> C'est bien le plus hault point de la perfection.

Characters and images from mythology, history and the animal kingdom serve artist and poet as they warn against rampant ambition. These admonitions address the general reader as well as the prince: "ambitieux humain" (XI), "les ambitieux" et "ambitieux humains" (XXXV). In sonnet XI, Chassignet reminds the would-be conqueror of "l'une et l'autre boule, / Soit des pays brulans, soit des pays glacés" of the punishment of Erysichthon, condemned to insatiable hunger for cutting down a grove sacred to Ceres (Ovid, *Met.* 8.847 ff.). In XXXV, the proofs assembled against the over ambitious are the crocodile and the dragon of the engraving and the allusion to the Roman emperor Jovian (Flavius Claudius Jovanius, 363-364 A.D.) made in the poetic composition. The engraving features a crocodile pursuing a man beside the Nile River and a kind of dragon or basilisk fleeing a man. The *devise* and couplet deliver the interpretation: the images from the animal kingdom represent honor or glory that flees "le superbe" but follows the person who himself flees self-importance. The sonnet omits the dragon of de Loisy's design; the crocodile fulfills both functions, symbolizing glory, which at once entices ("son lustre seduit") and eludes ("[elle] Fuit les ambitieux"). The historical "proof," the allusion to Jovian, makes it clear that the sonnet is directed not only to the "ambitieux humains" but also to the prospective ruler. Chassignet retells, in capsule form, Jovian's rise to power, acclaimed emperor "Quand moins il aspiroit à ce grade honorable."[12]

A mythical bird acts as a powerful image central to instruction in discernment and wise counsel. The Latin *devise* accompanying sonnet LXXV, "Sedat prudentia motus" [Prudence calms sedition], interprets the engraving's scene that depicts an alcyon in the midst of a rough sea, ships buffeted by a storm and the sun piercing the clouds.

Instead of beginning immediately with an identification of the emblematic elements, Chassignet instructs the "Princes qui praesidés à la race mortelle" to choose well "hommes de cervelle" for their councils. The instruction is both negative and positive; the princes should reflect on the calamities that "sappent journellement, et dehors et dedans" their states. To the storm of the artistic illustration, the poet adds the image of "une simple cordelle" by which hang the states. The negative image conveying precariousness prepares the way for the positive instruction, as "cordelle" rhymes with "cervelle." Another rhyme-word, "nouvelle" highlights yet another image; these prudent "hommes de cervelle" will provide "au mal nouveau medecine nouvelle." It is not until the final tercets that we have a careful, detailed, image-by-image interpretation of the entire emblem construction, underscored by a triple metaphor.

> Vos estats sont des mers, et les peuples mouvants
> Que vous tenés sujets sont les esprits des vents
> Qui courroucent les flots et souffrent les orages.
> Mais les vrays alcyons qui, nichans parmy vous,
> Peuvent rassoir vos flots et calmer les courroux
> Des vents de ceste mer, ce sont les hommes sages.

The Ideal Ruler and Subject

De Loisy and Chassignet do not only offer instruction or a "miroir du prince" throughout their volume, they also provide a contemporary example of the ideal prince, Clériadus de Vergy, governor of Franche-Comté (1602-1630), their dedicatee. Since the volume was composed around the middle of Clériadus's regime, the artist and poet had ample opportunity to observe first hand the peace, financial prosperity and artistic flowering that occurred under the ruler's guidance. Historical documents confirm the accuracy of the volume's praise. Letters of the period relating to military and governmental affairs reveal a courageous and talented ruler who sought to maintain internal peace and encouraged tolerance, for example toward the Savoyard refugees.[13] Similarly historians are unanimous in recognizing Clériadus's "courage…sens,…esprit fort et vif,…experience,…parfaite probité et… magnanimité."[14]

Ten engravings and their corresponding text address or refer to Clériadus, his wife or his family. Elsewhere I have treated in detail certain rich visual and poetic images found in several of these dedicatory units.[15] If Clériadus's portrait and the inaugural sonnet with its blason of the Vergy family evoke the volume's two centers of interest, the temporal and the eternal, the second emblematic unit, in parallel fashion, presents a complementary image of the ruler's wife.

Clériadus's blason may be placed on another more general image thus providing a reinforcement of the volume's instruction. The engraving accompanying sonnet XXVI, for example, features a luxuriant orange tree, itself symbolizing by its leaves and fruit the preeminent princely virtues as embodied in Clériadus and his family. The discerning "grands preux de Vergy" have wisely refused tempting offers and honors from foreign monarchs, demonstrating their loyalty to Burgundy. The family coat of arms, placed on one of the oranges of the engraving, creates a double image. The blason, a shield of azure with three golden cinquefoils or "quintefeuilles," already present in the volume's inaugural emblem where it embellishes a pedestal, identifies Clériadus and the Vergy with a primary princely virtue, steadfastness. The olfactory and gustatory appeal evoked in sonnet XXVI will undergo sustained analysis in this essay's section on sensory appeal. Steadfastness, symbolized by the fruit of the orange tree, is complemented by two other essential qualities of the ideal prince: duty and obedience. Although the sonnet identifies these qualities with the orange tree, duty with its leaves and obedience with its flowers, perhaps it is possible to suggest a further identification with the blason as well, since, as we recall, its charges or motifs are triple. In any case, the sonnet through its designation of three cardinal qualities of the ideal prince, sustains the ternary heraldic imagery.

It is clear from the emblematic units connected to the volume's dedicatee either by the Vergy *devise* or blason that the ideal prince is wise, dutiful and faithful. Like the entire Vergy line, he is also a brave warrior. Princely virtue, then, includes the essential *virtù*: "les preux de Vergy sont des foudres de guerre" (LXXXI). Clériadus's might is further underscored in the engraving associated with sonnet LXXXIV. Although both sonnet and engraving have been completely mangled, my examination of the intact engraving in the Besançon library (64466 Res. Ill.) reveals a double emphasis on Clériadus's bravery. Antiquity and myth lend their power to the emblem; Clériadus is depicted as a warrior of Antiquity, complete with breastplate, sword and shield, while his heroism is denoted by the mythic image of a ram or the Golden Fleece, evoking both Jason's mighty acts as well as the honor of "chevalier de la Toison d'Or" bestowed upon Clériadus in 1615. But the ideal prince is not alone in the emblem. The escutcheon is divided, featuring, in addition to his own, the armorial bearings of Clériadus's wife Madeleine. The previously mentioned ram frames the marital coat at the bottom, while a crown signaling princely power surmounts the impaled arms. To the right of Clériadus and kneeling as he does at the altar is Madeleine, here depicted in flowing robes and a modest head covering. Renaissance armorials often represented nobles and their wives kneeling at an altar, the prince bearing or accompanied by armor. However the wife more typically was richly dressed, with elaborate headdress and jewels.[16] Here Madeleine de Bauffremont, in modest robes and saintly pose, is instead reminiscent of numerous Renaissance paintings of her biblical namesake, Mary Madeleine. While we cannot be certain of the engraver's intent particularly in the absence of any interpretative sonnet, the Renaissance and early modern viewer would have readily been reminded of the prevalent artistic practice of depicting noble women as the Madeleine.[17] Allegorical figures accompany the prince and his wife: Hyménée, Cupid and a female figure holding a blazing heart and symbolizing conjugal love. Mythology and allegory thus join with heraldry, celebrating conjugal and sensual love alongside the merging of noble families.

The engraving accompanying sonnet II of our volume depicts Madeleine as a warrior in what may be a double image. A female warrior rings the alarm with her lance while another female warrior combats soldiers, the personification of vices. The blason of Madeleine de Bauffremont's family, reproduced with her husband's arms at the beginning of the volume as well as in several later engravings, features a series of vair bells. The coat of arms seems to authorize our identification of Madeleine with the warrior figure sounding the alarm, while the sonnet itself makes it amply clear that she is the other chaste warrior defending with "fermeté" the chateau's honor.

> Ah! Vous estes vroyement cette brave guerriere,
> Qui, descouvrant le vice au front de la barriere,
> Le combattés de prés et l'atterrés de loing.

The successful ruler's wife is expected to bear him children. Alas, that was not to be the destiny of Madeleine. The poet devotes an entire sonnet (XXVII) to the *desideratum*, interpreting de Loisy's engraving composed of the Vergy and Bauffremont blasons by the *devise* "Fructifica" [Be fruitful]. A final artistic representation of the subject, accompanying sonnet LV, pictures Madeleine as the Virgin Mary with the Infant Jesus on her knees and John the Baptist nearby, arms outstretched. The Vergy-Bauffremont union is symbolized not only by a Cupid complete with typical bow and arrow but also by the two family blasons (the flowers from the Vergy blason are in the hands of a lady-in-waiting while the bells of the Bauffremont blason are held by a winged child – another Cupid?). The poet loans his voice to Madeleine to deliver the lament of barrenness. Words of consolation follow the lament; if "le doux fruit de la conception" is denied, by contrast her legacy will consist of her numerous virtues, "l'honneur et la sagesse, / L'amour et la bonté, la grace et la caresse," all of which will be propagated throughout the world (LV).

Admonitions to subjects balance the warnings to "grands" and "puissants." Bolstered by historical, mythological and biblical allusions, the warnings transmit both practical and philosophical "vérités." A triple apostrophe to "Naboths audacieux" in sonnet XXIII and symbolic female figures in the accompanying engraving (one may well represent Jezebel of the biblical story recounted in I Kings 21) prepare the pragmatic instruction delivered through a maxim: "Les grands demeurent grands, mais dommage et mespris / Suit ordinairement celuy qui les provocque." But rulers, "Princes qui praesidés à la race mortelle," must value their subjects, choosing the wise among them (we have seen that the alcyon of the emblem confers a mythic quality to the instruction) to calm "les courroux / Des vents de ceste mer [the State]" (LXXV).

Images signifying subjects may seem to offer at times a contradictory message. Emblematic compositions featuring a small viper killing a large bull and a small generally faithful dog immobilizing a wild boar deliver a warning to princes; they must esteem their subjects (XXIX). A counter-warning in imperative form is issued to subjects: "garde-toy bien, sujet, de te mocquer et rire / Du roy ton souverain" (XXII). The corresponding engraving features a lion devouring a monkey while a "proof" from history is supplied by the poetic allusion to the legendary cruelty of Ramire I, ninth-century king of Asturias who executed his rebellious subjects. Sonnet LII makes it clear that Chassignet's overarching concern is the good of the state. The elephant in de Loisy's design symbolizes the state as well as the person of the ruler; the subject/serpent's rage toward the ruler/elephant is conveyed by an impressive example of verbal accumulation, "Il le presse, il l'estreint, il l'estrive, il le bat." The design represents one view of the final moments of the combat, the serpent plunges his head into the elephant's trunk, while the poem delivers, in complementary fashion, the final blow, the elephant with his massive weight crushes the serpent.

While the *devise* offers a balanced description of the emblem, "Vinci-tur et vincit" [He is conquered and he conquers], the couplet focuses on the disorder resulting from civil strife and the sonnet's final tercets furnish by means of a double imperative a warning to subjects. They must reflect on the disastrous consequences of discord.

> Factieux citoyens qui, divisés en deux,
> Vous livrés tous les jours mille combats hydeux,
> Quel fruict esperés-vous de vos guerres civiles?
> La mort de vostre estat, voire vos propres morts,
> Le desgast de vos champs et le sac de vos villes,
> Seront-ce pas le prix de vos fascheux discors?

While realistic in his instruction to prince and subject, Chassignet by his balanced admonitions to each holds up the ideal of a harmonious if not utopian political state. This vision connects the ideal ruler to the ideal subject, though indeed the motivation may well be often that of self-interest and self-preservation. If the ideal prince embodies duty, obedience and steadfastness to God and his country, the ideal subject must respond in a similar if not reciprocal manner, to his sovereign. A hint at this reciprocal relationship, itself to a degree reminiscent of feudal conditions between lord and vassal, may be found in sonnet LXI. Chassignet's realistic vein is seen in his recognition that subjects often test the prince, but double honor will redound when each treats the other with respect.

> Heureux le magistrat qui rencontre celuy
> Qui le veut exercer, si plein de suffisance
> Qu'en luy faisant honneur il en reçoit de luy.

Sensory Appeal

In addition to convincing through images or "proofs," the artistic and poetic instructions to princes and subjects made by de Loisy and Chassignet persuade through a sustained appeal to the five senses. I have written elsewhere at length of the interweaving of the senses with nature and with theology.[18] How, in particular, does this sensory appeal function in the exhortations to princes and subjects? First, all of the senses come into play, either to aid in the exposition of the engraving or to corroborate and underscore, often through rhyme-words, the artistic and poetic imagery. The lute of the engraving associated with sonnet VII represents, according to the *devise* "Regnum concordia firmat" [Concord strengthens the state], a pleasant sound suggestive of a harmonious government. Yet the sonnet's first line summons an unpleasant sound: "C'est un luth discordant qu'un peuple sans concorde." "Concorde" rhymes with "accorde," the latter the skillful work of the "accord-magistrat" who governs by both force and love. The poet offers a sustained metaphorical interpretation of the engraving in a quatrain that at once evokes the instrument's strings and the ruler's actions and talent.

> Ore il pince la basse, ore la haulte corde,
> Ore il bande le coeur privé d'ambition,
> Ore il lasche le coeur plein de praesomption,
> Ore il couppe à regret la corde qui discorde.

The sense of sight, whether literal or metaphorical, is quasi-omnipresent in the volume. Through a pictorial representation employing the chiaroscuro technique and including a tearful crocodile, Chassignet warns the prince of seeking after glory: "La gloire en est de mesme, et son ombre labile. / Fuit les ambitieux que son lustre seduit" (XXXV). Elsewhere an engraving featuring the sun's light penetrates the clouds, suggesting a peaceful government ruled by wise counselors (LXXV). The sense of touch comes into play in this emblem as well; we remember the metaphorical identification of the winds and rough seas as "les peuples mouvants" and the seditious states. Another exceedingly violent representation of touch is found in the combat between lion and monkey, king and subject (XXII). The animal imagery conveys the result of a ruler's vengeance, while the violent touch of an everyday object illustrates the consequence of a subject's lack of respect.

> Le mespris du vassal envers son souverain,
> Aiguisant le cousteau qui luy perce le sein,
> Engendre le lyon qui le singe devore.

Taste may be intertwined with an historical allusion or "proof." Although the focus of the emblem inspired by the banquet given by Dionysius I is the insecurity of an inhumane tyrant as illustrated by the sword hanging by a thread, Chassignet, in his poetic discourse, takes care to refer to the banquet or "table" itself, contrasting "les mets friands" with the "glaive redoutable" and the "filet incertain." The interrogative of the opening quatrain invites the prince to reflect on the opposition: "juge-tu bien heureux le roy fier et haultain...?" (LX). The gustatory and olfactory appeals are central to the volume's entire emblematic collection due to the attention given to the dedicatee's arms. Engravings including the depiction of an orange tree "chargé de fruits" (LXI) or the flower with three branches and three "quinte-feuilles" (LV) are to be understood metaphorically as they point to virtues and honor. The flowers and fruit may also allude to the fervent hope for an heir as the depiction of the Vergy arms provides the basis for the command/*devise* "Fructifica" [Be fruitful], the couplet "Fructi-fiés, puisque la fleur / Sans fruit est de peu de valeur," and the final poetic injunction: "Il faut...que tu [Madeleine] nous donne des fruits" (XXVII). The emphasis on taste, again metaphorical, is most evident in the engraving associated with sonnet XXVI. De Loisy's design makes a double reference to the orange tree that, with its abundant and extremely large, luscious fruit, occupies the center of the engraving. The Vergy arms are also placed on one of the oranges, at top and cen-ter. The "verd" of the fidelity of the "grand preux de Vergy" is located at the very center of the sonnet, as it, through sustained hyperbole, praises these princes who have continually refused foreign monarchs' offers and honors. The remarkable hyperbole of the *devise*, "Viret invariabilis illa" [It flourishes in every season] and the couplet, "En toute saison l'oranger / Porte et verdoye sans changer," finds, in the sonnet, further exposition and attention to the gustatory. The cold win-ter has no effect on "le jeune oranger" which bears "la fleur avec le fruit, la verte et meure orange." Finally, the fruit of the orange tree pro-vides the poet with an occasion to praise the Vergy "fermeté" as the sonnet culminates its encomium, established on a prolonged compari-son.

> [Ces grands preux de Vergy]...
> Ainsi que l'oranger, dez leurs prime naissance,
> Portent en mesme temps leurs fleurs d'obeissance,
> Les fueilles du devoir, les fruits de fermeté,
> Et si le noir glaçon des fortunes adverses,
> Le frimat des malheurs, le verglat des traverses,
> Jamais ne touche au verd de leurs fidelité.

The "grands preux de Vergy" are also frequently represented by "rochers en l'eau" or "cubes droicts" whose virtue resists tempests and revolts (I). An emblem that relies heavily on olfactory appeal illustrates the beneficial effect of tests on the prince's virtue. The engraving depicts a hand with a mortar and a pestle. The perfume evoked by the *devise*, "Redolet flagrantius icta" [The more it is pounded, the more it emits fragrance] and the sweet smell suggested by the couplet, "Plus la vertu sent de secousse, / Plus l'odeur qu'elle rend

est doulce," are echoed in the sonnet as Chassignet conveys the perse-
cution of the "groz rochers" or "hommes de merite." The poet adds to
the emblem the image of a knife that evil sharpens, producing in the
face of calamity "une odeur plus doulce." The final tercet returns to an
interpretation of the engraving and issues a triple olfactory appeal as
noun, adjective and adverb intensify the sweet smell of refined virtue.

> Le poivre ainsi pilé dans le mortier d'airain,
> Sous les coups redoublés du pilon cassegrain,
> Un parfum plus souef plus souefvement pousse.

Our examination of the images, arguments and examples from
history and the sensory appeal central to the *paideia* expressed and
portrayed by Chassignet and de Loysi has revealed a coherent, reflec-
tive thrust embracing the moral and the political. Indeed, as Anne-Elisabeth Spica argues, "la vocation de l'emblème est morale" ("Moralistes et emblématique" 171). An image in the engraving or in the
accompanying texts (*devise*, couplet, sonnet) may attract and furnish a
"proof"; an allusion to history or mythology may take its place in the
reader's *thesaurus* or "storage room" of "educated memory" (Carruthers 33), and an appeal to the senses may vivify a concept.[19] These
techniques of persuasion lead and challenge the reader to reflect on
both the virtuous and the pragmatic.

The Moral and Political Reflections

In his recent article "Éloge et instruction dans le *Télémaque*,"
Volker Kapp reminds us of the centrality of praise for the prince's
instruction ("ériger un homme en exemple à imiter...louer la pratique
gouvernementale") as well as for "toute la civilization depuis le Moyen
Age" (88, 95). In our volume, instruction through praise of Franche-
Comté's ruler challenges the reader to reflect on and imitate Clériadus's numerous virtues. The challenge is both implicit and explicit;
while the epidictic mode dominates, the more direct parenetic style is
also present. Emblems, coats of arms, and sonnets describe, demonstrate and praise the honor, magnanimity, charity, renown, courage and
power that characterized Clériadus (the Vergy are "foudres de guerre").
Emblematic illustrations, whether in the engravings or in the corresponding texts, call the prince who would govern well to reflect on
Clériadus' example. This ruler whose *devise*, "Sans varier," or "Variari
nescia virtus" [La vertu ne saurait subir de variation], is worthy of

imitation; his constancy and loyalty is contrasted with the disloyalty of revolting peoples, his virtue "despite la tempeste et rit de changement" (I).

In a somewhat more direct mode, the reader may be invited by interrogation, apostrophe and exclamation to reflect on the poet's praise of the Vergy's valorous deeds. Sonnet LXXXI interprets an engraving depicting a winged woman blowing two trumpets, the allegorical figure "La Renommée." Interrogations instruct explicitly as they call the reader as witness to the poet's contemplation of the phenomenon represented in the engraving: "Qu'est-ce que je voy là si haultement voler," "Ces deux trompes... / Qu'est-ce autre que le bruit de sa voix animée...?" and "Mais que dict-elle au ciel, qu'annonce-elle en terre?" If the Vergy princes' renown derives to a certain extent from their military valor and wisdom, it is above all due to their virtue. The poet makes this clear as he catalogs their many admirable qualities, only to follow the enumeration by a conjunction introducing the contrasting and most valued attribute: "mais [ils sont] fort hommes de bien." The final tercet ostensibly apostrophizes the idea represented by the allegorical figure in the engraving, but serves as well to instruct the reader/witness, compelling him or her by both apostrophe and exclamation to reflect on virtue.

> O renom glorieux en ce siècle où nous sommes,
> Qui part d'une vertu si rare entre les hommes
> Qu'honneurs, moyens, grandeurs, sans elle ne sont rien!

Positive instruction may be balanced by and contrasted with a direct exhortation to consider the sure and certain negative results of confrontation by opposing princes and foes to "ce comte porte-paix." As the poet interprets the anvil and hammer of the design accompanying sonnet LIV, he reiterates the Vergy *devise* "Sans varier." Direct address underscores the instruction; imperatives, an expressive interjection and an interrogation issue the challenge to miserable rebel princes: "Battés et rebattés ceste enclume massive / A grands coups de marteaux, chetifs, ah! Pensés-vous / Qu'elle ne rompra pas vos marteaux et vos coups [?]."

The emblematic compositions extolling the Vergy virtues present a microcosm or an important sample of the volume's moral and political (or pragmatic) reflections. As we examined the role of images, historical examples and sensory appeal, we observed a sustained parenetic style. Princes are called to consider carefully forces that undermine their kingdoms; they are admonished to choose for their councils intelligent and prudent men (LXXV). Rulers are exhorted to perfection as *devises* such as "Armis et legibus" (LXX) and "Pietate et justitia" (LXXVIII) communicate a balanced responsibility to the state and a prince's requisite personal qualities. In his article "Emblematic Structures in Sixteenth-Century French Poetry," Russell emphasizes the original pedagogical intent of the two columns or pillars, "probably invented" by Jacques Amyot, *précepteur* of Charles IX (68-69 and n. 43).[20] De Loisy's design, including in the background a maritime city, is somewhat more complex than the expected two columns exemplifying the eternal and the temporal. Yet the sonnet by its identification of justice and piety as "les deux pilotis… / Qui soustiennent l'estat du prince debonnaire," interprets the maritime allusion, since "pilotis" are pilings, appropriate supports for structures built on water. The astute early modern reader would also have been led to reflect on the implicit play on words between "pieux" and its homophone "pieu," the latter signifying a literal support complementary to the spiritual support that piety offers the state. The design with the maritime city is an example of the more elaborate and at first seemingly extraneous element that may occur in an emblem of this period, due to, as Russell points out, "the introduction of the more sophisticated technique of copperplate engraving." Similarly the play on words is an example of a "clever conceit [which could] open a space that invited independent speculation by a reader/viewer" ("Emblematic Structures" 7). The "riddle element" is typical of the early modern emblem, contributing to the reader's pleasure and intellectual challenge (*The Emblem and Device in France* 87, 173). In a recent issue of *Revue de Littérature Comparée* devoted to the emblem, Gisèle Mathieu-Castellani takes up "le défi de l'emblème" reminding us of Russell's application of the concept of "bricolage" to the creative process of both emblematist and reader (597-603).[21]

The prince must also reflect on God: "Dieu praeside aux combats, il commande aux vacarmes" (LXXX). Rulers are called to contemplate God's creation as poet and artist include a comet's warning in their instruction (LI). The early modern prince would have been receptive to this reasoning as there was a widespread fear of comets as omens of calamities or as warnings from God (Allen 74, n. 63, 3-100). The poet's thrust is both particular and general; he fears God's indignation at "nostre nation" while he exhorts all rulers to reflect on the comet and return to God. Although the poet will characterize God as "tres-patient et doux," he renders his hortative instruction exceptionally compelling by two imperatives, each occupying the first hemistich of the alexandrines while the second hemistich describes the disastrous consequences of disobedience.

> Empereurs, princes, roys, la comette reluit.
> Retournés-vous à Dieu, mort et perte vous suit.
> Demandés-luy pardon, votre gloire se passe.

Subjects are similarly exhorted to consider God; the emphasis here however is on their submission to the ruler. God has placed the prince in power and "veut que chacun [le] devotement honore" (XXII). Both epidictic and parenetic modes form the persuasive instruction. Demonstration by image, general argument and specific historical example, all, complement injunctions to subjects. The subject, as the prince, must reflect on the good of the state. The argument of the king as God's earthly representative is a constant, but the appeal to the subject's self-interest is frequent as well. The rebellious citizen is reminded that "Les roys sont dangereux quand, de cholere espris, / Ils desgorgent sur nous les bouillons de leurs ire" (XXII). The seditious subject should consider particular personal consequences, "vos propres morts, / Le desgast de vos champs et le sac de vos villes" (LII). Our earlier treatment of LII noted the diversity of this emblem's elements and a shifting, dual focus from seditious, attacking subject to massive, overpowering prince. Image and text combine as emphasis alternates between the subject/serpent's furious combat in the engraving and first quatrain of the sonnet and the prince/elephant's crushing blow in the second quatrain. This emblem "in two acts" appeals powerfully to the subject's self-preservation, as it illustrates "le prix de[s]…fascheux discors" so disastrous to both individual subject and state.

Harmonies and Disharmonies

In her masterful studies on sixteenth- and seventeenth-century emblem books, Alison Saunders has treated both theory and practice, noting that artists and authors or "practitioners," just as playwrights, were not constrained by the "elaborate rules and conventions" drawn up by theoreticians. Whether an emblem is made up of two, three or four parts, the appeal of the whole is both to eyes and to intelligence, as well as to memory. The form combines "the agreeable and the profitable, [...] serving to *plaire* and *instruire*" (*The Seventeenth-Century French Emblem* 19, 310, 337-38). Image and text may duplicate each other or the poet may choose to ignore certain elements of an illustration to concentrate on only one or two. Mid-seventeenth-century Jesuit theoretician Jakob Masen explains that while the relationship "between the *res significans* and the *res significata*...must be [one] of similitude," the emblematic form permits "various possible patterns" and the relationship between elements may range "from clear similarity to indirect allusion to direct opposition" (cited by Saunders in *The Seventeenth-Century French Emblem* 345).[22]

Our examination of the *Sonnets franc-comtois* has revealed considerable variety in the relationship between image and text. As we analyzed sonnet LXX, its accompanying engraving of scepter and lance, the Latin *devise* "Armis et legibus," and the couplet, we noted the balance of instruction throughout as artist and poet present the essential qualities of the perfect prince. We found that the poet's exposition of the illustration in the sonnet is detailed, balanced and elaborate, including rhyme-words and parallel maxims focusing on key elements. Positive and negative counsel converge to lead the reader-prince to "le plus hault point de la perfection." The only seemingly extraneous element would be the argument from "le bonheur" made in the couplet, "Les armes conjointes aux loix / Causent tout le bonheur des Roys." Yet the argument is highly appropriate as the primary means of persuasion, both from a general rhetorical perspective and with regard to princely instruction. We remember that Aristotle insists on happiness as the central aim of all deliberations (*Rhetoric* I.v. 1-18) and that authors of princely instruction such as Guillaume Budé similarly emphasize the prince's happiness as a powerful motivator. Since Chassignet would have been familiar with Budé's *Institution du prince*, presented to François I around 1519 and published posthumously in 1547, it is useful here to note the work's attention to happiness.[23]

As Budé argues from history, both profane and sacred, he exploits two key metaphors; history is a mirror of things past and present, and a mistress (85, 90-91). History is a "chose délectable" and the prince will gain honor, "se vostre plaisir s'adonne à oyr ceste maistresse" (85). Budé reminds his reader of the close association between happiness and wisdom in pagan Antiquity and in the Old Testament (138, 94, 95). As is the case with Chassignet, Budé devotes attention to subjects as well as to the prince, here also focusing on happiness that derives to them from the prince, "l'estat de félicité mondaine et béatitude publicque" (138). Finally, not only does Budé express his wish that God would grant the prince the grace of Titus, the renown and glory of Alexander and the long reign of Arganthonius, but also and in initial position, the happiness of Auguste: "Sire, Dieu vous doint la félicité d'Auguste" (79). The inclusion of "bonheur" then, in the couplet associated with sonnet LXX, rather than furnishing a distracting element to the emblematic composition serves to remind the early modern prince of the long and revered tradition of the appeal to happiness.

Instances of disharmony may be identified in the *Sonnets franc-comtois*, as in sonnet XLIII where the image of the corresponding engraving features a hand, writing on a block of marble. The Latin *devise* reproduces the image, specifying who is doing the writing: "Scribunt in marmore laesi" [The offended write on the marble], while the couplet substitutes "metal" for "marble" as indeed Chassignet's contemporary Jean Bertaut had done ("L'injure se grave en metal") (Courtaux 103 n.2). Courtaux not only supplies the alternative formulation by Bertaut but also indicates that the Chassignet manuscript included another marginal notation, "L'amour ne regne plus au monde, / Et le bienfait s'escrit en onde." The variants allow us a glimpse into the creative process as Chassignet, contemplating de Loisy's image, was reminded of maxims ancient and contemporary.[24] Instead of viewing the surfaces, marble and metal, as conflicting images, the reader might instead be impressed by a certain insistence on idea resulting from the two references to different surfaces, both however of a permanent nature. This permanent record of the ruler's unjust actions, the principal feature of the engraving, is decoded and elaborated on as its poetic interpretation commands the "grands" who would oppress the "petits,"

> Lisés et relisés les monuments anticques:
> Vous trouverés des roys ez siecles anciens
> Avoir estés tués de simples citoyens,
> Indignement traictés de leurs grandeurs iniques.

Verbal accumulation brings specificity to the interpretation: it is not permitted to "violenter ceux qui ne vous sont soubmis, / Les vexer, les fouler, les presser comme fange." The final word of the emblem's poetic text expresses the action of the mistreated subject who avenges himself; "vange" rhyming with "fange," insists on the cause and effect relationship of abusive princely power. Although not alluded to directly in the poetic exposition, the early modern reader would have undoubtedly been reminded of writing on another hard surface, the palace wall of King Belshazzar. Chapter five of the Old Testament Book of Daniel offers similar princely instruction as it paints a picture of this Babylonian king who had by his numerous misdeeds incurred God's wrath. Our emblematic composition, the image of the engraving with its hand, writing on a hard surface, and the poetic text, notably in the verses referring to the "pompes magnificques" of the "grands" who "par injustes moyens" oppress the "petits" and do violence to their subjects, could very well be an subtle reminder of the biblical account of an arrogant king, "weighed and found wanting" (Daniel 5: 27).

Conclusion

Our examination has demonstrated that the instruction of prince and, to a lesser degree, subject represents a major thrust of the *Sonnets franc-comtois*. A significant number of the emblems, over a third of the corpus, is devoted to a "miroir du prince." Building on the ten panegyric compositions that address or pertain to the volume's dedicatee, Clériadus de Vergy, his wife and family, our emblematists enlarge their aim consistently throughout the volume to describe and instruct the ideal prince.

Furthermore, instruction of the prince is not neglected in emblems of a more general nature addressing a variety of other readers, "l'homme ou la femme de bien," "l'homme vicieux," allegorical figures such as fortune, even material objects (a clock symbolizing sin or a millstone suggesting the "ambitieux mondain"). The prince can benefit as can the general reader, from multifaceted exhortations to virtue and warnings of vice, reflections on wisdom, fortune, patience, reason, experience, industry, true beauty, love, marriage, death, even gluttony. Yet, within the more generalized or "universal" compositions, our emblematists also insert specific, princely instruction or allusions to kings as *exempla*. In these often polysemic emblems, it might be said, adopting terminology that Roland Barthes applied to publicity, that the poetic text includes "relais" (44-45). Thus a brief allusion to Saul, the wisdom and prophetic spirit bestowed on him by God's spirit (the Old Testament record in I Samuel 10 has this immediately following his anointing by Samuel), would encourage the reader to return to the corresponding engraving of sonnet IX and rethink possible interpretations of the bull, with its horns attached to a laurel tree. The sacred, poetic "relais" involving Saul's prophesying could send the reader back specifically to the figure of the laurel tree. Though the poet does not make the explicit interpretation, the early modern reader would have been reminded that laurel leaves in profane Antiquity were reputed to confer prophetic powers (Tibulle, *Carmina* 2, 5, 63 in Lewis and Short 1043). Similarly two allusions in sonnet V to the contrasting character of two pairs of brothers, the Roman emperors Titus and Domitian on the one hand and Jacob and Esau on the other, are crucial to the intellectual challenge of the reader who would attempt to decipher the emblem's strange engraving featuring a gallows on which a lute is hung and, in the background, a woman carrying a sheaf of grain or flowers and standing beside a cart of dung – all highly varied symbolic evocations of man's diversity and God's sovereignty. Conduct in government and war are also touched upon in the more general emblems. Moderation in affairs of the state is counseled in sonnet XXX. The boastful yet cowardly soldier who "fait du Rodomont, et, vaillant à la table, / N'ose son ennemy sur le pré recevoir" symbolizes "le sçavoir sans l'usage" decried in sonnet LXXI. If Chassignet adduces here a Moorish king of Italian epic as the useless soldier, he takes care to include elsewhere a positive example, the magnanimous lion of legend and fable whose admirable and courteous behavior should be imitated by the prince (LIX).

The *Sonnets franc-comtois*, then, instruct the prince through what we might call today a "dialogue" between constituent elements of the emblematic compositions. To return to the quotation of Simonides in my chosen epigraph, "Poetry is a speaking picture, and a picture is a silent poem," we have noted the constant, unwavering intent to offer temporal and eternal instruction to the prince by figures and designs that appeal to the eye and text that appeals to the senses, memory and understanding. As David Graham puts it in his study of Menestrier's *L'Art des emblèmes* (1684), the text "devient littéralement la voix de l'image" (21). The dialogue between emblematic elements is enriched by the use of appropriate rhetorical strategies and figures, including *amplificatio* or the heaping of image upon image, antithesis, parallelism, hyperbole, apostrophe and particularly apt rhyme-words such as "loix" and "Roys" or "fort" and "accort" (LXX). The *paideia* of the *Sonnets franc-comtois* is highly varied, focusing on qualities to be avoided as well as those to be imitated, persuading by "proofs" from nature, history, mythology and the Scriptures, and providing a remarkable breadth of material for moral and political reflection. A sustained appeal to the senses underlies the appeal (and at times the challenge) to the reader's pleasure and intelligence. Our analysis of the collection has identified various patterns of these instructive emblems, from complete identification or duplication of word and image to the more frequent complementary model, where the text elucidates, or serves as "relais" to the engraving. Often an emblem will focus on one desirable quality or its opposite while occasionally, as in the emblems devoted to Franche-Comté's ruler, and in sonnet LXX, with its corresponding engraving of scepter and lance, all of the requisite qualities of the "perfect prince" will receive full and balanced exposition.

My previous studies of Chassignet's *Mespris* and the *Sonnets franc-comtois* have insisted on the Augustinian quality of this poetry that constantly appeals to the senses, invites the reader to contemplate key images and instructs him or her to action. The emphasis on the eternal and on the visible in the instruction featured in the de Loisy/Chassignet volume is highly resonant of passages such as chapter ten of the *Confessions* where the role of the senses is viewed as crucial in the transporting of images to the mind and memory. Similarly persuasion by the visible as "proofs" as well as the usefulness of pagan letters is authorized by Saint Augustine in *De Doctrina christiana* (I, iv, 4 and II, xviii, 28). The animal *exempla* of our emblems, numerous and varied, receive further sanction from the bestiary tradition replete with complex interpretations of moral significance.[25]

The volume's final sonnet weaves together the two-pronged, multifaceted instruction of Chassignet and de Loysi. The crowned reed of the engraving symbolizes the "prince du sang" while the sonnet recalls his "pouvoir haultain" and "vouloir souverain." Reminding the subject of the divine right of kings, the poet counsels reverence and endurance, "Puis qu'ils tiennent de Dieu leurs sceptre et leurs couronne." The ambiguity of this final line of the volume suggests an ultimate and powerful instruction for both princes and subjects. Lest the reader think that only the subject must submit to the higher power, the implicit message of the final line is delivered in an explicit manner elsewhere as kings are reminded that God is "leur gouverneur," "Dieu praeside aux combats… / Oste ou donne la peur au seul air de sa voix" (LXXX).

Engraving corresponding to Sonnet XXXV

Engraving corresponding to Sonnet LXXV

Portrait of Clèriadus de Vergy with quatrain by Chassignet

Engraving corresponding to Sonnet II

Engraving corresponding to Sonnet XXVI

Accompanying Sonnet LXXXIV

Engraving corresponding to Sonnet LV

Engraving corresponding to Sonnet XXI

Notes

[1] (Paris: 1892; rpt. Geneva: Slatkine, 1969). Subsequent references will appear in the text of the article.

[2] Others such as Daniel Russell and Gilles Banderier are less certain about their attribution. Russell, in his "Emblematic Structures in Sixteenth-Century French Poetry," states alternately that "nothing could be less certain" (89, n. 92) and that "these sonnets...indeed...well may be the work of Jean-Baptiste Chassignet" (90), while Banderier in "Le Bestiaire et l'herbier" includes a note indicating his reasons for questioning the attribution (154-55, n. 2).

[3] See my essay: "*Les Sonnets franc-comtois* de Jean-Baptiste Chassignet: la représentation du «premier lecteur» et la persuasion du lecteur idéal" in *La Poésie religieuse et ses lecteurs aux XVIe et XVIIe siècles.*

[4] Ortali 17-18, 137-40.

[5] See my essays: "L'entrelacement des sens et de la nature chez Jean-Baptiste Chassignet" in *Jean-Baptiste Chassignet,* and "*Les Sonnets franc-comtois* de Jean-Baptiste Chassignet" in *La Poésie religieuse.*

[6] The title of Boissard's work, *Theatrum vitae humanae* (1596), is indicative of the genre's scope. For the formation of the "grand citoyen," see the emblems of Schoonhoven (1618), for example. Jean-Marc Chatelain, *Livres d'emblèmes et de devises* 93, 145. The double mission of instruction to prince and subject was present in Alciati; his *Emblematum Liber* (1531) includes emblems instructing kings and princes as well as others relating to justice, equality and citizenship. For a highly useful review of the impressive corpus of works on "le modèle du prince," see Stegmann 117-33.

[7] Franche-Comté or Burgundy's sovereign was Isabelle-Claire-Eugénie, daughter of Philippe II, king of Spain. This is the same ruler in whose honor Tristan L'Hermite composed several poems including the well-known ode "A la Serenissime Princesse Isabelle" (XI, *Les Vers héroïques*) written during his residence along with his patron Gaston d'Orléans, at the court of Flanders.

[8] Henri's words are from d'Aubigné's "Lettres touchant quelques poincts de diverses sciences." Cited in Russell (1995) 225.

[9] For further details on versions of these fables, see Jeanne-Marie Boivin and Laurence Harf-Lancner, 312, 315. For a pertinent and comprehensive analysis of "Le Débat du ventre et des membres du corps," see Laurence Harf-Lancner, "L'Individu dans l'État" in *L'Individualisme* 51-71. Alison Saunders, in her masterful studies on the French emblem, has insisted, as have others such as Russell, on the genre's native French heritage. See her chapter, "Emblems and Associated Illustrated Didactic Literature in France," in *The Sixteenth-Century French Emblem Book* 29-70, and "Emblems and Emblematic Fables" in *The Seventeenth-Century French Emblem* 21-64.

[10] See his *Artisans of Glory* 17-19, 114-15, 255-59, 279-80, 336-37.

[11] Gelon was the 5th century B.C. tyrant of Gela who seized Syracuse, destroyed Camarina and Megara Hyblaea, and defeated Hamilcar's Carthaginian army (*Oxford Classical Dictionary* 460).

[12] De la Bléterie's *Histoire de Jovien* (Amsterdam, 1740) is often recommended as the best reference on the subject. Jovian is also remembered for his impartiality; professing Christianity and establishing it as a legal religion, he nevertheless protected the rights of non-Christians (see John McClintock and James Strong 4: 1037).

[13] The letters of Clériadus may be found in the Collections Chifflet and Granvelle of the Bibliothèque Municipale de Besançon; I refer in particular to the Collection Granvelle ms. 42, fol. 126, 154 and 170.

[14] André du Chesne, *Histoire de la Maison de Vergy* and Antoine Brun's funeral oration of Clériadus, published in *Les Mémoires de la Société d'Emulation du Jura* (1873), both referred to by Courtaux 8, 10-11, 34-38.

[15] The ten poems which treat Clériadus include: the quatrain under the dedicatee's portrait, I, II, XXVI, XXVII, LIV, LV, LXI, LXXXI and LXXXIV. I examine in some detail four of these poems, the dedicatory quatrain, I, XXVI, and LXI, in my article "Les *Sonnets franc-comtois* de Jean-Baptiste Chassignet."

[16] Stephen Slater, *The Complete Book of Heraldry* 101, 110-15.

[17] Although many images of the Madeleine represent her as ecstatic and seductive in keeping with the Mary of Luke 8 "out of whom went seven devils" or with the unnamed sinner who anointed Jesus' feet and wiped them with her hair (Luke 7:37-38), many other Renaissance and early modern representations depict her in modest clothing, often reading, a "symbol of the contemplative life." See, for example, Rogier van der Weyden's mid-fifteenth-century painting of the Madeleine as Lazarus's sister Mary of Bethany, reproduced in Susan Haskins's seminal *Mary Magdalen: Myth and Metaphor* 199, and note Haskins's discussion of noble women represented as the Madeleine 298-304.

[18] See my "L'entrelacement des sens" and "La littérature et l'art au service de la théologie."

[19] See the first chapter of Carruthers's seminal work for a thorough analysis of ancient models and metaphors for the memory.

[20] Russell notes that some scholars attribute the device to Michel de l'Hospital and that the straight columns "stress the claims of the French crown to the title of Holy Roman Emperor." For a full discussion of this point, see V. E. Graham and W. McAllister Johnson, eds. *The Paris Entries of Charles IX and Elisabeth of Austria* 64-75, as cited by Russell.

[21] In his discussion of the "profound influence" of emblematic forms on reading, Russell identifies the emblematist with the "bricoleur," referring to uses of the terminology by Lévi-Strauss and Gérard Genette (*Emblem and Device in France* 175-77). Else-

where Russell finds an expression of this "bricolage" in the description by Renaissance emblematist Gilles Corrozet of his own work as variation and adaptation, even disguise ("The Emblem and Authority" 82).

[22] Saunders refers to and summarizes important sections of Jakob Masen's work, *Speculum imaginum veritatis occultae.*

[23] All references in the text are to Claude Bontems's edition of Budé's work, a reproduction of the original text from ms. 5103 of the Bibliothèque de l'Arsenal (Appendice 77-140). See, for a pertinent discussion of "l'emblématique du pouvoir" and the relationship of "recueils d'emblèmes politiques" with "recueils humanistes," Anne-Elisabeth Spica's *Symbolique humaniste et emblématique* 362-65.

[24] Numerous related quotations may be found in Antiquity as well as in the Early Modern era, from Sophocles and Catullus to Shakespeare, Bacon and Sir Thomas More.

[25] For example, the elephant of the engraving accompanying sonnet LII, symbolizing the state and its ruler, typifies wisdom and intelligence as well as force. His combat with the dragon or serpent, representing the subject, is reminiscent, even to gory detail, of numerous bestiaries. See, for example Pierre de Beauvais, Guillaume le Clerc de Normandie and Brunetto Latini, *Bestiaires du Moyen Age*, ed. Gabriel Bianciotto.

Works Cited

Allen, Don Cameron. *The Star-crossed Renaissance*. New York: Octagon, 1973.

Aristotle. *Rhetoric*. Cambridge: Harvard University Press, 1967.

Augustine. *Confessions*. Vol. 2. Paris: Les Belles Lettres, 1994.

_____. *De Doctrina christiana*. Paris: Institut d'Etudes Augustiniennes, 1997.

Banderier, Gilles. "Le Bestiaire et l'herbier." *Jean-Baptiste Chassignet: Actes du Colloque du Centre Jacques-Petit*. Ed. Anne Mantero. Paris: Champion, 2003. 139-62.

Barthes, Roland. "Rhétorique de l'image." *Communications* 4 (1964): 40-51.

Bianciotto, Gabriel, ed. *Bestiaires du Moyen Age*. Paris: Stock, 1980.

Boivin, Jeanne-Marie and Laurence Harf-Lancner, eds. *Fables françaises du Moyen Age: Les Isopets*. Paris: Flammarion, 1996.

Brun, Antoine. *Les Mémoires de la Société d'Emulation du Jura*. Lons-le-Saunier, 1873.

Budé, Guillaume. *L'Institution du prince. Le Prince dans la France des XVIe et XVIIe Siècles*. Eds. Claude Bontems *et al*. Paris: Presses Universitaires France, 1965. Appendice: 77-140.

Bury, Emmanuel. "La *paideia* du *Télémaque*: Miroir d'un prince chrétien et lettres profanes." *Littératures classiques* 23 (1995): 69-81.

Carruthers, Mary. *The Book of Memory*. Cambridge, U.K.: Cambridge University Press, 1990.

Chassignet, Jean-Baptiste. *Le Mespris de la vie et consolation contre la mort*. Ed. Hans-Joachim Lope. Geneva: Droz, 1967.

———. *Sonnets franc-comtois*. Ed. Théodore Courtaux. Geneva: Slatkine, 1969 (rpt. of Paris edition of 1892).

Chatelain, Jean-Marc. *Livres d'emblèmes et de devises*. Paris: Klincksieck, 1993.

Cicero. *Tusculanae Disputationes*. Chicago: Bolchazy-Carducci, 1985.

Collection Granvelle. Ms. 42, fol. 126, 154, 170. Bibliothèque Municipale de Besançon.

Curtius, E. R. *European Literature and the Latin Middle Ages*. Princeton: Princeton University Press, 1983.

De la Bléterie. *Histoire de Jovien*. Amsterdam, 1740.

Du Chesne, André. *Histoire de la Maison de Vergy*. Paris: S. Cramoisy, 1625.

Graham, David. "Pour une rhétorique de l'emblème: *L'Art des Emblèmes* du Père Claude-François Menestrier." *Papers on French Seventeenth-Century Literature* 14 (1987): 13-36.

Graham, V. E. and W. McAllister Johnson, eds. *The Paris Entries of Charles IX and Elisabeth of Austria, 1571*. Toronto: University of Toronto Press, 1974.

Harf-Lancner, Laurence. "L'individu dans l'Etat: la fable des 'Membres et l'estomac' dans la littérature du Moyen Age." *L'Individualisme: permanence et métamorphoses*. Ed. Josiane Attuel. Paris: Presses Universitaires France, 1988. 51-71.

Haskins, Susan. *Mary Magdalen: Myth and Metaphor*. London: Harcourt Brace, 1993.

Kapp, Volker. "Eloge et instruction dans *le Télémaque*." *Littératures Classiques* 23 (1995): 83-97.

Lewis, Charlton T. and Charles Short. *A Latin Dictionary*. Oxford: Clarendon Press, 1966.

Masen, Jakob. *Speculum imaginum veritatis occultae, exhibens symbola, emblemata, hieroglyphica, aenigmata, omni, tam materiae, quam formae varietate, exemplis simul ac praeceptis illustratum*. Cologne: J. A. Kinchius, 1664.

Mathieu-Castellani, Gisèle. "Le Défi de l'emblème." *Revue de Littérature Comparée* 256 (1990): 597-603.

McClintock, John and James Strong, eds. *Cyclopedia of Biblical, Theological and Ecclesiastical Literature*. Vol. 4. Grand Rapids, MI: Baker, 1981.

McGowan, Margaret. "Prose Inspiration for Poetry: J. B. Chassignet." In *The French Renaissance and its Heritage: Essays Presented to Alan M. Boase*. Eds. D. R. Haggis, *et al.* London: Methuen, 1968. 139-65.

Ortali, Raymond. *Un Poète de la mort: Jean-Baptiste Chassignet*. Geneva: Droz, 1968.

Ovid. *Metamorphoses*. New York: Harcourt Brace, 1993.

Oxford Classical Dictionary. Oxford: Oxford University Press, 1970.

Plutarch. *De Gloria Atheniensium*. Paris: Presses de l'Université de Paris-Sorbonne, 1985.

Probes, Christine McCall. "L'entrelacement des sens et de la nature chez Jean-Baptiste Chassignet." *Jean-Baptiste Chassignet*. Ed. Anne Mantero. Paris: Champion, 2003. 163-80.

_____. "La littérature et l'art au service de la théologie: Le voyage terrestre et le voyage sprirituel, la poésie de Jean-Baptiste Chassignet mise en rapport avec les emblèmes de Pierre de Loysi." In *Spiritualité, l'épistolaire, le merveilleux au Grand Siècle*. Eds. David Wetsel and Frédéric Canovas. Tübingen: GunterNarr, 2003. 81-93.

_____. "*Les Sonnets franc-comtois* de Jean-Baptiste Chassignet: La représentation du 'premier lecteur' et la persuasion du lecteur idéal." In *La Poésie religieuse et ses lecteurs aux XVIe et XVIIe siècles*. Eds. Anne Mantero and Alain Cuillère. Dijon: Éditions Universitaires de Dijon, collection *Écritures*, 2005. 151-70.

Ranum, Orest. *Artisans of Glory*. Chapel Hill: University of North Carolina Press, 1980.

Russell, Daniel. "The Emblem and Authority." *Word and Image* 4.1 (1988): 81-99.

_____. *The Emblem and Device in France*. Lexington: French Forum Publishers, 1985.

_____. *Emblematic Structures in Renaissance French Culture*. Toronto: University of Toronto Press, 1995.

_____. "Emblematic Structures in Sixteenth-Century French Poetry." *Jahrbuch für Internationale Germanistik* 14 (1982): 54-100.

Saunders, Alison. *The Seventeenth-Century French Emblem: A Study in Diversity*. Geneva: Droz, 2000.

_____. *The Sixteenth-Century French Emblem Book: A Decorative and Useful Genre*. Geneva: Droz, 1988.

Slater, Stephen. *The Complete Book of Heraldry*. London: Hermes House, 2003.

Spica, Anne-Elisabeth. "Moralistes et emblématique." *DSS* 202 (1999): 169-80.

_____. *Symbolique humaniste et emblématique: L'évolution et les genres (1580-1700)*. Paris: Champion, 1996.

Stegmann, André. "Le Modèle du prince." In *Le Modèle à la Renaissance*. Eds. C. Balavoine *et al*. Paris: J. Vrin, 1986. 117-33.

Contributors

Anne L. Birberick (Northern Illinois University): Associate Professor of French and Chair of the Department of Foreign Languages and Literatures, she has published a monograph on Jean de La Fontaine (*Reading Undercover: Authority and Audience in Jean de La Fontaine*) as well as edited and contributed to two volumes of essays: *Refiguring La Fontaine* and *The Shape of Change*. Her current work focuses on the relationship between Racine and Saint-Cyr as well as the interconnections between knowledge and culture in the fairy tales of d'Aulnoy.

Claire Carlin (University of Victoria): Associate Professor of French and Associate Dean of Humanities, she has edited a volume of essays, *Imagining Contagion in Early Modern Europe* and completed a book-length monograph entitled "L'imaginaire nuptial en France, 1550-1715" that has been recently accepted for publication. In addition, she has published numerous essays on the representation of marriage and the conjugal couple in diverse genres. The most recent of these essays is one on Jeanne de Cambry that appeared in *EMF 11: Studies in Early Modern France* (2007).

Mark A. Cohen (Sarah Lawrence College): Assistant Professor of French, he is currently at work on a book-length study on the genre of fragmentary writing as it is used by seventeenth-century French moralists. His article, "La Bruyère and the 'Usage' of Childhood" appeared in the journal *French Forum* in 2001 and a review essay on Blanchot's *Book to Come* was published in the journal *Postmodern Culture* (2004).

Perry J. Gethner (Oklahoma State University): Professor of French and Head of the Department of Foreign Languages, he has published widely on seventeenth-century French drama, most notably the work of women playwrights. His critical edition, *Femmes dramaturges en France (1650-1750), Pièces choisies*, appeared in 2002 and was followed in 2003 with published translations of Montfleury's *Le Mary sans femme*, Gilbert's *Les Amours de Diane et d'Endimion*, and Poisson's *Les Fous divertissants*. In addition to his work as editor and translator, Professor Gethner has published over forty articles in journals and edited collections.

Twyla Meding (West Virginia University): Associate Professor of French, she has published articles on Honoré d'Urfé, Paul Scarron, and La Fontaine in *EMF: Studies in Early Modern France, Renaissance Quarterly*, and *Seventeenth-Century French Studies*. A recent essay, entitled "Translation as Appropriation"on María de Zayas and Paul Scarron appeared in *The Shape of Change* (Rodopi Press, 2002). At present, she is working on a project on representations of the pastoral in the Griselda story in Boccaccio and Perrault.

Nicholas Paige (University of California-Berkeley): Associate Professor of French, he is currently researching the concept of fictional discourse in seventeenth- and eighteenth-century France, and preparing a translation of Lafayette's *Zayde*. Publications include a scholarly monograph, *Being Interior: Autobiography and the Contradictions of Modernity in Seventeenth-Century France*, published with University of Pennsylvania Press and recent articles in *Representations* and *EMF: Studies in Early Modern France*.

Jennifer R. Perlmutter (Portland State University): Assistant Professor of French, she is presently researching a book-length monograph that examines the relationship between the *Ana* genre and an expanding reading public. Her interest in the creation of a broader and more popular reading public extends to her work on Donneau de Visé's *Le Mercure galant* presented at professional conferences. In 2004, she was the President of the North American Society for Seventeenth-Century French Literature.

Christine McCall Probes (University of South Florida): Associate Professor of French, she was one of the co-editors for the recent collection entitled *La Femme à l'âge classique: La Baroque, la musique et la liturgie* (Tübingen: Gunter Narr). Her numerous publications include articles on the sonnets of Jean-Baptiste Chassignet, the poetry of Tristan l'Hermite and Mlle de Scudéry, and the correspondence of Mme Palatine. The present essay grows out of her ongoing scholarship on the intersection between Chassignet's poetry and Loysi's emblems.

Larry Riggs (Butler University): Professor of French and Head of the Department of Modern Languages, he has published extensively on seventeenth-century French drama and moralism, early modern culture, and cultural studies. Recent publications include: *"Monstres Naissants*: Masculine Birth and Feminine Subversion in the *Theatrum Mundi*," "Dom Juan in the Country: Self-Fashioning Individual as Itinerant Fraud" and "Delusions of Self-Fashioning: *Moralisme* as Critique of Modernity." A first book on Molière, *Molière and Plurality*, appeared in 1989 and a second book on Molière, *Absent Mothers and Masculine Births* appeared most recently.

Index

Printed in the United States
122410LV00007B/113/A